OXFORD EARLY CHRISTIAN STUDIES

General Editors

Gillian Clark   Andrew Louth

THE OXFORD EARLY CHRISTIAN STUDIES series includes scholarly volumes on the thought and history of the early Christian centuries. Covering a wide range of Greek, Latin, and Oriental sources, the books are of interest to theologians, ancient historians, and specialists in the classical and Jewish worlds.

Titles in the series include:

Activity and Participation in Late Antique and Early Christian Thought
Torstein Theodor Tollefsen (2012)

Irenaeus of Lyons and the Theology of the Holy Spirit
Anthony Briggman (2012)

Apophasis and Pseudonymity in Dionysius the Areopagite
"No Longer I"
Charles M. Stang (2012)

Memory in Augustine's Theological Anthropology
Paige E. Hochschild (2012)

Orosius and the Rhetoric of History
Peter Van Nuffelen (2012)

Drama of the Divine Economy
Creator and Creation in Early Christian Theology and Piety
Paul M. Blowers (2012)

Embodiment and Virtue in Gregory of Nyssa
An Anagogical Approach
Hans Boersma (2013)

The *Chronicle of Seert*
Christian Historical Imagination in Late Antique Iraq
Philip Wood (2013)

Christ in the Life and Teaching of Gregory of Nazianzus
Andrew Hofer, O.P. (2013)

Ascetic Pneumatology from John Cassian to Gregory the Great
Thomas L. Humphries, Jr. (2013)

Contemplation and Classical Christianity
A Study in Augustine
John Peter Kenney (2013)

The Canons of Our Fathers
Monastic Rules of Shenoute
Bentley Layton (2014)

John Chrysostom on Divine Pedagogy
The Coherence of his Theology and Preaching
David Rylaarsdam (2014)

Gregory of Nyssa's Tabernacle Imagery in its Jewish and Christian Contexts

ANN CONWAY-JONES

OXFORD
UNIVERSITY PRESS

Great Clarendon Street, Oxford, OX2 6DP,
United Kingdom

Oxford University Press is a department of the University of Oxford.
It furthers the University's objective of excellence in research, scholarship,
and education by publishing worldwide. Oxford is a registered trade mark of
Oxford University Press in the UK and in certain other countries

© Ann Conway-Jones 2014

The moral rights of the author have been asserted

First Edition published in 2014

Impression: 1

All rights reserved. No part of this publication may be reproduced, stored in
a retrieval system, or transmitted, in any form or by any means, without the
prior permission in writing of Oxford University Press, or as expressly permitted
by law, by licence or under terms agreed with the appropriate reprographics
rights organization. Enquiries concerning reproduction outside the scope of the
above should be sent to the Rights Department, Oxford University Press, at the
address above

You must not circulate this work in any other form
and you must impose this same condition on any acquirer

Published in the United States of America by Oxford University Press
198 Madison Avenue, New York, NY 10016, United States of America

British Library Cataloguing in Publication Data
Data available

Library of Congress Control Number: 2014936850

ISBN 978-0-19-871539-9

Printed and bound by
CPI Group (UK) Ltd, Croydon, CR0 4YY

Links to third party websites are provided by Oxford in good faith and
for information only. Oxford disclaims any responsibility for the materials
contained in any third party website referenced in this work.

To my grandmothers:

Elsie Conway
and
Olive Daniel.

Elsie Conway was awarded a PhD in botany in 1925. During the Second World War she researched the potential of British seaweeds to provide agar-like compounds, as supplies from the Far East were becoming restricted. She was a founder member of the British Phycological Society.

Olive Daniel sailed to the Caribbean, on her own, in 1930, to marry a man she hadn't seen for three years. When once again separated by the Atlantic during the Second World War, they evaded the censor using a code based on the hymn numbers in the Methodist Hymn Book.

For their examples of scholarship and faith, and for their cherishing of me, I am profoundly grateful.

Preface

I first encountered Gregory of Nyssa at the very start of my theological studies, when told to write an essay on Cappadocian Trinitarian theology. On discovering that Gregory was known for depicting the ascent to God as an ascent into darkness, I was captivated. I subsequently wrote a dissertation titled 'The Cappadocian Sister', examining the ways in which Gregory used Macrina to exemplify his contemplative theology. I noticed, however, that *Life of Moses* didn't in fact say a great deal about darkness, whereas it contained pages and pages on something called 'the tabernacle not made with hands'; and I wondered about its significance. Years later, having studied for an MA in Jewish–Christian relations at the Centre for the Study of Jewish–Christian Relations in Cambridge (now the Woolf Institute), I entered into correspondence with Philip Alexander, Professor of Post-Biblical Jewish Literature at the University of Manchester, about writing a PhD thesis on early Jewish and Christian mystical exegesis. He sent me some as yet unpublished work heuristically comparing *Songs of the Sabbath Sacrifice* with *The Celestial Hierarchy* of Pseudo-Dionysius.[1] It occurred to me that Gregory of Nyssa lay, chronologically at least, somewhere between the two. I remembered 'the tabernacle not made with hands', and suggested it as the topic for my thesis. Once I had divided up Gregory's text, and given a title to each section, I felt more confident that the study might prove worthwhile. 'Darkness', 'names', 'heavenly powers', 'priestly vestments'...all were topics on which Jewish heavenly ascent texts had something to say.

I studied for my PhD part-time, over six years. My research was funded by a Postgraduate Award from the Arts and Humanities Research Council (AHRC), for which I am most grateful. Many people supported and encouraged me during that time. I would like to thank my dialogue partners in Birmingham—Birmingham Progressive Synagogue, Mosaic (the Birmingham Society for Jewish Studies), the Birmingham Council of Christians and Jews, and the Annual Birmingham Jewish–Christian Study Day—for kindling and sustaining my interest in the complex interactions between Judaism and Christianity, Jews and Christians. The Centre for the Study of Jewish–Christian Relations in Cambridge gave me the confidence to undertake serious study again, and to convert interest into sustained research. Studying midrash and Talmud with Margaret Jacobi has been a privilege. I am grateful to my colleagues at the University of Birmingham, particularly Philip Burton,

---

[1] Philip Alexander, 'The Qumran *Songs of the Sabbath Sacrifice* and the *Celestial Hierarchy* of Dionysius the Areopagite: A Comparative Approach', *Revue de Qumran*, 22: 87 (2006).

Hugh Houghton, Charlotte Hempel, and Deryn Guest, for their support. John Hall took an enthusiastic interest in this project from the start. Our meetings in the reception hall of Thimblemill Swimming Baths to translate *Life of Moses* must have amused the staff. Life has not always been straightforward, and John Austen helped me navigate some choppy waters. My friends Maggy and Marlene provided bolt-holes when I needed them. I was made welcome at two International Colloquia on Gregory of Nyssa, in Tübingen and Leuven, where I gained invaluable insights into Gregory's theology. My trips to Manchester were always a pleasure, with scholarly input and debate furnished by the Ehrhardt seminars. I am grateful to Kate Cooper for acting as my second supervisor; and I would like to thank my fellow students Maria, Penny, Katharina, David, and Sandra for their friendship. The staff at the John Rylands University Library Document Supply Service were fantastic—never complaining about the difficulties I created by living in Birmingham but studying in Manchester. Staff in the postgraduate office of the School of Arts, Histories and Cultures, notably Anna Bigland and Joanne Marsh, ensured that all went well with funding applications. My examiners, Morwenna Ludlow and George Brooke, combined encouragement with constructive criticism. Tom Perridge and Karen Raith from OUP have guided me expertly through the process of publication. Above all, my thanks go to Philip Alexander, for his wisdom and generosity. Conversations with him were a delight and an inspiration, always sending me home reinvigorated. And finally, I am indebted to Michael, Ben, and Simeon. Our family life sustains all my endeavours.

Contents

List of Abbreviations	xi
1. Gregory, the Tabernacle, and Heavenly Ascent	1
2. Gregory of Nyssa and *Life of Moses*	22
3. Biblical Contexts	29
4. Alexandrian Contexts	35
5. Heavenly Ascent Contexts	47
6. Darkness	63
7. The Tabernacle Not Made with Hands	82
8. Christological Interpretation	97
9. Divine Names	116
10. Heavenly Powers	134
11. The Earthly Tabernacle	154
12. Heavenly and Earthly Worship	171
13. The Holy of Holies	188
14. The Priestly Vestments	203
15. The Value of Heuristic Comparison	225
Conclusions	232
Appendix: Translation of Life of Moses 1.46–56, 61; 2.162–201	241
Glossary	253
Bibliography	257
Index of sources	283
General Index	295

List of Abbreviations

CRINT	Compendia rerum iudaicarum ad Novum Testamentum
FC	Fathers of the Church
GCS	Die griechische christliche Schriftsteller der ersten drei Jahrhunderte
GNO	Gregorii Nysseni opera, ed. Werner Jaeger, et al. (Leiden: Brill, 1952–)
JSNTSup	Journal for the Study of the New Testament Supplement Series
LXX	The Old Greek translation of the Hebrew Bible, known as the Septuagint
MT	Masoretic Text of the Hebrew Bible
NETS	A New English Translation of the Septuagint
NJPS	*Tanakh: The Holy Scriptures: The New JPS Translation according to the Traditional Hebrew Text*
NPNF[1]	Nicene and Post-Nicene Fathers, Series 1
NPNF[2]	Nicene and Post-Nicene Fathers, Series 2
PG	Patrologia graeca
RSV	Revised Standard Version
SBLSCS	Society of Biblical Literature Septuagint and Cognate Studies
SC	Sources chrétiennes

As suggested in *The SBL Handbook of Style: For Ancient Near Eastern, Biblical, and Early Christian Studies*, Greek and Latin works are referred to by English titles in the text, with the traditional Latin abbreviations being used in footnotes.[2] Abbreviations for Gregory of Nyssa's works are taken from *The Brill Dictionary of Gregory of Nyssa*, with additional full stops.[3] The abbreviations used for ancient texts can be found under 'primary literature' in the bibliography, apart from those for the works of Plato, Philo, and Josephus. These are, however, given in the index of citations from ancient sources.

---

[2] Patrick H. Alexander et al. (eds), *The SBL Handbook of Style: For Ancient Near Eastern, Biblical, and Early Christian Studies* (Peabody, Mass.: Hendrickson, 1999), 238.

[3] Lucas Francisco Mateo-Seco and Giulio Maspero (eds), *The Brill Dictionary of Gregory of Nyssa* (Leiden: Brill, 2010).

1

Gregory, the Tabernacle, and Heavenly Ascent

Having been first purified in mind by these laws, as it were, [Moses] was led to the more perfect mystical initiation, suddenly being shown a certain tabernacle by divine power. The tabernacle was a shrine, possessing beauty in indescribable variety: entrances, pillars and hangings; a table, lamps, and an incense altar; an altar and a mercy seat; and the secret and inaccessible core of the holy spaces. So that the wonder might not escape the memory, and might be shown to those below, he was counselled to transmit the beauty and arrangement of all these things not merely in writing, but by reproducing that immaterial creation in a material construction, obtaining the brightest and most radiant materials found on earth.[1]

1.1 INTRODUCTION

This study explores Gregory of Nyssa's tabernacle imagery, as found in *Life of Moses* 2.170–201. It does so by taking this section of *Life of Moses* to be an example of heavenly ascent, and then comparing and contrasting it with other accounts of heavenly ascent, in which privileged individuals gain access to the celestial realms, hoping to glimpse the divine glory. The book therefore initiates a conversation between two different fields of study: patristics and early Jewish mysticism. Whether the conversation bears fruit, in terms of a new understanding of Gregory's tabernacle imagery, as Gregory himself would say,

> Our speculative suggestions on the matter set before us we refer to the readers' judgement, to be deemed worthless or acceptable, as the mind of the competent judge shall determine.[2]

Gregory of Nyssa is probably best known for his depiction of apophatic darkness. As Andrew Louth writes,

> For Gregory of Nyssa the doctrine of God's unknowability means that the soul's ascent to God is an ascent into the divine darkness.... Gregory depicts vividly the

[1] *Vit. Moys.* 1.49.   [2] *Vit. Moys.* 2.173.

bewilderment, despair and longing that possesses the soul that seeks God. In the dark we can form no finished conception of what is there: this experience is interpreted by Gregory in terms of an endless longing for God, continually satisfied yet always yearning for more, which the soul knows that embarks on the search for the unknowable God.[3]

In *Life of Moses*, Gregory describes Moses entering into the darkness of Mount Sinai, where he sees God. This Gregory interprets as 'the seeing which consists in not seeing', for 'what is sought transcends all knowledge, cut off on all sides by incomprehensibility, as by a kind of darkness'.[4] He evokes the same theme in *On the Song of Songs*:

> Having left behind whatever is accessible to human nature, [the soul] enters within the innermost shrine of the knowledge of God and is entirely seized about by the divine darkness; and in this darkness, since everything that appears and is comprehended has been left outside, only the invisible and the incomprehensible remain for the soul's contemplation—and in them God is, just as the Word says concerning the Lawgiver: 'Moses entered into the darkness where God was'.[5]

However, within the darkness on Mount Sinai, Moses is shown a model of the tabernacle which the Israelites are to build (Exod. 25:8–9). *Life of Moses* conforms to the Exodus account: Moses enters the darkness and there he sees the tabernacle not made with hands (ἡ ἀχειροποίητος σκηνή). Whereas Gregory's interpretation of the darkness takes up three paragraphs of Jean Daniélou's Sources chrétiennes edition (2.162–4), his commentary on the tabernacle, including the priestly vestments, occupies thirty-two paragraphs (2.170–201). Yet commentators feel able to present an outline of the *Life of Moses* with little or no mention of the tabernacle. The aim of this study is to focus on this neglected part of *Life of Moses*, and draw attention to its significance.

The tabernacle was taken seriously by ancient writers. Exodus devotes ten chapters (25–28, 35–40) to Moses' vision of the model and the subsequent construction of the tabernacle. Detailed interpretations can be found in the works of Philo, Clement, and Origen. Josephus, Methodius, Jerome, and Theodoret also wrote about the tabernacle and the priestly vestments.[6] Moving forward in time, Bede produced a treatise with a verse-by-verse allegorical rendering of Exodus 24:12–30:21.[7] And 'perhaps the most learned and detailed treatises in the history of exegesis were called forth in the post-Reformation period in an effort to demonstrate the typology between the kingdom of God

---

[3] Andrew Louth, 'The Cappadocians', in Cheslyn Jones, Geoffrey Wainwright, and Edward Yarnold (eds), *The Study of Spirituality* (London: SPCK, 1986), 167.
[4] *Vit. Moys.* 2.163.   [5] *Cant.* 11 (GNO 6.323.2–9); trans. Norris, 341.
[6] Josephus *A.J.* 3.102–203, Methodius *Symp.* 5.7–8, Jerome *Epist.* 64, Theodoret *Quaest. in Ex.* 60.
[7] A translation can be found in Arthur G. Holder, *Bede: On the Tabernacle* (Liverpool: Liverpool University Press, 1994).

in the tabernacle and the church of Christ in its various forms as the invisible and visible, triumphant and militant, congregation of grace'.[8] Typology is still taken seriously in Evangelical Christian circles, as demonstrated by websites which proclaim the tabernacle to be a prophetic projection of God's redemptive plan.[9] Among liberal, academic readers, however, the tabernacle carries little resonance. As Brevard Childs writes,

> Most modern readers of the book of Exodus have difficulty understanding why the biblical description of the tabernacle has been regarded from the beginning with the greatest possible interest by Jewish and Christian scholars alike.[10]

It does not feature in the Revised Common Lectionary, the pattern of Sunday readings used by a wide range of Christian denominations.[11] The probable reason, therefore, that the tabernacle has been sidelined in studies of *Life of Moses* is that, unlike darkness, it does not appeal to contemporary sensibilities. The tabernacle was, after all, a place of animal sacrifice, a practice now rarely viewed with understanding or sympathy.[12] However, despite the cessation of Jewish animal sacrifice in CE 70, tabernacle/temple theology lived on. Christians transferred temple imagery to the church, and sacrificial imagery to the Eucharist.

Even before the destruction of the earthly temple, there was speculation about its heavenly counterpart. From the Book of the Watchers, dated to the third century BCE, onwards, temple structures were mapped onto the heavenly realms. It was widely assumed that the 'pattern' seen by Moses was the heavenly tabernacle—God's dwelling place. And privileged individuals, such as Enoch, Levi, and Isaiah, were assumed to have gained access to that divine seat of power. It features in the New Testament: Hebrews depicts Christ as the high priest of 'the greater and more perfect tabernacle (not made with hands, that is, not of this creation)';[13] and Revelation, drawing on Ezekiel's vision of the divine chariot, describes the celestial throne, the heavenly equivalent of the ark of the covenant. There is a rich tradition of heavenly ascent texts, running from Second Temple apocalyptic to the Hekhalot literature of Late Antiquity, in which an individual, or possibly a community (thinking of *Songs of the*

---

[8] Brevard S. Childs, *Exodus: A Commentary* (London: SCM, 1974), 548.
[9] See, for example, <http://www.the-tabernacle-place.com> or <http://www.tabernacletypology.com>.
[10] Childs, *Exodus*, 547.
[11] The exception which proves the rule is that extracts from the description of the priestly vestments (Exod. 28:1–4, 9–10, 29–30) may be used as an alternative reading for the seventh Sunday of Easter (year B) in the Church of Ireland and the Church in Wales.
[12] There is trenchant criticism of scholars' inability to investigate the sacrificial system sympathetically in Jonathan Klawans, *Purity, Sacrifice, and the Temple: Symbolism and Supersessionism in the Study of Ancient Judaism* (Oxford: Oxford University Press, 2006).
[13] Heb. 9:11.

Sabbath Sacrifice), ascends to heaven and glimpses the divine throne with its myriad attendant angels.[14] Some of these texts are Jewish, some Christian, some a mixture (such as a Jewish text reworked by Christian editors), and for some more nuanced definitions of identity are required.[15] Gregory's description of Moses' ascent into the darkness of Mount Sinai in order to see the tabernacle not made with hands fits into this paradigm.

According to modern scholars, there are no ascent narratives in the Bible: 'Nowhere in the Hebrew Bible is the gap between heaven and earth bridged in such a way that a human being leaves his place on earth and explores heaven.'[16] Gregory would not have agreed. According to him, not only was Moses vouchsafed a vision of the heavenly tabernacle, but other biblical figures had similar experiences:

> That is why the sublime *John*, who has been in this radiant darkness, says, 'No one has ever seen God'...[17]
>
> ...as *David* says, who was initiated into ineffable mysteries in the same secret place.[18]
>
> [*Paul*] himself probably experienced a vision of this tabernacle in the supercelestial secret places, he to whom through the Spirit the mysteries of paradise were revealed...[19]
>
> ...this is the name of the powers envisaged around the divine nature, as *Isaiah* and *Ezekiel* observed.[20]

And because those people saw what Moses saw, Gregory considers that their writings can be used to elucidate Exodus. He works within a framework in which exceptional individuals are believed to have been 'initiated into ineffable mysteries' in the supercelestial sanctuary. This is the framework of heavenly ascent, a framework which, in a wide variety of guises, was

---

[14] For an introduction to heavenly ascent texts, see Martha Himmelfarb, *Ascent to Heaven in Jewish and Christian Apocalypses* (Oxford: Oxford University Press, 1993).

[15] See David Frankfurter, 'Beyond "Jewish Christianity": Continuing Religious Sub-Cultures of the Second and Third Centuries and Their Documents', in Adam H. Becker and Annette Yoshiko Reed (eds), *The Ways that Never Parted: Jews and Christians in Late Antiquity and the Early Middle Ages* (Minneapolis: Fortress, 2007), 131–43.

[16] Peter Schäfer, *The Origins of Jewish Mysticism* (Tübingen: Mohr Siebeck, 2009), 53. See also Himmelfarb, *Ascent to Heaven*, 9; or George W. E. Nickelsburg, *1 Enoch 1: A Commentary on the Book of 1 Enoch, Chapters 1–36; 81–108* (Minneapolis: Fortress, 2001), 259–61. Paul Joyce demurs, suggesting that Ezekiel 40–42, the prophet's Temple vision, can be viewed as the first 'heavenly ascent' narrative. See Paul M. Joyce, 'Ezekiel 40–42: The Earliest "Heavenly Ascent" Narrative?', in H. J. de Jonge and J. Tromp (eds), *The Book of Ezekiel and Its Influence* (Aldershot: Ashgate, 2007). Christopher Morray-Jones warns not overstate the distinction between the visions of the biblical prophets and the heavenly ascents described by later apocalyptic writers. See Christopher Rowland and Christopher R. A. Morray-Jones, *The Mystery of God: Early Jewish Mysticism and the New Testament* (Leiden: Brill, 2009), 303–5.

[17] *Vit. Moys.* 2.163.   [18] *Vit. Moys.* 2.164.   [19] *Vit. Moys.* 2.178.

[20] *Vit. Moys.* 2.180.

common to all Late Antique cultures: pagan, Jewish, and Christian. Alan Segal states,

> It is possible to see the heavenly journey of the soul, its consequent promise of immortality and the corrolary necessity of periodic ecstatic journeys to heaven as the dominant mythical constellation of late classical antiquity.[21]

Bernard McGinn demurs only slightly: 'The claim to dominance aside, there can be no question of the importance of these visionary ascensions.'[22] The question therefore is not whether Gregory worked within a framework of heavenly ascent, but how he reconciled it with the biblical text, and then tailored it to his own needs. The heuristic comparison being embarked upon involves comparing his writings with other works produced or read during Late Antiquity, so that his particular shaping of the framework can be discerned.

McGinn writes,

> I am convinced that to neglect the Jewish roots of Christian mysticism and to see it, as many have done, as a purely Greek phenomenon is to risk misconstruing an important part of its history.[23]

He presents both the philosophical–religious tradition begun by Plato and the Jewish apocalypses as 'major components of the background of Christian mysticism'.[24] Philip Alexander suggests adding evidence from Qumran to the exploration of the Jewish matrix of Christian mysticism:

> The key ideas of Qumran mysticism—the celestial temple, the angelic liturgies, communion with the angels through liturgy and the ultimate angelification of the mystic—all had a vigorous afterlife specifically within Christian tradition.[25]

This study looks even further afield, and includes Jewish texts from Late Antiquity, in order to provide a wide variety of material with which to compare and contrast the tabernacle passage in *Life of Moses*. Gregory's relationship with Platonism has been thoroughly explored. Can heavenly ascent texts throw new light on his work? Some, such as *1 Enoch* or *Ascension of Isaiah*, he may have known, of others, such as *Songs of the Sabbath Sacrifice* or the Hekhalot literature, he cannot possibly have been aware. The aim of this study is not to prove that Gregory was influenced by particular heavenly ascent texts,

---

[21] Alan F. Segal, 'Heavenly Ascent in Hellenistic Judaism, Early Christianity and their Environment', in Wolfgang Haase (ed.), *Aufstieg und Niedergang der römischen Welt: Geschichte und Kultur Roms im Spiegel der neueren Forschung. 2. Principat. 23.2* (Berlin: Walter de Gruyter, 1980), 1388.
[22] Bernard McGinn, *The Foundations of Mysticism: Origins to the Fifth Century* (New York: Crossroad, 1991), 14.
[23] McGinn, *The Foundations of Mysticism*, 22.
[24] McGinn, *The Foundations of Mysticism*, 5.
[25] Philip Alexander, *The Mystical Texts: Songs of the Sabbath Sacrifice and Related Manuscripts* (London: T&T Clark, 2006), 138.

but to use comparison and contrast heuristically, so as to enhance the understanding of Gregory's ideas and use of imagery. Does Gregory's interpretation of the tabernacle come into focus when viewed through the lens of heavenly ascent?

Gregory works with the Platonic division between the sensible and intelligible worlds, even if he then superimposes upon it a gulf dividing Creator and creation. Daniélou points out that one of Gregory's favourite words for describing contemplation means 'to travel through the air' or 'to walk on high' (μετεωροπορέω/συμμετεωροπορέω).[26] One of the examples he cites is from Gregory's eulogy to his brother Basil:

> He...hastened with his soul into the beyond, and, overstepping the sensible boundary of the world, ever trod what is perceptible to the mind, and walked on high with the divine powers (συμμετεωροπορεῖν ταῖς θείαις δυνάμεσι), in no way hindered in the progress of his mind by the impediment of the body.[27]

The same verb is used by Plato in *Phaedrus*:

> Soul...traverses the whole heaven, appearing sometimes in one form and sometimes in another; now when it is perfect and fully winged, it mounts upward (ἐπτερωμένη μετεωροπορεῖ) and governs the whole world; but the soul which has lost its wings is borne along until it gets hold of something solid when it settles down, taking upon itself an earthly body...[28]

As Daniélou says, 'le Platon de Grégoire, c'est le Platon des mythes'.[29] But Gregory depends not only on Platonism for his imagery. When he describes Basil circulating with 'the divine powers', he conceives of those heavenly powers in personal terms. The Platonic *kosmos noētos* (the realm of Forms) has become the angelic world. This can be illustrated by an extract from *On the Song of Songs*:

> She [the bride/soul] bestirs herself again and in her understanding moves about the intelligible and supracosmic nature (which she calls *the city*), in which are the Rulers and Lordships and the Thrones set over the Powers and the assembly of the heavenly beings (which she calls *the square*) as well as the unnumbered multitude (which she denotes by the word *street*)—to see if she can find the Beloved among these. So she went about, searching every angelic order...[30]

---

[26] Jean Daniélou, *Platonisme et théologie mystique: Doctrine spirituelle de Saint Grégoire de Nysse*, 2nd edn (Paris: Aubier, 1954), 151.

[27] GNO 10,1.131.13–18; trans. Stein, 53 (amended).

[28] *Phaedr.* 246BC. There is a variant reading μετεωροπολεῖ (to range through the air). See Henry George Liddell, Robert Scott, and Henry Stuart Jones, *A Greek–English Lexicon*, 9th edn (Oxford: Clarendon, 1940), 1120. That word is used by Philo in *Spec.* 1.207; see 4.1.

[29] 'Gregory's Plato is the Plato of myths.' Daniélou, *Platonisme et théologie mystique*, 154.

[30] *Cant.* 6 (GNO 6.182.3–11); trans. Norris, 195. This is a commentary on Song of Songs 3:2.

Angels come from Christianity's biblical and apocalyptic heritage, not from Platonism. It therefore makes sense to explore Gregory's imagery in the context of other Jewish and Christian heavenly ascent texts which arise out of this heritage.

The primary questions motivating this study are: What is the significance of Gregory's tabernacle interpretation in *Life of Moses* 2.170–201? Why was it important to him? What was he trying to convey? How did he envisage the relationship between the heavenly and earthly tabernacles; in other words, between the divine and the human? Answering these questions, and taking seriously not only 'darkness' but also the vision revealed within it, may revise our understanding of *Life of Moses*, and of Gregory's mysticism more generally. One of the ways in which answers will be sought is by undertaking a heuristic comparison with heavenly ascent texts. A secondary question then emerges: How fruitful is it, even in the case of a fourth-century work clearly influenced by Platonic traditions, to take seriously the Jewish matrix of Christian mysticism? Recent scholarship has re-examined the boundaries between Judaism and Christianity in Late Antiquity, questioning whether a final parting of the ways ever happened. If this study does prove fruitful, it will provide yet another example of the value of studying Jewish and Christian texts alongside each other.

The 'meat' of the study is in Chapters 6 to 14, which undertake a close reading of *Life of Moses* 2.162–201. Each chapter focuses on a short section of Gregory's text, and analyses it according to a set pattern.[31] Firstly, Gregory's text is examined, and his biblical sources identified. The key biblical passages from which Gregory draws are introduced in Chapter 3. Secondly, there is a presentation of relevant passages in the work of his Alexandrian predecessors—Philo, Clement, and Origen. The Alexandrian texts which comment on the tabernacle, along with the Alexandrian use of the heavenly ascent paradigm, are introduced in Chapter 4. Thirdly, there is a discussion of the ways in which Gregory's fourth-century theological context has influenced his interpretation, often causing him to differ from his predecessors. The key theological ideas and disputes necessary for understanding *Life of Moses* are outlined in Chapter 2, where Gregory and *Life of Moses* are introduced. It is under this heading of 'theological context' that contemporary scholarly discussions about Gregory are most in evidence. Fourthly, a heuristic comparison with a number of heavenly ascent texts, both Jewish and Christian, is undertaken. The texts used are introduced in Chapter 5.

There is a clear difference between the first three parts in each of Chapters 6 to 14 and the last one. In the first three Gregory's sources and influences are identified, whether biblical texts, previous interpretations of the tabernacle

---

[31] *Life of Moses* 2.182 and 2.185 are examined together, out of sequence, in Chapter 12, 'Heavenly and Earthly Worship'.

(particularly from the Alexandrian tradition), or fourth-century debates and disagreements. Here we are on fairly solid ground. Part four, which uses heavenly ascent texts as a foil, is experimental. Gregory's work is compared and contrasted with other traditions about the heavenly tabernacle/temple in order to shed new light on his imagery; and the scholarship on these texts is mined for new questions to be asked of *Life of Moses*. Samuel Sandmel defines 'parallelomania' as 'that extravagance among scholars which first overdoes the supposed similarity in passages and then proceeds to describe source and derivation as if implying literary connection flowing in an inevitable or predetermined direction'.[32] Here, by contrast, differences are as important as similarities, and no literary connection is implied. In principle, such a heuristic comparison could be undertaken with traditions from any time or place. However, these heavenly ascent texts were produced and/or read in the Late Antique Eastern Mediterranean. Broadly speaking, they do come from Gregory's time and place. And, like Gregory's work, they take inspiration from biblical texts. Recent scholarship has suggested that the boundaries between Judaism and Christianity, up to and including the fourth century, were less fixed and more permeable than previously thought.[33] Ideas travelled across them in all sorts of ways, from casual meetings in the marketplace, to attendance at each other's festivals, to the scholarly reading of texts. Much of the imagery in apocalyptic literature is graphic and memorable, and could easily have been passed on by word of mouth. Therefore, it is not impossible that Gregory was influenced by, and perhaps reacted against, the kind of ideas contained in heavenly ascent texts. By undertaking a heuristic comparison, influence is not being ruled out. But proving influence is not the aim. The aim of this study is to sharpen our understanding of Gregory's use of tabernacle imagery.

Segal states, 'Christianity, the mystery cults, Emperor cult, magic, theosophy, late classical philosophy, and even rabbinic Judaism, to a lesser extent, were committed to the ascension pattern, tailored to their own needs'.[34] The net for this heuristic comparison could therefore have been cast even wider. There are significant traditions which are not represented. One is the Syriac tradition, a route by which near-Eastern ideas and imagery could have reached Gregory. There is mention of Pseudo-Macarius and Messalian tendencies in 11.3 (in connection with the earthly tabernacle), and of fourth-century neoplatonism in 9.3 (when examining divine names), but no systematic comparison with either. Valentinian ideas are included in some of the discussions of Gregory's Alexandrian predecessors, but no other so-called Gnostic texts are

---

[32] Samuel Sandmel, 'Parallelomania', *Journal of Biblical Literature*, 81: 1 (1962), 1.
[33] See, for example, Adam H. Becker and Annette Yoshiko Reed (eds), *The Ways that Never Parted: Jews and Christians in Late Antiquity and the Early Middle Ages* (Minneapolis: Fortress, 2007); or Daniel Boyarin, *Border Lines: The Partition of Judaeo-Christianity* (Philadelphia: University of Pennsylvania Press, 2004).
[34] Segal, 'Heavenly Ascent', 1388.

considered. And there is no engagement with Greek pagan traditions of heavenly ascent. Even the comparison with Jewish and Christian heavenly ascent texts is not exhaustive. A selection of texts has been made, based on their usefulness for this study.

Given that it is experimental, this methodology of heuristic comparison is reviewed in Chapter 15, with the following questions in mind: Has Gregory's use of tabernacle imagery come into sharper focus as a result of the comparison? Which heavenly ascent texts have proved particularly useful? And have any of the concepts developed by scholars of Jewish mysticism been of value in examining Gregory's text?

1.2 PREVIOUS SCHOLARSHIP ON GREGORY'S TABERNACLE IMAGERY

Gregory's tabernacle imagery has received far less scholarly attention than that conferred on his apophatic darkness imagery. This sidelining is illustrated by Everett Ferguson, Anthony Meredith, and Verna Harrison, all of whom summarize *Life of Moses* without mentioning the tabernacle.[35] Harrison quotes *Life of Moses* 2.163, which includes the phrase 'the seeing that consists in not seeing', and asks, 'What then is seen?' She answers her question with an extract from *On the Song of Songs*, which refers to 'some sense of His presence', even though in *Life of Moses* it is clearly the heavenly tabernacle that is seen.[36] Colin Macleod is an exception to the general neglect, pointing out that 'the reverse side of Gregory's negative theology is Christian faith: in the very darkness which surrounds God we see the "tabernacle", Christ'; but he doesn't explore this in any detail.[37] Thanks to another text from *On the Song of Songs*, Daniélou divides Gregory's mysticism into three stages: light, cloud, and darkness.[38] Ronald Heine points out that the details of *Life of Moses* do not follow this scheme:

> [Daniélou] pictures the soul as moving from gnosis in the second stage, to mystic contemplation of God in darkness in the third stage. It is after Moses has gone into

---

[35] Everett Ferguson, 'Progress in Perfection: Gregory of Nyssa's *Vita Moysis*', in Elizabeth A. Livingstone (ed.), *Papers Presented to the Sixth International Conference on Patristic Studies Held in Oxford 1971*, part 3: *Tertullian, Origenism, Gnostica, Cappadocian Fathers, Augustiniana* (Berlin: Akademie-Verlag, 1976), 307–14; Anthony Meredith, *Gregory of Nyssa* (London: Routledge, 1999), 99–109; Verna E. F. Harrison, *Grace and Human Freedom according to St. Gregory of Nyssa* (Lewiston, NY: Edwin Mellen, 1992), 73–85.
[36] Harrison, *Grace and Human Freedom*, 76–7.
[37] Colin W. Macleod, 'Allegory and Mysticism in Origen and Gregory of Nyssa', *Journal of Theological Studies*, 22: 2 (1971), 378.
[38] Daniélou, *Platonisme et théologie mystique*, 18–19. For further details see 6.3.

the darkness, however, that he has the vision of the tabernacle which, Daniélou acknowledges, is presented in terms of gnosis. He, therefore, puts the vision of the tabernacle in the second stage in the structure of his book. Gregory, however, presents the vision of the tabernacle as a step beyond Moses' entering 'the invisible sanctuary of the knowledge of God'.[39]

Daniélou's commentary on the vision of the tabernacle according to Gregory focuses on the way in which Gregory replaces the Platonic *kosmos noētos* with the angelic world.[40] Heine homes in on the 'repeated emphasis on the leadership of the church throughout the treatise', pointing out Gregory's use of the earthly tabernacle to highlight church leaders, and of the priestly vestments to teach about priestly virtue.[41] Michael Lieb includes *Life of Moses* in his survey of traditions stemming from Ezekiel's *visio Dei*. He presents Gregory's depiction of Moses' experience as culminating with the ark of the covenant:

> Having ascended the mountain of knowledge, the seer penetrates the luminous darkness of the tabernacle to find himself before the ark of the covenant upon which reside those cherubim whose significance is to be seen in the respective visions of Isaiah and Ezekiel. Within the tabernacle Gregory's seer beholds his own version of the *merkabah*.[42]

This distorts Gregory's narrative, which cannot really be said to climax at that point, but it does provide a precedent for examining *Life of Moses* against the background of traditions of heavenly ascent inspired by Ezekiel's vision. Lieb is right in saying that the biblical texts relating the visions of Isaiah and Ezekiel 'represent a locus classicus in Gregory for the kind of visionary enactment that expressed what Moses was made to undergo in his ascent of the mount'.[43]

Hans Boersma has recently emphasized the centrality of anagogy—the ascent into the heavenly or eschatological reality of divine life—in Gregory's theology.[44] He links this upward movement to participation in divine virtue. What Boersma terms 'anagogy' is, in this study, designated 'heavenly ascent'; Chapter 14 (on the priestly vestments) will corroborate his analysis of Gregory's anagogical understanding of virtue. He makes no mention, however, of any Jewish background to the concept of anagogy, considering it purely in Platonic and Christian terms. He argues, against most contemporary scholars,

---

[39] Ronald E. Heine, *Perfection in the Virtuous Life: A Study in the Relationship Between Edification and Polemical Theology in Gregory of Nyssa's De Vita Moysis* (Cambridge, Mass.: Philadelphia Patristic Foundation, 1975), 3 n. 2.

[40] Daniélou, *Platonisme et théologie mystique*, 162–72.

[41] Heine, *Perfection in the Virtuous Life*, 23–4.

[42] Michael Lieb, *The Visionary Mode: Biblical Prophecy, Hermeneutics, and Cultural Change* (Ithaca: Cornell University Press, 1991), 225–6. *Merkabah*, pronounced *merkavah*, the Hebrew term for 'chariot', is the name given to the vision described in Ezekiel 1.

[43] Lieb, *The Visionary Mode*, 226.

[44] Hans Boersma, *Embodiment and Virtue in Gregory of Nyssa: An Anagogical Approach* (Oxford: Oxford University Press, 2013).

that Gregory considers the angelic, paradisal life of before the Fall, and after the eschaton, to be beyond the limits of space and time found in material existence. Since Gregory understands the heavenly tabernacle, which for him represents Christ, to be infinite, Moses can progress infinitely as regards participation in and knowledge of Christ.[45]

As well as the previous scholarship on Gregory's interpretation of the tabernacle, just outlined, this study draws on a number of areas of current research, four of which will now be introduced.

1.3 RETHINKING GREGORY OF NYSSA

A collection of essays, edited by Sarah Coakley, entitled *Rethinking Gregory of Nyssa*, was published in 2003. In her introduction, Coakley notes 'the myriad differences of style and *genre* with which Gregory plays in his various works, and his often infuriatingly inconsistent modes of argument'.[46] She calls for an integrated approach to his work, in which false disjunctions, such as 'theology'/'spirituality' or 'philosophy'/'exegesis', are laid aside.[47] In particular, she argues for 'the significance of Gregory's wider *exegetical* corpus for the assessment and understanding of his doctrinal contribution'.[48] Another contributor to that volume is Martin Laird, who draws attention to Gregory's designation of the holy of holies as 'the apophatic space of the inner sanctuary, the hidden chamber of the heart'.[49] In his own book, *Gregory of Nyssa and the Grasp of Faith: Union, Knowledge and Divine Presence*, he emphasizes the exegetical character of Gregory's work, insisting that the theme of divine darkness is not introduced 'apart from scriptural texts which lend themselves to such an interpretation'.[50] In the context of other scriptural texts Gregory is equally capable of presenting a mysticism of light.[51] This study continues the trend of re-examining Gregory's exegesis, and allowing it to inform more nuanced and complex understandings of his doctrinal positions. It also seeks to break down the divide between his propositional statements and his poetic use of imagery.

---

[45] Boersma, *Embodiment and Virtue*, 243–4.
[46] Sarah Coakley (ed.), *Re-Thinking Gregory of Nyssa* (Oxford: Blackwell, 2003), 11.
[47] Coakley (ed.), *Re-Thinking Gregory of Nyssa*, 2.
[48] Coakley (ed.), *Re-Thinking Gregory of Nyssa*, 5.
[49] Martin Laird, 'Under Solomon's Tutelage: The Education of Desire in the Homilies on the Song of Songs', in Coakley (ed.), *Re-Thinking Gregory of Nyssa*, 85.
[50] Martin Laird, *Gregory of Nyssa and the Grasp of Faith: Union, Knowledge, and Divine Presence* (Oxford: Oxford University Press, 2004), 180.
[51] Laird, *Gregory of Nyssa and the Grasp of Faith*, 174.

In *Gregory of Nyssa: Ancient and (Post)modern*, Morwenna Ludlow examines the ways in which Gregory has been read by twentieth- and twenty-first-century theologians. She insists that she is not rejecting the techniques of traditional patristic scholarship: 'The methods of traditional patristic scholarship (historical and philological) can be used to advise on the limits or scope of meaning; the use of other recent readings can be used continually to stretch the limits of what patristic scholars consider possible.'[52] This study is stretching the limits in a different direction, by a comparison with Jewish texts, but it too stays in dialogue with patristic scholarship. Ludlow characterizes Gregory's theological method as one of 'keeping questions in play, or forcing readers continually to reassess their answers': a method which arises out of 'the fruitful ambiguity of Scripture'.[53] This is why 'there are still some surprises to be found in his texts'.[54] One of the theologians analysed by Ludlow is Scot Douglass, who develops the concept of a '*metadiastemic* intrusion', which will be examined in 8.3. Although he approaches Gregory from the perspective of post-Heideggerian philosophy, he emphasizes Gregory's reliance on biblical traditions of 'impenetrable, circumscribed spaces within which dwelt the inaccessible presence of God', notably the holy of holies.[55] It is gratifying that this postmodern reading of Gregory underlines the significance of tabernacle imagery.

1.4 DEBATES AROUND MYSTICISM

'Mysticism' is a problematic term. It tends to imply the personal experience of individuals who take active steps to draw closer to the divine; but 'there is no such thing as a universally recognized definition of mysticism'.[56] Harrison observes that the word 'mysticism' 'is notoriously difficult to pin down', but says that she keeps the term 'because of its extensive use in the literature'.[57] Similarly, in the context of Jewish mysticism, Peter Schäfer says that he uses the word 'only because it is the label that scholarly tradition has long attached to the texts I will be treating'.[58] For texts such as *Life of Moses*, Macleod prefers the term 'mystical theology', given that 'Gregory never speaks of any religious experiences of his own'.[59] One focus for discussion is the notion of *unio*

---

[52] Morwenna Ludlow, *Gregory of Nyssa, Ancient and (Post)modern* (Oxford: Oxford University Press, 2007), 290.
[53] Ludlow, *Gregory of Nyssa, Ancient and (Post)modern*, 288–9.
[54] Ludlow, *Gregory of Nyssa, Ancient and (Post)modern*, 290.
[55] Scot Douglass, *Theology of the Gap: Cappadocian Language Theory and the Trinitarian Controversy* (New York: Peter Lang, 2005), 133.
[56] Schäfer, *The Origins of Jewish Mysticism*, 1.
[57] Harrison, *Grace and Human Freedom*, 61–2.
[58] Schäfer, *The Origins of Jewish Mysticism*, 23–4.
[59] Macleod, 'Allegory and Mysticism in Origen and Gregory of Nyssa', 363.

mystica—mystical union with the divine. Gershom Scholem, who founded the academic study of Jewish mysticism, insisted that the term had 'no particular significance':

> Numerous mystics, Jews as well as non-Jews, have by no means represented the essence of their ecstatic experience, the tremendous uprush and soaring of the soul to its highest plane, as a union with God.[60]

Most scholars of Jewish mysticism have agreed with him, and attempted to produce alternative definitions. Alexander mentions suggestions that, in theistic systems, 'which are conscious of an unbridgeable ontological gap between the Creator and the created', 'communion' is a more appropriate term than 'union' for a relationship with the transcendent presence.[61] Schäfer proposes replacing *unio mystica* with *unio liturgica* (see 12.4), arguing that the liturgical union of the mystic with the angels 'is one of the most important characteristics shared by the Hekhalot literature and the ascent apocalypses'.[62] And Elliot Wolfson argues that Jewish sources provide a model of mysticism based on 'the "angelification" of the human being who crosses the boundary of space and time and becomes part of the heavenly realm'.[63] One aspect of this study will be to see whether these scholarly reflections on Jewish mysticism provide useful tools with which to examine Gregory's tabernacle imagery.

There has been a fault line in Gregorian scholarship between those who label *Life of Moses* and *On the Song of Songs* as 'mystical', and those who categorize them as 'theological'. Harrison places Daniélou, Walther Völker, and Aloysius Lieske among the former, and Hans Langerbeck, Ekkehard Mühlenberg, Heine, and Bernard Barmann among the latter.[64] Those on the 'mystical' side are happy to talk in terms of 'union with God',[65] 'a sense of presence',[66] or 'participation in the divine life'.[67] The first two expressions are drawn from *On the Song of Songs*. Laird, for example, justifies talking of 'union' by quoting from its first homily, which describes the soul being escorted like a bride to

---

[60] Gershom G. Scholem, *Major Trends in Jewish Mysticism*, 3rd edn (New York: Schoken Books, 1961), 5.
[61] Alexander, *The Mystical Texts*, 8.
[62] Schäfer, *The Origins of Jewish Mysticism*, 341.
[63] Elliot R. Wolfson, 'Mysticism and the Poetic-Liturgical Compositions from Qumran: A Response to Bilhah Nitzan', *Jewish Quarterly Review*, 85: 1–2 (1994), 186.
[64] Harrison, *Grace and Human Freedom*, 62.
[65] Jean Daniélou, 'Introduction', in Herbert Musurillo, *From Glory to Glory: Texts from Gregory of Nyssa's Mystical Writings* (New York: Scribner, 1961; repr., Crestwood, NY: St Vladimir's Seminary Press, 2001), 31; Laird, *Gregory of Nyssa and the Grasp of Faith*, 53.
[66] Mariette Canévet, 'La perception de la présence de Dieu à propos d'une expression de la XIe homélie sur le Cantique des Cantiques', in Jacques Fontaine and Charles Kannengiesser (eds), Ἐπέκτασις: *Mélanges patristiques offerts au Cardinal Jean Daniélou* (Paris: Beauchesne, 1972); Daniélou, 'Introduction', 32; Laird, *Gregory of Nyssa and the Grasp of Faith*, 199.
[67] Harrison, *Grace and Human Freedom*, 79.

an incorporeal, spiritual, and pure union (συζυγία) with God.⁶⁸ Mühlenberg, however, states:

> Die Unmöglichkeit der Vereinigung hat Gregor von Nyssa von dem Inneren seines Systems aus begründen können, von seinem Gottesbegriff aus.⁶⁹

He objects to the language of *unio mystica* on three grounds. Firstly, he sees it as an anachronistic reading back of a medieval concept into Gregory's work; secondly, Gregory clearly delineates an ontological gulf between created human beings and the infinite uncreated God, making union impossible; and thirdly, union implies an endpoint to the spiritual journey, whereas Gregory talks of perpetual progress.⁷⁰ Heine suggests that 'the polemical theology of Gregory's debate with Origenism and Eunomianism provides the base from which the *De vita Moysis* can be properly interpreted'.⁷¹ By way of rejoinder, it is argued that it is still possible to talk of union or presence or participation despite the fact that God's essence can never be known, and the infinity of God means that there is no stopping point. Harrison, for example, writes that 'by faith, hope and love, the impasse of divine incomprehensibility is overcome. The person...makes a breakthrough into eternal growth and starts climbing the endless ladder of ever increasing knowledge and participation.'⁷² Similar debates have taken place over heavenly ascent texts, often couched in terms of 'exegesis' versus 'experience'. Michael Stone and Martha Himmelfarb have had a long-running disagreement over whether the pseudepigraphic ascent apocalypses are 'literary documents',⁷³ or reflections of 'actual visionary activity or analogous religious experience'.⁷⁴ David Halperin and Schäfer insist that the accounts of *ma'aseh merkavah* (the work of the chariot) in rabbinic literature are referring to the exegetical activity of interpreting the first chapter of Ezekiel,⁷⁵ whereas Wolfson and Morray-Jones object to the sharp

---

⁶⁸ GNO 6.15.13–15; quoted Laird, *Gregory of Nyssa and the Grasp of Faith*, 101 n. 197.

⁶⁹ 'Gregory of Nyssa has been able to justify the impossibility of union from within his systematic understanding, from his conceptualisation of God.' Ekkehard Mühlenberg, *Die Unendlichkeit Gottes bei Gregor von Nyssa: Gregors Kritik am Gottesbegriff der klassischen Metaphysik* (Göttingen: Vandenhoeck & Ruprecht, 1966), 199.

⁷⁰ Mühlenberg, *Die Unendlichkeit Gottes*, 147, 199, 152.

⁷¹ Heine, *Perfection in the Virtuous Life*, 5.

⁷² Harrison, *Grace and Human Freedom*, 86; cf. Laird, *Gregory of Nyssa and the Grasp of Faith*, 209.

⁷³ Himmelfarb, *Ascent to Heaven*, 98; cf. Martha Himmelfarb, 'The Practice of Ascent in the Ancient Mediterranean World', in John J. Collins and Michael Fishbane (eds), *Death, Ecstasy and Otherworldly Journeys* (Albany: State University of New York Press, 1995), 132.

⁷⁴ Michael E. Stone, 'A Reconsideration of Apocalyptic Visions', *Harvard Theological Review*, 96: 2 (2003), 167; cf. Michael E. Stone, 'Apocalyptic, Vision or Hallucination?', in *Selected Studies in Pseudepigrapha and Apocrypha with Special Reference to the Armenian Tradition* (Leiden: Brill, 1991), 428.

⁷⁵ David J. Halperin, *The Merkabah in Rabbinic Literature* (New Haven: American Oriental Society, 1980), 179; Schäfer, *The Origins of Jewish Mysticism*, 211.

distinction between exegetical activity and visionary mysticism.[76] Alexander points out that 'there is constant ebb and flow between text and experience'.[77] Experience suggests exegetical moves, exegesis provides the language and images with which to express experience. However, whereas the exegetical moves behind a text can be deciphered, decoding the experience involved is another matter: 'L'historien ne sait que ce qu'on lui dit. Il ne pénètre pas le secret des cœurs'.[78] This study concerns literary texts, not the phenomenology of mysticism. It is not, therefore, attempting to discover what experiences lie behind the texts. Instead, it examines their language and imagery, asking how the human relationship to the divine is being configured. In particular, it enquires into whether Gregory's tabernacle imagery, looked at through the lens of heavenly ascent, fits with notions of 'union', 'presence', or 'participation'.

1.5 REASSESSMENT OF JEWISH/CHRISTIAN BOUNDARIES

The Ways that Never Parted: Jews and Christians in Late Antiquity and the Early Middle Ages includes an article by Martin Goodman in which he presents a series of diagrams illustrating the changes that have occurred in scholarly understandings of Jewish–Christian relations. He starts with a standard view of 'the parting of the ways' (see fig. 1.1); and ends with an attempt to portray the current recognition of complexity (see fig. 1.2). A prominent advocate of the re-evaluation of Jewish–Christian boundaries is Daniel Boyarin. He has questioned the use of the terms 'Judaism' and 'Christianity', arguing that 'there is no nontheological or nonanachronistic way at all to distinguish Christianity from Judaism until institutions are in place that make and enforce this distinction, and even then, we know precious little about what the nonelite and nonchattering classes were thinking or doing'. He tries 'to show that there is at least some reason to think that, in fact, vast numbers of people around the empire made no such firm distinctions at all until fairly late in the story'.[79] Our encounter with Jewish and Christian traditions is, for the most part, through literary texts, and the new thinking recognizes that 'what the texts were doing is sometimes as, if not more, important than what they

---

[76] Elliot R. Wolfson, *Through a Speculum That Shines: Vision and Imagination in Medieval Jewish Mysticism* (Princeton: Princeton University Press, 1994), 121–4; Rowland and Morray-Jones, *The Mystery of God*, 258–9.

[77] Alexander, *The Mystical Texts*, 60.

[78] A. J. Festugière, *La révélation d'Hermès Trismégiste*, vol. 5: *Le Dieu inconnu et la gnose* (Paris: Gabalda, 1954), 267; quoted Macleod, 'Allegory and Mysticism', 362.

[79] Daniel Boyarin, 'Rethinking Jewish Christianity: An Argument for Dismantling a Dubious Category (to which is Appended a Correction of my *Border Lines*)', *Jewish Quarterly Review*, 99: 1 (2009), 28.

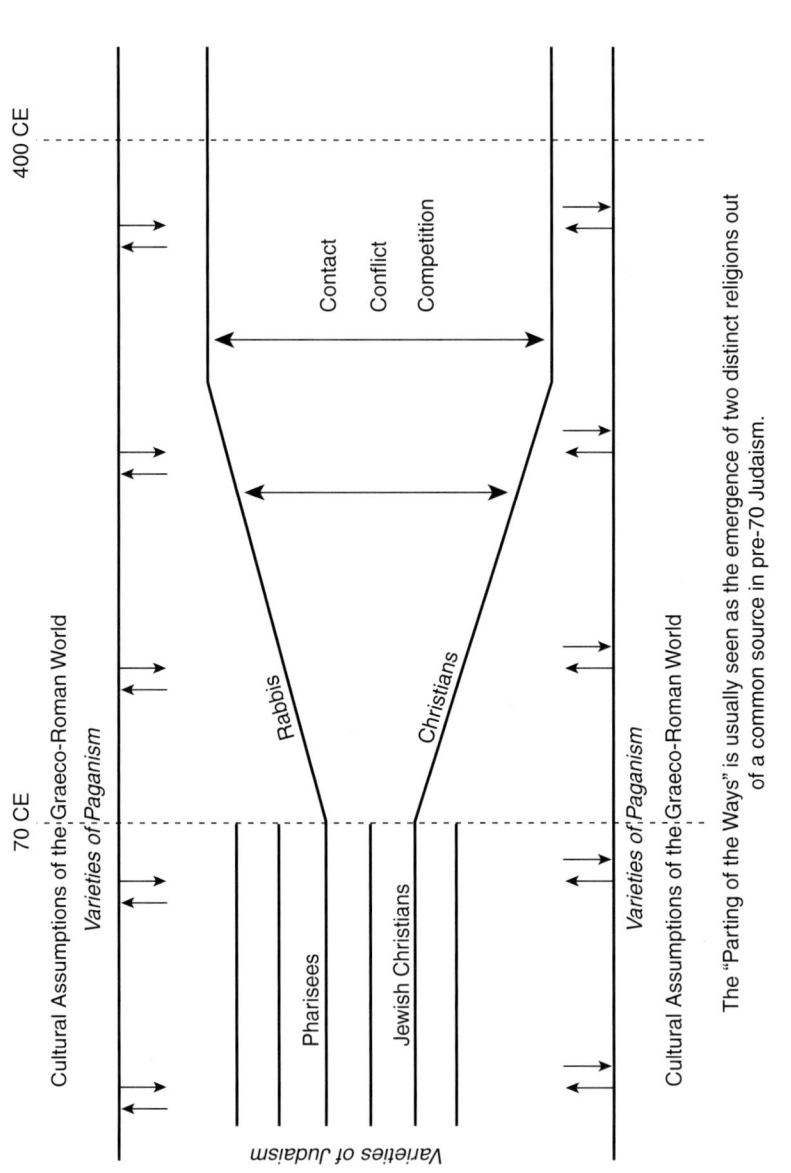

Figure 1.1 Standard view of 'the parting of the ways'.

Source: from Martin Goodman, 'Modeling the "Parting of the Ways"', in *Judaism in the Roman World: Collected Essays*, Ancient Judaism and Early Christianity, 66 (Leiden: Brill, 2007), p. 177 [first published as Martin Goodman, 'Modeling the "Parting of the Ways"', in Adam H. Becker and Annette Yoshiko Reed (eds), *The Ways that Never Parted: Jews and Christians in Late Antiquity and the Early Middle Ages* (Tübingen: Mohr Siebeck, 2003; repr., Minneapolis: Fortress, 2007)].

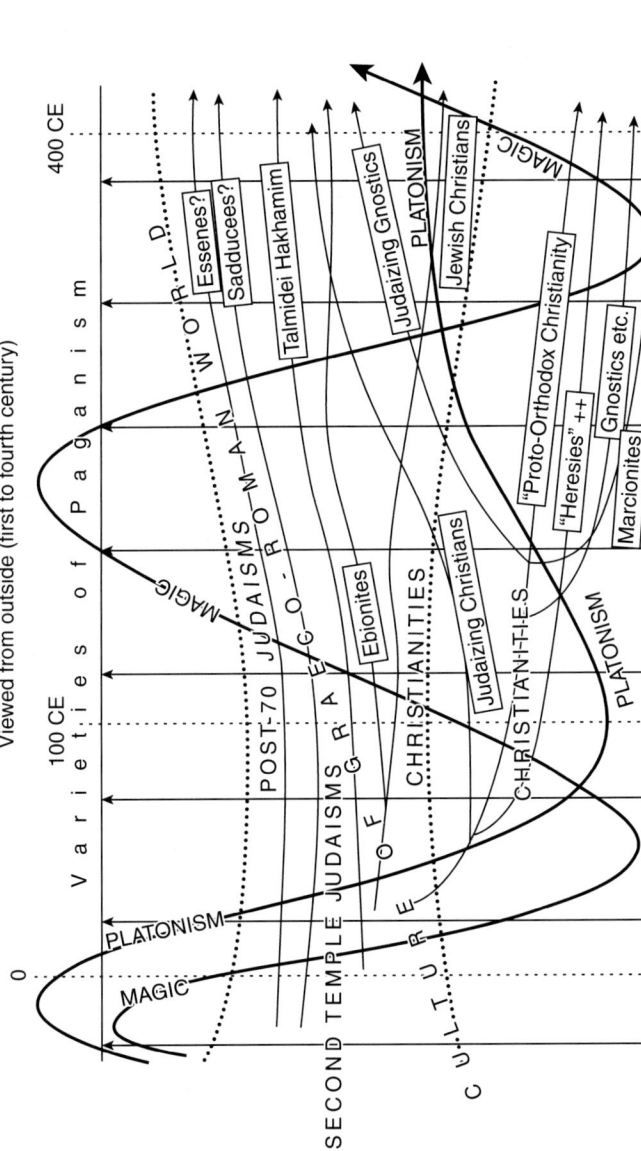

The relationships betwee Judaism, Christianity, and the surrounding culture was complex. The designation of each group in this diagram is that used by modern scholars rather that that used by insiders: no Christian group ever described itself as a "heresy". The significance of convergence between groups is that particular groups had ideas or practices close to those of other groups: it should not be concluded that closeness of ideas promoted cooperation or even social contact. Groups may reserve their greatest hostility for similar enthusiasts who happen to diverge from them in some small but (in their eyes) immensely significant detail.

Figure 1.2 The complexity of the relationships between Judaism, Christianity and the surrounding culture

Source: from Martin Goodman, 'Modeling the "Parting of the Ways"', in *Judaism in the Roman World: Collected Essays*, Ancient Judaism and Early Christianity, 66 (Leiden: Brill, 2007), p. 185 [first published as Martin Goodman, 'Modeling the "Parting of the Ways"', in Adam H. Becker and Annette Yoshiko Reed (eds), *The Ways that Never Parted: Jews and Christians in Late Antiquity and the Early Middle Ages* (Tübingen: Mohr Siebeck, 2003; repr, Minneapolis: Fortress, 2007)].

were saying'.⁸⁰ Heresiological literature, in particular, is not a reflection of reality, but an attempt to reconfigure reality. Megan Williams describes how its redefinition of the content of orthodoxy typically took place in two stages:

First, what was once comfortably within the parameters of the acceptable is designated 'heretical', so that it can be expelled from 'orthodoxy'. These rejected elements are then further identified with some category that can safely be assumed to have always already been outside the bounds of orthodoxy. For Christians, of course, that category was 'Judaism'.⁸¹

The fourth century is now seen 'as the critical era for Jewish and Christian self-definition'.⁸² Only then did church fathers, such as Gregory of Nyssa, and the rabbis of Palestine have the institutional mechanisms to impose firm boundaries.

Heavenly ascent texts are caught up in this re-evaluation. They provide prime examples of the inadequacy of the labels 'Jewish' and 'Christian'. James Davila has criticized the assumption that pseudepigrapha which 'lack explicitly Christian content or elements, or whose explicitly Christian elements can be easily excised on redaction-critical grounds, were originally Jewish compositions'.⁸³ *2 Enoch*, for example, has been designated a Jewish pseudepigraphon dating from the first century CE,⁸⁴ and yet it was preserved by Christians, and is now studied thanks to medieval Slavonic manuscripts. The *Aramaic Levi Document*, fragments of which were found in the Cairo Genizah and at Qumran, may well be a source behind *Testament of Levi*. But, in its present form, *Testament of Levi* includes explicitly Christian passages. Does removing these 'interpolations' make it Jewish? Marinus de Jonge has argued that 'a Jewish *Grundschrift*, if it existed at all, cannot possibly be reconstructed. The Testaments must be studied as a Christian composition which makes use of a surprising number of Jewish traditions, probably on the basis of acquaintance with written Jewish sources'.⁸⁵ David Frankfurter has suggested that texts such as Revelation, *Ascension of Isaiah*, and *Testaments of the Twelve Patriarchs*

---

⁸⁰ Judith M. Lieu, *Neither Jew nor Greek? Constructing Early Christianity* (London: T&T Clark, 2002), 3.

⁸¹ Megan Hale Williams, 'No More Clever Titles: Observations on Some Recent Studies of Jewish–Christian Relations in the Roman World', *Jewish Quarterly Review*, 99: 1 (2009), 48.

⁸² Becker and Reed, *The Ways that Never Parted*, 17; cf. Daniel Boyarin, *Dying for God: Martyrdom and the Making of Christianity and Judaism* (Stanford: Stanford University Press, 1999), 18; Philip Alexander, ' "The Parting of the Ways" from the Perspective of Rabbinic Judaism', in James D. G. Dunn (ed.), *Jews and Christians: The Parting of the Ways, A.D. 70 to 135* (Tübingen: Mohr Siebeck, 1992), 1–25.

⁸³ James R. Davila, *The Provenance of the Pseudepigrapha: Jewish, Christian, or Other?* (Leiden: Brill, 2005), 3.

⁸⁴ Andrei A. Orlov, *The Enoch–Metatron Tradition* (Tübingen: Mohr Siebeck, 2005), 9.

⁸⁵ Marinus de Jonge, 'Levi in Aramaic Levi and in the Testament of Levi', in Esther G. Chazon and Michael Stone (eds), *Pseudepigraphic Perspectives: The Apocrypha and Pseudepigrapha in Light of the Dead Sea Scrolls* (Leiden: Brill, 1999), 71.

might be 'the work of *continuous* communities of halakhically-observant Jewish groups—perhaps of a sectarian nature—that incorporated Jesus into their cosmologies and liturgies while retaining an essentially Jewish, or even *priestly*, self-definition'.[86]

The paradigm of heavenly ascent was common to Jews, Christians, and pagans. It could provide another wavy line, like 'magic', crossing the whole of Goodman's final diagram. Different texts developed its potential in different ways, not all of which can be labelled straightforwardly 'Jewish' or 'Christian'. It is no surprise that Gregory of Nyssa bought into heavenly ascent—it was part of the zeitgeist: 'The antithesis of the heavens and the earth, closer to the stars, closer to the heavy matter of our world, *epouranios* and *epigeios*, runs obsessively through the literature of the period.'[87] The question is how Gregory manipulated that paradigm in the service of orthodox Christian self-definition. This will come into focus by comparing his interpretation of heavenly ascent with a spectrum of other possibilities.

1.6 JEWISH ROOTS OF CHRISTIAN MYSTICISM

McGinn writes,

> The religious world of late Second Temple Judaism provided a matrix for Christian mysticism in two related ways—through the mystical, or at least protomystical, ascents to the vision of God found in the apocalypses, and through the movement toward the establishment of a canon of the sacred texts of Israel and the creation of the tools and techniques to render it continuously alive for the believing community.[88]

He is careful, however, not to overstate the influence of post-Second Temple Jewish texts, saying that 'Merkavah mysticism...would form a major topic for comparative study with early Christian mysticism, especially since both shared so much common background, but there is little evidence for any direct contact'.[89] One forum for the discussion of pre-Kabbalistic Jewish and pre-Dionysiac Christian mysticism 'across the traditional boundaries that have separated the study of Judaism and Christianity from each other' has been the Early Jewish and Christian Mysticism Group of the Society of Biblical Literature.[90] To celebrate its tenth anniversary, it published *Paradise*

---

[86] Frankfurter, 'Beyond "Jewish Christianity"', 134–5.
[87] Peter Brown, *The Making of Late Antiquity* (Cambridge, Mass.: Harvard University Press, 1978), 16. *Epouranios* is 'heavenly' and *epigeios* 'earthly'.
[88] McGinn, *The Foundations of Mysticism*, 22.
[89] McGinn, *The Foundations of Mysticism*, 20.
[90] April D. DeConick (ed.), *Paradise Now: Essays on Early Jewish and Christian Mysticism* (Atlanta: Society of Biblical Literature, 2006), xvii.

Now: Essays on Early Jewish and Christian Mysticism. In her introductory essay, April DeConick talks of the internalization of the apocalyptic heritage, the collapse of the cosmic into the personal: 'The period-literature indicates that some Jews and Christians hoped to achieve *in the present* the eschatological dream, the restoration of God's Image *within themselves*—the resurrection and transformation of their bodies into the glorious bodies of angels and their minds into the mind of God.'[91] Another overview of scholarly explorations is provided by the website 'Jewish Roots of Eastern Christian Mysticism'.[92] It contains a cornucopia of articles, including sections on 'Jewish Temple Traditions and Christian Liturgy', 'Instruction, Initiation, and Special Knowledge: Jewish and Christian Traditions', and 'Ascent to Heaven in Jewish and Christian Mysticism'. Under 'Jewish Temple Traditions and Christian Liturgy' are a number of articles by Margaret Barker. She argues that a secret tradition, 'rooted in the symbolism of the temple and the teachings of the ancient priesthood', was passed down orally in the early church.[93] According to her, the theology of the Jerusalem temple was first obscured by 'the seventh-century BCE "reformers" in the time of Josiah', a situation reinforced 'by the triumph of the group who returned from Babylon in the sixth century and set up the second temple'. Nevertheless, 'the world of the first temple and its high priestly tradition survived into the early Church'.[94] She is right to highlight the influence of temple imagery on early Christianity. However, as this book will demonstrate, there is no need to posit a secret oral tradition which maintained First Temple theology intact in order to account for the influence. Evolving traditions of biblical interpretation are sufficient explanation. This study will show that the idea of a 'tabernacle not made with hands' does indeed have biblical and apocalyptic roots. And the issues with which Gregory wrestles, such as who has access to the heavenly mysteries, whether God can be seen or not, and the relationship between God's essence and God's names, also crop up in other traditions arising from the same heritage. But ideas about the tabernacle and temple are not static; they develop differently in different contexts. The influence of Platonism on Christianity in general, and Gregory in particular, is enormous; and this leads to a divergence between Jewish and Christian mysticism. Guy Stroumsa argues that, thanks to Platonism, Christian theologians—but not Jewish thinkers after Philo—'could claim the vision of God to be a spiritual vision, which had nothing to do with the vision of the corporal eyes'.[95] Jews retained archaic

---

[91] April D. DeConick, 'What Is Early Jewish and Christian Mysticism?', in DeConick (ed.), *Paradise Now*, 24.
[92] <http://www.marquette.edu/maqom>.
[93] Margaret Barker, *The Great High Priest: The Temple Roots of Christian Liturgy* (London: T&T Clark, 2003), 11.
[94] Barker, *The Great High Priest*, 315.
[95] G. G. Stroumsa, 'To See or Not to See: On the Early History of the *Visio Beatifica*', in Peter Schäfer (ed.), *Wege mystischer Gotteserfahrung: Judentum, Christentum und Islam/Mystical approaches to God: Judaism, Christianity, and Islam* (Munich: Oldenbourg, 2006), 72.

patterns of thought for much longer, so that it is hard 'to find a serious disengagement from anthropomorphic conceptions of God among Jews before Maimonides'.[96] These differences in context, philosophical background, and language must be taken seriously, but it is still possible to trace the trajectory of apocalyptic ideas through both Jewish and Christian mystical traditions.

---

[96] Stroumsa, 'To See or Not to See', 71.

2

Gregory of Nyssa and *Life of Moses*

Let us put forth Moses as our example for life.[1]

2.1 GREGORY'S LIFE AND WORKS

Gregory of Nyssa was born around CE 335 to a pious, wealthy, well-educated family of Pontus and Cappadocia, which had been Christian for at least three generations. Gregory, his oldest brother, Basil of Caesarea, and their friend, Gregory of Nazianzus, are known collectively as the Cappadocian fathers. Thanks to Gregory's biography of his sister, *Life of Macrina*, Gregory of Nazianzus' oration *In Praise of Basil*, and the letters of all three Cappadocian fathers, more is known about Gregory's life and family background than is the case with many patristic authors. Anna Silvas provides a biography in the introduction to her translation of the letters by and about Gregory; and Raymond Van Dam probes Cappadocian family relationships and friendships.[2] Despite the comparative wealth of source material, however, questions remain, not least because the Cappadocian fathers carefully manipulated their self-presentation. The date of Basil's death, a crucial event for Gregory, has been the subject of debate.[3] Gregory probably married; did he even perhaps have a son?[4] His rhetoric is not easy to decipher. Silvas comments that 'Gregory manages to reveal himself and yet remain somehow elusive'.[5] When, in *Letter* 10, he writes, 'we are very distressed at the present state of affairs and

---

[1] *Vit. Moys.* 1.15; trans. Malherbe and Ferguson, 33.
[2] Anna M. Silvas, *Gregory of Nyssa: The Letters: Introduction, Translation and Commentary* (Leiden: Brill, 2007), 1–57; Raymond Van Dam, *Families and Friends in Late Roman Cappadocia* (Philadelphia: University of Pennsylvania Press, 2003).
[3] See Pierre Maraval, 'Retour sur quelques dates concernant Basile de Césarée et Grégoire de Nysse' *Revue d'histoire ecclésiastique* 99 (2004), and Silvas, *The Letters*, 32–9.
[4] See Jean Daniélou, 'Le Mariage de Grégoire de Nysse et la Chronologie de sa Vie', *Revue des études augustiniennes*, 2 (1956); M. Aubineau, *Grégoire de Nysse: Traité de la Virginité* (Paris: Cerf, 1966), 65–77; and Silvas, *The Letters*, 15–25.
[5] Silvas, *The Letters*, 1.

our affliction has no end,'[6] is he talking about the situation in Nyssa in 375,[7] or his difficulties in Sebasteia in 380,[8] or the tensions between Helladius of Caesarea and himself in 383?[9] As Pierre Maraval remarks, 'on aimerait moins de plaintes et plus de faits!'[10]

Of the five boys born to Gregory's parents, Basil the Elder and Emmelia, three—Basil, Gregory, and Peter—became bishops; one, Naucratius, lived as a hermit and died in a hunting accident; and one must have died in infancy. The eldest child, Macrina, one of five daughters, resolved to stay single after the death of her fiancé, and persuaded her widowed mother 'to share a common way of life with the virgins, making sisters and equals of the slave girls and domestics who were with her'.[11] Gregory credits her with taking Basil in hand after he had become 'excessively puffed up with the thought of his own eloquence'.[12] Unlike Basil, who studied in Constantinople and Athens, Gregory seems to have been educated nearer to home, acquiring nevertheless a sophisticated knowledge of philosophy and rhetoric: 'He read deeply and retentively in Plato, Aristotle, the Stoics, Plotinus and other platonizing philosophers, Philo of Alexandria and Christian authors, above all Origen.'[13] According to Gregory of Nazianzus, Gregory of Nyssa embarked on an ecclesiastical career, taking up the minor position of lector, but abandoned it in order to become a rhetorician.[14] He returned to the church, however, for in 371 or 372, Basil, by then bishop of Caesarea and locked into a power struggle with the neighbouring bishop of Tyana, appointed him bishop of Nyssa. Basil reports that Gregory accepted the position reluctantly, being 'constrained, under every necessity, to undertake the ministry'.[15] In 375/6 he was accused of financial irregularities, deposed from his see, and sent into exile, probably as part of attempts by the Arian emperor, Valens, to intimidate Basil. Gregory was able to return to Nyssa in 378, shortly before Basil's death.[16] Within a year, Macrina too had died.

Daniélou divides Gregory's works into three groups: those written before Basil's death, starting with *On Virginity*; those written between 379 and 385, at

---

[6] GNO 8,2.40; trans. Silvas, 148.

[7] See Jean Daniélou, 'Grégoire de Nysse à travers les lettres de Saint Basile et de Saint Grégoire de Nazianze', *Vigiliae christianae*, 19 (1965), 34.

[8] See Pierre Maraval, *Grégoire de Nysse: Lettres* (Paris: Cerf, 1990), 30, 184 n. 1; and Silvas, *The Letters*, 146–7.

[9] See Jean Daniélou, 'La chronologie des oeuvres de Grégoire de Nysse', in F. L. Cross (ed.), *Papers Presented to the Fourth International Conference on Patristic Studies Held at Christ Church, Oxford, 1963, Part 1* (Berlin: Akademie-Verlag, 1966), 165.

[10] 'We would like fewer complaints and more facts!' Maraval, *Lettres*, 30.

[11] *Macr.* (GNO 8,1.378.2–5); trans. Silvas, 118.

[12] *Macr.* (GNO 8,1.377.11–12); trans. Silvas, 117.   [13] Silvas, *The Letters*, 8.

[14] Gregory of Nazianzus *Epist.* 11; trans. Silvas, 91–2.

[15] Basil *Epist.* 225; trans. Silvas, 84.

[16] For difficulties over the dating see Silvas, *The Letters*, 32–9.

the height of his ecclesiastical career; and those written after 386.[17] The dating of his writings is not an exact science—there are few references to external datable events. Daniélou himself could change his mind: in 1955 he assigned *On the Lord's Prayer, On the Beatitudes,* and *On the Titles of the Psalms* to the end of Gregory's life; but by 1966 he had moved them to the first period, on the basis of their Platonic and Origenist themes, which become modified in later works.[18] It does seem, however, that with Basil's death, Gregory came into his own. He continued Basil's dispute with the neo-Arian Eunomius of Cyzicus, writing four treatises against him: *Against Eunomius* 1–3 and *Refutation of the Confession of Faith of Eunomius*. He also produced a number of shorter works on the Trinity, and refuted the Christology of Apollinarius. With *On the Making of Humankind, On the Soul and Resurrection,* and *On Infants' Early Deaths* he provided a series of reflections on anthropological themes. There is no record of Gregory's part in the debates of the Council of Constantinople in 381, but he was clearly an influential figure. He may have given the opening address; he certainly delivered the funeral oration for Meletius, the first president of the council, who died shortly after it opened. He was named, along with Helladius of Caesarea and Otreius of Melitene, as a guardian of orthodoxy in Cappadocia and Pontus. He also seems to have been sent by the council on an official mission to Arabia, after which he visited Jerusalem. *Letter 3* suggests that a bitter doctrinal dispute took place there. In 385 Gregory was chosen to deliver the funeral orations of the emperor's young daughter Pulcheria and, a few weeks later, of his wife Flacilla. His *Great Catechetical Oration*, written around that time, provides a comprehensive account of Christian theology.

The Council of Nicaea, in 325, declared the Son to be *homoousios* (sharing the same being or essence) with the Father. This was reaffirmed by the Council of Constantinople in 381. For much of the intervening period, however, the concept was the subject of intense debate. In the 320s and 330s the leading opponent of the Nicene party was Arius, a priest and teacher from Alexandria, who died in 337. By the 360s a radical neo-Arian grouping had arisen, led by Aetius of Antioch, and then by his disciple Eunomius of Cyzicus, which insisted that the Father and Son were unlike in *ousia* (being or essence). Gregory championed a Trinitarian formula of one *ousia* and three *hypostases* (persons), and his fiercest arguments were with Eunomius. Eunomius declared the Begotten Son to be subordinate to the Unbegotten God, whose essence was defined by that name 'Unbegotten'. Gregory, by contrast, insisted both on the true deity of Christ, and on the radical unknowability of God's essence, positing an ontological gap between Creator and creation. In the process he developed

---

[17] Daniélou, 'La chronologie des oeuvres de Grégoire de Nysse'.
[18] See Jean Daniélou, 'La chronologie des sermons de Grégoire de Nysse', *Revue des sciences religieuses*, 29 (1955), 372; and Daniélou, 'La chronologie des oeuvres de Grégoire de Nysse', 160–2.

a sophisticated understanding of the nature of language in relation to God. Gregory also argued against the Christology of Apollinarius of Laodicea, who described Jesus as the divine Logos within human flesh. Gregory insisted on the full humanity of Jesus, including a human mind. But his own Christology was later judged untenable, as it did not fit fifth-century criteria. According to these Chalcedonian standards, he managed to be 'Nestorian' and 'Monophysite' at the same time. He talked of Jesus as a human being (an *anthrōpos*) who was 'taken up' or 'appropriated' by Christ; but then suggested that at the resurrection, his entire humanity was 'swallowed up in the eternal reality of the glorified Son, like a drop of water lost in a boundless ocean'.[19]

Gregory lived at a turning point in Christian history. By the time he was born, the days of persecution were over, but it was by no means clear that paganism was a spent force. The reign of Julian the Apostate (360–362), when practising Christians were forbidden to teach in schools and universities, took place when Gregory was in his late twenties. It was only in 391, at the end of Gregory's life, that pagan sacrifices were prohibited. Adrian Hastings characterizes the sixty years from CE 370 to 430 as 'a moment of genius'. He attributes this to the fact that many of the key patristic writers of that time, including the Cappadocian Fathers,

> had been deeply educated in the traditional learning of Athens and Rome before turning to theology. That may have had something to do with the freshness of their thought, a sense of diverse stimulation possible only for those inhabiting a philosophical frontier. Several of them, too, had quite chequered careers in other ways as well. Where they became monks it was out of an entirely adult decision. The tension in many of their lives between ecclesiastical service, in the episcopate or otherwise, and the call to contemplative prayer remains evident.[20]

The fourth century saw a shift from individual Christian asceticism to cenobitic living, with the widespread establishment of monastic communities. Living a monastic lifestyle replaced martyrdom as the way of witnessing to Christianity's defiance of the world. Members of Gregory's family were key players, with both his sister Macrina and his brother Basil establishing monasteries. Basil's *Rules* laid the foundations of Eastern monasticism. One of Basil's aims was to contain ascetic fervour within the confines of the institutional church. From Constantine's reign onwards, there was an explosion of ecclesiastical construction. Worship could now be held in public, in purpose-built basilicas. Gregory commissioned an octagonal *martyrion* at Nyssa, which he

---

[19] Brian E. Daley, ' "Heavenly Man" and "Eternal Christ": Apollinarius and Gregory of Nyssa on the Personal Identity of the Savior', *Journal of Early Christian Studies*, 10: journalIssue4/journalIssue (2002), 471.

[20] Adrian Hastings, '150–550', in Adrian Hastings (ed.), *A World History of Christianity* (London: Cassell, 1999), 58.

described in a letter to Amphilochius of Iconium.[21] To go with the new buildings, more and more elaborate liturgies were devised, drawing on both Old Testament priestly traditions and imperial court ritual.

Daniélou suggests that from around 387 Gregory 'turned himself wholly towards the life of the spirit', as exemplified by *Life of Moses* and *On the Song of Songs*.[22] Not everyone agrees, as will be discussed in 2.2. Jerome, in his *Lives of Illustrious Men*, dated to 393, writes of Gregory as though he is still alive. He is known to have been present at a synod in 394; but no more is heard of him after that.

2.2 LIFE OF MOSES

Daniélou assigns *Life of Moses* to the end of Gregory's life. Heine disagrees, and demolishes Daniélou's arguments one by one.[23] Gregory's reference to his grey hairs (τῇ πολιᾷ) in *Life of Moses* 1.2 is a red herring, as he also mentions them in *Against Eunomius* 2, dated to before the Council of Constantinople.[24] Heine concludes that the treatise may have been written

> when (1) Eunomius' attacks on Basil and the whole Eunomian problem were very much alive in Gregory's mind and (2) when Eunomianism was still causing many problems in the Cappadocian churches. The mid 380's would be the most probable date for the first of these conditions; the second probably continued for some time thereafter. Although the exact date of writing remains obscure, we believe that the evidence for a late date is so tenuous that the treatise should not be approached with the *a priori* assumption that it was written at a time when theological controversy was far removed from Gregory's thoughts.[25]

The real disagreement is not about dating, but about the nature of the treatise. Is it mysticism or polemical theology? Agreeing with Daniélou's dating does not preclude seeing the treatise differently.[26] Alden Mosshammer, for example, by comparing *On the Beatitudes* with *On the Song of Songs*, charts Gregory's intellectual development not so much as a turning towards mysticism, as the discovery

---

[21] *Epist.* 25 (GNO 8,2.79–83).

[22] Jean Daniélou, 'Introduction', in Herbert Musurillo, *From Glory to Glory: Texts from Gregory of Nyssa's Mystical Writings* (New York: Scribner, 1961; repr., Crestwood, NY: St Vladimir's Seminary Press, 2001), 9.

[23] Ronald E. Heine, *Perfection in the Virtuous Life: A Study in the Relationship Between Edification and Polemical Theology in Gregory of Nyssa's De Vita Moysis* (Cambridge, Mass.: Philadelphia Patristic Foundation, 1975), 10–15.

[24] *Eun.* 2.605 (GNO 1.403.3).   [25] Heine, *Perfection in the Virtuous Life*, 15.

[26] See also G. May, 'Die Chronologie des Lebens und des Werkes Gregors von Nyssa', in Marguerite Harl (ed.), *Écriture et culture philosophique dans la pensée de Grégoire de Nysse* (Leiden: Brill, 1971), 63–4. May concurs with Daniélou's dating.

of an incarnational theology which takes the church seriously. In the earlier work, 'Gregory's focus is on the upward journey of the individual soul from the cave of earthly darkness and deception towards the pure intelligence of the heavens'.[27] In the later one, 'the soul no longer stands alone'.[28] It becomes truly itself by receiving Christ. And 'each bridal soul both in her own progress and in her love for other souls contributes to the building of the Body of Christ'.[29]

The *Life of Moses* is divided into two parts: *Historia* (historical narrative) and *Theōria* (interpretation). In part one Gregory summarizes the life of Moses as told in Exodus, selected passages from Numbers, and Deuteronomy 34. In part two he seeks out 'the spiritual understanding (*dianoia*) which corresponds to the history in order to obtain suggestions of virtue'.[30] In the case of the tabernacle, the *historia* is set out in 1.49–56, 61, and the *theōria* given in 2.170–201. Gregory reflects on the three theophanies experienced by Moses: at the burning bush, in the darkness of Mount Sinai, and as a result of his request to see God's glory, when he is shown the back of God. Macleod comments on 'the freedom with which Gregory handles the text of Exodus and Numbers... The work omits many episodes narrated of Moses in the Bible; it is concerned simply with his life as a model of virtue.'[31] Heine, on the other hand, notes that Gregory 'deviates from the order of events in the Biblical text only three times in the entire treatise, and only one of these deviations seems to be of any significance as an intentional rearrangement of the order of the story'.[32] There is truth in both comments. Gregory does make a selection from the biblical material. In the narrative about Mount Sinai, for example, he omits the covenant ceremony of Exodus 24, and the instructions about sacrifices and the Sabbath in Exodus 29–31. He chooses just ten episodes from the book of Numbers. And, as Daniélou points out, even in his *historia* Gregory amplifies the biblical text, emphasizing the miraculous.[33] However, Heine is right that Gregory follows the biblical outline of Moses' story. He certainly does not manipulate it into the threefold schema of light, cloud, and darkness put forward by Daniélou.[34] As Ludlow comments,

> This leads to a slightly odd ending to *The Life of Moses* from a dramatic point-of-view—a gentle *diminuendo* rather than a grand finale—however, it fits with

---

[27] Alden A. Mosshammer, 'Gregory's Intellectual Development: A Comparison of the *Homilies on the Beatitudes* with the *Homilies on the Song of Songs*', in H. R. Drobner and A. Viciano (eds), *Gregory of Nyssa: Homilies on the Beatitudes* (Leiden: Brill, 2000), 360.
[28] Mosshammer, 'Gregory's Intellectual Development', 379.
[29] Mosshammer, 'Gregory's Intellectual Development', 385.
[30] *Vit. Moys.* 1.15; trans. Malherbe and Ferguson, 33.
[31] Colin W. Macleod, 'Allegory and Mysticism in Origen and Gregory of Nyssa', *Journal of Theological Studies*, 22: journalIssue2/journalIssue (1971), 372–3.
[32] Heine, *Perfection in the Virtuous Life*, 99.
[33] Jean Daniélou, *Grégoire de Nysse: La Vie de Moïse, ou Traité de la perfection en matière de vertu* (Paris: Cerf, 2000), 17–19.
[34] See 6.3.

Gregory's belief that knowing and loving God is a journey to be travelled eternally. This is symbolized by Moses' death on the brink of the promised land: he has reached his goal and yet he will never quite be there.[35]

Gregory seeks the 'mind' of scripture. This includes not only the interpretation of individual episodes, but also the overarching aim (*skopos*) of the text, which is revealed in the orderly sequence (*akolouthia*) of events: 'What sets apart Gregory's treatment of allegory is the attempt to find a structure and a sequence in the texts that he deals with.'[36] Gregory is influenced by Origen in his use of allegory, but, as Ludlow argues, 'he is much more cautious than Origen about offering several interpretations of one text, or seeking out several layers of meaning', because 'over-speculative exegesis is ruled out by the controlling concept of the *akolouthia*, which is itself determined by the divine *skopos* in the text'.[37] Abraham Malherbe and Everett Ferguson discuss the criteria that Gregory, in common with other Alexandrian exegetes, employs for finding spiritual interpretations of the sacred text: an allegorical meaning becomes necessary when the literal meaning is unnecessary, superfluous, or out of place; when something morally wrong is enjoined in the biblical text; or when anything unworthy of God is suggested; as well as when it is impossible to reduplicate the exact historical circumstances.[38] Examples of all these considerations can be found in *Life of Moses*. However, Gregory's main concern should not be seen as making sense of the difficulties of the biblical text. He is doing something more creative, as Macleod recognizes:

> The biblical life of Moses offers a framework and a collection of symbols within it. It stands to the allegorist as a myth to a poet or dramatist; it can both embody and shape his thought or feeling. And it is clear above all from *Comm. in Cant.*, where Moses and the wanderings of the Israelites often appear in significant contexts, that the patriarch had lain for some time as a symbol in Gregory's mind.... Allegory then might be positively valued as a kind of artistic form, capable of suggesting and expressing fresh connections of thought.[39]

The life of Moses is 'a springboard for [Gregory's] theology'.[40] He is constrained by the biblical text: by the order of events and the many peculiarities of the stories. Like a woodcarver, he has to incorporate these 'knots' into his creation. But his aim is to provide inspiration for a life of Christian virtue.

---

[35] Morwenna Ludlow, 'Theology and Allegory: Origen and Gregory of Nyssa on the Unity and Diversity of Scripture', *International Journal of Systematic Theology*, 4: journalIssue1/journalIssue (2002), 56.
[36] Macleod, 'Allegory and Mysticism', 372.   [37] Ludlow, 'Theology and Allegory', 65.
[38] Abraham J. Malherbe and Everett Ferguson, *Gregory of Nyssa: The Life of Moses* (New York: Paulist Press, 1978), 7–8.
[39] Macleod, 'Allegory and Mysticism', 376.   [40] Macleod, 'Allegory and Mysticism', 374.

3

Biblical Contexts

It seems good to me to make use of Scripture as a counselor.[1]

Heavenly ascent texts, including the tabernacle passage in *Life of Moses*, abound with biblical allusions. Wherever one stands in the scholarly debates about the balance of exegesis and personal experience in apocalyptic and other heavenly ascent traditions, there is no doubt that a number of key biblical texts have shaped those traditions. As McGinn says, referring to both Jewish and Christian mystical traditions, the Bible served 'as the inexhaustible living source from which the book of experience drew its sustenance'.[2] Below are short introductions to the tabernacle narrative in Exodus, Ezekiel Chapter 1, and the Pauline material mined by Gregory, indicating those features of interest to subsequent interpreters. These are not the only biblical passages elaborated upon by heavenly ascent texts: Gregory also quotes from the Psalms; *Songs of the Sabbath Sacrifice* alludes to the 'still small voice' of 1 Kings 19:12; nearly everywhere Isaiah's seraphim merge with Ezekiel's cherubim. But these texts require some introductory remarks for the later developments to make sense.

3.1 EXODUS 25–28

On Mount Sinai, surrounded by the divine cloud, Moses is shown the pattern of the tabernacle which the Israelites are to build. The Hebrew word that is translated as 'tabernacle' is *mishkan*, derived from the verb *shakhan* 'to dwell'. It simply means 'dwelling place', and in the MT is used to denote both the tabernacle and the temple.[3] Biblical scholars assign Exodus 25–8 to P, the Priestly source:

> The idealized blueprint that P presents in Exodus 25–39 draws on two architectural models: on portable tent sanctuaries used by ancient Semitic nomads, and

---

[1] *Vit. Moys.* 1.11; trans. Malherbe and Ferguson, 31.
[2] Bernard McGinn, 'Selective Affinities: Reflections on Jewish and Christian Mystical Exegesis', in Rachel Elior and Peter Schäfer (eds), *Creation and Re-Creation in Jewish Thought: Festschrift in Honor of Joseph Dan on the Occasion of his Seventieth Birthday* (Tübingen: Mohr Siebeck, 2005), 87.
[3] For *mishkan* used to denote the temple see Pss. 43:3, 84:2, Ezek. 37:27.

on the Solomonic temple. Indeed, in some respects the tabernacle's plan is closer to that of a genuine ancient Semitic tent shrine than to Solomon's temple.⁴

In this Exodus narrative, the LXX translates *mishkan* as *skēnē*, 'tent'. Wilhelm Michaelis suggests that it seemed to the translators that *skēnē* was the predestined word for *mishkan* 'because the two terms contain the same three consonants skn in the same sequence'.⁵

The detailed instructions for the tabernacle are no longer entirely comprehensible: the measurements are unclear and some of the technical terms obscure. As Menahem Haran remarks, 'We are faced with a unique combination of long-winded description on the one hand and total omission of various particulars on the other.'⁶ The basic layout, however, is clear: an outer courtyard within which stands a tent divided into two. The tent has three or four layers of coverings. The inner curtains are made of 'fine twined linen and blue and purple and scarlet' with a design of cherubim worked into them.⁷ Over them are placed curtains of goats' hair.⁸ Then there is a covering of tanned rams' skins, along with the skins of some other animal, which cannot be identified from its Hebrew designation (תחשים).⁹ The King James version has 'badger', the RSV 'goat', and the NJPS 'dolphin'; the LXX opts for blue skins (δέρματα ὑακίνθινα). The larger compartment of the tabernacle is the holy place, the smaller one the holy of holies, and between them hangs a veil—*parokhet* in Hebrew, *katapetasma* in Greek—made of the same material as the inner curtains.¹⁰ In the courtyard stand an altar and a bronze washbasin.¹¹ In the holy place is the table for the 'bread of the Presence', the seven-branch lampstand, and the altar of incense.¹² In the holy of holies is the ark containing the 'testimony' (עדת; τὰ μαρτύρια): the two stone tablets inscribed by the finger of God.¹³ It is covered by the 'mercy seat' (כפרת; ἱλαστήριον), which is adorned by two golden cherubim, one at each end.¹⁴ The wings of the cherubim overshadow the mercy seat; their faces are turned to one another, but facing downwards towards the ark. Moses is told that God will speak with him 'from above the mercy seat'.¹⁵ 'The Divine Presence was believed to settle, as it were, in the space between the two cherubim

---

⁴ Benjamin D. Sommer, *The Bodies of God and the World of Ancient Israel* (Cambridge: Cambridge University Press, 2009), 93.

⁵ W. Michaelis, 'σκηνή, σκῆνος, σκήνωμα, σκηνόω, ἐπισκηνόω, κατασκηνόω, σκηνοπηγία, σκηνοποιός', in Gerhard Friedrich (ed.), *Theological Dictionary of the New Testament* (Grand Rapids, Mich.: Eerdmans, 1971), 7.371.

⁶ Menahem Haran, *Temples and Temple-Service in Ancient Israel: An Inquiry into the Character of Cult Phenomena and the Historical Setting of the Priestly School* (Oxford: Clarendon, 1978), 150.

⁷ Exod. 26:1.   ⁸ Exod. 26:7.   ⁹ Exod. 26:14.   ¹⁰ Exod. 26:31.
¹¹ Exod. 27:1–8; 30:17–21.   ¹² Exod. 25:23–30; 25:31–40; 30:1–10.
¹³ Exod. 31:18, 34:1.   ¹⁴ Exod. 25:10–22.   ¹⁵ Exod. 25:22.

above the Ark', which fits with a conception of the ark 'as a footstool beneath the invisible throne of God'.[16]

After describing the tabernacle, the text details the high priest's clothing. He was to wear eight items, six of them listed in Exodus 28:4: a breastpiece (חשן; περιστήθιον),[17] an ephod (אפוד; ἐπωμίς), a robe (מעיל; ποδήρης),[18] a tunic (כתנת; χιτών), a turban (מצנפת; κίδαρις),[19] and a girdle (אבנט; ζώνη). Two items are mentioned later: a *petalon* (thin plate) of pure gold (ציץ זהב טהור; πέταλον χρυσοῦν καθαρόν),[20] and linen breeches (מכנסי־בד; περισκελῆ λινᾶ).[21] The ephod was to be of the same fine linen and coloured yarns as the tabernacle curtains, with the addition of gold thread. It is unclear 'whether the ephod covered the lower and/or upper parts of the body and whether the back and/or front'.[22] It had two shoulder pieces, each with a stone engraved with the names of six of the sons of Israel. Fastened to the ephod was the breastpiece, probably a pouch of some sort. It too was made of the multicoloured fabric with gold thread. Set onto it were twelve stones; and contained within it were the Urim and Thummin, which the LXX calls the 'disclosure' and the 'truth' (ἡ δήλωσις καὶ ἡ ἀλήθεια).[23] These 'constituted a device for determining the will of God in specific matters that were beyond human ability to decide'.[24] Underneath the ephod, the high priest wore the blue robe; and inside that the tunic. In the MT the bottom of the robe is ornamented with pomegranates made of blue, purple, and scarlet, and golden bells.[25] The bells are to tinkle as the high priest officiates.[26] In the LXX there are three kinds of ornament: golden pomegranates, bells, and pomegranates made of blue, purple, scarlet, and linen. These fabric pomegranates are also referred to as 'flower-work' (ἄνθινον), translated 'blossom' by NETS.[27] The MT describes the tunic as 'chequered' (תשבץ), which the LXX translates as 'tasselled' (κοσυμβωτόν).[28] Like other priests, the high priest wore linen breeches. His turban was surmounted by a gold plate, engraved with the words 'Holy to the Lord'. The Hebrew word translated 'plate' (ציץ) usually means 'a blossom, flower'. Elsewhere this plate is referred to as a diadem/crown (נזר).[29] The brilliant, colourful nature of these clothes is in sharp contrast to the plain linen (בד; λίνεος)

---

[16] Nahum M. Sarna, *Exploring Exodus: The Origins of Biblical Israel* (New York: Schocken, 1996), 210.
[17] Translated 'oracle' (λόγιον) in LXX Exod. 28:15.
[18] Translated 'foot-length undergarment' (ὑποδύτης ποδήρης) in LXX Exod. 28:27.
[19] Translated 'headdress' (μίτρα) in LXX Exod. 28:33.
[20] Exod. 28:36, LXX Exod. 28:32.   [21] Exod. 28:42, LXX Exod. 28:38.
[22] Nahum M. Sarna, *The JPS Torah Commentary: Exodus* (Philadelphia: Jewish Publication Society, 1991), 178.
[23] Exod. 28:30, LXX Exod. 28:26.   [24] Sarna, *Exodus*, 181.   [25] Exod. 28:33–34.
[26] Exod. 28:35.   [27] LXX Exod. 28:29–30.   [28] Exod. 28:4.
[29] Exod. 29:6.

garments prescribed in Leviticus 16:4 for the high priest's yearly entry into the holy of holies.

In chapters 35–40 of the MT the description of the tabernacle and vestments is repeated, as their fabrication takes place. The LXX departs radically from the MT, both in terms of order and content, with some substantial blocks of material omitted.[30] At the end of Exodus, however, the MT and the LXX converge again as they describe the descent of God's glory:

> Then the cloud covered the tent of meeting, and the glory of the Lord filled the tabernacle (וכבוד יהוה מלא את־המשכן; καὶ δόξης κυρίου ἐπλήσθη ἡ σκηνή).[31]

3.2 EZEKIEL 1

In the first chapter of Ezekiel, the prophet has a vision of a mobile throne supported by four 'living creatures' (*ḥayyot*). This subsequently became known as the *merkavah*, 'chariot', as shown by Ben Sira and *Pseudo-Ezekiel*, both dated to the second century BCE:

> Ezekiel beheld the vision and described the different creatures of the chariot throne (זני מרכבה)[32]

> The vision which Ezeki[el] saw [...] the gleam of the chariot (נגה מרכבה) and four living creatures[33]

The earliest witness to this designation may be the LXX translation of Ezekiel, dating from the third or second century BCE. At 43:3 it reads, '...and the vision of the chariot (ἡ ὅρασις τοῦ ἅρματος) which I saw was like the vision which I saw at the river Chebar...' Halperin favours the view 'that the translator's text was...the same as MT; and that ["the chariot"] is a midrashic rendering that presupposes *merkābâh* as a standard designation for the entity seen by Ezekiel at the River Chebar'.[34] The term *merkavah* is also used in 1 Chronicles 28:18,

---

[30] The numerous problems of the LXX text were noted by Origen, in his *Letter to Africanus*: 'What needs there speak of Exodus, where there is such diversity in what is said about the tabernacle and its court, and the ark, and the garments of the high priest and the priests, that sometimes the meaning even does not seem to be akin?' (trans. Crombie, 374). For a detailed examination see John William Wevers, *Text History of the Greek Exodus* (Göttingen: Vandenhoeck & Ruprecht, 1992), 117–46, or Martha Lynn Wade, *Consistency of Translation Techniques in the Tabernacle Accounts of Exodus in the Old Greek* (Atlanta: Society of Biblical Literature, 2003). Wade concludes, 'it seems likely that the second tabernacle account was produced by a second translator who used the translation of the first tabernacle account as a point of reference' (p. 245).

[31] Exod. 40:34.   [32] Ben Sira 49:8; text Beentjes, 88; trans. Skehan and Lella, 540.
[33] 4Q385 4 5–6; text and trans. Martínez and Tigchelaar, 2.769.
[34] David J. Halperin, 'Merkabah Midrash in the Septuagint', *Journal of Biblical Literature*, 101: 3 (1982), 354.

in the course of David's instructions to Solomon about the construction of the temple:

> …also his plan for the golden chariot of the cherubim (ולתבנית המרכבה הכרובים זהב) that spread their wings and covered the ark of the covenant of the Lord.

These references would seem to be drawing on a much older Israelite tradition of God 'enthroned on the cherubim'.[35] The 'living creatures' of Ezekiel 1 are identified as cherubim in 10:20. The exact relationship between Chronicles and Ezekiel is unclear. Did Ezekiel draw upon the tradition recorded in Chronicles of a 'chariot' in the holy of holies to imply that God could leave the temple and appear in Babylon? However, as Alexander points out, 'it is odd that [Ezekiel] does not actually take over the useful term *merkabah*'.[36] Or was the Chronicler alluding to Ezekiel's vision, already known as the *merkavah*? Either way, Ezekiel's vision of the *merkavah* became a key biblical text for later Jewish mystics. Its influence can be seen in Revelation's description of the heavenly throne with its four living creatures.

3.3 PAULINE EPISTLES[37]

Gregory interprets 2 Corinthians 12:2–5, which refers to a man in Christ being caught up to the third heaven, as a description of Paul's ascent to the supercelestial sanctuary. He therefore considers Paul to be a reliable guide to 'the mysteries of paradise'.[38] He refers to him—the great apostle—twelve times in his tabernacle interpretation,[39] and manages to include a quotation from, or allusion to, every Pauline letter other than 2 Thessalonians, 2 Timothy, Titus, and Philemon.[40] He assumes that Hebrews was written by Paul, and therefore includes its interpretation of the tabernacle curtain as the flesh of Jesus, even though it does not fit his overall scheme. He makes particularly creative use of

---

[35] Pss. 80:2 (RSV 80:1); 99:1; cf. 18:11 (RSV 18:10).
[36] Philip Alexander, *The Mystical Texts: Songs of the Sabbath Sacrifice and Related Manuscripts* (London: T&T Clark, 2006), 68.
[37] This study does not distinguish between authentic Pauline letters and those written pseudonymously, since Gregory, like other church fathers, did not do so.
[38] *Vit. Moys.* 2.178.
[39] *Vit. Moys.* 2.173, 174, 178, 179, 182 (twice), 184 (twice), 192, 193, 194 (twice).
[40] The full list of quotations/allusions is as follows: 1 Cor. 2:10, 1 Cor. 14:2 (2.173); 1 Cor. 1:24 (2.174); Col. 1:17 (2.175); Col. 2:9 (2.177); Heb. 10:20, 2 Cor. 12:3–4 (2.178); Col. 1:16 (2.179); Rom. 3:25, Phil. 2:10, Heb. 13:15 (2.182); Rom. 12:4–5, 1 Cor. 12:12–13, Eph. 1:22–23, 1 Cor. 12:28, Gal. 2:9, Phil. 2:15, 1 Cor. 15:58, 1 Tim. 3:15 (2.184); Heb. 13:15, Eph. 5:2, Phil. 4:18 (2.185); 1 Cor. 9:27 (2.187); Rom. 12:1, 1 Thess. 4:17 (2.191); 1 Tim. 1:19 (2.192); Heb. 12:11 (2.193); 1 Cor. 9:13–14, 1 Cor. 9:18, 1 Cor. 4:11 (2.194); 2 Cor. 6:7 (2.198).

Colossians 1:15–20: He seems to take the 'fullness' (*plērōma*) in 1:19 and 2:9 as linked to the verb 'to fill' (*plēthō*) in Exodus 40:34—Christ, like the tabernacle, is filled with the fullness/glory of God.[41] Gregory then uses Colossians 1:16 to argue that the heavenly powers created in Christ are represented by the furniture in the tabernacle.[42]

---

[41] For more details see 8.1, and also Ann Conway-Jones, 'Filled with the Glory of God: The Appropriation of Tabernacle Imagery in the New Testament and Gregory of Nyssa', in Michael Tait and Peter Oakes (eds), *Torah in the New Testament: Papers Delivered at the Manchester–Lausanne Seminar of June 2008* (London: T&T Clark, 2009), 231–3.

[42] See 10.1.

4

Alexandrian Contexts

> Certain of those who have previously examined the word say that the dye signifies the air.[1]

The cosmopolitan Greek city of Alexandria in Egypt was, for centuries, a centre of culture and learning. First Jews, and then Christians, there harnessed Hellenistic rhetoric and philosophy in the service of their religious belief systems. Three figures in particular stand out: Philo, Clement, and Origen. All three adapted for biblical use the allegorical approach developed to make sense of Homeric myths. They found 'spiritual' meanings hidden behind the literal details of the biblical text. During the fourth century Alexandrian exegesis came under fire from Antiochene 'literalists', who preferred to view the Old Testament as prophetic typology. Perhaps because of that controversy, Gregory very rarely uses the term *allēgoria* (allegory).[2] But he readily employs other terms typical of Alexandrian exegesis, such as *anagōgē* (elevation, lifting up), *theōria* (contemplation, insight, interpretation), *dianoia* (thought, understanding, deeper meaning), and *ainigma* (riddle, figure, symbol, sign). He says of *Life of Moses*,

> First we shall go through in outline [Moses'] life as we have learned it from the divine Scriptures. Then we shall seek out the spiritual understanding (*dianoia*) which corresponds to the history (*historia*)...[3]

As Manlio Simonetti argues, despite some concessions, Gregory 'was fundamentally an exegete of the Alexandrian tendency'.[4] And, as Boersma has pointed out, his understanding of *anagōgē* reached beyond the realm of exegesis, with the purpose of life itself being anagogical in character. For Gregory, anagogy was 'our own increasing participation in divine virtue and thus our own ascent into the life of God'.[5]

---

[1] *Vit. Moys.* 2.191.
[2] For a discussion of the six times that Gregory does use either *allēgoria* or a cognate word, see Hubertus R. Drobner, 'Allegory', in Lucas Francisco Mateo-Seco and Giulio Maspero (eds), *The Brill Dictionary of Gregory of Nyssa* (Leiden: Brill, 2010), 21.
[3] *Vit. Moys.* 1.15; trans. Malherbe and Ferguson, 33.
[4] Manlio Simonetti, 'Exegesis', in Mateo-Seco and Maspero (eds), *The Brill Dictionary of Gregory of Nyssa*, 335.
[5] Hans Boersma, *Embodiment and Virtue in Gregory of Nyssa: An Anagogical Approach* (Oxford: Oxford University Press, 2013), 3.

Philo, Clement, and Origen all developed elaborate explanations of the tabernacle's symbolism, assigning meaning to each piece of furniture and each high priestly vestment. These interpretations are important background to Gregory's tabernacle imagery, even though he made considerable adjustments, in terms of both exegetical technique and content. The melting pot of Alexandria, however, was not just home to these 'mainstream' figures. There were other seekers after knowledge, such as the followers of Basilides and Valentinus, who tend to be known by the catch-all label of 'Gnostics'. They were vituperatively condemned by the heresiologists Justin Martyr, Irenaeus, and Hippolytus. By contrast, Clement and Origen 'made real attempts to understand their opponents'.[6] Clement's *Excerpts from Theodotus*, in which he collects and comments on the teachings of the Valentinian Theodotus, testifies to further possible uses for tabernacle imagery. They may well represent the kind of possibilities that Gregory wished to guard against. This chapter contains short introductions to uses of the heavenly ascent paradigm and interpretations of the tabernacle in the works of Philo, Clement, and Origen; along with glimpses into the Valentinian use of tabernacle imagery, gained from *Excerpts from Theodotus* and Irenaeus' *Against Heresies*.

4.1 PHILO

Philo (*c*.20 BCE–CE 50) was an Alexandrian Jew who used allegorical interpretation to reconcile the Jewish scriptures with Hellenistic philosophy. He came from a wealthy, distinguished family, and was a member, possibly the head, of the Jewish delegation to the emperor, Gaius Caligula, in Rome, following a pogrom in Alexandria in CE 38.[7] He was a prolific author, and even though around a third of his works have been lost, we 'have thirty-six treatises fully or mainly extant in Greek, with fragments of another; plus an additional thirteen treatises fully or mainly extant in Armenian, with fragments of two others'.[8] Philo had an advanced grasp of Greek philosophy, and a thorough knowledge of the LXX, but probably didn't know Hebrew. His writings were not preserved by rabbinic Jews, but had an enormous influence on Christian exegesis. In some Byzantine catenae he is even referred to as a 'bishop'.[9] His works must have been in the library of the Alexandrian catechetical school of which Clement became a member. When Origen moved from Alexandria to

---

[6] Birger A. Pearson, *Ancient Gnosticism: Traditions and Literature* (Minneapolis: Fortress, 2007), 20.
[7] Philo *On the Embassy to Gaius* (*Legatio ad Gaium*), cf. Josephus *A.J.* 18.257–260.
[8] Gregory E. Sterling, et al., 'Philo', in John J. Collins and Daniel C. Harlow (eds), *Early Judaism: A Comprehensive Overview* (Grand Rapids, Mich.: Eerdmans, 2012), 253.
[9] David T. Runia, *Philo in Early Christian Literature: A Survey* (Assen: Van Gorcum, 1993), 3.

Palestinian Caesarea in 233, he took copies of Philo's works with him: 'These copies were absorbed into the library of the Episcopal school at Caesarea, and form the basis for the text of Philo's works that we today still possess.'[10]

According to Segal, 'Philo... represents a full actualization of philosophic possibilities of the ascension structure which were developed in the Hellenistic Age'.[11] Philo uses it to describe both his own experience:

> There was a time when I had leisure for philosophy... [I] seemed always to be borne aloft into the heights with a soul possessed by some God-sent inspiration, a fellow-traveller with the sun and moon and the whole heaven and universe. Ah then I gazed down from the upper air, and straining the mind's eye beheld, as from some commanding peak, the multitudinous world-wide spectacles of earthly things, and blessed my lot in that I had escaped by main force from the plagues of mortal life.[12]

and that of others:

> The soul of the lover of God does in truth leap from earth to heaven and wing its way on high (πτερωθεῖσα μετεωροπολεῖ), eager to take its place in the ranks and share the ordered march of sun and moon and the all-holy, all-harmonious host of the other stars, marshalled and led by the God Whose kingship none can dispute or usurp...[13]

He ties this Hellenistic ascent structure to the Bible by allegorizing the lives of biblical figures. *On Abraham* presents Enosh, Enoch, and Noah as a 'first trinity of those who yearn for virtue', and Abraham, Isaac, and Jacob as a second greater trinity, who stretch 'the eyesight of the soul' to reach God, the Father and Maker of all.[14] In *On the Posterity of Cain* he suggests that Moses is superior to the patriarchs:

> Moses, the man wise in all things... does not, like those before him, haunt the outer court of the Holy Place as one seeking initiation, but as a sacred Guide (ἱεροφάντης) has his abode in the sanctuary (ἐν τοῖς ἀδύτοις).[15]

This sanctuary is the darkness of Mount Sinai:

> ...entering the darkness, the invisible region, [Moses] abides there while he learns the secrets of the most holy mysteries. There he becomes not only one of the congregation of the initiated, but also the hierophant and teacher of divine rites, which he will impart to those whose ears are purified.[16]

---

[10] Runia, *Philo in Early Christian Literature*, 158.
[11] Alan F. Segal, 'Heavenly Ascent in Hellenistic Judaism, Early Christianity and their Environment', in Wolfgang Haase (ed.), *Aufstieg und Niedergang der römischen Welt: Geschichte und Kultur Roms im Spiegel der neueren Forschung. 2. Principat. 23.2* (Berlin: Walter de Gruyter, 1980), 1354.
[12] *Spec.* 3.1–3.   [13] *Spec.* 1.207.   [14] *Abr.* 48, 58.   [15] *Post.* 173.
[16] *Gig.* 54.

In *Questions on Exodus* the entry into the darkness becomes an ascent to God:

> What is the meaning of the words, 'Come up to Me to the mountain and be there' [Exod. 24:12]? This signifies that a holy soul is divinized[17] by ascending not to the air or to the ether or to heaven (which is) higher than all but to (a region) above the heavens. And beyond the world there is no place but God. And He determines the stability of the removal by saying 'be there', (thus) demonstrating the placelessness and the unchanging habitation of the divine place.[18]

On Moses is not thought to be typical of Philo's writing. Albert Geljon characterizes it as an 'introductory treatise' which 'seems to be intended for a general readership'.[19] There is less use of allegory than in his other biblical works. In part one Philo presents a comparatively straightforward biography of Moses, depicting him as a philosopher–king; in part two he discusses his offices of legislator, priest, and prophet. As part of his portrayal of Moses as priest, he gives lengthy commentaries on the cosmological symbolism of both the tabernacle and the high priestly vestments.[20] He says, for example, that the lampstand figures 'the movements of the luminaries above';[21] and that the colours of the woven work relate to the four elements: linen for earth, purple for water, blue for air, and scarlet for fire.[22] Josephus gives a similar cosmological interpretation,[23] but there are differences in detail, and Philo presents his interpretation within a Platonic framework: Moses sees 'with the soul's eye the immaterial forms (ἀσωμάτους ἰδέας) of the material objects about to be made'.[24] Roger Arnaldez and colleagues insist that Philo's tabernacle interpretation is to be seen as symbolic, rather than allegorical:

> point de ces élans mystiques capable de conduire comme à une perception des valeurs spirituelles ou à la presence de Dieu.[25]

On the whole, Geljon agrees, but he does point out two examples of allegorical exegesis, 'namely the interpretation of the Cherubim as God's two powers, and the explanation of the mercy seat of the ark as God's gracious power (2.96, 99)'.[26] *Questions on Exodus*, meanwhile, has only survived in Armenian. The

---

[17] Marcus notes: 'Arm. *astouacanal* usu. renders θεοῦσθαι, a word that seems not to occur elsewhere in Philo. Perhaps the original here was θεοφορεῖσθαι.' Ralph Marcus, *Philo: Questions and Answers on Exodus*, supplementary volume 2 in F. H. Colson, G. H. Whitaker, and R. Marcus, *Philo in Ten Volumes (and Two Supplementary Volumes)* (London: Heinemann, 1929–1962), 82 n. n.

[18] *QE* 2.40.

[19] Albert Geljon, *Philonic Exegesis in Gregory of Nyssa's De Vita Moysis* (Providence: Brown Judaic Studies, 2002), 40.

[20] *Mos.* 2.71–135.   [21] *Mos.* 2.102.   [22] *Mos.* 2.88.   [23] *A.J.* 3.179–187.

[24] *Mos.* 2.74.

[25] 'none of those mystical flights capable of leading as to a perception of spiritual values or to the presence of God'. Roger Arnaldez, et al., *Philon d'Alexandrie: De vita Mosis I–II* (Paris: Cerf, 1967), 13.

[26] Geljon, *Philonic Exegesis in Gregory of Nyssa's De Vita Moysis*, 38.

questions closely follow the biblical text, and the answers contain both literal and allegorical exegesis, often moving from the literal to a deeper meaning, as in the exegesis of LXX Exodus 25:7:

> What is the meaning of the words, 'Thou shalt make for Me a sanctuary, and I shall appear among you'? Clear indeed is the literal meaning, for the shrine is spoken of (as) the archetype of a sort of shrine, (namely, as) the tent. But as for the deeper meaning, God always appears in His work, which is most sacred; by this I mean the world. For His beneficent powers are seen and move around in all its parts, in heaven, earth, water, air and in what is in these.... If, however, thou art worthily initiated and canst be consecrated to God and in a certain sense become an animate shrine of the Father, (then) instead of having closed eyes, thou wilt see the First (Cause)... For the beginning and end of happiness is to be able to see God. But this cannot happen to him who has not made his soul, as I said before, a sanctuary and altogether a shrine of God.[27]

In *Questions on Exodus* 2.51–124, Philo works systematically through Exodus 25–28. He presents some of the same symbolism as in *On Moses*, often adding more detail. When commenting on the ark and cherubim within the holy of holies he puts forward a hierarchy of powers from the Speaker (in other words, God) through the Logos down to the world of Ideas. And as can been seen from the above quote, he also elaborates on the soul as a shrine of God.[28] Geljon has shown that Gregory studied Philo's *On Moses*.[29] There are places where *Life of Moses* may be reflecting *Questions on Exodus*, but in no case is that treatise the only possible source.

4.2 CLEMENT

Clement of Alexandria (c.150–c.215) was 'the first Christian author to make explicit mention of Philo'.[30] He also borrowed extensively from Philo's works. As Annewies van den Hoek says, with regard to *Miscellanies*,

> [Clement] hungrily swallowed Philo's words and eagerly absorbed his thoughts; he used Philo's inventions and misused them to provide his own. Many of the twisting threads of Clement's theological thinking are taken from Philo but they are woven into a very different tapestry.[31]

---

[27] *QE* 2.51.   [28] *QE* 2.51, 53–55.
[29] Geljon, *Philonic Exegesis in Gregory of Nyssa's De Vita Moysis*, 160.
[30] Runia, *Philo in Early Christian Literature*, 132.
[31] Annewies van den Hoek, *Clement of Alexandria and His Use of Philo in the Stromateis: An Early Christian Reshaping of a Jewish Model* (Leiden: Brill, 1988), 229–30.

Clement, it seems, was neither born nor died in Alexandria, but spent some twenty-five years there, from around 175 to the Severian persecution of 202. According to Eusebius, he was first a pupil at and then the head of the catechetical school founded (or taken over) by Pantaenus.[32] His best-known works are the trilogy *Exhortation to the Greeks* (*Protrepticus*), *Christ the Educator* (*Paedagogus*), and *Miscellanies* (*Stromata*): 'A Platonic philosopher, polymath, and Christian apologist, Clement was the first Christian to attempt a thoroughgoing synthesis of the Bible and Greek philosophy.'[33] He saw the Christian life as a journey towards perfect knowledge (*gnōsis*). But in his *Excerpts from Theodotus*, introduced futher in 4.3, he comments critically on passages written by a Valentinian Gnostic author.

Clement's use of the heavenly ascent theme can be illustrated from *Miscellanies* 5.32–40, in which he discusses the symbolism of the temple as one example of the way in which scripture speaks in riddles (*ainigmata*). As van den Hoek demonstrates, he is dependent on Philo's *On Moses*, but more for its structure than for the direction of its thought: 'He remodels Philo's cosmology in a Christological, gnostic and eschatological sense.'[34] Van den Hoek suggests that Clement's allegorical interpretations of the temple's furnishings and the high priest's vestments 'are centered on two complementary themes that form two sides of the same coin: the incarnation of Christ and the rise of the gnostic to the higher regions'.[35] Clement quotes not only from Philo, but also from Plato and Pseudo-Euripides;[36] and from other sources which cannot now be identified. At times he piles up interpretations, some of them contradictory, as when he discusses the cherubim. Claude Mondésert is dismissive about the coherence of the passage: 'il n'y a là que des pierres détachées'.[37] Van den Hoek, on the other hand, argues that the Christological comments which Clement interjects into the Philonic and classical material act as 'preludes to the decisive, concluding Christian interpretation'.[38]

For Clement, as for Philo, the holy of holies represents the *kosmos noētos*.[39] He gives three different, though not incompatible, interpretations to the ark within it. It might be 'the eighth region and the world of thought (*noētos kosmos*)', or 'God, all-embracing, and without shape, and invisible', or 'the repose

---

[32] *Hist. eccl.* 5.10–11, 6.6.

[33] Judith L. Kovacs, 'Clement of Alexandria', in Robert Benedetto et al. (eds), *The New SCM Dictionary of Church History*, vol. 1: *From the Early Church to 1700* (London: SCM, 2008), 156.

[34] Van den Hoek, *Clement of Alexandria and His Use of Philo*, 145–6. I have amended quotations from van den Hoek and Kovacs to conform to my use of 'gnostic' for a seeker after knowledge, and 'Gnostic' for traditions declared 'heretical' by 'orthodox' church fathers.

[35] Van den Hoek, *Clement of Alexandria and His Use of Philo*, 146.

[36] See *Strom.* 5.33.5 and 5.36.1.

[37] 'There are there but detached stones.' Claude Mondésert, *Clément d'Alexandrie: Introduction à l'étude de sa pensée religieuse à partir de l'Écriture* (Paris: Aubier, 1944), 182.

[38] Van den Hoek, *Clement of Alexandria and His Use of Philo*, 142.

[39] *Strom.* 5.34.7, cf. *QE* 2.94.

which dwells with the adoring spirits'.[40] His interpretations of the cherubim seem more confused. In *Miscellanies* 5.35.6–7 he associates them with the constellations of the two Bears, or the two hemispheres, saying, 'both together have twelve wings and by zodiac and by time, which moves on it, point to the world of sense'.[41] In the next paragraph, however, they are identified with the intelligible realm:

> But the face is a symbol of the rational soul, and the wings are the lofty ministers and energies of powers right and left; and the voice is delightsome glory in ceaseless contemplation.[42]

Clement, again like Philo, is relating the 'physical' heaven of the constellations to the 'spiritual' heaven of the intelligible realm. Much of the emphasis in his tabernacle interpretation, however, is not on the significance of the furniture, but on who is allowed where. He describes the outer covering as 'a barrier against popular unbelief'.[43] This covering was stretched over five pillars, which Clement sees as symbolic of the five senses; and the crowd 'adheres to the things of sense'.[44] Priests were allowed to enter the intermediate space between the covering and the veil.[45] The high priest alone was permitted behind the veil. The passage ends with a commentary on Leviticus 16, in which the high priest, described as gnostic (γνωστικός), represents the 'spiritual and perfect man' who becomes 'replenished with insatiable contemplation face to face'.[46] Section 27 of *Excerpts from Theodotus* elaborates further on the entry of the high priest into the holy of holies as the ascent of the gnostic soul to the highest level of the celestial hierarchy. Whatever the relationship between the two passages, they illustrate how the theme of heavenly ascension can be mapped onto the entry of the high priest into the holy of holies. Judith Kovacs has remarked, 'As far as I know, no one has investigated the question of how much of Clement's work was read by Gregory and the other Cappadocians.'[47] But whether Gregory knew this passage from *Miscellanies* or not, it demonstrates

---

[40] *Strom.* 5.36.3; trans. Wilson, 242.

[41] Trans. van den Hoek, *Clement of Alexandria and His Use of Philo*, 130. Note the influence of the seraphim (Isa. 6:2).

[42] *Strom.* 5.36.4; trans. Wilson, 242–3.

[43] *Strom.* 5.33.3; trans. van den Hoek, *Clement of Alexandria and His Use of Philo*, 122. Clement uses the word κάλυμμα for the curtain stretched over five pillars at the entrance to the tabernacle. In this he follows Philo (cf. *Mos.* 2.87). The LXX uses ἐπίσπαστρον, along with καταπέτασμα, for that curtain (Exod. 26:36–37), and κάλυμμα for the curtain at the entrance to the court (Exod. 27:16).

[44] *Strom.* 5.33.4; trans. van den Hoek, *Clement of Alexandria and His Use of Philo*, 124.

[45] Clement uses the term παραπέτασμα for the veil at the entrance to the holy of holies.

[46] 5.40.1; trans. van den Hoek, *Clement of Alexandria and His Use of Philo*, 141.

[47] Judith L. Kovacs, 'Clement of Alexandria and Gregory of Nyssa on the Beatitudes', in H. R. Drobner and A. Viciano (eds), *Gregory of Nyssa: Homilies on the Beatitudes* (Leiden: Brill, 2000), 323 n. 40.

how Philo's cosmological interpretation was remoulded by second-century Alexandrian theology.

4.3 EXCERPTS FROM THEODOTUS

DeConick describes Valentinianism as 'one of the earliest Alexandrian schools of Christian theology'.[48] Valentinus himself was educated in Alexandria, and probably began his teaching activity there, before moving to Rome sometime before 140. *Excerpts from Theodotus* contains extracts from the writings of Theodotus, assumed to be a pupil of Valentinus, together with comments by Clement, and possibly other material as well. It is not always easy to discern where quotations from Theodotus end and comments by Clement begin; and the presentation of Theodotus' teachings is extremely disjointed: 'No coherent account of Theodotus' system can be seen in the material presented, but a basic Valentinian myth lies in the background and is reflected here and there.'[49] More detail of that Valentinian myth is supplied by Irenaeus: *Against Heresies* 1.1–8 seems to be drawing on the same source as *Excerpts from Theodotus* 42–65, although, given Irenaeus' polemical intent, his statements need to be treated with caution.[50] *Excerpts* 27 interprets the entry of the high priest into the holy of holies as the soul's passage into the spiritual realm (τὰ πνευματικά). There is no agreement as to whether it belongs to Theodotus or Clement. Salvatore Lilla and DeConick assign it to Theodotus (or some other Gnostic writer); Robert Pierce Casey, François Sagnard, Birger Pearson, and Kovacs disagree.[51] Kovacs argues that it represents 'the further elaboration of Clement's exegesis of the tabernacle'.[52]

---

[48] April D. DeConick, 'Heavenly Temple Traditions and Valentinian Worship', in Carey C. Newman, James R. Davila, and Gladys S. Lewis (eds), *The Jewish Roots of Christological Monotheism: Papers from the St. Andrews Conference on the Historical Origins of the Worship of Jesus* (Leiden: Brill, 1999), 308.

[49] Pearson, *Ancient Gnosticism*, 165.

[50] See Elaine H. Pagels, 'Conflicting Versions of Valentinian Eschatology: Irenaeus' Treatise vs. the Excerpts from Theodotus', *Harvard Theological Review*, 67: 1 (1974); or Ismo Dunderberg, *Beyond Gnosticism: Myth, Lifestyle, and Society in the School of Valentinus* (New York: Columbia University Press, 2008), 197–8.

[51] Salvatore R. C. Lilla, *Clement of Alexandria: A Study in Christian Platonism and Gnosticism* (Oxford: Oxford University Press, 1971), 177–9; April D. DeConick, 'The True Mysteries: Sacramentalism in the *Gospel of Philip*', *Vigiliae christianae*, 55: 3 (2001), 261 n. 73; Robert Pierce Casey, *The Excerpta ex Theodoto of Clement of Alexandria* (London: Christophers, 1934), 9–16; F. Sagnard, *Clément d'Alexandrie: Extraits de Théodote* (Paris: Cerf, 1948), 11; Pearson, *Ancient Gnosticism*, 165.

[52] Judith L. Kovacs, 'Concealment and Gnostic Exegesis: Clement of Alexandria's Interpretation of the Tabernacle', in Elizabeth A. Livingstone (ed.), *Papers Presented at the Twelfth International Conference on Patristic Studies Held in Oxford 1995*, part 3: *Preaching, Second Century, Tertullian to Arnobious, Egypt before Nicaea* (Leuven: Peeters, 1997), 433.

Irenaeus provides evidence that the Valentinians envisaged the divine world as a complex structure resembling a series of temple rooms, with the 'Pleroma' (Fullness) as the holy of holies. According to the Valentinian myth which he relates, in the Pleroma is the invisible and incomprehensible First-Being, who is responsible for a series of emanations, or aeons (eternities). The last of these aeons, Sophia, produces a crisis in the Godhead by wishing to comprehend the greatness of the First-Being. Although Sophia is enabled to stay within the Pleroma, the crisis results in the formation of a Lower Sophia, named Achamoth, who is excluded from the Pleroma. Achamoth goes on to produce the Demiurge (Creator), who resides one stage lower:

> [The Demiurge] made also seven heavens, above which he himself exists. On this account they style him the Hebdomad, but his mother Achamoth is the Ogdoad... Her dwelling is the intermediate region. She is indeed above Demiurge, but below or outside the Fullness until the consummation.[53]

Irenaeus says that the Valentinians divided people into three classes—spiritual (πνευματικόν), ensouled (ψυχικόν), and earthly (χοϊκόν).[54] For the ensouled, salvation consists of reaching the intermediate region, whereas the spiritual are destined for the Pleroma.[55] In *Excerpts from Theodotus*, by contrast, the faithful souls first join the spiritual beings in the Ogdoad, 'then comes the marriage feast, common to all who are saved, until all are equal and know each other. Henceforth the spiritual elements (τὰ πνευματικά) having put off their souls, together with the Mother... pass into the bride chamber within the Limit and attain to the vision of the Father...'[56] Elaine Pagels argues that the spiritual elements are envisaged as being taken from both the previously ensouled and spiritual beings. She accuses Irenaeus of substituting an exclusive eschatology in place of an inclusive one.[57]

4.4 ORIGEN

Origen (c.185–c.253) is 'arguably the most influential interpreter of the Bible in Christian tradition', as well as being 'a key figure in the history of Christian spirituality'.[58] But he was always controversial, as a result of which most of

---

[53] *Haer.* 1.5.2–3; trans. Unger and Dillon, 34.   [54] *Haer.* 1.7.5.   [55] *Haer.* 1.7.1.
[56] *Exc.* 63.2; trans. Casey, 83.
[57] Pagels, 'Conflicting Versions of Valentinian Eschatology', 46; cf. Dunderberg, *Beyond Gnosticism*, 139. This is contra Casey, for whom the marriage feasts represents a stage in which the psychics and pneumatics are together, but after which the pneumatics advance into the Pleroma, leaving the psychics in the Ogdoad. See Casey, *The Excerpta ex Theodoto*, 152 n. 2.
[58] Joseph W. Trigg, 'Origen', in Robert Benedetto, et al. (eds), *The New SCM Dictionary of Church History*, vol. 1: *From the Early Church to 1700* (London: SCM, 2008), 479.

his works have been lost, with only some surviving in ancient translations. Origen was brought up in Alexandria, and began his teaching career there, but left around 231 after coming into conflict with the city's bishop. He spent his last two decades based in Palestinian Caesarea, as 'the leading intellectual of the age'.[59] One of his pupils there was a Gregory, later named 'Thaumaturgus' (the wonderworker), who went on to become a bishop in his native Pontus, and whose sayings were passed down to Gregory of Nyssa by his grandmother, Macrina the elder.[60] Hence the influence of Origen on Cappadocian Christianity generally, and on Gregory of Nyssa in particular. Origen himself combined a search for spiritual meaning with a 'nearly obsessive attention' to the details of the biblical text: 'No other ancient author was more aware of the Bible's many inconsistencies at the literal level, and no other ancient author worked harder to resolve them.'[61]

Ascent is an important theme for Origen. His controversial doctrine of *apokatastasis* (restoration) involved a return of all things to the Father through Christ, based on Paul's words that in the end God will be 'all in all' (πάντα ἐν πᾶσιν).[62] McGinn writes,

> The central metaphor Origen uses for this process of return is that of a journey upward, an ascension—the notion that may well be taken as the main motif of his mysticism. This mode of presenting the life of the spirit, of course, is one common to many religious traditions, and there can be no doubt that Origen's adaptation of it was dependent on a generalized Platonic world view; but his *theologia ascendens* (to use von Balthasar's phrase) departs from Platonism both in its Christocentrism and in its biblical foundation. The whole message of scripture is the descent and ascent of the Incarnate Word to rescue the fallen intellects. Thus, the history of Israel and the other nations recounted in the Old Testament is to be read as an account of the fall and rise of souls. The New Testament recounts the Word's descent and ascent more directly, though still mysteriously.... Though it would be incorrect to ascribe the popularity of the ascent motif in Christian mysticism to Origen alone, there can be no doubt that his emphasis on itinerary had great influence on many later mystics.[63]

Macleod agrees that 'Origen's mysticism is intimately connected with his central activity as an exegete.'[64] He quotes from the *Fragment on 1 Thessalonians*, in which Origen comments on 1 Thessalonians 4:17:

---

[59] John Anthony McGuckin, *The Westminster Handbook to Origen* (Louisville, Ken.: Westminster John Knox Press, 2004), 22.
[60] Eusebius *Hist. eccl.* 6.30, 7.14, 7.28.1; Basil *Epist.* 204.6.
[61] John J. O'Keefe, 'Scriptural Interpretation', in McGuckin (ed.), *The Westminster Handbook to Origen*, 194–5.
[62] 1 Cor. 15:28.
[63] Bernard McGinn, *The Foundations of Mysticism: Origins to the Fifth Century* (New York: Crossroad, 1991), 115–16.
[64] Colin W. Macleod, 'Allegory and Mysticism in Origen and Gregory of Nyssa', *Journal of Theological Studies*, 22: 2 (1971), 369.

But we must examine more closely how these who are 'caught up in the clouds' go 'to meet the Lord'. We know that the clouds are the prophets...and since God set in the church first the apostles and then the prophets, the clouds must be understood not only as the prophets but also the apostles. So if anyone is caught up to Christ, he ascends above the clouds of the law and the gospel, above the prophets and apostles: and taking the wings of a dove, and raised by their doctrine to the heights, he meets (Christ) not below but in the air and the spiritual understanding of the Scriptures.[65]

Elsewhere Origen says,

> I return to the wide open fields of the Holy Scripture: I would seek the spiritual meaning of the word of God, and in it no narrowness of distress will confine me. I shall ride through the most spacious places of the mystical and spiritual understanding.[66]

The process of exegesis has become an ascent.

Origen consistently interprets the tabernacle as symbolic of the church and its members. He appeals to his congregation to 'make a sanctuary for the Lord both collectively and individually'.[67] In *Homilies on Exodus* 9 and 13, and *Homilies on Numbers* 5, he unpacks the symbolism of each item that makes up the tabernacle, paying close attention to the details of the biblical text. In *Homilies on Exodus* 9.3, for example, he identifies the pillars of the tabernacle as teachers and ministers; the interposed bars as the right hand of fellowship; the bases of the pillars as the prophets; and their capitals as Christ. In *Homilies on Exodus* 13.4–5 he picks up on two details of LXX Exodus 25:4: the 'scarlet doubled' (κόκκινον διπλοῦν) and the 'twisted linen' (βύσσον κεκλωσμένην). The 'scarlet doubled' he links with two kinds of fire: the fire that enlightens, and the fire that burns; and he finds biblical verses relating to each. The 'twisted linen' he sees as symbolic of weakening the flesh 'by abstinence, by vigils, and by the exertion of meditations'.[68] In *Homilies on Numbers* 5 Origen comments on Numbers 4, in which the duties of the Levites when packing up the tent of witness are enumerated. He says that 'the tabernacle of testimony [refers] to all the saints who are assessed under God's covenant. In this tabernacle are some who are more exalted in their merits and superior in grace.'[69] The lampstand represents the apostles, the holy table those who feed souls that hunger for justice, the incense altar those who pray for the entire people, the ark those to whom God has entrusted the secret mysteries, the mercy seat those who intercede for the sins of the people, and the cherubim those who have merited the wealth of the knowledge of God. The biblical context of packing up and moving on allows him to talk of those represented by these symbols as being carried

---

[65] PG 14.1302C; trans. Macleod, 'Allegory and Mysticism', 370.
[66] *Comm. Rom.* 7.11.3; trans. Scheck, 2.97.   [67] *Hom. Exod.* 9.3; trans. Heine, 338.
[68] *Hom. Exod.* 13.5; trans. Heine, 383.   [69] *Hom. Num.* 5.3.2; trans. Scheck, 19.

on the shoulders of angels to the promised land. In *Commentary on Romans* 3.8 Origen interprets the mercy seat as the soul of Jesus, and the ark of the covenant as his holy flesh. The cherubim signify 'that the Word of God, who is the only begotten Son, and his Holy Spirit always dwell in the propitiatory, that is, in the soul of Jesus'.[70] God speaks from between the cherubim (Exod. 25:22) because it is only through the Son and the Spirit that God becomes known.[71] Origen says, with regard to a similar interpretation of the seraphim, that he learnt this from his Hebrew teacher.[72] In *Homilies on Leviticus* 6 he tackles the priestly vestments, taking them to represent the virtues with which believers should adorn themselves. John McGuckin suggests that the homilies 'generally represent a simpler and more pastoral face of Origen' but that 'this argument ought not to be forced too much, as the students of his Schola would have been in constant attendance on him'.[73] The homilies on Exodus, Leviticus, and Numbers now only exist in Rufinus' Latin translation. There are a few Greek fragments of *Commentary on Romans*, but for most of this we are still reliant on Rufinus. McGuckin says of him:

> Rufinus is generally a reliable translator, but...many scholars regard his translations as having been largely 'sense related' and, for long works, reductively paraphrastic.[74]

This makes it impossible to compare the wording of Origen, and Gregory's tabernacle interpretations in detail.

---

[70] *Comm. Rom.* 3.8.5; trans. Scheck, 1.220.   [71] *Comm. Rom.* 3.8.8; trans. Scheck, 1.221.
[72] *Princ.* 1.3.4, 4.3.14.   [73] McGuckin, *Handbook to Origen*, 28.
[74] McGuckin, *Handbook to Origen*, 31.

5

Heavenly Ascent Contexts

> After this he finds himself in the tabernacle not made with hands. Who will follow one who travels through such places, and elevates his mind so high, who as he goes on from peak to peak becomes, through the ascent of the heights, ever higher than before?[1]

In his account of Moses' ascent of Mount Sinai to view the heavenly tabernacle, Gregory of Nyssa is working with the structure and language of heavenly ascent. Traditions of heavenly ascent were widespread within Hellenistic and Late Antique cultures, but they were flexible, and could be shaped in a variety of ways. From his Alexandrian predecessors Gregory inherited a tradition of heavenly ascent which combined Platonic notions with biblical narratives. Philo allegorized the lives of biblical characters so that they represented the soul's search for God. Clement and the Valentinians portrayed the rise of the spiritual gnostic to insatiable contemplation in terms of an entry into the holy of holies. Origen made the process of scriptural interpretation an ascent in itself. Their legacies can be seen in Gregory's work. He did not, however, take them over uncritically. The theological context of the fourth century made some of these earlier formulations problematic.

In order to discern Gregory's shaping of the heavenly ascent paradigm, his writing will be compared and contrasted with a number of heavenly ascent texts. These can be divided into three categories. Firstly, there are the ascent apocalypses: *1 Enoch, 2 Enoch, Testament of Levi,* and *Ascension of Isaiah,* which are pseudonymous accounts of the heavenly journeys of biblical heroes. The descriptions of what was seen in heaven draw on biblical texts, such as Exodus 25–28, Isaiah 6, and Ezekiel 1, but the journeys are not in themselves biblical. These texts are not straightforward exegesis, but new narratives, written back into the biblical period, often using enigmatic phrases in the biblical text as starting points. These narratives encapsulate new understandings of the relationship between the divine and the human. As Himmelfarb points out, 'The vision of 1 Enoch 14 marks a crucial departure in the history of ancient Jewish literature.' There is a 'central difference between Enoch's vision and the

[1] *Vit. Moys.* 2.167.

visions of the prophets, including Ezekiel's: unlike any of the prophets, Enoch ascends to heaven'.[2] Secondly, there are texts which contain liturgical or theurgic material: *Songs of the Sabbath Sacrifice* and the later Hekhalot texts. It may have been believed that those who recited them experienced the journey for themselves. As Alexander writes,

> The fundamental difference between [Sabbath] Songs and apocalyptic is that Songs *performs* [the] vision: it is not merely literary description; it is liturgy—a feature which binds Sabbath Songs tightly to the later Heikhalot tradition, with its evident stress on theurgy and mystical ascent.[3]

Thirdly, there is the rabbinic material from tractate *Ḥagigah* (11b–16a) of the Babylonian Talmud. This construes the 'work of the chariot' as rabbinic exegetical activity, but displays a profound ambivalence towards it, and is anxious to stress its dangers. *3 Enoch* spans the three categories. It 'belongs to the late phase of the Hekhalot literature', but also 'reveals strong affinities to apocalyptic and classical rabbinic traditions'.[4]

Roughly speaking—qualifications will need to be added later—the climax of both apocalyptic and theurgic texts is a vision of the divine glory on the *merkavah* throne. Scholem writes,

> [The essence of the earliest Jewish mysticism] is not absorbed contemplation of God's true nature, but perception of His appearance on the throne, as described by Ezekiel, and cognition of the mysteries of the celestial throne-world.[5]

From *1 Enoch* to the Hekhalot literature, the ascent through the layers of heaven 'is depicted as a journey through increasingly holy rooms of the Temple to the holiest of the chambers, the *devir* or Holy of Holies, where the manifestation of God is enthroned on his *merkavah* or chariot'.[6] In *Testament of Levi*, for example, the angel tells Levi that 'in the highest [heaven] of all dwells the Great Glory in the holy of holies far beyond all holiness'.[7] In mapping heavenly ascent onto the temple plan, Clement and the Valentinians were drawing 'from a deep reservoir of imagery'.[8]

---

[2] Martha Himmelfarb, *Ascent to Heaven in Jewish and Christian Apocalypses* (Oxford: Oxford University Press, 1993), 9.

[3] Philip Alexander, *The Mystical Texts: Songs of the Sabbath Sacrifice and Related Manuscripts* (London: T&T Clark, 2006), 128.

[4] Peter Schäfer, *The Origins of Jewish Mysticism* (Tübingen: Mohr Siebeck, 2009), 315–16.

[5] Gershom G. Scholem, *Major Trends in Jewish Mysticism*, 3rd edn (New York: Schoken Books, 1961), 44.

[6] April D. DeConick, 'Heavenly Temple Traditions and Valentinian Worship', in Carey C. Newman, James R. Davila, and Gladys S. Lewis (eds), *The Jewish Roots of Christological Monotheism: Papers from the St. Andrews Conference on the Historical Origins of the Worship of Jesus* (Leiden: Brill, 1999), 311.

[7] *T. Levi* 3:4; trans. Hollander and de Jonge, 136.

[8] DeConick, 'Heavenly Temple Traditions and Valentinian Worship', 310.

It is the heuristic comparison between *Life of Moses* and heavenly ascent texts which is the innovative aspect of this study. One of the issues to be faced in this comparison is the tension between propositional statements and the use of imagery. Gregory makes vivid and creative use of biblical narrative and imagery. Mariette Canévet comments on 'la difficulté que l'on éprouve à donner un sens philosophique à des images plus poétiques que rigoureuses'.[9] Similarly, Coakley acknowledges 'the myriad differences of style and *genre* with which Gregory plays in his various works, and his often infuriatingly inconsistent modes of argument'.[10] It is Gregory's use of imagery which makes his writing captivating for the reader. Macleod comments that if 'mystical imagery—the language of ecstasy, vision or union... is vividly enough employed, the reader naturally feels an experience is being communicated to him, because to create such a feeling is a characteristic of good writing'.[11] But Gregory can also use propositional statements. He works within a Platonic philosophical framework, which deals in logic and argument, and he often provides interpretations to his images. As well as describing the beauties of the heavenly tabernacle, he tells us that it symbolizes Christ. The heavenly ascent texts, by contrast, do not make use of abstract philosophical terms. They present their ideas solely through vivid, not to say lurid or bizarre, imagery. The challenge is to interpret that imagery, and decide whether the authors of these texts were wrestling with some of the same questions as Gregory: questions in particular about human access to the divine.

Below are introductions to each of the heavenly ascent texts used. It is not an exhaustive list. Other texts, such as the Similitudes of Enoch (*1 Enoch* 37–71), the *Apocalypse of Abraham*, *3 Baruch*, or the *Apocalypse of Paul* could have been included. But those chosen span a range of dates, genres, and religious affiliation, and they include features which have proved useful for the purposes of this book. In particular, some of their content relates to the topics addressed by Gregory, such as 'darkness', 'the tabernacle not made with hands', 'divine names', and 'priestly vestments'.

5.1 *1 ENOCH* 14

1 Enoch has been described as 'perhaps the single most important non-canonical Jewish text to have survived from Second Temple times'. It is a

---

[9] 'the difficulty we experience in giving philosophical meaning to images more poetic than rigorous.' Mariette Canévet, 'La perception de la présence de Dieu à propos d'une expression de la XIe homélie sur le Cantique des Cantiques', in Jacques Fontaine and Charles Kannengiesser (eds), Ἐπέκτασις: *Mélanges patristiques offerts au Cardinal Jean Daniélou* (Paris: Beauchesne, 1972), 443.

[10] Sarah Coakley (ed.), *Re-Thinking Gregory of Nyssa* (Oxford: Blackwell, 2003), 11.

[11] Colin W. Macleod, 'Allegory and Mysticism in Origen and Gregory of Nyssa', *Journal of Theological Studies*, 22: 2 (1971), 362.

long composite work of 108 chapters, 'made up of separate treatises originating at very different periods'.[12] Chapter 14 falls within the Book of the Watchers (chapters 1–36), dated to the third century BCE. Fragments of the Book of the Watchers in Aramaic, including some of Chapter 14, were found at Qumran; and most scholars think that Aramaic, rather than Hebrew, was its original language. Complete copies of the Book of the Watchers have been preserved in Greek and Ethiopic. Elaborating upon the enigmatic story in Genesis 6:1–4, it tells of fallen angels, named 'Watchers', who come to earth, have sexual intercourse with human women, and pass on illicit knowledge to humankind. Enoch, of whom the Bible says, he 'walked with God; and he was not, for God took him' (Gen. 5:24), is asked to draw up a petition on their behalf, requesting forgiveness.[13] He then dreams of being whirled up to heaven, where he passes through a threefold structure to behold the Great Glory sitting on a crystalline throne, surrounded by myriads of angels. This vision in *1 Enoch* 14 represents 'an important transition from the older Ezekiel tradition of the prophetic call to the much later tradition of Jewish Merkabah mysticism'.[14] In particular, the Book of the Watchers is the first Jewish text to describe an ascent to heaven in unequivocal terms. Himmelfarb sees in its description of the Watchers a mild condemnation of the Jerusalem priesthood.[15] Schäfer goes further, and understands Enoch's heavenly temple 'as a devastating critique of the Temple in Jerusalem', since Enoch's vision could imply that the holy of holies in the earthly temple is empty, God having withdrawn himself to his temple in heaven.[16] *1 Enoch*, which is cited in the New Testament—Jude 1:14–15 quotes *1 Enoch* 1:9—was held in high regard by second-century Christians, but Origen exhibits doubts about it, and Jerome associates it with the teachings of the Manicheans.[17]

5.2 SONGS OF THE SABBATH SACRIFICE

Songs of the Sabbath Sacrifice was unknown until its discovery at Qumran. Fragments of ten manuscripts have survived: eight from Cave 4 (4Q400–407), one from Cave 11 (11Q17), and one from Masada (Mas1k). The oldest

---

[12] Philip Alexander, 'Essay with Commentary on Post-Biblical Jewish Literature', in John Barton and John Muddiman (eds), *The Oxford Bible Commentary* (Oxford: Oxford University Press, 2001), 794.

[13] *1 En.* 13:3–6.

[14] George W. E. Nickelsburg, *1 Enoch 1: A Commentary on the Book of 1 Enoch, Chapters 1–36; 81–108* (Minneapolis: Fortress, 2001), 259.

[15] Himmelfarb, *Ascent to Heaven*, 22.

[16] Schäfer, *The Origins of Jewish Mysticism*, 66.

[17] William Adler, 'Introduction', in James C. VanderKam and William Adler (eds), *The Jewish Apocalyptic Heritage in Early Christianity* (Assen: Van Gorcum, 1996), 23.

manuscript has been dated to the late Hasmonean period (*c*.75–50 BCE), and the youngest to the middle of the first century CE. The first editor, John Strugnell, coined the title *Shirot 'Olat Ha-Shabbat* (*Songs of the Sabbath Sacrifice*), on the basis of the headings which introduce each song. Carol Newsom's 1985 edition made all the material available.[18] She reconstructed the fragmentary manuscripts into thirteen songs, which she suggested were designed to be sung on the first thirteen Sabbaths of the year. The first songs focus on the liturgy of praise performed by angelic beings, referred to as 'priests of the highest heights' (כוהני מרומי רום), 'priests of the inner sanctum' (כוהני קורב), or even 'godlike beings of all the Most Holy Ones' (אלוהי כול קדושי קדושים).[19] From song 7 onwards, the emphasis shifts to the structure of the heavenly temple. Songs 9 to 12 spiral inwards from the outer vestibules of the temple to its central inner sanctuary, with song 12 invoking the manifestation of the divine glory upon the *merkavah*. There is some debate about the structure of the song cycle. Newsom argues that the seventh song plays 'a central and climactic role in the composition', whereas Morray-Jones maintains that the twelfth song 'forms the true climax of the liturgical cycle as a whole'.[20] Song 13 describes the sacrifices offered by the angelic high priests, along with their ritual garments, which has seemed to some scholars something of an anti-climax.

Initially Newsom suggested that *Sabbath Songs* was a sectarian composition, but later changed her mind.[21] Alexander proposes that it 'may be a Qumranian reworking of an originally Jerusalemite temple liturgy'.[22] It has been suggested by Newsom, Bilhah Nitzan, Alexander, and Morray-Jones that the liturgical poetry of *Sabbath Songs* aims to create a mystical experience of communion with the angels in their heavenly worship:

> The hypnotic quality of the language and the vividness of the description of the celestial temple cause even the modern reader of these fragments to feel the power of the language to create a sense of the presence of the heavenly temple.[23]

---

[18] Carol A. Newsom, *Songs of the Sabbath Sacrifice: A Critical Edition* (Atlanta: Scholars Press, 1985). This study uses the text and translation in James H. Charlesworth and Carol A. Newsom, *Angelic Liturgy: Songs of the Sabbath Sacrifice* (Tübingen: Mohr Siebeck, 1999).

[19] 4Q400 1 i 20, 19, 2.

[20] Carol A. Newsom, 'Merkabah Exegesis in the Qumran Sabbath Shirot', *Journal of Jewish Studies*, 38: 1 (1987), 14; Christopher R. A. Morray-Jones, 'The Temple Within', in April D. DeConick (ed.), *Paradise Now: Essays on Early Jewish and Christian Mysticism* (Atlanta: Society of Biblical Literature, 2006), 162.

[21] Compare Newsom, *Songs of the Sabbath Sacrifice*, 4, with Charlesworth and Newsom, *Angelic Liturgy*, 4.

[22] Alexander, *The Mystical Texts*, 97.

[23] Newsom, *Songs of the Sabbath Sacrifice*, 72. See also Bilhah Nitzan, 'Harmonic and Mystical Characteristics in Poetic and Liturgical Writings from Qumran', *Jewish Quarterly Review*, 85: 1–2 (1994), 183; Alexander, *The Mystical Texts*, 44; Christopher Rowland and Christopher R. A. Morray-Jones, *The Mystery of God: Early Jewish Mysticism and the New Testament* (Leiden: Brill, 2009), 325–6.

Crispin Fletcher-Louis disagrees, arguing that its language refers not to the heavenly temple, but 'to the Qumran community members who now have a heavenly, angelic and divine identity'.[24] Alexander points out that this view is beset by a number of problems, not least that without a heavenly temple there are no angels for an angelomorphic community to resemble.[25] Schäfer accuses Morray-Jones of confusing the textual level (the heavenly ritual) and the performative level (the enacting of the text in the worship of the sectarians). He argues that the earthly community urgently calls on the angels to praise God and offer the celestial sacrifice (now crucial, given that earthly sacrifices have become corrupt), but is reluctant to associate this with an ascent to heaven.[26]

5.3 TESTAMENT OF LEVI

Testament of Levi is part of a longer work—the *Testaments of the Twelve Patriarchs*, which purports to relate the final utterances of Jacob's twelve sons. Each patriarch gathers his family around him, reflects on his life, and exhorts his offspring to virtue. Special honour is given to Levi and Judah, as heads of the priestly and kingly lines respectively. The *Testaments* were written in Greek, and contain some Christian material. Howard Clark Kee argues that the Christian interpolations 'may be readily differentiated from the original Greek text', and attributes the 'basic writing' to a Hellenized Jew living in the Maccabean period.[27] Harm Hollander and Marinus de Jonge argue that 'it is practically impossible to answer the question whether there ever existed Jewish Testaments', and that 'our first and foremost task is to try to interpret the Testaments as they lie before us'.[28] They suggest that the *Testaments* received their present form during the second half of the second century in Christian circles. In the case of *Testament of Levi*, however, some of the source material has been identified. Fragments of an Aramaic document dealing with Levi were discovered in the Cairo Genizah, and at Qumran. The *Aramaic Levi Document* is generally thought to be a non-sectarian treatise, dating from the third or early second century BCE, and highly prized by the Qumran community. Its exact relationship with the Greek *Testament of Levi* has

---

[24] Crispin H. T. Fletcher-Louis, 'Heavenly Ascent or Incarnational Presence? A Revisionist Reading of the *Songs of the Sabbath Sacrifice*', *Society of Biblical Literature Seminar Papers*, 37 (1998), 369.

[25] Alexander, *The Mystical Texts*, 46.

[26] Schäfer, *The Origins of Jewish Mysticism*, 144–6.

[27] H. C. Kee, 'Testaments of the Twelve Patriarchs', in James H. Charlesworth (ed.), *The Old Testament Pseudepigrapha*, vol. 1: *Apocalyptic Literature and Testaments* (New York: Doubleday, 1983), 777–8.

[28] H. W. Hollander and M. de Jonge, *The Testaments of the Twelve Patriarchs: A Commentary* (Leiden: Brill, 1985), 85.

been much discussed.[29] Unfortunately, most of the key material on Levi's vision(s) of heaven is missing. It is, therefore, by and large the Greek *Testament of Levi* which will be used in this study. Both Origen and Jerome refer to the *Testaments of the Twelve Patriarchs*, although not *Testament of Levi* specifically.[30]

In *Testament of Levi* Levi ascends to heaven twice (2:5–5:2 and 8:1–19). The first time he falls asleep and beholds the heavens opened, with an angel inviting him to enter. The contents of the various heavens through which he needs to pass are described.[31] In the highest heaven dwells the Great Glory, and just below are 'the angels of the presence of the Lord', who 'offer to the Lord a pleasant odour, a reasonable and bloodless offering'.[32] The climax to Levi's vision is to see 'the holy temple and the Most High upon a throne of glory', after which he is given his priestly commission and returns to earth.[33] Three chapters later he ascends to heaven again, although this time there is no sign of the Most High. Instead he is taken through an investiture ceremony, during which he is anointed and clothed by 'seven men in white clothing'.[34]

5.4 *2 ENOCH*

2 Enoch is an enigmatic work, until recently found only in Slavonic manuscripts dating from the fourteenth century onwards. It has been suggested that it represents 'one of the earliest specimens of Merkabah mysticism, manifesting a portentous transition between early apocalyptic and mystical currents'.[35] It seems to show an awareness of earlier Enochic traditions, but probably not a direct literary dependency on *1 Enoch*. In 2009 Joost Hagen announced the discovery of four Coptic fragments, preliminarily dated to the eighth to tenth centuries.[36] Both the Slavonic and Coptic versions are most probably

---

[29] See Robert A. Kugler, *From Patriarch to Priest: The Levi-Priestly Tradition from Aramaic Levi to Testament of Levi* (Atlanta: Scholars Press, 1996); Marinus de Jonge, 'Levi in Aramaic Levi and in the Testament of Levi', in Esther G. Chazon and Michael Stone (eds), *Pseudepigraphic Perspectives: The Apocrypha and Pseudepigrapha in Light of the Dead Sea Scrolls* (Leiden: Brill, 1999); and Michael E. Stone, 'Aramaic Levi Document and Greek Testament of Levi', in Shalom M. Paul, et al. (eds), *Emanuel: Studies in Hebrew Bible, Septuagint and Dead Sea Scrolls in Honor of Emanuel Tov* (Leiden: Brill, 2003).
[30] See Hollander and de Jonge, *The Testaments of the Twelve Patriarchs*, 15.
[31] There has been some debate over the manuscript evidence as to whether the text describes three heavens or seven. The text and translation used here adopt the seven heaven schema.
[32] *T. Levi* 3:4–6; trans. Hollander and de Jonge, 136.
[33] *T. Levi* 5:1–2; trans. Hollander and de Jonge, 143.
[34] *T. Levi* 8:1–10; trans. Hollander and de Jonge, 149.
[35] Andrei A. Orlov and Gabriele Boccaccini (eds), *New Perspectives on 2 Enoch: No Longer Slavonic Only* (Leiden: Brill, 2012), 2.
[36] Joost L. Hagen, 'No Longer "Slavonic" Only: 2 Enoch Attested in Coptic from Nubia', in Orlov and Boccaccini (eds), *New Perspectives on 2 Enoch*, 7–34.

translations from the Greek. But the text contains many Semitisms, indicating either Hebrew (or Aramaic) sources behind the Greek, or the adoption of a biblical style in the Greek, or interpolated material translated directly from the Hebrew.[37] Robert Charles assigned *2 Enoch* to between 30 BCE and CE 70, Józef Milik to the ninth or tenth centuries CE.[38] Milik's dating has been finally disproved by the Coptic fragments. Orlov agrees with Charles, arguing that 'the text was composed at a time when the Second Temple was still standing'.[39] André Vaillant and Milik argued for a Christian authorship, but most scholars have concluded that *2 Enoch* started life as a Jewish text.[40] Lawrence Schiffman, however, waves 'the necessary red flag of caution', based on the complete absence of *halakhah* (Jewish law) in *2 Enoch*.[41] Opinions on the place of writing have also been divided. Francis Andersen comments, '2 Enoch could derive from any region in which Jewish, Greek, Egyptian, and other Near Eastern ideas mingled'.[42] A majority of scholars, however, 'tends to locate the original of Greek 2 Enoch in the important Jewish metropolis of Alexandria', their case now strengthened by the discovery of Coptic fragments.[43] But given the time lag between the proposed date of composition and the date of the manuscripts, there is no certainty that any particular element of the text was there in the 'original'. The problems are compounded by variation in the manuscripts. The text never exists on its own, only as part of larger anthologies. Two recensions have been proposed, a long and a short one, with further possible subdivisions. Even within manuscripts supposedly of the same recension, there is much variation. There has been debate about which recension is the earlier, and whether the division happened before or after the translation from Greek into Slavonic. Andersen cautions,

---

[37] For the last possibility, see Liudmila Navtanovich, 'The Provenance of 2 Enoch: A Philological Perspective', in Orlov and Boccaccini (eds), *New Perspectives on 2 Enoch*, 80–2.

[38] R. H. Charles, *The Apocrypha and Pseudepigrapha of the Old Testament in English*, vol. 2: *Pseudepigrapha* (Oxford: Clarendon, 1913), 429; J. T. Milik, *The Books of Enoch: Aramaic Fragments of Qumrân Cave 4* (Oxford: Clarendon, 1976), 112.

[39] Andrei A. Orlov, *The Enoch–Metatron Tradition* (Tübingen: Mohr Siebeck, 2005), 330.

[40] A. Vaillant, *Le livre des secrets d'Hénoch: Texte slave et traduction française* (Paris: Institut d'études slaves, 1952), viii–xiii; Milik, *The Books of Enoch*, 112. For a list of scholarly supporters of the idea of Jewish authorship see Andrei A. Orlov, 'The Sacerdotal Traditions of 2 Enoch and the Date of the Text', in Orlov and Boccaccini (eds), *New Perspectives on 2 Enoch*, 106 n. 19.

[41] Lawrence H. Schiffman, '2 Enoch and Halakhah', in Orlov and Boccaccini (eds), *New Perspectives on 2 Enoch*, 228.

[42] Francis I. Andersen, '2 (Slavonic Apocalypse of) Enoch', in Charlesworth (ed.), *The Old Testament Pseudepigrapha*, vol. 1: *Apocalyptic Literature and Testaments*, 96.

[43] Christfried Böttrich, 'The "Book of the Secrets of Enoch" (2 En): Between Jewish Origin and Christian Transmission: An Overview', in Orlov and Boccaccini (eds), *New Perspectives on 2 Enoch*, 58–9.

The textual history of this work is probably beyond recovery; it is very complicated, and in all likelihood there have been deletions and interpolations in both recensions.[44]

The newly discovered Coptic fragments, however, clearly represent the short recension.

2 Enoch divides into three sections: Enoch's ascent to heaven (1–36), Enoch's last words to his sons (37–68), and the stories of Enoch's descendants, principally Methuselah and Melchizedek (69–73). It is the heavenly ascent which is of interest here. Enoch, 'a wise man, a great scholar',[45] is woken from sleep by two angels, huge men with fiery faces and golden wings. They carry him up through six heavens, showing him sights both cosmological and angelic, and imparting calendrical information. At the edge of the seventh heaven they withdraw, and the archangels Gabriel and Michael bring him 'in front of the face of the LORD'.[46] At the command of God, he is anointed and reclothed, becoming transformed, 'like one of the glorious ones'.[47] Hugo Odeberg and Andrei Orlov take this to mean that he is made a 'Prince of the Divine Presence'.[48] Jonas Greenfield and Alexander argue for a less dramatic interpretation, in which Enoch assumes the same kind of spiritual body as that that the righteous dead receive in heaven.[49] The archangel Vereveil is summoned, and told to give Enoch a pen, so that he can write down all the secrets which are about to be revealed to him. God himself explains creation to him, and then gives him thirty days to return to earth and share his new-found knowledge with his sons. In order to be able to do so, his face has to be chilled by an angel with hands like ice. After Enoch has imparted his wisdom, angels grasp him, and carry him up to the highest heaven, where 'the LORD [receives] him and [makes] him stand in front of his face for eternity'.[50]

5.5 ASCENSION OF ISAIAH

Ascension of Isaiah is often described as a Jewish–Christian apocalypse. Frankfurter cautions that it is texts like *Ascension of Isaiah* which expose the

---

[44] Francis I. Andersen, 'Enoch, Second Book of', in David Noel Freedman (ed.), *The Anchor Bible Dictionary* (New York: Doubleday, 1992), 2.519.
[45] *2 En.* 1a:1; trans. Andersen, 103.
[46] *2 En.* 22:6; trans. Andersen, 139. In the long recension there are ten heavens.
[47] *2 En.* 22:10; trans. Andersen, 139.
[48] Hugo Odeberg, *3 Enoch or the Hebrew Book of Enoch* (Cambridge: Cambridge University Press, 1928; repr., New York: Ktav, 1973), 55; Orlov, *The Enoch–Metatron Tradition*, 156.
[49] Jonas C. Greenfield, 'Prolegomenon', in Odeberg, *3 Enoch or the Hebrew Book of Enoch*, xxiii; Philip Alexander, 'The Historical Setting of the Hebrew Book of Enoch', *Journal of Jewish Studies*, 28 (1977), 160.
[50] *2 En.* 67:2; trans. Andersen, 195.

deficiencies of such theological categories as 'Christian', 'Jewish', or 'Jewish–Christian', and challenge us 'to reconstruct historical nuances of identity'.[51] He suggests that *Ascension of Isaiah*, like Revelation, might have emerged 'from a guild of self-defined prophets maintaining visionary traditions within some Jewish milieu who at some point in the later first century [arrived] at the conclusion that Christ is the visible portion of God'.[52] The text falls into two parts—an account of Isaiah's martyrdom, in which he is sawn in two at the behest of King Manasseh (1–5) and a report of his visionary ascent through seven heavens (6–11)—leading to speculation about two (or more) sources. Earlier scholarship assumed that the basic material on Isaiah's martyrdom came from a Jewish text, whereas the vision was a later Christian addition.[53] Recently a more unitary approach has emerged. Robert Hall argues that the final redaction 'stems from an early Christian prophetic school' of 'the end of the first or more probably the beginning of the second century CE'.[54] Jonathan Knight, building on the work of Italian scholars such as Enrico Norelli, suggests that 'what we find in the earliest stratum...is an original first-person account of heavenly ascension written by an unknown author in the first century CE (chapters 7–11)', dating, in other words, 'from the period when the later New Testament documents were being written'.[55] Chapters 1–5 'were added in the early second century to address a more pessimistic situation'.[56] Although almost certainly originally written in Greek, only one Greek fragment of 2:4–4:4 has survived. The most complete surviving translation is in Ethiopic. There are also two Latin translations, a Slavonic version, fragments in two Coptic dialects, and a medieval Greek recasting. These are collected together in the edition by Paolo Bettiolo and colleagues.[57] Michael Knibb's translation into English, which has been used in this study, was made before the Bettiolo edition, on the basis of a collation of five Ethiopic manuscripts. It is Isaiah's vision of ascending through the seven heavens to see the Great Glory flanked by the Beloved and the angel of the Holy Spirit which interests us here.

---

[51] David Frankfurter, 'Beyond "Jewish Christianity": Continuing Religious Sub-Cultures of the Second and Third Centuries and their Documents', in Adam H. Becker and Annette Yoshiko Reed (eds), *The Ways that Never Parted: Jews and Christians in Late Antiquity and the Early Middle Ages* (Minneapolis: Fortress, 2007), 137.

[52] Frankfurter, 'Beyond "Jewish Christianity"', 138.

[53] See, for example, M. A. Knibb, 'Martyrdom and Ascension of Isaiah', in James H. Charlesworth (ed.), *The Old Testament Pseudepigrapha*, vol. 2: *Expansions of the 'Old Testament' and Legends, Wisdom and Philosophical Literature, Prayers, Psalms, and Odes, Fragments of Lost Judeo-Hellenistic Works* (New York: Doubleday, 1985), 143.

[54] Robert G. Hall, 'The *Ascension of Isaiah*: Community Situation, Date, and Place in Early Christianity', *Journal of Biblical Literature*, 109: 2 (1990), 306.

[55] Jonathan Knight, 'The Origin and Significance of the Angelomorphic Christology in the Ascension of Isaiah', *The Journal of Theological Studies*, 63: 1 (2012), 70, 71.

[56] Knight, 'Angelomorphic Christology in the Ascension of Isaiah', 70.

[57] Paolo Bettiolo, Alda Giambelluca Kossova, Claudio Leonardi, Enrico Norelli, and Lorenzo Perrone, *Ascensio Isaiae: Textus* (Turnhout: Brepols, 1995).

The culmination of Isaiah's vision is to be shown Christ's descent, followed by his birth, life, death, and resurrection, and finally his ascension back to heaven. During the descent, the Lord Christ makes his own form to be like that of the angels in each of the heavens he passes through, so as not to be recognized. Gregory's sermon *On the Ascension of Christ* also tells how, in his descent, Christ 'proportions himself wherever he goes to those who receive him' so that 'coming amongst angels he likens himself to their nature'.[58] However, Gregory's version includes words from LXX Psalm 23 (MT 24), not found in *Ascension of Isaiah*. Therefore, although he knows of this tradition, he probably drew upon a different source.

5.6 HEKHALOT TEXTS

The Hekhalot literature has survived in medieval manuscripts—the most important having been produced by the *Ḥasidei Ashkenaz*[59]—and in fragments found in the Cairo Genizah. The name refers to the palaces (*hekhalot*) through which the adept, sometimes referred to as the 'descender to the chariot' (*yored merkavah*), must journey.[60] It is an extremely fluid literature, 'which has reached different literary expressions in different manuscripts at different times and in different places'.[61] Schäfer therefore refers not to 'works' or 'texts' but 'macroforms', composed of smaller 'microforms'. These reflect a long process of evolution, from circles of mystics in Palestine to the shaping of the literature in Talmudic and post-Talmudic Babylonia, making dating highly controversial. Morray-Jones argues that 'the process of compilation and redaction of the [*Hekhalot Zutarti*] macroform must...have begun no later than the second or third centuries CE. Several of the microforms contained within this macroform may well be even older'.[62] Schäfer, on the other hand, emphasizes that the literature, as we have it, is 'a late rabbinic or even postrabbinic phenomenon (sixth century and later)'.[63] He therefore insists that the attributions within the literature to the second-century rabbis Ishmael and

---

[58] GNO 9.326; trans. Jean Daniélou, *The Development of Christian Doctrine before the Council of Nicaea*, vol. 1: *The Theology of Jewish Christianity* (London: Darton, Longman & Todd, 1964), 209 n. 10.

[59] The Ḥasidei Ashkenaz were Jewish pietists and mystics who lived in Germany and northern France in the late twelfth and thirteenth centuries. They may have heavily edited the texts.

[60] No satisfactory explanation has been found for this terminology of 'descent', used in *Hekhalot Rabbati*. See Peter Schäfer, *The Hidden and Manifest God: Some Major Themes in Early Jewish Mysticism* (Albany: State University of New York Press, 1992), 2–3 n. 4.

[61] Peter Schäfer, 'Tradition and Redaction in Hekhalot Literature', in *Hekhalot-Studien* (Tübingen: Mohr Siebeck, 1988), 15.

[62] Rowland and Morray-Jones, *The Mystery of God*, 234.

[63] Schäfer, *The Origins of Jewish Mysticism*, 245.

Aqiva are pseudepigraphic. Attempts to identify the circles of mystics behind the texts, and their sociological background, have not proved convincing. Schäfer's *Synopse zur Hekhalot-Literatur* is a synoptic edition of seven of the best manuscripts containing the major macroforms. References to the *Synopse* are made according to paragraph number. Not all the macroforms have yet been translated into English. This study will refer to *Hekhalot Rabbati* ('The Greater Palaces', §§81–306), *Hekhalot Zutarti* ('The Lesser Palaces', §§335–517), *Ma'aseh Merkavah* ('The Work of the Chariot', §§544–596), and *3 Enoch* (§§1–79).

The Hekhalot texts are not a straightforward read. Descriptions of ascent are intertwined with prayers, hymns, and magical adjurations containing long lists of nonsensical names. Halperin writes,

> Open Schäfer's *Synopse* at any point…and you find yourself plunged into a swirl of hymns, incantations, divine names, and fantastic descriptions of heavenly beings. All of this seems to be assembled in no discernable pattern and to no discernable purpose. Every now and again the name of a rabbi, usually 'Ishmael' or 'Akiba' or 'Nehuniah b. ha-Qanah', floats to the surface. Very occasionally, there is something that looks like a narrative.[64]

The most complete narrative of an ascent is in *Hekhalot Rabbati* (§§198–268), where R. Nehuniah ben ha-Qannah instructs R. Ishmael, along with 'the greater and the lesser Sanhedrin', who have gathered at the entrance to the temple.[65] He tells them that anyone wishing to descend to the *merkavah* should invoke Suryah, Prince of the Divine Presence, by adjuring him 112 times, using variations of the divine name. Here we see how heavenly ascent and adjuration are intertwined. The description of the journey through the seven palaces to gaze on 'the king and his throne, his majesty and his beauty' (§198) is not coherent—several fragmentary accounts have obviously been combined—but there are many references to fearful gatekeepers, and to the names and 'seals' needed to get past them. At the climax of the account the *yored merkavah* stands before the throne of glory and recites a long series of hymns, thus joining the angelic liturgy.

3 Enoch, also known as *Sepher ha-Hekhalot* ('Book of the Palaces'), contains no theurgic incantations, and thus stands apart from the other macroforms. It appears to be 'a late fusion of Hekhalot and apocalyptic narrative traditions'.[66] It opens with a first-person narrative by Rabbi Ishmael, telling of his ascent 'to

---

[64] David J. Halperin, *The Faces of the Chariot: Early Jewish Responses to Ezekiel's Vision* (Tübingen: Mohr Siebeck, 1988), 367.

[65] There is a translation of a slightly abbreviated version of this narrative in Philip Alexander, *Textual Sources for the Study of Judaism* (Manchester: Manchester University Press, 1984), 120–5.

[66] Michael D. Swartz, 'Mystical Texts', in Shmuel Safrai, et al. (eds), *The Literature of the Sages*, second part: *Midrash and Targum, Liturgy, Poetry, Mysticism, Contracts, Inscriptions, Ancient Science and the Languages of Rabbinic Literature* (Assen: Royal Van Gorcum, 2006), 411.

the height to behold the vision of the chariot'.⁶⁷ He passes through six concentric palaces, and at the door of the seventh utters a prayer, invoking the merit of Aaron. God sends Metatron, Prince of the Divine Presence (שׂר הפנים), to his aid. Ishmael is presented before the throne of glory, where he sings praises, to which the creatures above and below the throne respond with the *Qedushah* (Isaiah 6:3 and Ezekiel 3:12). Ishmael goes on to question Metatron about his identity. Metatron reveals that he is Enoch, son of Jared, who was conveyed to heaven 'in great glory on a fiery chariot'.⁶⁸ Once there, his body changed beyond all recognition: '[The Holy One, blessed be he] made to grow on me 72 wings, 36 on one side and 36 on the other, and each single wing covered the entire world. He fixed in me 365,000 eyes and each eye was like the Great Light.'⁶⁹ The Holy One made him 'a throne like the throne of glory', which was placed 'at the door of the seventh palace'.⁷⁰ Metatron was then given a majestic robe and a kingly crown. And after receiving homage from all the angelic princes in charge of the cosmos, he underwent a further transformation, this time into blazing fire. Chapter 16 tells of Metatron's dethroning and punishment, as a result of being seen by Aḥer, who exclaimed 'There are indeed two powers in heaven!'⁷¹ This intrudes into the narrative, which continues by relating Metatron's knowledge of angelic names, hierarchies, and cosmological duties.

5.7 B. ḤAGIGAH 11b-16a

The Babylonian Talmud is structured as a commentary upon the Mishnah, which is the foundation document of rabbinic Judaism, edited around CE 200. The Mishnah contains mostly legal material, organized into sixty-three tractates. The rabbis who feature in the Mishnah, and are therefore assumed to have flourished before CE 200, are known as the *tanna'im*. There are two Talmuds: the Palestinian Talmud, known as the Yerushalmi, edited in Palestine in the fifth century, and the Babylonian Talmud, known as the Bavli, edited in the rabbinic academies of Babylonia in the sixth century. The rabbis who feature in either Talmud, but who lived after the final redaction of the Mishnah are known as *amora'im*. The Bavli is vast—the Soncino Hebrew–English edition is made up of thirty-two volumes—and its contents are much more diverse than those of the Mishnah, encompassing legal debates, biblical interpretation,

---

⁶⁷ *3 En.* 1:1; §1; trans. Alexander, 255.   ⁶⁸ *3 En.* 6:1; §9; trans. Alexander, 261.
⁶⁹ *3 En.* 9:2–4; §12; trans. Alexander, 263.
⁷⁰ *3 En.* 10:1–2; §13; trans. Alexander, 263–4.
⁷¹ *3 En.* 16:3; §20; trans. Alexander, 268. Aḥer (which means 'another') was the name given to Elisha b. Avuyah, the rabbinic arch-heretic of the second century CE.

legends, parables, and prayers. A fourth rabbinic document which needs to be mentioned is the Tosephta, edited in the fourth century, which contains additional Tannaitic material, as well as later discussions.[72] We here are concerned with the few folios of tractate *Ḥagigah* in the Bavli dealing with *m. Ḥagigah* 2:1. The mishnaic text reads as follows:

> '*Arayot*[73] may not be expounded by three, nor *ma'aśeh běrešit* [the work of creation] by two, nor the *merkabah* [chariot] by an individual, unless he is a scholar and has understood on his own.
>
> Anyone who gazes at four things, it would be merciful to him if he had not come into the world: what is above and what is below, what is before and what after.
>
> Anyone who has no concern for the honor of his Creator, if would be merciful to him if he had not come into the world.[74]

Halperin suggests that the restriction on expounding the *merkavah* originally circulated independently (without the restrictions on *'arayot* and *ma'aseh bereshit*), and was a prohibition on private study of the *merkabah*:

> Private study is permitted only to a competent 'scholar' who can 'understand on his own'; another might, without a teacher's guidance, blunder into idiosyncratic exegeses of the text. It is implied that one not a 'scholar' *would* be permitted to study the *merkabah* with a teacher, or in some sort of established framework.[75]

Once combined with the other two restrictions, however, the meaning of the ruling was reversed: 'solitary study of the *merkabah* was no longer the object of the restriction, but a concession granted to certain individuals'.[76] The privileged few could study Ezekiel 1 on their own; no one else was to go near it. The Bavli's commentary changes the preposition from 'by' (ב) to 'to' (ל), thus changing the setting to that of a teacher–student relationship. The *merkabah* may only be expounded by a teacher to a single student, and only if that student is wise and already understands on his own. This situation is illustrated by the story of R. Yoḥanan b. Zakkai dismounting from his ass in order to listen to his student, R. Eleazar b. Arakh, prove that he has already understood 'the work of the chariot' on his own (*b. Ḥag.* 14b).

---

[72] The relationship between the Mishnah and the Tosephta is the subject of debate. See Amram Tropper, 'The State of Mishnah Studies', and Ronen Reichman, 'The Tosefta and Its Value for Historical Research: Questioning the Historical Reliability of Case Stories', in Martin Goodman and Philip Alexander (eds), *Rabbinic Texts and the History of Late-Roman Palestine* (Oxford: Oxford University Press, 2010), 96–7, 118–19.

[73] Forbidden sexual relations: Leviticus 18 and 20.

[74] Trans. David J. Halperin, *The Merkabah in Rabbinic Literature* (New Haven: American Oriental Society, 1980), 11–12.

[75] Halperin, *The Merkabah in Rabbinic Literature*, 35.

[76] Halperin, *The Merkabah in Rabbinic Literature*, 36.

M. Ḥagigah 2:1 is commented upon by the Tosephta and both Talmuds. All three, for example, tell the story of the four who entered a mysterious garden (*pardes*) and their respective fates.[77] But the Bavli's discussion of *m. Ḥagigah* 2:1 'is much more comprehensive and complex than any of its parallels'.[78] In the story of *pardes*, it inserts a reference to a water test, which is described in more detail in *Hekhalot Zutarti*. And, like *3 Enoch*, it tells of Aḥer's ascent to heaven, where he sees Metatron seated and exclaims 'Perhaps, God forbid, there are two Divine powers'.[79] There has been much debate about what 'expounding (the work of) the chariot' might mean. Halperin and Schäfer insist that in the Mishnah, Tosephta, and Yerushalmi it refers to the exegetical activity of interpreting the first chapter of Ezekiel.[80] Only in the Bavli, where there is influence from apocalyptic and Hekhalot texts, is there a 'slow and still rudimentary infiltration of a tradition that identifies the Merkavah *exegesis* with an *ascent* to the Merkavah'.[81] *M. Ḥagigah* forbids 'expounding' (דרש) the chariot; and in the stories that follow in *b. Ḥagigah* there is talk of transmitting (מסר), instructing (Aramaic גמר), studying (Aramaic תני), reading (קרא), teaching (למד,שנה), beginning an exposition (פתח), and discoursing (רצה). This is quintessential rabbinic vocabulary. The 'rabbinization' can also be seen in the fact that the exposition of *ma'aseh merkavah* is traced back to Yoḥanan b. Zakkai and his disciples, giving it an impeccable rabbinic pedigree (*b. Ḥag.* 14b).[82] In the stories about Yoḥanan b. Zakkai's disciples expounding the 'work of the chariot', heavenly approval is signalled by miraculous phenomena: fire coming down from heaven, a rainbow appearing in the cloud, ministering angels assembling. Many of these phenomena duplicate those of the revelation at Sinai, as described in Exodus 19, Psalm 68, and associated rabbinic legends.[83] 'The supernatural expertise of R. [Yoḥanan] and his disciples may have been believed to show that they, and through them the rabbis, had inherited the mantle of Moses.'[84] Schäfer insists that the rabbis 'understood the respective biblical texts (Genesis 1 and Ezekiel 1) as material for exegetical exercises and not for ecstatic experiences that aim at an ascent to the Merkavah in heaven'.[85] But the stories of miraculous phenomena seem to indicate that,

---

[77] *T. Ḥag.* 2:3–4; *y. Ḥag.* 2:1 fol. 77b; *b. Ḥag.* 14b, 15a,b. Translations of these three versions of the story, set out in parallel columns, can be found in Halperin, *The Merkabah in Rabbinic Literature*, 86–7. The *pardes* story will be discussed in 13.4.

[78] Schäfer, *The Origins of Jewish Mysticism*, 222.

[79] Trans. Halperin, *The Merkabah in Rabbinic Literature*, 168. The story of Aḥer and Metatron will be discussed in 8.4.

[80] Halperin, *The Merkabah in Rabbinic Literature*, 179; Schäfer, *The Origins of Jewish Mysticism*, 211.

[81] Schäfer, *The Origins of Jewish Mysticism*, 194; cf. Halperin, *The Faces of the Chariot*, 37.

[82] Yoḥanan b. Zakkai is credited with reconstituting Jewish religious authority after the destruction of the temple.

[83] For details, see Halperin, *The Merkabah in Rabbinic Literature*, 128–33.

[84] Halperin, *The Merkabah in Rabbinic Literature*, 138.

[85] Schäfer, *The Origins of Jewish Mysticism*, 31.

at its highest, exegesis could turn into an ecstatic experience, dissolving the boundaries between heaven and earth. Morray-Jones therefore objects to 'a sharp distinction between the exegetical activity described in the Talmudic sources and the visionary mysticism of the hekhalot writings'.[86] He argues that what the rabbinic writers called *ma'aseh merkavah* was the tradition of 'performative exegesis' represented by *Hekhalot Zutarti*.[87] And Wolfson writes,

> As a result of their exegetical activity [Yohanan ben Zakkai and his disciples] experienced paranormal states of religious inspiration frequently involving the phenomenon of fire. Even though the experiences related in the rabbinic sources typically do not involve a heavenly journey or consequent vision of the enthroned glory, the fact that the exposition of the biblical text occasions a mystical state is significant.[88]

Rabbinic midrash is very different to Origen's allegorical exegesis; but, for the rabbis too, exegesis can become an ascent in itself. Alongside their positive reception of *merkavah* traditions, however, come dire warnings of its dangers. The restriction of *m. Ḥag.* 2:1 is reinforced in the Bavli by a number of cautionary tales warning of the dangers of *ma'aseh merkavah*. Twice (once in Aramaic, once in Hebrew) it tells of a child who studied the references in Ezekiel to the mysterious *ḥashmal*, and 'fire came forth from *ḥašmal* and burned him up'.[89] Ben Azzai, Ben Zoma, and Aḥer come to sticky ends after trying to enter *pardes*.[90] The overall impression given of the 'work of the chariot' is 'of something mysterious and wonderful, but terrifyingly dangerous and forbidden'.[91]

---

[86] Rowland and Morray-Jones, *The Mystery of God*, 258; cf. Elliot R. Wolfson, *Through a Speculum That Shines: Vision and Imagination in Medieval Jewish Mysticism* (Princeton: Princeton University Press, 1994), 121–2.
[87] Rowland and Morray-Jones, *The Mystery of God*, 259.
[88] Wolfson, *Through a Speculum That Shines*, 122.
[89] B. Ḥag. 13a; trans. Halperin, *The Merkabah in Rabbinic Literature*, 155–6.
[90] B. Ḥag. 14b.
[91] Christopher R. A. Morray-Jones, 'Paradise Revisited (2 Cor 12:1–12): The Jewish Mystical Background of Paul's Apostolate. Part 1: The Jewish Sources', *Harvard Theological Review*, 86: 2 (1993), 183.

6

Darkness

What does it mean that Moses found himself inside the darkness and thus saw God in it? For what is now recorded seems somehow contrary to the first theophany; for the divine is then perceived in light, but now in darkness.[1]

6.1 *LIFE OF MOSES* 2.162–169: BIBLICAL CONTEXT

According to Exodus, three days after the people of Israel had arrived at Mount Sinai, 'the Lord descended upon it in fire; and the smoke of it went up like the smoke of a kiln, and the whole mountain quaked greatly'.[2] A trumpet was heard, growing louder and louder. Moses spoke, and God answered him in thunder. Chapter 19 reports that Moses ascended and descended Mount Sinai several times, taking Aaron with him at least once.[3] The beginning of Chapter 20 has God speaking the words of the Ten Commandments; it is unclear whether the people heard them or not.[4] The people then 'stood afar off, while Moses drew near to the thick darkness [ערפל; the LXX simply has 'darkness'—γνόφος] where God was'.[5] After more ordinances, Chapter 24 describes the covenant ceremony, involving Moses and Aaron, Nadab and Abihu, and seventy elders of Israel. They see the God of Israel, under whose feet is 'as it were a pavement of sapphire stone, like the very heaven for clearness'.[6] The end of the chapter reads:

> Then Moses went up on the mountain, and the cloud covered the mountain. The glory of the Lord settled on Mount Sinai, and the cloud covered it six days; and on the seventh day he called to Moses out of the midst of the cloud. Now the appearance of the glory of the Lord was like a devouring fire on the top of the mountain in the sight of the people of Israel. And Moses entered the cloud, and went up on the mountain. And Moses was on the mountain forty days and forty nights.[7]

This is when Moses is shown the pattern of the tabernacle in all its detail.

---

[1] *Vit. Moys.* 2.162.   [2] Exod. 19:18.   [3] See Exod. 19:24.
[4] Contrast Exod. 19:9 with 20:18–19.   [5] Exod. 20:21.   [6] Exod. 24:10.
[7] Exod. 24:15–18.

Gregory simplifies the Exodus account. According to him, Moses led the men, suitably purified, to the mountain slopes.[8] Then

> the clear light of the atmosphere was darkened so that the mountain became invisible, wrapped in a dark cloud. A fire shining out of the darkness presented a fearful sight to those who saw it. It hovered all around the sides of the mountain so that everything which one could see smouldered with the smoke from the surrounding fire.[9]

There was a terrible sound, 'harsh and intolerable to every ear', 'like the blaring of trumpets'.[10] It was laying down divine ordinances. The people as a whole 'were incapable of enduring what was seen and heard', and therefore requested that the law be mediated through Moses: 'So when all went down to the foot of the mountain, Moses alone remained.'[11] His fear dissolved and he boldly entered the darkness. There he received the divine commandments, and 'having been first purified in mind by these laws, as it were, he was led to the more perfect mystical initiation, suddenly being shown a certain tabernacle by divine power'.[12] Gregory mentions the fire, the smoke, and the terrifying trumpet-like sound, but emphasizes the darkness of Exodus 20:21. In part 2 of *Life of Moses* he reflects on the difference between this theophany and the first one—the burning bush—when the divine was 'perceived in light'.[13] He portrays the ascent to God as an ascent into darkness:

> Religious knowledge at first appears as light to those in whom it springs up. Therefore the opposite of piety is thought to be obscurity; and the escape from obscurity comes with participation in the light. But as the mind advances, and through an ever greater and more perfect attentiveness comes to envisage an understanding of all existence, the nearer it draws to contemplation, the more it sees that the divine nature is not to be contemplated.[14]

In this progression, the mind must leave behind 'everything visible, not only what the senses grasp but also what the mind seems to see'. The aim is to gain access to 'the unseen and incomprehensible'.[15] Despite quoting John 1:18 ('No one has ever seen God'), Gregory does not abandon all light and vision imagery: he still writes about 'seeing God'.[16] But he resorts to paradox: 'the seeing which consists in not seeing (τὸ ἰδεῖν ἐν τῷ μὴ ἰδεῖν)', and 'radiant darkness (λαμπρῷ γνόφῳ)'.[17]

Gregory's interpretations of the entry into darkness, the giving of divine ordinances, and the vision of the tabernacle are linked by the theme of divine incomprehensibility. That which is sought 'transcends all knowledge, cut off

---

[8] *Vit. Moys.* 1.42. [9] *Vit. Moys.* 1.43; trans. Malherbe and Ferguson, 42.
[10] *Vit. Moys.* 1.44; trans. Malherbe and Ferguson, 42.
[11] *Vit. Moys.* 1.45; trans. Malherbe and Ferguson, 42–3. [12] *Vit. Moys.* 1.49.
[13] *Vit. Moys.* 2.162. [14] *Vit. Moys.* 2.162. [15] *Vit. Moys.* 2.163.
[16] *Vit. Moys.* 2.162, 163, 164. [17] *Vit. Moys.* 2.163.

on all sides by incomprehensibility (τῇ ἀκαταληψίᾳ), as by a kind of darkness'.[18] This is reinforced by the divine voice:

> The divine word first forbids that human beings liken the divine to anything known, since every concept which derives from a recognisable (περιληπτικὴν) image by whatever thought process, and by speculation on the divine nature, fashions an idol of God, and does not proclaim God.[19]

Gregory describes the darkness as an *aduton*, the innermost room of a temple or shrine:

> [Moses] then boldly approached the darkness itself and found himself inside the invisible realities, where he was no longer discernible to those watching. Stealing into the secret place (*aduton*) of the divine mystical initiation, there, unseen, he was with the invisible.[20]

He uses *aduta*, in the plural, to designate the tabernacle: '[Moses] slipped into the inner sanctuary (*ta aduta*) of the tabernacle not made with hands',[21] and *adutos*, the adjective, to describe the holy of holies: 'By these [veils] were separated that part of the tabernacle which was visible and accessible to some of those conducting ceremonies from that which was secret (*aduton*) and inaccessible.'[22] This holy of holies is symbolic of divine incomprehensibility, for 'the truth of all existence is truly a holy matter, a holy of holies, incomprehensible (ἄληπτόν) and unapproachable for the multitude'.[23] Once again, we are faced with paradox. Moses 'steals into the invisible secret place (ἄδυτον παραδύεται) of divine knowledge': he enters the unenterable.[24] He is in the darkness, and yet he 'sees (βλέπει) that tabernacle not made with hands'.[25] Macleod undercuts the scholarly emphasis on Gregory's apophaticism by stating, 'the reverse side of Gregory's negative theology is Christian faith: in the very darkness which surrounds God we see the "tabernacle", Christ'.[26] It is not, however, that straightforward, for as well as contrast there is intensification: within the *aduton* of the darkness is the tabernacle (*ta aduta*), within which is the *aduton* of the holy of holies. And within the holy of holies are the cherubim who 'cover with their wings the mysteries lying in the ark'.[27] There is an incomprehensibility within the tabernacle not made with hands, to which even Moses does not have access.

Gregory's reflections on darkness start from Exodus 20:21. He also, at 2.164, quotes from LXX Psalm 17:12:[28]

> And he made darkness [σκότος translating חשׁך] his hideaway [ἀποκρυφήν translating סתרו]...[29]

---

[18] *Vit. Moys.* 2.163. [19] *Vit. Moys.* 2.165. [20] *Vit. Moys.* 1.46.
[21] *Vit. Moys.* 2.229; trans. Malherbe and Ferguson, 114. [22] *Vit. Moys.* 2.172.
[23] *Vit. Moys.* 2.188. [24] *Vit. Moys.* 2.167. [25] *Vit. Moys.* 2.169.
[26] Colin W. Macleod, 'Allegory and Mysticism in Origen and Gregory of Nyssa', *Journal of Theological Studies*, 22: 2 (1971), 378.
[27] *Vit. Moys.* 2.180. [28] MT 18:12; RSV 18:11. [29] Trans. NETS.

He uses the same verse in *On the Song of Songs*:

> Now the word *night* points to contemplation of things unseen, just like Moses, who entered into the darkness in which God was—God, who, as the prophet says, 'Made darkness his hiding place round about him.'[30]

In both cases, he only quotes the first clause, but the next phrase may also have been in his mind:

> ...around him was his tent [σκηνή translating סכתו]...[31]

In the Greek, the darkness around God is a *skēnē*, a tabernacle. This verse, therefore, lends biblical weight to Gregory's interplay between darkness and tabernacle.

6.2 LIFE OF MOSES 2.162–169: ALEXANDRIAN CONTEXT

Gregory's depiction of the ascent of the soul is often contrasted with Origen's:

> Whereas for Origen the soul pursues a path of increasing light—the darkness it encounters is dissolved as it progresses further—with Gregory the soul travels deeper and deeper into darkness.[32]

The difference with Origen can be illustrated by looking at Origen's use of Exodus 20:21 and LXX Psalm 17:12 in *Against Celsus* 6.17:

> It is said...that 'God made darkness his hiding-place'. This is a Hebrew way of showing that the ideas of God which men understand in accordance with their merits are obscure and unknowable, since God hides Himself as if in darkness from those who cannot bear the radiance of the knowledge of Him and who cannot see Him, partly because of the defilement of the mind that is bound to a human 'body of humiliation', partly because of its restricted capacity to comprehend God. To make it clear that the experience of the knowledge of God comes to men on rare occasions, and is to be found by very few people, Moses is said in scripture to have entered into 'the darkness where God was'....
> Moreover, our Saviour and Lord, the Logos of God, shows the depth of the knowledge of the Father, and that, although a derived knowledge is possessed by those whose minds are illuminated by the divine Logos himself, absolute understanding and knowledge of the Father is possessed by himself alone...By participation in him who took away from the Father what is called darkness, which he

---

[30] *Cant.* 6 (GNO 6.181.4–8); trans. Norris, 193. This is a commentary on Song of Songs 6:1.
[31] Trans. NETS.
[32] Andrew Louth, *The Origins of the Christian Mystical Tradition: From Plato to Denys*, 2nd edn (Oxford: Oxford University Press, 2007), 81.

made 'his hiding place',... thus revealing the Father, anyone whatever who has the capacity to know Him may do so.'[33]

Origen argues that God conceals himself from those who are unworthy, but that Christ has taken away the darkness, and unveiled the Father. As Louth comments, 'the soul does not have to do with a God who is ultimately unknowable. Darkness is only a phase we pass through: it is not ultimate as in Philo, Gregory of Nyssa, or Denys the Areopagite.'[34]

If Gregory has broken with Origen, it is by returning to Philo. Philo at times uses imagery of light and seeing. He repeatedly comments on Israel as 'he who sees God'.[35] And, like the heavenly ascent texts examined in 6.4, he can portray God as shielded not by darkness but by dazzling light:

> ... [the mind] seems to be on its way to the Great King Himself; but, amid its longing to see Him, pure and untempered rays of concentrated light stream forth like a torrent, so that by its gleams the eye of the understanding is dazzled.[36]

But Exodus 20:21 is an important text for him.[37] In *On Moses* 1.158, he says:

> [Moses] entered, we are told, into the darkness where God was, that is into the unseen, invisible, incorporeal and archetypal essence of existing things.

In *On the Posterity of Cain* 14–16 and *On the Change of Names* 7–10 Moses' entry into the darkness becomes a fruitless search, and a comment on the unknowability of God:

> When...the God-loving soul probes the question of the essence of the Existent Being, he enters on a quest of that which is beyond matter and beyond sight. And out of this quest there accrues to him a vast boon, namely to apprehend that the God of real Being is apprehensible by no one, and to see precisely this, that He is incapable of being seen.[38]

Geljon argues that 'Gregory's interpretation of the darkness as God's incomprehensibility is Philonic', with both of them 'calling God ἀκατάληπτος [incomprehensible] and ἀόρατος [invisible]'.[39] Others insist on a contrast between Gregory and Philo:

> Plato, Philo and Plotinus would all agree that the soul cannot express God in image or concept; it is Gregory who grounds this incapacity in a *metaphysical* gulf between God and the created self.[40]

---

[33] Trans. Chadwick, 330–1.
[34] Louth, *The Origins of the Christian Mystical Tradition*, 70.
[35] See, for example, *Abr.* 57.   [36] *Opif.* 71; cf. *Fug.* 165.
[37] He comments on it in *Post.* 14, *Gig.* 54, *Mut.* 7, and *Mos.* 1.158.   [38] *Post.* 15.
[39] Albert Geljon, *Philonic Exegesis in Gregory of Nyssa's De Vita Moysis* (Providence: Brown Judaic Studies, 2002), 134.
[40] Rowan Williams, *The Wound of Knowledge: Christian Spirituality from the New Testament to St. John of the Cross* (London: DLT, 1979), 60.

The measure of similarity between Gregory and Philo, though striking enough, should not be overstressed. Both employ the same passage of Exodus to suggest the transcendence of the divine nature. But, whereas for Philo the text points to the superiority of God to sense, Gregory uses the same passage to assert the superiority of God to intellect as well. For Philo God is above all sensory shape, for Gregory he is above all form. For Philo incomprehensibility seems to mean 'incapable of being seen', for Gregory the same expression means 'incapable of being understood'.[41]

Philo posits the Logos as an intermediary between the unknowable 'Being' (τὸ ὄν) and the created world. In *On the Confusion of Tongues*, he uses Exodus 24:10—'And they saw the place, there where the God of Israel stood'[42]—to suggest that the goal of Moses' ascent was the Logos:

> It is the special mark of those who serve the Existent (τὸ ὄν) that...in their thoughts [they] ascend to the heavenly height, setting before them Moses, the nature beloved of God, to lead them on the way. For then they shall behold the place which in fact is the Word, where stands God the never changing, never swerving...[43]

Origen develops this understanding in a Christian direction, by making Christ the one who dispels the darkness around the Father. For Gregory, Christ is not an intermediary, but fully divine, and therefore as incomprehensible as the Father, hence the metaphysical gulf referred to by Rowan Williams. The contrast between Gregory and Philo, however, is not as great as Meredith implies. Philo does not use 'seeing' simply to refer to sensual perception, but as a metaphor for noetic comprehension.

Clement refers to Exodus 20:21 in *Miscellanies* 2.6.1, where he quotes from *On the Posterity of Cain* 14–16:

> Whence Moses, convinced that God is never to be known by human wisdom, says: '*Show yourself to me*' and he is pressed *to enter into the darkness, where God's voice was, that is into the inaccessible* (ἀδύτους) *and invisible conceptions of the Existent. For God is not in darkness or in space but above both space and time* and peculiarities of created things.[44]

This enables Geljon to say that 'Clement explains the darkness in the same way as Philo does'.[45] Lilla agrees that 'Clement follows Philo' in the interpretation

---

[41] Anthony Meredith, *The Cappadocians* (Crestwood, NY: St Vladimir's Seminary Press, 1995), 74.
[42] LXX; trans. NETS.   [43] *Conf.* 95–6.
[44] Trans. Annewies van den Hoek, *Clement of Alexandria and His Use of Philo in the Stromateis: An Early Christian Reshaping of a Jewish Model* (Leiden: Brill, 1988), 149. The italics designate words taken over from Philo.
[45] Geljon, *Philonic Exegesis in Gregory of Nyssa's De Vita Moysis*, 131.

of Exodus 20:21.⁴⁶ However, Clement alludes to *On the Posterity of Cain* 14–16 again in *Miscellanies* 5.71.5:

> Moses says *'reveal yourself to me'* (Ex. 33:13), hinting *most plainly* that God cannot be *taught*, or spoken by human beings, but is knowable only through the *power* that proceeds from him. For *the quest is formless and unseen*, but the grace of his knowledge comes from him through the Son.⁴⁷

André Méhat comments,

> Au dernier terme, Clément ne peut accepter que Dieu soit inconnaissable. Si parfois il semble reprendre la thèse philonienne que Dieu ne peut être connu que par ses manifestations et *dans sa puissance*, au fond, guidé par l'espérance, qu'il tient de saint Paul, de la vision 'face à face', il retourne les expressions de Philon. Jouant sur les mots, il croit plutôt que Dieu ne peut être connu que *par sa puissance*, par un effet de sa grâce et la médiation du Logos.⁴⁸

David Runia agrees:

> Clement agrees with Philo that God cannot be known as he really is.... But when Moses asks that God reveal himself, the answer is not negative, as it is by implication in Philo. God *is* knowable, but only through his power, which Clement does not connect with divine forces in the cosmos, but with the knowledge that comes through the Son. God is unknowable, yet he is made known by grace and in Christ.⁴⁹

Geljon points out that Clement took over Philo's exegesis of the darkness, and therefore that Gregory might have been influenced by Clement rather than Philo.⁵⁰ Studies such as Geljon's have shown, however, that Gregory read Philo, whereas there is no comparable data on Gregory and Clement.⁵¹ It seems more likely that Gregory took the interpretation direct from Philo, especially as he shows none of Clement's ambivalence towards apophaticism.

---

⁴⁶ Salvatore R. C. Lilla, *Clement of Alexandria: A Study in Christian Platonism and Gnosticism* (Oxford: Oxford University Press, 1971), 217.
⁴⁷ Trans. David T. Runia, 'Clement of Alexandria and the Philonic Doctrine of the Divine Power(s)', *Vigiliae christianae*, 58: 3 (2004), 266–7.
⁴⁸ 'In the end, Clement can not accept that God is unknowable. Although he sometimes seems to take up the Philonic argument that God can only be known by his manifestations and in his power, guided by the hope of the vision "face to face" received from St Paul, he turns Philo's phrases around. Playing on words, he believes rather that God can only be known by his power, that is, as a result of his grace and by the mediation of the Logos.' André Méhat, *Étude sur les 'Stromates' de Clément d'Alexandrie* (Paris: Seuil, 1966), 203.
⁴⁹ Runia, 'Clement of Alexandria and the Philonic Doctrine of the Divine Power(s)', 267.
⁵⁰ Geljon, *Philonic Exegesis in Gregory of Nyssa's De Vita Moysis*, 131, 134.
⁵¹ See Judith L. Kovacs, 'Clement of Alexandria and Gregory of Nyssa on the Beatitudes', in H. R. Drobner and A. Viciano (eds), *Gregory of Nyssa: Homilies on the Beatitudes* (Leiden: Brill, 2000), 323 n. 40.

6.3 LIFE OF MOSES 2.162–169: THEOLOGICAL CONTEXT

The darkness surrounding God is a biblical theme. As McGinn notes,

> The mysticism of darkness is not found among pagan Neoplatonists. Indeed, we may even surmise that this distinctively biblical apophaticism serves as a critique of late antique pagan theology with its heavy use of light imagery.[52]

All the Alexandrian writers, including Origen, commented on Exodus 20:21; Gregory was adhering 'with singular fidelity to an inherited exegetical tradition'.[53] He was living, however, within a new theological context. What exactly, therefore, did darkness symbolize for him?

Daniélou insists that Gregory gives new meaning to 'darkness':

> In Gregory of Nyssa, and especially in his later works, as the *Life of Moses*, and the *Commentary on the Canticle of Canticles*, the term 'darkness' takes on a new meaning and an essentially mystical connotation. It expresses the fact that the divine essence remains inaccessible even to the mind that has been enlightened by grace, and that the awareness of this inaccessibility constitutes the highest form of contemplation. Gregory's originality consists in the fact that he was the first to express this characteristic of the highest stages of mystical experience.[54]

As Henri Crouzel has pointed out, one explanation for the contrast between Origen and Gregory is their differing polemical contexts:

> Origen and Gregory of Nyssa have often been contrasted by attributing to the former a mysticism of light and to the latter a mysticism of darkness... Now it is not impossible that Origen's mysticism of light is influenced by his polemic against the Montanist conception of trance as unconsciousness, while the mysticism of darkness favoured at Nyssa perhaps arises in part from Gregory's reaction, following his brother Basil, against the neo-Arianism of Eunomius who maintained that the divine nature was strictly defined by the fact that the Father was unbegotten.[55]

Eunomius argues 'that God is knowable—indeed, completely comprehensible because God is simple unity.... [He] concludes that this definition of God as simple unity can only be safeguarded by isolating the Supreme and Absolute One from the second and third, which came after and are therefore inferior and derivative. Ἀγεννησία [unbegottenness] becomes for him the essentially

---

[52] Bernard McGinn, *The Foundations of Mysticism: Origins to the Fifth Century* (New York: Crossroad, 1991), 175.

[53] Martin Laird, *Gregory of Nyssa and the Grasp of Faith: Union, Knowledge, and Divine Presence* (Oxford: Oxford University Press, 2004), 200.

[54] Jean Daniélou, 'Introduction', in Herbert Musurillo, *From Glory to Glory: Texts from Gregory of Nyssa's Mystical Writings* (New York: Scribner, 1961; repr., Crestwood, NY: St Vladimir's Seminary Press, 2001), 27.

[55] Henri Crouzel, *Origen* (San Francisco: Harper & Row, 1989), 121.

divine attribute which guarantees God's simplicity and uniqueness.'[56] Gregory responds by insisting that God's being (*ousia*), 'what he essentially is, eludes all attempt at comprehension and investigation.'[57] He derides Eunomius for thinking otherwise: 'It is therefore futile to claim that knowledge vainly puffed up is able to know the divine Being.'[58] Although 'all the words found in holy scripture to indicate God's glory describe some feature of God', his being itself

> scripture leaves uninvestigated, as beyond the reach of mind and inexpressible in word, decreeing that it should be honoured in silence by prohibiting enquiry into the deepest things and by saying that one ought not to 'utter a word in the presence of God' (Eccl 5:1).[59]

This incomprehensibility becomes associated, in Gregory's exegesis, with the darkness surrounding God.

At the beginning of *Platonisme et théologie mystique*, Daniélou quotes from Gregory's *On the Song of Songs*:

> The revelation of God to the great Moses began with light as its medium, but afterwards God spoke to him through the medium of a cloud, and when he had become more lifted up and more perfect, he saw God in darkness.[60]

He then comments:

> Nous trouvons ici résumées les étapes de la vie de Moïse, telles que Grégoire nous les expose par ailleurs dans le traité qui porte ce nom.[61]

He structures Gregory's mysticism into three stages: light/purification (κάθαρσις), cloud/contemplation (θεωρία), darkness/love (ἀγάπη). He has to admit, however, that they are not an obvious feature of *Life of Moses*:

> C'est à l'Exode que Grégoire emprunte dans le *Commentaire sur le Cantique* les grands symboles des trois voies. Or ce commentaire sur l'Exode, qu'est la *Vie de Moïse*, nous permet-il de les retrouver? Il faut reconnaître que si les grandes lignes apparaissent, nous ne sommes pas en présence de divisions à caractère bien déterminé. Ceci d'ailleurs ne sera pas pour nous étonner. Grégoire n'est pas l'homme des divisions rigides. Et sa composition, conformément à l'esthétique de son temps, ne présente aucun souci de systématisation.[62]

---

[56] Frances M. Young and Andrew Teal, *From Nicaea to Chalcedon: A Guide to the Literature and Its Background*, 2nd edn (London: SCM, 2010), 157.
[57] *Eun.* 2.12 (GNO 1.230); trans. Hall, 62.
[58] *Eun.* 2.93 (GNO 1.254); trans. Hall, 80.
[59] *Eun.* 2.105 (GNO 1.257); trans. Hall, 83.
[60] *Cant.* 11 (GNO 6.322.9–12); trans. Norris, 339.
[61] 'We find summarised here the stages of the life of Moses, as Gregory expounds them for us elsewhere, in the treatise of that name.' Jean Daniélou, *Platonisme et théologie mystique: Doctrine spirituelle de Saint Grégoire de Nysse*, 2nd edn (Paris: Aubier, 1954), 19.
[62] 'It is from Exodus that Gregory has borrowed the great symbols of the three tracks found in *On the Song of Songs*. Do we find them again in *Life of Moses*, his commentary on Exodus? It

Gregory's account of the tabernacle, in particular, does not fit Daniélou's scheme. It comes after Moses' entry into the darkness, and Gregory explicitly states that it is a further progression:

> First he leaves behind the foot of the mountain, separated out from all those unsuited for the ascent. Then as he rises to the summit of the ascent he hears the sounds of the trumpets. At these he steals into the invisible secret place of divine knowledge. And he does not stay there, but carries on to the tabernacle not made with hands. For there the one who is elevated through such ascents truly arrives at the limit.[63]

For Daniélou, however, darkness is the final stage, and he assigns the tabernacle to the summit of the second stage, contemplation.[64] In contrast to this threefold schema, Heine insists that

> there is neither a set number of stages in Moses' progress nor a set order in which things are discussed. The stages Gregory sets forth are based on the chronology of Moses' life, and what he discusses in each stage is controlled by what the imagery of the Biblical text suggests. Each episode in Moses' life takes us beyond the preceeding one in showing us the way of perfection in the virtuous life. Gregory never attempts to impose any systematic order on the progression of the Biblical story.[65]

Laird too emphasizes the exegetical character of Gregory's work, insisting that he does not introduce the theme of divine darkness 'apart from scriptural texts which lend themselves to such an interpretation'.[66]

There is a sharp divide between those commentators who think that Gregory simply uses darkness as a code for divine incomprehensibility, and those who argue that it symbolizes something more. The first group can be represented by Heine:

> Gregory's statements about seeing God in the darkness do not point to an intuitive knowledge of God...but only to a recognition that God's essence is beyond comprehension.[67]

and the second by Daniélou:

> God, as He is in Himself, is Darkness for the intellect, but can be grasped by faith. In this way it is clear that the knowledge of God in the darkness is not merely negative. It is truly an experience of the presence of God as He is in Himself, in such wise that this awareness is completely blinding for the mind, and all the more so, the closer it is to Him.[68]

---

needs to be recognised that although the essential outlines appear, we do not encounter clearly demarcated divisions. This should not surprise us. Gregory is not a man of rigid divisions. And his composition, in accordance with the aesthetics of his time, does not attempt a systematic presentation.' Daniélou, *Platonisme et théologie mystique*, 22.

[63] *Vit. Moys.* 2.167. [64] Daniélou, *Platonisme et théologie mystique*, 162–72.

[65] Ronald E. Heine, *Perfection in the Virtuous Life: A Study in the Relationship Between Edification and Polemical Theology in Gregory of Nyssa's De Vita Moysis* (Cambridge, Mass.: Philadelphia Patristic Foundation, 1975), 107–8.

[66] Laird, *Gregory of Nyssa and the Grasp of Faith*, 180.

[67] Heine, *Perfection in the Virtuous Life*, 110. [68] Daniélou, 'Introduction', 32.

This time, Laird agrees with Daniélou:

> Gregorian darkness... is much more a metaphor of presence than one of absence, a metaphor which emphasizes the mind's capacity for union (supranoetic) with God, who is most intimately present, and yet who is not grasped by the mind in comprehension (grasped rather by faith).... Gregorian darkness is a metaphor of union and presence.[69]

The way in which Mount Sinai's darkness in *Life of Moses* is interpreted partly depends on whether it is viewed through the lens of *Against Eunomius* or the lens of *On the Song of Songs*. Heine compares a number of passages in *Life of Moses*, including 2.163, with passages in *Against Eunomius* 'to show how the doctrine about knowledge of God in the *De vita Moysis* echoes the central concepts and concerns of the debate about the essence of God between Gregory and Eunomius'.[70] Laird and Harrison, on the other hand, pick up on the passage from *On the Song of Songs* in which the bridegroom gives to the soul a 'sense of presence (αἴσθησιν ... τῆς παρουσίας)'.[71] It is therefore not surprising that Heine concludes that *Life of Moses* 2.163 'parallels in all its essential points the "orthodox" statement about God which Gregory intended as a sharp contrast to the Eunomian view', whereas Harrison, like Laird, agrees with Daniélou that the seeing which consists in not seeing denotes 'a profound kind of mystical awareness'.[72]

Laird points out that, in Homily 12 of *On the Song of Songs*, Gregory does not stop at Moses' entry into the darkness, but adds that 'Moses becomes like the sun and is unable to be approached by those who are drawing near because of the light beaming from his face (cf. Exod. 34: 29–30)'.[73] Laird comments:

> Moses enters the darkness where God is but becomes luminous; he moves ever deeper in unknowing but grows increasingly in light. Whether the luminous quality surrounding the Patriarch is the light of knowledge consequent upon union beyond knowledge, or whether it is the light of divinized virtue, Gregory does not say with any precision.

He therefore concludes that although Gregory 'is an exponent of the so-called "mysticism of darkness"... he also expounds a "mysticism of light"'.[74] In *Life of Moses* there is a similar interplay, not between darkness and light, but between

---

[69] Laird, *Gregory of Nyssa and the Grasp of Faith*, 198–9.
[70] Heine, *Perfection in the Virtuous Life*, 150.
[71] *Cant.* 11 (GNO 6.324.10–11); Laird, *Gregory of Nyssa and the Grasp of Faith*, 199; Verna E. F. Harrison, *Grace and Human Freedom according to St. Gregory of Nyssa* (Lewiston, NY: Edwin Mellen, 1992), 77.
[72] Heine, *Perfection in the Virtuous Life*, 157; Harrison, *Grace and Human Freedom*, 77.
[73] GNO 6.355.11–14; trans. Laird, *Gregory of Nyssa and the Grasp of Faith*, 204.
[74] Laird, *Gregory of Nyssa and the Grasp of Faith*, 204.

darkness and the tabernacle. As already mentioned, Macleod notes 'the complex texture of Gregory's writing': 'in the very darkness which surrounds God we see the "tabernacle", Christ'.[75]

6.4 *LIFE OF MOSES* 2.162–169: HEAVENLY ASCENT CONTEXT

Heavenly ascent texts work primarily with imagery of light, not darkness. From biblical texts onwards, that of the divine which humans perceive is described as 'glory', *kavod* in Hebrew. Once the earthly tabernacle has been constructed, it becomes filled with 'the glory of the Lord'.[76] Ezekiel has a vision of 'the appearance of the likeness of the glory of the Lord'.[77] In the ascent apocalypses, Enoch sees 'the Great Glory', as do Levi and Isaiah.[78] *2 Enoch* talks of the 'face' of the Lord:

> I saw the view of the face of the Lord, like iron made burning hot in a fire and brought out, and it emits sparks and is incandescent. Thus even I saw the face of the Lord. But the face of the Lord is not to be talked about, it is so very marvellous and supremely awesome and supremely frightening.[79]

Orlov argues that this 'represents the divine *kavod*'.[80] As Schäfer comments, 'We do not learn much about the physical shape of God's face, only that it looks like white-hot iron—quite a prosaic image for the brightness of God's face.'[81] The Hekhalot texts too refer to the divine *panim* (face, sometimes translated 'countenance' or 'presence'):

> Lovely countenance,
> adorned countenance,
> countenance of beauty,
> countenance of flame[s]
> is the countenance of the Lord, the God of Israel,
> when he sits upon the throne of his glory.[82]

---

[75] Macleod, 'Allegory and Mysticism', 377–8. [76] Exod. 40:34. [77] Ezek. 1:28.
[78] *1 En.* 14:20; *T. Levi* 3:4; *Ascen. Isa.* 9:37.
[79] *2 En.* 22:1, longer recension; trans. Andersen, 136.
[80] Andrei A. Orlov, 'God's Face in the Enochic Tradition', in April D. DeConick (ed.), *Paradise Now: Essays on Early Jewish and Christian Mysticism* (Atlanta: Society of Biblical Literature, 2006), 186.
[81] Peter Schäfer, *The Origins of Jewish Mysticism* (Tübingen: Mohr Siebeck, 2009), 80.
[82] *Hekhalot Rabbati* §159; trans. Peter Schäfer, *The Hidden and Manifest God: Some Major Themes in Early Jewish Mysticism* (Albany: State University of New York Press, 1992), 16.

In these later writings, 'glory' is also sometimes replaced by the *Shekhinah*, a rabbinic designation for the divine presence, which, like *mishkan* (tabernacle), is derived from the verb *shakhan* (to dwell):

> Anyone who gazed at the brightness of the Šekinah was not troubled by flies or gnats, by sickness or pain; malicious demons were not able to harm him, and even the angels had no power over him.[83]

What, however, exactly is 'glory'? It seems to be a visible manifestation of the invisible God, which is dangerous to look at, and impossible to describe: 'This manifestation has neither shape nor colour nor sound: it is aniconic; it is the dazzling void at the centre of things.'[84] Benjamin Sommer argues that in the Priestly literature of the Hebrew Bible '*kavod* refers to God's body and hence to God's very self.... [It] consists of unspeakably bright light, and for this reason, it is surrounded by a cloud. Normally, this cloud protects humans, so that they see only some of the *kavod*'s deadly brightness as it shines through the cloud.'[85] The figure on the chariot throne in Ezekiel 1 is described as being composed of a mysterious fiery substance called *ḥashmal*:

> And upward from what had the appearance of his loins I saw as it were gleaming *ḥashmal*, like the appearance of fire enclosed round about; and downward from what had the appearance of his loins I saw as it were the appearance of fire, and there was brightness round about him.[86]

'God's body is of human shape, but its essence is fire.'[87] In Daniel 7 and *1 Enoch* 14 the figure on the throne is wearing a garment—once again a covering—to which some luminosity has been transferred. As Alexander remarks in regard to *1 Enoch* 14,

> The description of the raiment baffles visualization; it is like the glare of the sun's orb, or of a snow-field, both of which overwhelm and 'whiteout' human vision.[88]

Neither *Testament of Levi* nor *Ascension of Isaiah* attempts any description of the 'Great Glory'. *Ascension of Isaiah*, which survives only in translation, seems uncertain as to whether it can be seen or not. In 9:37 Isaiah says,

> And I saw the Great Glory while the eyes of my spirit were open, but I could not thereafter see...[89]

---

[83] *3 En.* 5:3; §7; trans. Alexander, 259–60.

[84] Philip Alexander, 'The Qumran *Songs of the Sabbath Sacrifice* and the *Celestial Hierarchy* of Dionysius the Areopagite: A Comparative Approach', *Revue de Qumran*, 22: 87 (2006), 358.

[85] Benjamin D. Sommer, *The Bodies of God and the World of Ancient Israel* (Cambridge: Cambridge University Press, 2009), 68.

[86] Ezek. 1:27. The RSV translates *ḥashmal* as 'bronze', the NJPS as 'amber'. 'The word is unique to Ezekiel and essentially untranslatable.' Paul M. Joyce, *Ezekiel: A Commentary* (London: T&T Clark, 2009), 68.

[87] Schäfer, *The Origins of Jewish Mysticism*, 47.

[88] Alexander, '*Songs of the Sabbath Sacrifice* and the *Celestial Hierarchy*', 358 n. 15.

[89] Trans. Knibb, 172, from the Ethiopic. The Slavonic and one of the Latin versions deny even this glimpse.

Knight suggests that this is 'a fleeting glimpse of the deity but not a vision as such'.[90] The text goes on to specify that none of the angels can see the Great Glory, but that the righteous dead do behold 'with great power the glory of that one'.[91] So a vision of the divine glory is promised for the afterlife. Andersen notes that, concerning *2 Enoch* 22:1, 'The state of the MSS betray the embarrassment of scribes over this attempt to describe the appearance of the Lord.'[92] Orlov, however, argues that here, as elsewhere, 'luminosity... represents the screen that protects the Deity from the necessity of revealing its true form'.[93]

Ithamar Gruenwald states that 'despite the daring modes of expression one can find in [the Hekahlot] literature about the contents of the mystical experience, the possibility of a direct visual encounter with God is generally ruled out'.[94] Schäfer is more nuanced, pointing out the paradoxes. A section from *Hekhalot Rabbati* reads:

> A heavenly punishment [shall befall] you,
> you who descend to the Merkavah,
> if you do not report and say,
> what you have heard,
> and if you do not testify,
> what you have seen upon the countenance:
> countenance of majesty and might,
> of pride and eminence,
> which elevates itself,
> which raises itself,
> which rages [and] shows itself great.
> The countenance shows itself mighty and great
> Three times daily in the heights,
> and no man perceives and knows it,
> so, as is written:
> Holy, holy, holy.[95]

The conclusion stresses that no one can perceive the divine countenance and yet 'the *yored merkavah*, nonetheless, does see and "perceive" it, for he is called upon

---

[90] Jonathan Knight, 'The Origin and Significance of the Angelomorphic Christology in the Ascension of Isaiah', *The Journal of Theological Studies*, 63: 1 (2012), 78.
[91] 9:38; trans. Knibb, 172.
[92] Francis I. Andersen, '2 (Slavonic Apocalypse of) Enoch', in James H. Charlesworth (ed.), *The Old Testament Pseudepigrapha*, vol. 1: *Apocalyptic Literature and Testaments* (New York: Doubleday, 1983), 136 n. c.
[93] Orlov, 'God's Face in the Enochic Tradition', 183.
[94] Ithamar Gruenwald, *Apocalyptic and Merkavah Mysticism* (Leiden: Brill, 1980), 94.
[95] §169; trans. Schäfer, *The Hidden and Manifest God*, 17–18.

to give an account of it'.⁹⁶ Another section gives a graphic account of what happens to anyone who looks at the divine garment:

> Of no creature are the eyes
> able to observe it,
> not the eyes [of a human being] of flesh and blood,
> and not the eyes of his servants.
> But one who does observe,
> beholds exactly and sees it,
> his eyeballs are seized and contorted,
> and his eyeballs flash
> and shoot forth torches of fire.
> And they scorch him
> and they burn him.⁹⁷

Schäfer concludes:

> One is well-advised not to harmonize these two texts too hastily, but rather to view the tension between the 'ability to see' (or 'wanting to see') God's beauty on his throne and the danger that arises from this seeing as one of the fundamental statements of *Hekhalot Rabbati* and the Hekhalot literature as a whole.⁹⁸

To see God is not impossible, but it would be unbearable. *Ma'aseh Merkavah* is less ambivalent, stating, at the end of a long prayer section:

> Anyone who recites this prayer with all his strength can behold the radiance of the Shekhinah, and the Shekhinah loves him.⁹⁹

There is, however, no description of the *Shekhinah*. *Hekhalot Zutarti* is the only Hekhalot text to directly ask the question whether one can see God, answering it with a medley of biblical texts:

> Who is able to explain, who is able to see?
>   Firstly, it is written [Exodus 33:20]: For man may not see me and live.
>   And secondly, it is written [Deuteronomy 5:21–24]: That man may live though God has spoken to him.
>   And thirdly, it is written [Isaiah 6:1]: I beheld my Lord seated upon a high and lofty throne.¹⁰⁰

It implies that Isaiah 6:1 provides the solution to the contradiction between the verses from Exodus and Deuteronomy. Isaiah, representing a 'descender

---

⁹⁶ Schäfer, *The Hidden and Manifest God*, 18.
⁹⁷ *Hekhalot Rabbati* §102; trans. Schäfer, *The Hidden and Manifest God*, 19–20.
⁹⁸ Schäfer, *The Hidden and Manifest God*, 20.
⁹⁹ §591; trans. Schäfer, *The Hidden and Manifest God*, 89.
¹⁰⁰ §350; trans. Schäfer, *The Hidden and Manifest God*, 57–8.

to the chariot', sees God on the throne and comes to no harm. But, as Schäfer points out,

> It is surely no mere coincidence that directly following the quotation from Isaiah, no description of God's appearance on the throne is provided, but rather the question 'and what is his name?' is posed. This entails that the name of God is the crucial revelation for the Merkavah mystic.... The 'vision' of God consists, so to speak, of the communication of his names.[101]

A little further on, Rabbi Aqiva's words are reported:

> But R. ['Aqiva] said:
> He is, so to say, as we are,
> but he is greater than everything
> and his glory consists in this,
> that he is concealed from us.[102]

This theme of concealment occurs elsewhere in the Hekhalot literature, forming a counterpoint to the suggestion that God can be seen:

> What does YHWH, the God of Israel, the glorious King, do?... The glorious King covers his face, otherwise the heaven of 'Arabot would burst open in the middle, because of the glorious brilliance, beautiful brightness, lovely splendour, and radiant praises of the appearance of the Holy One, blessed be he.[103]

The covering takes different forms. Sometimes God is concealed by the *pargod*, the heavenly curtain equivalent to the *parokhet* in the earthly tabernacle/temple which divides off the holy of holies:

> R. Ishmael said: Meṭaṭron said to me:
> Come and I will show you the curtain (*pargod*) of the
> Omnipresent One, which is spread before the Holy
> One, blessed be he...[104]

Sometimes the divine garment, which in *Hekhalot Rabbati* is termed the *ḥaluq* provides the covering:

> Measure of holiness,
> measure of might,
> frightful measure,
> terrible measure,
> measure of trembling,
> measure of shaking,
> measure of terror,
> measure of vibration,

---

[101] Schäfer, *The Hidden and Manifest God*, 58.
[102] *Hekhalot Zutarti* §352; trans. Schäfer, *The Hidden and Manifest God*, 58.
[103] *3 En.* 22B:5–6; trans. Alexander, 305.   [104] *3 En.* 45:1; §64; trans. Alexander, 296.

[that emanates] from the garment (*ḥaluq*) of ZHRRY'L,
the Lord, the God of Israel,
who comes crowned to the throne of his glory.[105]

Wolfson suggests that the glory is hidden 'precisely because it is potentially visible, that is, inasmuch as the vision of the glory can prove fatal to any mortal, it must be hidden from sight'.[106]

B. Ḥagigah 12b names and describes each of the seven heavens. For the seventh heaven, *'Arabot*, it has a long list of contents, including 'the Ofannim and the Seraphim and the holy creatures and the ministering angels and the throne of glory, (and) the King, the living God, high and exalted'.[107] At the climax of the account, however, it quotes Psalm 18:12, the same verse as used by Gregory:

> And darkness (חֹשֶׁךְ) and cloud (עָנָן) and mist (עֲרָפֶל) surround him, as it is written: He made darkness his hiding place, (as) his hut around him, darkness of water, thick clouds of the sky.[108]

Schäfer concludes from this:

> Our author, having reached the climax of his description of the seven heavens, wants to emphasize that the God who, as we (now) know, resides in the uppermost heaven, is utterly invisible, hidden as it were behind thick and impenetrable darkness. So the bottom line of his 'revelation' about the seven heavens and about God's place in the heavenly realm is that in the end we can know nothing. We only know that he is there, but he is and remains concealed; nobody can approach, let alone see him.[109]

The Talmud records a dissenting voice, aware of the biblical imagery of light associated with God:

> But is there any darkness before heaven? For behold it is written: He reveals deep and hidden things, knows what is in the darkness, and light dwells with him (Dan 2:22).[110]

This contradiction is resolved by distinguishing between the outer chambers (darkness) and the inner chambers (light), assuming, presumably, that human beings cannot get through the darkness to reach the light. Another dissenting

---

[105] §102; trans. Schäfer, *The Hidden and Manifest God*, 19.

[106] Elliot R. Wolfson, *Through a Speculum That Shines: Vision and Imagination in Medieval Jewish Mysticism* (Princeton: Princeton University Press, 1994), 96.

[107] B. Ḥag. 12b; trans. Peter Schäfer, 'From Cosmology to Theology: The Rabbinic Appropriation of Apocalyptic Cosmology', in Rachel Elior and Peter Schäfer (eds), *Creation and Re-Creation in Jewish Thought: Festschrift in Honor of Joseph Dan on the Occasion of his Seventieth Birthday* (Tübingen: Mohr Siebeck, 2005), 47.

[108] B. Ḥag. 12b; trans. Schäfer, 'From Cosmology to Theology', 48.

[109] Schäfer, 'From Cosmology to Theology', 50.

[110] B. Ḥag. 12b; trans. Schäfer, 'From Cosmology to Theology', 48.

voice—R. Aḥa b. Jacob—suggests that there might be yet another heaven above the heads of the living creatures, based on Ezekiel 1:22. This, however, is silenced with a quotation from Ben Sira (3:21–22):

> Do not investigate things that are too wonderful for you and do not explore what is hidden from you! Consider what you have been permitted (to consider), but the concealed things are not your concern![111]

echoing the ending of *m. Ḥagigah* 2:1:

> Anyone who gazes at four things, it would be merciful to him if he had not come into the world: what is above and what is below, what is before and what after.
> Anyone who has no concern for the honor of his Creator, if would be merciful to him if he had not come into the world.[112]

In the Hekhalot literature, the various coverings concealing the divine seem to be a protection from danger. It is not so much that God cannot be seen, but that to do so can lead to a terrible fate. B. *Ḥagigah* too has stories of danger, but the tone is different. Schäfer argues that the purpose of the restriction in *m. Ḥagigah* 2:1 is to protect God's honour:

> Improper, unbridled exegesis of Gen. 1 and Ezek. 1 [might] infringe on God's privacy, so to speak, God's own sovereign realm, spatially and temporally, and... such an exegesis might bring one too close to God, in any event, too close to accommodate the rabbis' sense of decency.[113]

Despite their use of light imagery, heavenly ascent texts are more apophatic than might at first appear. Glory does not reveal God: it conceals the divine by dazzling the onlooker. These texts also tend to stress the danger of attempting to perceive the divine. The appropriate human response is fear and trembling. The biblical imagery of darkness surrounding God is picked up by the Talmud. The rabbis do not consider it appropriate for human beings to try and approach God. They therefore describe God as 'hidden behind an impenetrable thicket of darkness.'[114]

6.5 *LIFE OF MOSES* 2.162–169: CONCLUSIONS

Darkness is a biblical theme. In Exodus 20:21, Moses draws near to the thick darkness where God is. Another important verse is Psalm 18:12 (LXX 17:12). Gregory

---

[111] B. *Ḥag.* 13a; trans. Schäfer, 'From Cosmology to Theology', 48.
[112] Trans. David J. Halperin, *The Merkabah in Rabbinic Literature* (New Haven: American Oriental Society, 1980), 12.
[113] Schäfer, *The Origins of Jewish Mysticism*, 185.
[114] Schäfer, 'From Cosmology to Theology', 56.

continues the Alexandrian tradition of commenting on these verses, picking up particularly on Philo's apophaticism. He does so in a new theological context, in which he has to counter Eunomius' claim that the essence of God is defined by its unbegottenness. His use of darkness symbolism, however, is nuanced and paradoxical. He talks of 'radiant darkness', and of 'the seeing which consists in not seeing'.[115] And within the darkness, Moses is vouchsafed a vision of the tabernacle.

Gregory uses darkness as a symbol of divine incomprehensibility, in line with his arguments against Eunomius. He does not, however, use it as consistently and as systematically as Daniélou suggests. He invokes its symbolism in exegetical contexts where the theme of darkness has already been introduced by the scriptural text. And darkness is not the summit of the soul's journey. Within the darkness is a presence, symbolized in *Life of Moses* by the tabernacle not made with hands. This does not completely undercut his apophaticism, however, for within the heavenly tabernacle is the ark shielded by the wings of the cherubim: another symbol of divine incomprehensibility.

The heavenly ascent texts tend to pick up on a different biblical theme—that of glory. There is not, however, as much difference between glory and darkness as might at first appear. Daniélou says of Gregory's 'darkness mysticism':

> The knowledge of God in the darkness...is truly an experience of the presence of God as He is in Himself, in such wise that this awareness is completely blinding for the mind, and all the more so, the closer it is to Him. In fact, one might almost say that the darkness expresses the divine presence, and that the closer He comes to the soul, the more intense is the darkness. The image of darkness is merely a way of expressing the fact that the awesomeness of the divine essence is more than human nature can endure.[116]

The word 'darkness' could easily be replaced by 'glory'. Whereas Gregory engages in philosophical arguments about divine incomprehensibility, the heavenly ascent texts, particularly the Hekhalot literature, use vivid, not to say lurid, imagery of consuming fire to illustrate the dangers of thinking that human beings can approach the divine. The nearest parallel to Gregory's use of darkness imagery comes in *b. Ḥagigah* 12b, which quotes Psalm 18:12 and uses it to emphasize that God is hidden from human view. Gregory denounces Eunomius' hubris: 'It is...futile to claim that knowledge vainly puffed up is able to know the divine Being.'[117] Similarly, the rabbis are 'fiercely protective' of God's privacy.[118]

---

[115] *Vit. Moys.* 2.163. [116] Daniélou, 'Introduction', 32.
[117] *Eun.* 2.93 (GNO 1.254); trans. Hall, 80.
[118] Schäfer, *The Origins of Jewish Mysticism*, 211.

7

The Tabernacle Not Made with Hands

> What then is that tabernacle not made with hands, which was shown to Moses on the mountain, and which he was commanded to look upon as an archetype, so that he might present the wonder not made with hands by means of a hand-made structure?[1]

7.1 *LIFE OF MOSES* 2.170–172: BIBLICAL CONTEXT

Moses boldly approached the darkness, where he stole into 'the secret place of the divine mystical initiation'.[2] There he received the divine ordinances, and 'having been first purified in mind by these laws, as it were, he was led to the more perfect mystical initiation, suddenly being shown a certain tabernacle by divine power'.[3] Gregory repeatedly describes this tabernacle as 'not made with hands'.[4] The adjective 'not made with hands' (ἀχειροποίητος) is not found in the LXX: it 'seems to be a New Testament coinage'.[5] In Mark 14:58 Jesus is accused of saying, 'I will destroy this temple that is made with hands, and in three days I will build another, not made with hands.' And in 2 Cor. 5:1 Paul writes that 'we have a building from God, a house not made with hands, eternal in the heavens'. This is in contrast to 'the earthly tent we live in', where the word 'tent' is *skēnos*, a cognate of *skēnē*, 'tabernacle'.[6] Hebrews uses two words rather than one, but envisages a 'greater and more perfect tent' which is 'not made with hands (οὐ χειροποιήτου), that is, not of this creation'.[7]

---

[1] *Vit. Moys.* 2.170.   [2] *Vit. Moys.* 1.46.   [3] *Vit. Moys.* 1.49.
[4] 2.167 (twice), 169, 170, 229. The adjective also occurs alone or with another noun in 1.51; 2.168, 170, 173, 174, 245.
[5] J. P. M. Sweet, 'A House Not Made with Hands', in William Horbury (ed.), *Templum Amicitiae: Essays on the Second Temple presented to Ernst Bammel* (Sheffield: Sheffield Academic Press, 1991), 371. Van der Horst states that, as far as he knows, the word does not occur either in pagan Greek literature and epigraphy or in the LXX and Jewish pseudepigrapha. Pieter Willem van der Horst, 'A New Altar of a Godfearer?', *Journal of Jewish Studies*, 43 (1992), 33.
[6] 'Not made with hands' occurs a third time in the NT in Col. 2:11, with reference to circumcision.
[7] Heb. 9:11, cf. 9:24.

'Made with hands' (χειροποίητος) is employed in the LXX pejoratively, to designate idolatrous buildings or objects, often translating the Hebrew for 'idol' (אליל).⁸ This is in line with its wider use as a 'standard epithet in religious discussions, Jewish, pagan, and Christian' with 'pointed polemical connotations, contrasting mere human contrivances with what is not "made with hands", or is of divine origin'.⁹ In the Hebrew Bible, the cosmos as a whole is sometimes contrasted with man-made buildings:

> Thus says the Lord: 'Heaven is my throne and the earth is my footstool; what is the house which you would build for me, and what is the place of my rest?'¹⁰

Sometimes even the cosmos is seen as inadequate for God:

> But will God indeed dwell on the earth? Behold, heaven and the highest heaven cannot contain thee; how much less this house which I have built!¹¹

Many scholars argue that there gradually evolved the notion of a 'heavenly' temple, 'heaven' being not so much the physical heavens as another dimension, either of space or time.¹² The development of this idea of a sanctuary not made with hands can be illustrated from the exegetical afterlife of Exodus 15:17–18. In the MT this reads:

> Thou wilt bring them in, and plant them on thy own mountain, the place (מכון), O Lord, which thou hast made for thy abode, the sanctuary, O Lord, which thy hands have established. The Lord will reign for ever and ever.

There is here an 'ambivalence between temple, heaven and mountain', which William Propp suggests was inherited from Canaanite traditions.¹³ In the LXX Exodus 15:17 reads:

> Lead them in, and plant them in the mountain of your inheritance, in your prepared dwelling place (εἰς ἕτοιμον κατοικητήριόν σου) that you made, O Lord, a holy precinct, O Lord, that your hands prepared (ὃ ἡτοίμασαν αἱ χεῖρές σου).¹⁴

As William Horbury comments, the LXX translation 'suggests that this verse was already taken to promise a pre-existent God-given temple in the third

---

⁸ See, for example, Lev. 26:1; Isa. 2:18, 16:12, 46:6.
⁹ Harold W. Attridge, *The Epistle to the Hebrews* (Philadelphia: Fortress, 1989), 247.
¹⁰ Isaiah 66:1.   ¹¹ 1 Kings 8:27.
¹² See Carol A. Newsom, *Songs of the Sabbath Sacrifice: A Critical Edition* (Atlanta: Scholars Press, 1985), 59–72; Martha Himmelfarb, *Ascent to Heaven in Jewish and Christian Apocalypses* (Oxford: Oxford University Press, 1993), 9–13; or Philip Alexander, *The Mystical Texts: Songs of the Sabbath Sacrifice and Related Manuscripts* (London: T&T Clark, 2006), 52–5. Fletcher-Louis disagrees, arguing that there is no clear evidence of a belief in the heavenly temple in Hellenistic Judaism. See Crispin H. T. Fletcher-Louis, *All the Glory of Adam: Liturgical Anthropology in the Dead Sea Scrolls* (Leiden: Brill, 2002), 267–8, especially nn. 46, 47, 48.
¹³ William H. C. Propp, *Exodus 1–18* (New York: Doubleday, 1999), 563.
¹⁴ Trans. NETS.

century BCE'.¹⁵ The 'notion of a pre-existent divinely prepared heavenly temple' also 'pervades the LXX versions of Solomon's temple prayer':¹⁶

> ...then you shall listen from heaven from your established dwelling place (ἐξ ἑτοίμου κατοικητηρίου σου)...¹⁷

Wisdom 9:8 picks up on this divinely prepared sanctuary and, presumably with Exodus 25–27 in mind, suggests that the earthly temple was a copy of it:

> You said that I should build a shrine on your holy mountain, an altar in the city of your encamping, a copy of the holy tent that you prepared beforehand from the beginning (μίμημα σκηνῆς ἁγίας ἣν προητοίμασας ἀπ' ἀρχῆς).¹⁸

It is not only in Greek sources, however, that Exodus 15:17 was interpreted in this way. Thanks to the link word 'plant', *4QFlorilegium* (4Q174), a text discovered at Qumran, uses it in an interpretation of 2 Samuel 7:10–11a—'And I will appoint a place for my people Israel, and will plant them, that they may dwell in their own place, and be disturbed no more...'—which it says refers to:

> the house which [he will establish] for [him] in the last days, as is written in the book of [Moses: 'The temple of] YHWH your hands will est[a]blish. YHWH shall reign for ever and ever.'¹⁹

Exodus 15:17 is taken to refer to 'an eschatological temple to be built by God himself at the End of Days'.²⁰ The *Mekhilta* plays on the word for place (מכון),²¹ turning it into 'corresponding to' (מְכֻוָּן), so as to bring out the correspondence between earthly and heavenly sanctuaries:

> *The place for Thee to Dwell In* (מכון לשבתך). Corresponding to Thy dwelling place (מְכֻוָּן לְשִׁבְתְּךָ). This is one of the statements to the effect that the Throne below corresponds to and is the counterpart of the Throne in heaven. And so it also says: 'The Lord is in His holy Temple, the Lord, His throne is in heaven' (Ps. 11.4). And it also says: 'I have surely built Thee a house of habitation, a place [מכון, which again could be taken as מְכֻוָּן] for Thee to dwell in for ever' (1 Kings 8.13).²²

The history of the exegesis of Exodus 15:17 shows how a tradition developed of a temple not built by human hands but by God, which was already prepared

---

¹⁵ William Horbury, 'Land, Sanctuary and Worship', in John Barclay and John Sweet (eds), *Early Christian Thought in its Jewish Context* (Cambridge: Cambridge University Press, 1996), 210.
¹⁶ William Horbury, 'The Wisdom of Solomon', in John Barton and John Muddiman (eds), *The Oxford Bible Commentary* (Oxford: Oxford University Press, 2001), 660.
¹⁷ LXX 1 Kings 8:39; trans. NETS. Cf. LXX 1 Kings 8:43, 49; 2 Chr. 6:30, 33, 39.
¹⁸ Trans. NETS.   ¹⁹ 4Q174 1 i, 21 2–3; trans. Martínez and Tigchelaar, 1.353.
²⁰ Devorah Dimant, '4QFlorilegium and the Idea of the Community as Temple', in A. Caquot, M. Hadas-Lebel, and J. Riaud (eds), *Hellenica et Judaica: Hommage à Valentin Nikiprowetzky* (Leuven: Peeters, 1986), 173.
²¹ One of the earliest collections of rabbinic midrash, usually dated to the third century CE.
²² *Mekhilta* Shirata 10.24–28; text and trans. Lauterbach, 2.78.

in heaven, and which would become available to human beings at the end of time. It was to this tradition that the saying in Mark probably refers: by promising to destroy the temple and build another not made with hands, Jesus was heralding the last days. The saying could, however, be interpreted in other ways: as referring to 'the temple of his body' (John 2:21), or to the community of the church. John Sweet argues that in 2 Corinthians 5:1 Paul alludes to a saying from the Jesus tradition (Paul was, of course, writing before Mark's gospel) in order to bring 'a corporate emphasis into what might seem merely individualistic':

> Our physical body, like the earthly Temple, is under sentence of demolition; as a dwelling it is more like a *tent*, a familiar metaphor for the body which also evokes the Temple as the place of God's presence and glory, but with the suggestion of flimsiness... On the other hand we already have a heavenly dwelling or clothing awaiting us, the Temple-community of the New Age, which is none other than the body of the risen Christ...[23]

Hebrews picks up both on the correspondence between earthly and heavenly sanctuaries and on the idea that Jesus has ushered in a new phase of history. Now that Christ has entered 'not into a sanctuary made with hands, a copy of the true one, but into heaven itself,... to appear in the presence of God on our behalf' we have reached 'the end of the age' and there is no longer any need for the earthly copy.[24] As Craig Koester comments,

> While the author of Hebrews wanted to move his readers beyond the Jewish practices associated with the tabernacle, he preserved Christianity's continuity with Israel's heritage by portraying Christ as a priest in the heavenly tabernacle.[25]

What did Moses see in the darkness? According to Exodus 25:9, 40, he was shown a pattern/plan of what he was to build. The Hebrew word is *tavnit*, and in the LXX it is translated as *paradeigma* in verse 9 and *tupos* in verse 40. *Tavnit/paradeigma* also occurs four times in 1 Chronicles 28:11–19, where David gives Solomon the plan for the temple. This passage is unique to the Chronicler, and Hugh Williamson suggests that the choice of wording 'is clearly intended as an echo of the "pattern" of the tabernacle and its furnishings, shown to Moses on Mount Sinai in Exod. 25.9, 40'.[26] 1 Chronicles 28:19 appears to be a summarizing statement by David: 'All this have I been made to understand in writing by the hand of the Lord upon me, all the works of the pattern', which 'probably implies that David wrote the plans under conscious

---

[23] Sweet, 'A House Not Made with Hands', 384, 383.   [24] Heb. 9:24, 26.
[25] Craig R. Koester, *The Dwelling of God: The Tabernacle in the Old Testament, Intertestamental Jewish Literature, and the New Testament* (Washington, DC: Catholic Biblical Association of America, 1989), 185.
[26] H. G. M. Williamson, 'The Temple in the Books of Chronicles', in Horbury (ed.), *Templum Amicitiae*, 26.

divine inspiration'.[27] For Moses, however, the situation was different: according to Exodus, he was shown something. 'Pattern' could simply refer to architectural plans, or a scale model;[28] but, as we have seen, Wisdom 9:8 assumes that the 'pattern' he saw was the heavenly sanctuary itself, an assumption which seems to have become widespread. It is found, for example, in Hebrews:

> They serve a copy and shadow of the heavenly sanctuary (τῶν ἐπουρανίων); for when Moses was about to erect the tent, he was instructed by God, saying, 'See that you make everything according to the pattern (κατὰ τὸν τύπον) which was shown to you on the mountain.'[29]

For Jewish sources, Solomon's temple was the successor to the tabernacle, both being copies of the heavenly sanctuary. Williamson suggests that, according to the Chronicler, 'since there was so much in common between the basic plan of the tabernacle and the temple, and since they stood in continuous tradition with each other, David did not need to see the heavenly pattern afresh: he could visit it at Gibeon'.[30] Not everyone was happy with the leadership of the second temple, and some of the holiest artefacts from the first temple, such as the ark, were no longer extant; but the same ideal, of the earthly sanctuary mirroring the heavenly one, remained. It would make no sense, therefore, to ask whether the heavenly sanctuary was a tabernacle or a temple. Some Christian polemic, however, distinguished between the tabernacle and the temple, notably Stephen's speech in Acts:

> Our fathers had the tent of witness in the wilderness, even as he who spoke to Moses directed him to make it, according to the pattern that he had seen. Our fathers in turn brought it in with Joshua when they dispossessed the nations which God thrust out before our fathers. So it was until the days of David, who found favour in the sight of God and asked leave to find a habitation for the God of Jacob. But it was Solomon who built a house for him. Yet the Most High does not dwell in houses made with hands (ἐν χειροποιήτοις); as the prophet says,
>
> > Heaven is my throne, and earth my footstool.
> > What house will you build for me, says the Lord,
> > or what is the place of my rest?
> > Did not my hand make all these things?[31]

This argues that the Jerusalem temple was 'made with hands', whereas it views the desert tabernacle more positively. There has been much discussion of why

---

[27] Williamson, 'The Temple in the Books of Chronicles', 26 (including the translation of Chr. 28:19).

[28] 'In my opinion, the plain meaning of the verses referring to Moses' revelation is that he was shown an exact model of the Tabernacle which he was to make. If so, he was *not* shown the divine heavenly dwelling.' Victor Avigdor Hurowitz, *I Have Built You an Exalted House: Temple Building in the Bible in Light of Mesopotamian and Northwest Semitic Writings* (Sheffield: Sheffield Academic Press, 1992), 168.

[29] Heb. 8:5.   [30] Williamson, 'The Temple in the Books of Chronicles', 26.

[31] Acts 7:44–49.

Hebrews does not mention the temple (which may or may not have been standing when the epistle was written) but consistently refers to the earthly place of worship as the tabernacle. This too may have been a Christian attempt to draw on Israel's traditions whilst ignoring its current institutions. Gregory, of course, is commenting on Exodus, so he naturally talks of the tabernacle, although he does refer to it as a 'shrine'/'temple' (ναός).[32]

Where does Gregory think that Moses went, and what does he think he saw? He tells us that on Mount Sinai Moses participated in 'eternal life', and 'lived in a state beyond nature', with 'no need of food'.[33] The tabernacle was suddenly shown to him by divine power.[34] Gregory also refers to 'the wonders (θαυμάτων) shown to him in the theophany' and to 'the wonder (θαῦμα) not made with hands'.[35] He lovingly describes the pillars and veils, the ark and the lampstand.[36] The impression is of a colourful, gleaming vision. Gregory calls it the tabernacle above (ἡ ἄνω σκηνή),[37] but nowhere does he refer to it as the dwelling of God. He does, however, talk of Moses being 'enclosed by the heavenly tabernacle'.[38] It is certainly more than simply the blueprint for the tabernacle below. The vision carries meanings, which need to be deciphered: 'Of what things not made with hands are these imitations?'[39] Gregory consistently associates it with 'mystery' (μυστήριον); and once refers to it as a theophany (θεοφάνεια).[40] He is very clear that 'the divine nature...transcends all knowable concepts and models, and cannot be likened to any known thing'.[41] And yet he tentatively suggests that this tabernacle not made with hands conveys something about Christ. Moses was educated 'by a type (ἐν τύπῳ) in the mystery of the tabernacle which encloses everything. This would be Christ, "the power of God and the wisdom of God"'.[42] His repeated use of the adjective 'not made with hands'—it occurs eleven times in the treatise—is part and parcel of his apophaticism. He wishes to stress not only that Moses' vision was a divine gift, but that the mysteries to which it points are not within human grasp.

7.2 LIFE OF MOSES 2.170–172: ALEXANDRIAN CONTEXT

The LXX, whose traditional associations with Egypt have been confirmed by modern scholarship,[43] translates *tavnit* as *paradeigma* at Exodus 25:9 and

---

[32] *Vit. Moys.* 1.49, 50, 51, 56.   [33] *Vit. Moys.* 1.58; trans. Malherbe and Ferguson, 46.
[34] *Vit. Moys.* 1.49.   [35] *Vit. Moys.* 1.56; 2.170.
[36] *Vit. Moys.* 1.49–50; 2.170–172.   [37] *Vit. Moys.* 2.184, 312.
[38] *Vit. Moys.* 2.312; trans. Malherbe and Ferguson, 134.   [39] *Vit. Moys.* 2.173.
[40] *Vit. Moys.* 2.174, 188, 315; 1.56.   [41] *Vit. Moys.* 1.47.   [42] *Vit. Moys.* 2.174.
[43] See Emanuel Tov, 'The Septuagint', in Martin Jan Mulder and Harry Sysling (eds), *Mikra: Text, Translation, Reading and Interpretation of the Hebrew Bible in Ancient Judaism and Early Christianity* (Assen: Van Gorcum, 1988), 164, 180.

tupos at 25:40.⁴⁴ At Exodus 26:30, the MT has a word (מִשְׁפָּט) whose more usual meaning is 'judgement', but here suggests 'manner, fashion, plan'. The LXX translates it as *eidos*, 'form'. *Paradeigma, tupos,* and *eidos* are key words in middle Platonist terminology. Pseudo-Justin, in *Exhortation to the Greeks*,⁴⁵ quotes all three verses (Exod. 25:9, 40, 26:30) in order to prove that '[Plato] discovered the word *form* (τὸ τοῦ εἴδους ὄνομα) in the writings of Moses'.⁴⁶ The word *paradeigma* is particularly significant, because in *Timaeus* 28–29 Plato used it to designate the model after which the Demiurge constructed the universe. Turning Pseudo-Justin's argument on its head, therefore, did the translators responsible for the LXX deliberately use *paradeigma, tupos,* and *eidos* in order to give a Platonist spin to Moses' vision? James Barr thinks not:

> Where LXX used [*paradeigma*] for *tabnit* the sense was that of the 'plan' or 'design' of a building, a sense well established in Greek from Herodotus (v. 62) and still used much later, and a sense which corresponded exactly to that of the Hebrew. It seems therefore unlikely that either the LXX intended, or was unconsciously influenced by, or was taken by its readers to intend, any suggestion of Platonism, merely on the ground that this word, which was used in the LXX in its straightforward sense…, was also used by Plato in a rather transferred sense to describe the nature of the forms.⁴⁷

Robert Hayward, however, whilst agreeing that one cannot be certain that the translators intended to use *paradeigma* in its Platonic sense, argues that 'the word stands out by being used only once in the entire Pentateuch, and it might certainly have invited the very first *readers* of LXX to see in it a Platonic sense'.⁴⁸ The use of *paradeigma* at Exodus 25:9 by the LXX translators made it easy for writers in the Alexandrian tradition to interweave Biblical and Platonic imagery: the heavenly tabernacle plan became the Platonic world of Forms.

Philo talks of the whole universe as the temple of God:

> The highest, and in the truest sense the holy, temple of God is…the whole universe, having for its sanctuary the most sacred part of all existence, even heaven, for its votive ornaments the stars, for its priests the angels who are servitors to His powers…⁴⁹

---

⁴⁴ Philo's LXX, however, appears to have *paradeigma* at 25:40 (cf. *Leg.* 3.102).
⁴⁵ This is usually dated to the second half of the third century CE. See Miroslav Marcovich, *Pseudo-Iustinus: Cohortatio ad Graecos, De monarchia, Oratio ad Graecos* (Berlin: Walter de Gruyter, 1990), 3–4.
⁴⁶ *Cohortatio ad Graecos* 29; text Marcovich, 65; trans. Falls, 411–12.
⁴⁷ James Barr, *The Semantics of Biblical Language* (Oxford: Oxford University Press, 1961; repr., London: SCM, 1983), 153–4.
⁴⁸ C. T. R. Hayward, 'Understandings of the Temple Service in the Septuagint Pentateuch', in John Day (ed.), *Temple and Worship in Biblical Israel: Proceedings of the Oxford Old Testament Seminar* (London: T&T Clark, 2007), 397 n. 26.
⁴⁹ *Spec.* 1.66.

In *On Planting* he interprets Exodus 15:17 along these lines, arguing that 'the mountain of Thine inheritance' refers to the world:

> The world, we read, is God's house in the realm of sense-perception, prepared and ready for Him. It is a thing wrought, not, as some have fancied, uncreate. It is a 'sanctuary', an outshining of sanctity, so to speak, a copy of the original (μίμημα ἀρχετύπου); since the objects that are beautiful to the eye of the sense are images of those in which the understanding recognizes beauty. Lastly, it has been prepared by the 'hands' of God, his world-creating powers.[50]

Elsewhere he argues that there are 'two temples of God: one of them this universe... and the other the rational soul'.[51] As van den Hoek comments,

> Cosmology and anthropology are extensions of each other... The human soul represents a second sanctuary after a first sanctuary, which is the universe; the second sanctuary is transformed into a microcosm in tune with the cosmic harmony.[52]

The quotation from *On Planting* also refers to an 'original', an archetype, of which the sanctuary of the world is a copy. This ties in with Philo's description of the process of creation in *On the Creation of the World*:

> For God, being God, assumed that a beautiful copy would never be produced apart from a beautiful pattern (καλοῦ παραδείγματος), and that no object of perception would be faultless which was not made in the likeness of an original discerned only by the intellect (πρὸς ἀρχέτυπον καὶ νοητὴν ἰδέαν). So when He willed to create this visible world He first fully formed the intelligible world (τὸν νοητὸν κόσμον), in order that He might have the use of a pattern wholly God-like and incorporeal (ἀσωμάτῳ καὶ θεοειδεστάτῳ παραδείγματι) in producing the material world, as a later creation, the very image of an earlier, to embrace in itself objects of perception of as many kinds as the other contained objects of intelligence.[53]

He is picking up on Plato's reference to a model (*paradeigma*) for the cosmos in *Timaeus* 28–29; does he also have in mind the pattern of the tabernacle shown to Moses? He draws attention to the parallels between creation and the building of the tabernacle when he compares Bezalel (the craftsman who built the tabernacle, according to Exodus 31:1–5) with the Logos:

> Bezalel means, then, 'in the shadow of God'; but God's shadow is His Word, which he made use of like an instrument, and so made the world.[54]

---

[50] *Plant.* 48, 50.
[51] *Somn.* 1.215.
[52] Annewies van den Hoek, *Clement of Alexandria and His Use of Philo in the Stromateis: An Early Christian Reshaping of a Jewish Model* (Leiden: Brill, 1988), 117.
[53] *Opif.* 16.
[54] *Leg.* 3.96.

When Philo describes Moses' experience on Mount Sinai, he says:

> [Moses] saw with the soul's eye the immaterial forms (ἀσωμάτους ἰδέας) of the material objects about to be made, and these forms had to be reproduced in copies perceived by the senses, taken from the original draught (ἀρχετύπου γραφῆς), so to speak, and from patterns conceived in the mind (νοητῶν παραδειγμάτων).... So the shape of the model (τύπος τοῦ παραδείγματος) was stamped upon the mind of the prophet, a secretly painted or moulded prototype, produced by immaterial and invisible forms (ἄνευ ὕλης ἀοράτοις εἴδεσι)...[55]

The same vocabulary is used here as in *On the Creation of the World* 16. But what exactly is the relationship between the *paradeigma* of creation and the *paradeigma* of the tabernacle? Only in *Questions on Exodus* (for which we do not have the original Greek) does he imply that they are one and the same:

> What is the meaning of the words, 'Thou shalt make (them) according to the pattern which has been shown to thee on the mountain'? [Ex 25:40] Through the 'pattern' He again indicates the incorporeal heaven, the archetype of the sense-perceptible, for it is a visible pattern and impression and measure.[56]

That Philo thinks of the tabernacle as constructed from the same model as the cosmos makes sense, given his cosmological interpretation of the tabernacle, in which he describes the tabernacle layout and furniture as representative of the universe.

When Philo was writing, the Jerusalem temple still stood, and it was for him a sacred building—*the* sacred building. By Origen's time, it had been destroyed. Unlike some earlier Christian authors,[57] Origen does not condemn the temple with its sacrificial laws, but considers that its time has passed. Thanks both to Hebrews and to the Johannine identification of the temple with the body of Christ (John 2:19–21), he associates the new era simultaneously with Jesus Christ and with the heavenly temple:

> First, there was Jerusalem, that great, royal city, where the most renowned Temple had been constructed for God. But after that, one who was the true Temple of God came and said about the Temple of his body, 'Destroy this Temple'; and began to open the mysteries 'of the heavenly Jerusalem,' this earthly place was destroyed and the heavenly became visible, and in that Temple 'stone' did not remain 'upon stone' from the time when the flesh of Christ was made the true Temple of God. First there was a high priest who purified the people 'by the blood of bulls and goats'; but when the true high priest who 'sanctifies' believers 'by his own blood,' came, that first high priest exists no more and neither was any place left for him.[58]

---

[55] *Mos.* 2.74, 76. [56] *QE* 2.82, cf. 2.52.
[57] See, for example, *Barn.* 16. [58] *Hom. Lev.* 10.1.3; trans. Barkley, 203.

He consistently argues for the superiority of the celestial temple over the earthly one:

> If therefore, O Jew, coming to the earthly city of Jerusalem, you find it overthrown and reduced to ashes and embers, do not weep as you do now 'as if with the mind of a child'; do not lament; but search for a heavenly city instead of an earthly one. Look above! And there you will discover 'the heavenly Jerusalem that is the mother of all'.[59]

This then informs his exegesis. The aim of his commentary on the description of the tabernacle in Exodus 25–28 is to 'ascend to heaven and there seek the magnificence of the eternal tabernacle whose form is imperfectly represented on earth by Moses', since 'things which are introduced in the divine books are said not of earthly things, but of heavenly, and are forms not of present but "of future goods", not of corporeal things, but of spiritual'.[60] Despite this statement of intent, however, Origen cannot in fact describe 'the eternal tabernacle'. Instead, in the body of the sermon, he discusses the earthly copy. For him, unlike Philo, this is neither the cosmos nor the Jerusalem temple, but the church. He picks up on Philo's macrocosm–microcosm relationship:

> For if, as some before us have said, this tabernacle represents the whole world, and each individual also can contain an image of the world, why can not each one also complete a form of the tabernacle in himself?[61]

Origen is not talking about human beings in general, however, but of the believers who make up the church.

If the heavenly *paradeigma* is the Platonic world of Ideas, it cannot be described directly in human language. All that can be described and discussed is the earthly copy. For Philo that copy is the universe. The tabernacle/temple is a symbolic representation of the universe; of which the human being is a microcosm. Philo talks of all three (the tabernacle/temple, the universe, and the human soul) as sanctuaries of God. Origen too, for all his talk of ascending to the heavenly heights, can only describe the earthly copy, which for him is the church, and its microcosm, the individual believer. The nearest either of them come to describing the heavenly world is when they talk about the holy of holies and its contents. For Philo, God speaking from above the cherubim over the ark represents the hierarchy of the 'Alone truly existent One', the divine Logos, the creative and kingly powers, and the gracious and punitive powers.[62] For Origen, the cherubim and the propitiatory represent 'the science of the Trinity'.[63] These interpretations will be looked at in more detail in 10.2, when discussing heavenly powers.

---

[59] *Hom. Josh.* 17.1; trans. Bruce, 158.
[60] *Hom. Exod.* 9.2; trans. Heine, 337.
[61] *Hom. Exod.* 9.4; trans. Heine, 340–1.
[62] *Fug.* 100–101; *QE* 2.68.
[63] *Hom. Num.* 10.3.4; *Comm. Rom.* 3.8.

7.3 LIFE OF MOSES 2.170–172: THEOLOGICAL CONTEXT

The Alexandrian tradition worked with the Platonic notion of the *kosmos noētos*. The aim of heavenly ascent was for the soul to return to its true home there:

> The Platonic tradition…generally assumed that the intellect, when sufficiently purified, led back from the multiplicity of things to pure simplicity, would naturally 'gravitate' to its proper 'home' in the transcendent.[64]

Gregory superimposed upon this a gulf between Creator and creation:

> When all that is non-rational is put aside, and the soul or intellect is naked before God, it confronts a stranger: the uncreated Lord is still and always will be on the far side of an unbridgeable gulf, and the soul will not ever be able to rest in the security of perfect union in the Platonic sense. Plato, Philo and Plotinus would all agree that the soul cannot express God in image or concept; it is Gregory who grounds this incapacity in a *metaphysical* gulf between God and the created self.[65]

Mosshammer shows how the idea of this 'double antithesis' develops over the course of Gregory's writing, particularly as a result of his debate with Eunomius. In his early works, 'a dualism between intelligible and sensible predominates'.[66] In his later works, however, Gregory

> proceeds to subdivide the intellectual nature into the uncreated maker of all being and the created nature dependent upon it. He defines the uncreated nature as being always the same, beyond distinctions of greater or less as to possession of the good. That nature which is brought into being by creation, on the other hand, is never complete, but ever creating itself, by a process of perpetual increase in participation of a superior good. Thus there can be no limit to its increase, but the present good—however complete it may seem—is always but the beginning of something more.[67]

Where does the tabernacle not made with hands fit into this scheme? According to Daniélou, Gregory replaces the Platonic *kosmos noētos* with the world of angels.[68] This is certainly part of his tabernacle interpretation, and

---

[64] Rowan Williams, *The Wound of Knowledge: Christian Spirituality from the New Testament to St. John of the Cross* (London: DLT, 1979), 59.

[65] Williams, *The Wound of Knowledge*, 60.

[66] Alden A. Mosshammer, 'The Created and the Uncreated in Gregory of Nyssa: *Contra Eunomium* 1,105–113', in Lucas F. Mateo-Seco and Juan L. Bastero (eds), *El 'Contra Eunomium I' en la producción literaria de Gregorio de Nisa. VI Coloquio Internacional sobre Gregorio de Nisa* (Pamplona: Ediciones Universidad de Navarra, 1988), 360.

[67] Alden A. Mosshammer, 'Gregory's Intellectual Development: A Comparison of the *Homilies on the Beatitudes* with the *Homilies on the Song of Songs*', in H. R. Drobner and A. Viciano (eds), *Gregory of Nyssa: Homilies on the Beatitudes* (Leiden: Brill, 2000), 367.

[68] Jean Daniélou, *Platonisme et théologie mystique: Doctrine spirituelle de Saint Grégoire de Nysse*, 2nd edn (Paris: Aubier, 1954), 162.

will be examined further in 10.3. But Gregory also describes Moses' experience as a theophany.⁶⁹ He has inherited from Origen an interpretation of the earthly tabernacle as symbolic of the body of Christ, the church.⁷⁰ In *Life of Moses* 1.51, the expression he uses to refer to what Moses has seen (τὸ ... τῆς δημιουργίας ὑπόδειγμα) could simply refer to 'the design for manufacture'; but it seems likely that he is playing on words, and picking up on the cosmological symbolism of the tabernacle by referring to it as 'the pattern of creation'. If the heavenly tabernacle is not made with hands, in other words is uncreated, if it is the model, the source, of creation, and if the earthly tabernacle, its copy, is the church, then the heavenly tabernacle must be Christ. Chapter 8 will examine how Gregory tries to unpack and make sense of this.

7.4 *LIFE OF MOSES* 2.170–172: HEAVENLY ASCENT CONTEXT

As Himmelfarb has pointed out, when Enoch ascends to heaven in the Book of the Watchers 'the heavenly edifices through which [he] passes to reach the divine throne are a temple'.⁷¹ And this sets a trend for subsequent heavenly ascent texts:

> The Book of the Watchers was an extremely influential work, and one aspect of its influence is the picture of heaven as a temple that explains so many features of the other ascent apocalypses, whether it stands in the foreground or in the background.⁷²

1 Enoch 14 describes two 'houses', one leading on into the next, surrounded by a wall, corresponding to the ground plan of the tabernacle. The ceiling of the first house is 'like shooting stars and lightning flashes' among which are 'fiery cherubim', just as cherubim decorate the walls of the tabernacle, Solomon's temple, and Ezekiel's vision of the rebuilt temple.⁷³ Inside the second house the 'Great Glory' sits upon a throne guarded by cherubim, equivalent to the cherubim over the ark in the holy of holies.⁷⁴ The style of *Songs of the Sabbath Sacrifice* is very different, but it too describes heaven using temple terminology. There are pillars (עמודים) and corners (פנות).⁷⁵ Song 10 describes the *parokhet* (veil), and seems to allude to the figures of cherubim woven into it. The Hebrew of the phrase 'works of wondrous mingled colours' (מעשי רוקמות פלא)

---

⁶⁹ *Vit. Moys.* 1.56.   ⁷⁰ This will be explored in Chapter 11.
⁷¹ Martha Himmelfarb, 'Apocalyptic Ascent and the Heavenly Temple', *Society of Biblical Literature Seminar Papers*, 26 (1987), 210.
⁷² Himmelfarb, *Ascent to Heaven*, 14.
⁷³ *1 En.* 14:11; trans. Nickelsburg and VanderKam, 34. Cf. Exod. 26:1; 1 Kgs 6:29; Ezek. 41:20.
⁷⁴ *1 En.* 14:18–20.   ⁷⁵ 4Q403 1 i 41.

echoes the 'embroidered work' (מעשה רקם) of the hangings at the entrances of the tabernacle and its court, and of the high priest's girdle.[76] Other technical terms, such as 'inner room' (דביר),[77] 'lofty abode' (זבול),[78] 'vestibule' (אולם),[79] and 'chariot' (מרכבה)[80] come from the descriptions of Solomon's temple in Kings and Chronicles. Newsom argues that Ezekiel's vision of the rebuilt temple in Ezekiel 40–48 has influenced the structure of Songs 9 to 12.[81] Some later texts, such as *Testament of Levi* (in some manuscripts), the *Ascension of Isaiah*, and *b. Ḥagigah* work with a structure of seven heavens. There has been discussion as to where this notion came from, with Adela Yarbro Collins arguing for the influence of Babylonian magic.[82] Fletcher-Louis, however, suggests that it relates to 'the traditional separation of the temple into seven spheres of holiness' as described in *m. Kelim* 1:8 and Josephus *Jewish War* 1.26.[83] In *Testament of Levi* the top four heavens function as a temple. In *b. Ḥagigah* 12b there is a temple and altar in the fourth heaven.

The heavenly ascent texts do not work with philosophical categories, but with vivid imagery. In the Platonic tradition, the divide between heaven and earth is the divide between intelligible and sensible, with the sensible being a copy of the intelligible ideal. Philo and Origen cannot describe the heavenly *paradeigma*, only its earthly copy and representation. Ascent texts do describe the heavenly realms; their heroes travel through them and describe what they see: God on a throne within a temple. However, as Himmelfarb acknowledges, 'while it is clear that the heavenly temple of 1 Enoch 14 corresponds to the earthly temple, it does not seem to correspond in detail to any particular temple described in the Hebrew Bible', and 'the heavenly temples of later apocalypses are also characterized by an absence of technical terminology and by an even more limited correspondence of detail between the earthly and the heavenly temples'.[84] She argues that this limited correspondence 'seems to reflect the belief that the heavenly temple so transcends the earthly that the correspondence cannot be exact'.[85] The paradoxical imagery makes it clear that the heavenly temple is 'not made with hands'. In *1 Enoch* 14 the outer wall is built of hailstones surrounded by tongues of fire (14:9). The second house is 'greater than the former one' (14:15), and yet seems to be contained within it: 'Heaven is a totally paradoxical, topsy-turvy world where the terrestrial laws of nature do not apply'.[86] In *Songs of the Sabbath Sacrifice* there

---

[76] 4Q405 14–15 i 6, cf. Exod. 26:36, 27:16, 28:39.
[77] E.g. 4Q403 1 ii 13, cf. 1 Kgs 6:20.   [78] 4Q403 1 i 41, cf. 1 Kgs 8:13.
[79] 4Q405 14–15 i 4, cf. 1 Kgs 6:3.   [80] E.g. 4Q405 20–22 ii 8, cf. 1 Chr. 28:18.
[81] Newsom, *Songs of the Sabbath Sacrifice*, 53–5.
[82] Adela Yarbro Collins, 'The Seven Heavens in Jewish and Christian Apocalypses', in John J. Collins and Michael Fishbane (eds), *Death, Ecstasy and Otherworldly Journeys* (Albany: State University of New York Press, 1995), 86–7.
[83] Fletcher-Louis, *All the Glory of Adam*, 57 n. 6.
[84] Himmelfarb, *Ascent to Heaven*, 15.   [85] Himmelfarb, *Ascent to Heaven*, 16.
[86] Philip Alexander, 'The Dualism of Heaven and Earth in Early Jewish Literature and its Implications', in Armin Lange, et al. (eds), *Light against Darkness: Dualism in Ancient*

is an inconsistent use of singulars and plurals. Sometimes there is one *merkavah*, sometimes several *markavot*.[87] They are also plural sanctuaries (מקדשי),[88] temples (היכלי),[89] vestibules (אולמי),[90] inner rooms (דבירי),[91] veils (פרכות),[92] firmaments (רקיעי),[93] and thrones (כסאי),[94] existing alongside singular forms. Sometimes a sevenfold plurality is specified, as in 'seven exalted holy places' (לשבעת קודשי רום),[95] or 'seven inner rooms of priesthoods' (שבעת דבירי כהונות),[96] but not always. This interchangeable use of singular and plural forms may have been a deliberate rhetorical device designed to disorientate the reader, making it 'virtually impossible to extract a coherent and stable image of the heavenly sphere or the heavenly Temple structures that are said to inhabit it'.[97] Newsom talks of 'intentional violations of ordinary syntax and meaning in a text which is attempting to communicate something of the elusive transcendence of heavenly reality'.[98] Whereas in *1 Enoch* the heavenly temple seems to constructed of the primordial elements of fire and water, albeit in impossible combinations, in *Songs of the Sabbath Sacrifice* 'the architectural structures of the Temple are animated and become living and praising creatures':[99]

> With these let all fo[undations of...]° holies praise, the uplifting pillars of the supremely lofty abode, and all the corners of its structure. Sin[g-praise].[100]

This is not a 'material', but a 'spiritual' temple, composed of living angelic beings. In the later Hekhalot texts 'there seems to be an implication that the seven concentric palaces grow progressively larger as one moves inwards'.[101] There are dire warnings about how dangerous the heavenly realms are for human beings, who survive only if they themselves are transformed. Ascending on high involves being able 'to walk in rivers of fire'.[102]

Mediterranean Religion and the Contemporary World (Göttingen: Vandenhoeck & Ruprecht, 2011), 173.

[87] Compare 4Q405 20–22 ii 8 with 4Q405 20–22 ii 3.   [88] E.g. 4Q404 5 5.
[89] E.g. 4Q400 1 i 13.   [90] E.g. 4Q405 14–15 i 4.   [91] E.g. 4Q405 14–15 i 7.
[92] E.g. 4Q405 15–16 ii 5.   [93] E.g. 4Q405 23 i 7.   [94] E.g. 4Q405 23 i 3.
[95] 4Q403 1 ii 11.   [96] 4Q405 7 7 as restored.
[97] Ra'anan S. Boustan, 'Angels in the Architecture: Temple Art and the Poetics of Praise in the *Songs of the Sabbath Sacrifice*', in Ra'anan S. Boustan and Annette Yoshiko Reed (eds), *Heavenly Realms and Earthly Realities in Late Antique Religions* (Cambridge: Cambridge University Press, 2004), 210.
[98] Newsom, *Songs of the Sabbath Sacrifice*, 49.
[99] Peter Schäfer, *The Origins of Jewish Mysticism* (Tübingen: Mohr Siebeck, 2009), 133.
[100] Song 7.12 (4Q403 1 i 41, 4Q405 6 2); trans. Charlesworth and Newsom, 163.
[101] Alexander, 'The Dualism of Heaven and Earth', 176.
[102] *Hekhalot Zutarti* §349; trans. Christopher Rowland and Christopher R. A. Morray-Jones, *The Mystery of God: Early Jewish Mysticism and the New Testament* (Leiden: Brill, 2009), 278.

7.5 *LIFE OF MOSES* 2.170–172: CONCLUSIONS

On Mount Sinai Moses was shown the 'pattern' of the tabernacle. This came to be interpreted as the divinely prepared sanctuary ready for the end of time. And the earthly tabernacle/temple was seen as a copy of the heavenly one. The words used by the LXX to translate 'pattern' (*paradeigma, eidos, tupos*) made it easy for the heavenly plan to become the Platonic world of Forms. Ascent texts use temple imagery in their pictures of heaven, but with paradoxical twists, as they are aware that heaven is 'a different dimension...where things can happen that defy the laws operating in this world'.[103] In other words, the Alexandrian tradition and heavenly ascent texts both refer to a world beyond this one, a world which human language is not adequate to describe. Moses was given a glimpse of that world on Mount Sinai, and then did his best to reproduce it with the tabernacle. For Gregory, the paradoxical tabernacle 'not made with hands', the source of creation, the fountainhead of life and power, becomes a type of Christ.

---

[103] Alexander, 'The Dualism of Heaven and Earth', 170.

8

Christological Interpretation

> Paul partially disclosed the secret meaning of these things, and therefore, taking a little clue from his words, we say that Moses was educated beforehand by a type in the mystery of the tabernacle which encloses everything. This would be Christ, 'the power of God and the wisdom of God', which in its own nature is not made by hands, yet allows itself to be physically fashioned when this tabernacle needs to be pitched among us, so that, in a certain way, the same is both unfashioned and fashioned: uncreated in pre-existence, but becoming created in accordance with this material composition.[1]

8.1 *LIFE OF MOSES* 2.173–179: BIBLICAL CONTEXT

'What then is that tabernacle not made with hands?' asks Gregory.[2] He describes the vision, and then returns to his question:

> Of what things not made with hands are these imitations? And what benefit does the material reproduction of the things seen there by Moses bring to those viewing it?[3]

He professes a reluctance to answer it:

> It seems good to me to leave the precise word on these things to those who through the Spirit have the power to search the depths of God,[4] if indeed there be anyone able to speak 'mysteries in the Spirit',[5] as the apostle says. Our speculative suggestions on the matter set before us we refer to the readers' judgement, to be deemed worthless or acceptable, as the mind of the competent judge shall determine.[6]

1 Corinthians 2:10 is used by both Origen and Gregory to justify their allegorical interpretations of scripture.[7] Gregory, unlike Origen, 'stops short of asserting that he has the spiritual understanding which Paul had'.[8] Instead, he relies on Paul to back up his interpretations. One reason for his professed

---

[1] *Vit. Moys.* 2.174. [2] *Vit. Moys.* 2.170. [3] *Vit. Moys.* 2.173.
[4] Cf. 1 Cor. 2:10. [5] 1 Cor. 14:2. [6] *Vit. Moys.* 2.173.
[7] For details, see Ronald E. Heine, 'Gregory of Nyssa's Apology for Allegory', *Vigiliae christianae*, 38: 4 (1984).
[8] Heine, 'Gregory of Nyssa's Apology for Allegory', 364.

reluctance is that 'mysteries' (μυστήρια) are only to be spoken of by the spiritual elite. The second sentence, however, carries a different tone. It suggests an awareness that he is about to say something not well established, and which may be controversial. He states that the heavenly tabernacle is a type of the pre-existent Christ, and the earthly tabernacle a type of the incarnate Christ. This, according to Daniélou, is 'une vue personnelle de Grégoire, comme il le dit lui-même'.[9] There are precedents for the tabernacle being interpreted as a type of the church,[10] and for particular elements within it to be seen as symbols of Christ,[11] but not for the heavenly tabernacle as a whole to be construed as a type of Christ. Where, therefore, did Gregory get the idea?

Christians scrutinized the Old Testament for signs of Christ. Some of the typologies used by Gregory, such as the bronze serpent erected by Moses as a type of the cross,[12] were established early on. Here he is producing a new one. It is natural that at a climactic point in the narrative he would wish to find Christ. He interprets the burning bush as symbolic of the incarnation, and there too he is innovative: 'Gregory appears to be the first to make the bush a figure of Mary's virginity unaffected by the birth of Jesus'.[13] Since the tabernacle has two manifestations: a celestial and an earthly one, there is a natural correspondence with the pre-existent and the incarnate Christ. There is, however, more to Gregory's interpretation than this. He is drawing on a number of tabernacle traditions, particularly those concerning its relationship with wisdom, and reinterpreting them for a new theological context. The result is a tightly woven complex of allusions.

Throughout this section Gregory stresses his dependence on Paul: 'as the apostle says'; 'Paul partially disclosed the secret meaning of these things'; 'since therefore the great apostle says'; 'elucidation...may come to us through the very words of the apostle'.[14] This is because Paul, like Moses, has seen the heavenly tabernacle (2 Cor. 12:2–5), and therefore can be relied upon to give at least hints about its mysteries. Hebrews (which Gregory believes to have been written by Paul) says that 'the veil of the lower tabernacle is the flesh of Christ'.[15] Gregory dubs this a 'partial interpretation':

> it would be good, by paying attention to the partial interpretation, to harmonise the whole understanding of the tabernacle with this part.[16]

---

[9] 'Gregory's personal view, as he says himself,' Jean Daniélou, *Grégoire de Nysse: La Vie de Moïse, ou Traité de la perfection en matière de vertu* (Paris: Cerf, 2000), 221 n. 1.

[10] See Origen *Hom. Exod.* 9.3, *Hom. Num.* 5.3; and Methodius *Symp.* 5.7–8.

[11] E.g. Clement *Strom.* 5.35.1, where the golden lampstand is designated a sign of Christ.

[12] *Vit. Moys.* 1.67–68; 2.271–277. Cf. John 3:14–15, *Barn.* 12, Justin Martyr *Dial.* 91, 94, 112, 131.

[13] Abraham J. Malherbe and Everett Ferguson, *Gregory of Nyssa: The Life of Moses* (New York: Paulist Press, 1978), 159–60 n. 28.

[14] *Vit. Moys.* 2.173, 174, 178, 179.   [15] *Vit. Moys.* 2.178, cf. Heb. 10:20.

[16] *Vit. Moys.* 2.178.

Christological Interpretation

For the 'whole understanding', in which not only the veil, but the entire tabernacle is related to Christ, he turns to two other Pauline texts. The first, quoted at the beginning of his interpretation, is 1 Corinthians 1:24, the other is Colossians 1:15–20. To these he adds John 1:14 and allusions to Proverbs 8:22. The net result is to link Christ and the tabernacle, via wisdom, in three different ways: a) as becoming present on earth, b) as the agent/pattern of creation, and c) as the dwelling of God.[17] The parallels he implies are best shown in tabular form, see table 8.1. The entries in bold are statements made by Gregory. The biblical verses will be discussed here, and the antecedents in Philo in 8.2, on the Alexandrian context.

a) Christ Present on Earth

Gregory starts by quoting 1 Corinthians 1:24, which establishes the reference to wisdom. He continues by talking about the tabernacle as both unfashioned and fashioned (ἀκατάσκευον, κατεσκευασμένην), uncreated and created (ἄκτιστον, κτίστην). This alludes to LXX Proverbs 8:22: 'The Lord created (ἔκτισέν) me as the beginning of his ways...',[18] a verse which was exploited by the Arians:

> Because this saying is uttered by Wisdom, and the Lord is called Wisdom by great Paul (*1 Cor* 1.24), they advance this verse as meaning that the Only-begotten God himself, speaking as Wisdom, confesses that he was created by the Maker of all things.[19]

Gregory counters their arguments in *Against Eunomius* 1, *Against Eunomius* 3, and again in *Refutation of the Confession of Faith of Eunomius*.[20] In the

---

[17] These characterizations of wisdom/Christ can already be found in *Against Eunomius* 3,1. In *Life of Moses* Gregory adds the connection to the tabernacle. See Ann Conway-Jones, 'Uncreated and Created: Proverbs 8 and *Contra Eunomium* III/I as the Background to Gregory's Interpretation of the Tabernacle in *Life of Moses* II 173–7', in Johan Leemans and Matthieu Cassin (eds), *Gregory of Nyssa: Contra Eunomium III: An English Translation with Commentary and Supporting Studies* (Leiden: Brill, 2014).

[18] Trans. NETS.

[19] *Eun.* 3,1.21 (GNO 2.11.4–8); trans. Hall. For the early history of debates around Proverbs 8:22–5 see Sara Parvis, 'Christology in the Early Arian Controversy: The Exegetical War', in Andrew T. Lincoln and Angus Paddison (eds), *Christology and Scripture: Interdisciplinary Perspectives* (London: T&T Clark, 2007). Parvis sets out the interpretations of Arius, Eusebius of Nicomedia, Asterius the Sophist, and Marcellus of Ancyra. The relationship between Gregory's argument and those earlier debates is explored in Michel J. van Parys, 'Exégèse et théologie trinitaire: Prov. 8:22 chez les Pères Cappadociens', *Irénikon*, 43 (1970), 362–79, and 'Exégèse et théologie dans les livres contre Eunome de Grégoire de Nysse: Textes scripturaires controversés et élaboration théologique', in Marguerite Harl (ed.), *Écriture et culture philosophique dans la pensée de Grégoire de Nysse* (Leiden: Brill, 1971), 169–96.

[20] *Eun.* 1.298–305 (GNO 1.114–117); *Eun.* 3,1.21–65 (GNO 2.10–27); *Ref. Eun.* 110–113 (GNO 2.358–360).

Table 8.1 Parallels between the tabernacle, wisdom and Christ, in the Bible, Philo and Gregory of Nyssa

	Tabernacle	Wisdom	Christ
a) present on earth	• The tabernacle was set up on earth (Exod. 35–40)	• Wisdom became created (Prov. 8:22) • 'Wisdom has built her house' (Prov. 9:1) • 'In a holy tent I (wisdom) ministered before him' (Sir. 24:10) • The Logos within the holy of holies (*Fug.* 100–101, *QE* 68)	• 'and the Word became flesh and tabernacled among us' (John 1:14) • **'yet pitched his own tabernacle among us'** (2.175)
b) agent/ pattern of creation	• *Paradeigma* as the pattern for both the tabernacle and creation (*Mos.* 2.76, *Opif.* 16, *QE* 52, 82) • The tabernacle as a microcosm of creation (*Mos.* 2.81–108, *QE* 83–85)	• God by wisdom founded the earth (Prov. 3:19) • Wisdom as the agent/pattern for creation (Prov. 8:22 combined with Gen. 1:1) • Wisdom holds all things together (Wis. 1:7) • The *paradeigma* as the *kosmos noētos*, either identified with the Logos or placed within it (*Opif.* 20, 25, 36) • The Logos as the instrument of creation (*Leg.* 3.96)	• 'all things were made through him' (John 1:3) • **'in him all things were created, visible and invisible'** (2.179; Col. 1:16) • 'in him all things hold together' (Col. 1:17) • **'enclosing everything within himself'** (2.177)
c) dwelling of God	• 'the glory of the Lord filled the tabernacle' (Exod. 40:34)	• The Logos as the house of God (*Migr.* 4) • Wisdom as the palace of the All-ruler (*Congr.* 116) • The Logos containing all God's fullness (*Somn.* 1.75)	• 'And from his fullness have we all received' (John 1:16) • **'in whom dwells the whole fullness of divinity'** (2.177; Col. 1:19, 2:9)

Refutation he mentions translations which read 'acquired' (ἐκτήσατο) rather than 'created' (ἔκτισε),[21] but says that he is happy to stick with 'the reading which prevails in the Churches' because:

> He Who for our sakes became like as we are, was in the last days truly *created*,— He Who in the beginning being Word and God afterwards became Flesh and Man.[22]

---

[21] 110 (GNO 2.358.13–15). Gregory does not specify the 'more ancient copies' he has seen; but Eusebius (*Eccl. theol.* 3.2) mentions Aquila, Symmachus, and Theodotion, all of which use 'acquired' rather that 'created'.

[22] 111 (GNO 2.358.23–26); trans. NPNF² 5.117.

According to Gregory, Proverbs 8:22 refers to the pre-existent Christ becoming incarnate. In his discussion in *Against Eunomius* 1 he brings together John 1:3 and Colossians 1:17:

> [the Evangelist] says that all things that have come to be have come to be through him and are constituted (συνεστάναι) in him.[23]

The same passages lie behind his statement in *Life of Moses* 2.175: 'For there is one out of us all who both existed before the ages and came into being at the end of the ages.' Malherbe and Ferguson take this as an allusion to Colossians 1:17; but it could equally be seen as a summary of the prologue to John's gospel.[24] The paragraph ends with an unambiguous reference to John 1:14:

> This one is the Only Begotten God, who encompasses everything in himself but who also pitched his own tabernacle among us (πηξάμενος δὲ καὶ ἐν ἡμῖν τὴν ἰδίαν σκηνήν).

Most commentators agree that both Colossians and John are reusing Jewish wisdom traditions.[25] The idea of wisdom dwelling on earth in a tent/tabernacle can be found in Sirach 24, itself a meditation on Proverbs 8:

> ... he who created me put down my tent (τὴν σκηνήν μου)
> and said, 'Encamp (κατασκήνωσον) in Iakob...'
> ... In a holy tent (ἐν σκηνῇ ἁγίᾳ) I ministered before him...[26]

In *Against Eunomius* 3,1, Gregory quotes Proverbs 9:1 ('Wisdom has built her house'), saying that it hints at the building of the Lord's flesh:

> It was not in someone else's building that the true Wisdom dwelt, but she constructed for herself a dwelling from the body of the Virgin.[27]

He argues that Proverbs, John, and the tabernacle narrative all display the same structure, talking first of the pre-existent Christ's role in creation, and then of the incarnation. As he says with regard to Proverbs:

> It is... possible to see Solomon... presenting the whole mystery of the Economy. He speaks earlier of the pre-temporal power and activity of Wisdom, when in a way he agrees even verbally with the Evangelist. Just as John in comprehensive language proclaims him Cause and Designer of all things, so Solomon says that every single thing in the universe was made by him (*Prov* 3.19)... Having presented these and similar matters he brings in also the doctrine of the human Economy, why the Word became flesh.[28]

---

[23] *Eun.* 1.301–302 (GNO 1.115.25–116.1); trans. Hall, 79.
[24] Malherbe and Ferguson, *The Life of Moses*, 180 n. 220.
[25] Barrett, for example, states, 'Col. 1.15–20 shows as clearly as does John 1.1–18 the use of language drawn from Jewish speculations about Wisdom'. C. K. Barrett, *The Gospel according to St John*, 2nd edn (London: SPCK, 1978), 154.
[26] Sir. 24:8–10; trans. NETS.   [27] *Eun.* 3,1.44 (GNO 2.19.6–8); trans. Hall.
[28] *Eun.* 3,1.46–48 (GNO 2.19–20); trans. Hall.

In *Life of Moses* Gregory follows his interpretation of the heavenly and earthly tabernacles with an allegorization of the priestly vestments in terms of virtue. Similarly, he continues his interpretation of Proverbs by saying that the 'mountains', 'hills', 'deeps', and 'earth' of Proverbs 8:24–26 signify 'the manifold gifts of the Holy Spirit'.[29]

b) Christ as the Agent/Pattern of Creation

Variations on the phrase 'who encloses (περιέχων) everything within himself' are repeated three times in *Life of Moses* 2.173–179.[30] The phrase was used by Philo, and its theological implications will be explored in 8.3. It also alludes to Colossians 1:16: 'for in him all things were created…'—which Gregory quotes in 2.179—and John 1:3: 'all things were made through him'. These New Testament reflections on Christ seem to have linked the 'beginning' in Proverbs 8:22 with the 'beginning' in Genesis 1:1, so as to make wisdom/Christ the agent of creation: through wisdom God created the heavens and the earth. Alexander argues that although Hellenistic Jewish works, such as Wisdom, Ben Sira, and Philo, come close to doing so, Colossians was the first text to make this exegetical move.[31] Colossians combines this idea of Christ as the agent of creation with an image of Christ as the continuing sum and foundation of creation: 'in him all things hold together (τὰ πάντα ἐν αὐτῷ συνέστηκεν)'.[32] This echoes Wisdom 1:7: 'that which holds all things together (τὸ συνέχον τὰ πάντα)'. Gregory may be referring to this image of Christ as 'the power which encloses all existence (ἡ περιεκτικὴ τῶν ὄντων δύναμις)' and 'the common shelter of all (ἡ κοινὴ τοῦ παντὸς σκέπη)' in the context of the heavenly tabernacle because it is the function of a tent/tabernacle to enclose and protect.[33] He may also be aware of the Philonic tradition of the tabernacle as the pattern and microcosm of creation.

c) Christ as the Dwelling of God

The purpose of the earthly tabernacle built by the people of Israel was to provide a dwelling place for the glory of God:

> And the cloud covered the tent of witness, and the tent was filled with the glory of the Lord (καὶ δόξης κυρίου ἐπλήσθη ἡ σκηνή).[34]

---

[29] *Eun.* 3,1.56 (GNO 2.23); trans. Hall.   [30] *Vit. Moys.* 2. 174, 175, 177.
[31] Philip Alexander, '"In the Beginning": Rabbinic and Patristic Exegesis of Genesis 1:1', in Emmanouela Grypeou and Helen Spurling (eds), *The Exegetical Encounter between Jews and Christians in Late Antiquity* (Leiden: Brill, 2009), 23.
[32] Col. 1:17.   [33] *Vit. Moys.* 2.177.
[34] LXX Exod. 40:34; trans. NETS. Cf. 1 Kgs 8:10–11.

John 1:14–16 reworks the key concepts of that verse—glory, filling, and tabernacle:

> And the Word became flesh and dwelt (ἐσκήνωσεν) among us, full (πλήρης) of grace and truth; we have beheld his glory (δόξαν), glory as of the only Son from the Father.
> ... And from his fullness (ἐκ τοῦ πληρώματος) have we all received, grace upon grace.

Colossians 1:19 also refers to fullness:

> For in him all the fullness was pleased to dwell (ὅτι ἐν αὐτῷ εὐδόκησεν πᾶν τὸ πλήρωμα κατοικῆσαι).

In 2:9 this seems to be commented upon and clarified:

> For in (Christ) the whole fullness of deity dwells bodily (ὅτι ἐν αὐτῷ κατοικεῖ πᾶν τὸ πλήρωμα τῆς θεότητος σωματικῶς)...[35]

Gregory relates these references to the tabernacle:

> For the power... in whom 'dwells the whole fullness of divinity (ἐν ᾗ κατοικεῖ πᾶν τὸ πλήρωμα)'... enclosing everything within himself, is rightly called 'tabernacle'.[36]

He is taking 'fullness' as linked to the verb 'fill' in Exodus 40:34. Christ, like the tabernacle, is filled with the fullness/glory of God. Gregory quotes from Colossians 2:9, but omits 'bodily'. It would seem that, unlike John 1:14–16, he is referring to the divine, not the earthly, Christ. This is confirmed by his reference to 'fullness' in *Against Eunomius* 3,1. There he brings together John 1:1, 1:16, and 1:18:

> The one who is in the bosom of the Father [John 1:18] never allows the Paternal bosom to be thought empty of himself. So it is not as something external put into his bosom, but because he is the fullness [John 1:16] of all goodness, that the one who is 'in the beginning' (*Jn* 1.1) is deemed to be always in the Father, not waiting to be generated in him by creation, so that the Father might not ever be deemed wanting in good things.[37]

---

[35] Commentators on Colossians debate the meaning of 'bodily', given the present tense of 'dwells'. Rowland suggests that it refers to Christ's glorious heavenly body. Christopher Rowland and Christopher R. A. Morray-Jones, *The Mystery of God: Early Jewish Mysticism and the New Testament* (Leiden: Brill, 2009), 161. Similarly, according to Stroumsa, the imagery of Col. 1:1–20 'clearly suggests the macrocosmic conception of Christ as the image, or form, of the invisible God'. G. G. Stroumsa, 'Form(s) of God: Some Notes on Meṭaṭron and Christ: For Shlomo Pines', *Harvard Theological Review*, 76: 3 (1983), 284.

[36] *Vit. Moys.* 2.177.

[37] *Eun.* 3,1.49 (GNO 2.20–21); trans. Hall. In *Refutation of the Confession of Faith of Eunomius* 191–192 (GNO 2.393; NPNF² 5.129), Gregory combines John 1:16 with John 20:21 (Jesus breathing the Holy Spirit upon the disciples) to prove that the fullness of God dwells in the Holy Spirit.

From Colossians and John, therefore, Gregory pulls out two strands of tradition about the tabernacle/wisdom reapplied to Christ: the tabernacle/Christ as the dwelling place of the fullness of God, and wisdom/Christ as the agent/pattern of creation. To these he adds the theme of the tabernacle/wisdom/Christ becoming created among us, taken from Exodus 35–40, Proverbs 8:22, 9:1, and John 1:14. In naming Christ as 'tabernacle', therefore, Gregory creates three pictures: Christ dwelling within the tabernacle of a human body at the incarnation; Christ as a tabernacle enclosing, protecting, and patterning the universe; and Christ as a tabernacle containing the fullness of God. He is aware of the potential misunderstanding and misuse of these pictures, which is why he includes a digression on the subject of divine names, to be examined in Chapter 9.

8.2 LIFE OF MOSES 2.173–179: ALEXANDRIAN CONTEXT

Within Philo's cosmological interpretation of the tabernacle, the Logos crops up in a number of guises: it is the central branch of the lampstand,[38] the 'middle bar' of Exodus 26:28,[39] and the veil separating off the holy of holies.[40] Within the holy of holies Philo places a hierarchy of divine powers, culminating in the Logos.[41] His interpretation of the high priest's breastpiece (*logeion*) involves the Stoic distinction between the internal and the uttered logos.[42] Clement links Christ with the lampstand,[43] and uses the breastpiece as a springboard for comments on Christ's roles in creation, prophecy and judgement.[44] In his *Commentary on Romans*, Origen identifies the cherubim with the Word of God and his Holy Spirit, and the mercy seat with the soul of Jesus.[45] None of these interpretations of the tabernacle furniture are acceptable to Gregory, however, because they imply that the Word of God is inferior to the Father. Nowhere in his allegorical description of the tabernacle does he mention the Logos, and rather than associating Christ with one particular element, he turns the tabernacle as a whole into a type of Christ.

As we have seen, Gregory links the tabernacle to Christ in three different ways, relying heavily on the prologue to John's gospel and Colossians 1:16–19, passages which draw on Hellenistic Jewish wisdom traditions. All three ideas can also be found in Philo's work, with reference either to the tabernacle, wisdom, or the Logos:

---

[38] *Her.* 216, 225. [39] *QE* 2.89. [40] *QE* 2.91. [41] *Fug.* 100–101; *QE* 2.68.
[42] *Mos.* 2.127. [43] *Strom.* 5.35.1. [44] *Strom.* 5.38.2, 5.39.1.
[45] *Comm. Rom.* 3.8.5.

a) Philo draws on LXX Exodus 25:21—'I will speak to you from above the propitiatory in between the two cheroubim'—to envisage the Logos at the top of a hierarchy of divine powers within the holy of holies of the earthly tabernacle.[46]

b) Philo talks of a heavenly *paradeigma* in connection with both creation and the tabernacle. In *Questions on Exodus* (2.52, 82) he seems to imply that it is the same *paradeigma*, which would make sense, given that he presents the earthly tabernacle as a microcosm of creation.[47] In *On the Creation of the World* 16 he identifies the *paradeigma* with the intelligible world, which in turn he either identifies with the Logos: 'it is manifest that the archetypal seal also, which we aver to be the world descried by the mind, would be the very Word of God',[48] or places within the Logos: 'The incorporeal world, then, was now finished and firmly settled in the Divine Reason....'.[49] In some of his other works, he describes the Logos as the instrument of creation: '[God] made use of [His Word] like an instrument (ὀργάνῳ), and so made the world'.[50] He does not, however, make the Logos the agent of creation, stressing that God himself created the world 'with no counsellor to help Him'.[51]

c) Philo says that 'God, the Mind of the universe, has for His house His own Word'.[52] In the context of the tabernacle, he also talks of wisdom as the dwelling of God:

> [Moses] will speak of God's dwelling place, the tabernacle, as being 'ten curtains' (αὐλαίας), for to the structure which includes the whole of wisdom the perfect number ten belongs, and wisdom is the court (αὐλή) and palace of the All-ruler, the sole Monarch, the Sovereign Lord.[53]

He brings themes b and c together when he says, talking of the creation of light, that 'the model or pattern was the Word which contained all [God's] fullness (πληρέστατος ἦν αὐτοῦ)'.[54]

The ideas with which Gregory is working, therefore, have precedents in Philo's work, although it is not clear to what extent Gregory is aware of them. One phrase of Gregory's, however, has direct links to Philo: 'who encloses (περιέχων) everything within himself'.[55] One of the ways in which Philo expresses God's transcendence is with the words 'enclosing, not enclosed (περιέχων, οὐ περιεχόμενος)'. He produces them when dealing with a biblical text which either includes the word 'place' (τόπος), or implies that God can be found at a particular place:

---

[46] This will be looked at in more detail in 10.2.   [47] See 7.2.   [48] *Opif.* 25.
[49] *Opif.* 36, cf. 20.   [50] *Leg.* 3.96, cf. *Migr.* 6.   [51] *Opif.* 23.   [52] *Migr.* 4.
[53] *Congr.* 116.   [54] *Somn.* 1.75.   [55] *Vit. Moys.* 2.174, 175, 177.

For not even the whole world would be a place fit for God to make His abode, since God is His own place, and He is filled by Himself, filling and containing (πληρῶν καὶ περιέχων) all other things in their destitution and barrenness and emptiness, but Himself contained (περιεχόμενος) by nothing else, seeing that He is Himself One and the Whole.[56]

This has theological implications, to which we now turn.

8.3 *LIFE OF MOSES* 2.173–179: THEOLOGICAL CONTEXT

Gregory accuses Eunomius of 'plagiarism from the actual works of Philo', and promises to demonstrate 'the affinity between Eunomius' doctrines and the words of Jews'.[57] Paradoxically, however, he combats what he sees as Eunomius' collusion with the Jewish Philo by making use of two doctrines whose roots go back to Philo: the incomprehensibility and the infinity of God. The incomprehensibility of God has been discussed in Chapter 6, in connection with the imagery of darkness. Gregory indicates the infinity of God with his phrase 'who encloses everything within himself', echoing Philo's 'enclosing, not enclosed'. William Schoedel shows how this formula 'enclosing, not enclosed' focused the early church debates about the infinity of God, eventually resulting 'in a reversal of the Greek evaluation of the infinite'.[58] Philo's use of it indicates 'an impulse to go beyond the Greek tradition in emphasizing the divine transcendence', but he has 'an ambivalent attitude toward the infinite as such'.[59] For Irenaeus it is a weapon against Gnostic dualism.[60] It is Gregory of Nyssa who uses it as a clear statement of God's infinity. In the context of Moses' request to see God (Exod. 33:18), he says:

> [Moses] learns from what was said that the Divine is by its very nature infinite (ἀόριστον), enclosed (περιειργόμενον) by no boundary.... Since what is encompassed (περιεχομένου) is certainly less than what encompasses (περιέχοντος), it would follow that the stronger prevails. Therefore, he who encloses the Divine by any boundary makes out that the Good is ruled over by its opposite. But that is out of the question. Therefore, no consideration will be given to anything enclosing infinite nature.[61]

---

[56] *Leg.* 1.44.   [57] *Eun.* 3,7.8 (GNO 2.217); trans. Hall.
[58] William R. Schoedel, 'Enclosing, not Enclosed: The Early Christian Doctrine of God', in William R. Schoedel and Robert L. Wilken (eds), *Early Christian Literature and the Classical Intellectual Tradition: In Honorem Robert M. Grant* (Paris: Beauchesne, 1979), 75.
[59] Schoedel, 'Enclosing, not Enclosed', 76.   [60] See *Haer.* 2.1.2.
[61] *Vit. Moys.* 2.236, 238; trans. Malherbe and Ferguson, 115–16.

Christological Interpretation

So it would seem that in his interpretation of the tabernacle, Gregory has transformed the understanding of the tabernacle as a structure enclosing the universe, as in earlier cosmological interpretations, into a representation of Christ participating in the infinity of God, and therefore encompassing everything. We have the paradoxical picture of an infinite tent.

Turning now to the incarnation, John 1:14 reads, 'And the Word became flesh and dwelt among us...', where the verb 'to dwell' is *skēnoō*. Raymond Brown says of this verse, 'we are being told that the flesh of Jesus Christ is the new localization of God's presence on earth, and that Jesus is the replacement of the ancient Tabernacle'.[62] It is what gives Gregory permission to talk of the incarnate Christ as *skēnē*. There is, however, an important difference between John 1:14 and Gregory's reference to it. Whereas John 1:14 uses the verb *skēnoō*, which leaves open the exact nature of the relationship between 'Word' and 'flesh', Gregory uses the phrase 'to pitch a tabernacle' (πήγνυναι σκηνήν),[63] which is more in line with John 2:19–21, in which Jesus' body is described as a temple. *Skēnos*, a cognate of *skēnē*, also meaning 'tent', had long been used to designate the human body.[64] It is used in this way in Wisdom (9:15) and by Paul (2 Cor. 5:1–4). In the LXX *skēnōma* and *skēnē* are synonymous, both being used to translate *mishkan* (tabernacle). By Gregory's time they too have acquired associations with the human body. He uses all three words (*skēnē*, *skēnos*, *skēnōma*) to refer to the body.[65] With respect to Christ, he talks of the *skēnōma* formed when the Spirit came upon the Virgin;[66] and says that Christ brought the human race back to immortal life through the man in whom he tabernacled (διὰ τοῦ ἀνθρώπου ᾧ κατεσκήνωσεν).[67] Koester argues that the use of *skēnoō* in John 1:14 is 'a play on words that embraces both "flesh" and "glory"': 'flesh' because it resembles *skēnos*, and 'glory' because it resembles *skēnē*.[68] Michaelis thinks that the most important background to its use is the Hebrew verb *shakhan* 'to dwell', which denotes not a fleeting stay, but a longer or more permanent residence:

> It would appear that ἐσκήνωσεν ἐν ἡμῖν [dwelt among us] in Jn. 1:14 does not refer to the temporary and transitory element in the earthly existence of

---

[62] Raymond E. Brown, *The Gospel According to John, I–XII* (New York: Doubleday, 1966), 33.
[63] *Vit. Moys.* 2.174, 175.
[64] It occurs in Democritus and in Pseudo-Plato *Axiochos*. See W. Michaelis, 'σκηνή, σκῆνος, σκήνωμα, σκηνόω, ἐπισκηνόω, κατασκηνόω, σκηνοπηγία, σκηνοποιός', in Gerhard Friedrich (ed.), *Theological Dictionary of the New Testament* (Grand Rapids, Mich.: Eerdmans, 1971), 7.381; and Jean Daniélou, *The Bible and the Liturgy* (Notre Dame, Ind.: University of Notre Dame Press, 1956), 345 n. 27.
[65] See *Virg.* 4 (GNO 8,1.270.25, 271.2), and *Inscr.* 2.6 (GNO 5.87.10).
[66] *Epist.* 3.20 (GNO 8,2.25.12).   [67] *Eun.* 3,3.51 (GNO 2.126.5).
[68] Craig R. Koester, *The Dwelling of God: The Tabernacle in the Old Testament, Intertestamental Jewish Literature, and the New Testament* (Washington, DC: Catholic Biblical Association of America, 1989), 102.

the Logos but is designed to show that this is the presence of the Eternal in time.[69]

In Gregory, however, the *skēnē* of the earthly tabernacle would seem to be invoking the temporary human body within which Christ consents to be confined: 'becoming created in accordance with this material composition (τῷ δὲ κατὰ τὴν ὑλικὴν ταύτην σύστασιν κτίστην γενομένην)'.[70] This explains why his imagery was not taken up by later patristic authors: it implied too extrinsic a relationship between the human and divine natures of Christ. From the fifth century onwards, 'tabernacle' was used as a metaphor for the Virgin Mary, in whose case an extrinsic relationship with deity was more appropriate.[71]

Brian Daley argues that although Gregory's Christology 'does not easily fit into the taxonomy of fifth-century controversy' and has therefore been seen as 'puzzling and unsatisfactory', when considered on its own terms is 'remarkably powerful and also remarkably consistent, both in itself and with the rest of his thought on God, creation, and the mystery of salvation'.[72] Gregory developed his conception of Christ's person and work in controversy with Apollinarians. In his *Reply to the Teachings of Apollinarius*, he says:

> Who does not know that the God revealed to us in flesh, according to the word of pious tradition, is immaterial and invisible and uncompounded, and that he was and is infinite and uncircumscribed, existing everywhere and penetrating all creation, but that he has been seen, as far as appearance goes, in human circumscription (ἐν ἀνθρωπίνῃ περιγραφῇ)?[73]

The eternal Christ never changes, but by his 'taking up' of human form the transformation of humanity was made possible:

> He mingled with what is human and received our entire nature within himself, so that the human might mingle with what is divine and be divinized with it, and that the whole mass of our nature might be made holy through that first-fruit.[74]

---

[69] Michaelis, 'σκηνή, σκῆνος, σκήνωμα, σκηνόω, ἐπισκηνόω, κατασκηνόω, σκηνοπηγία, σκηνοποιός', 386.

[70] *Vit. Moys.* 2.174. Daniélou's text here differs slightly from Musurillo's.

[71] See, for example, Proclus of Constantinople *Homily* 6.17.9: Αὕτη ἡ σκηνὴ τοῦ μαρτυρίου, ἀφ' ἧς νεὼς ὢν ὁ ἀληθινὸς Ἰησοῦς μετὰ τὸν ἐνναμηνιαῖον τοῦ ἐμβρύου χρόνον, ἐξεπορεύετο; text Leroy, 323.

[72] Brian E. Daley, 'Divine Transcendence and Human Transformation: Gregory of Nyssa's Anti-Apollinarian Christology', in Sarah Coakley (ed.), *Re-Thinking Gregory of Nyssa* (Oxford: Blackwell, 2003), 67–8.

[73] *Antirrh.* (GNO 3,1.156.14–18); trans. Daley, 'Divine Transcendence and Human Transformation', 70.

[74] *Antirrh.* (GNO 3,1.151.16–20); trans. Brian E. Daley, '"Heavenly Man" and "Eternal Christ": Apollinarius and Gregory of Nyssa on the Personal Identity of the Savior', *Journal of Early Christian Studies*, 10: 4 (2002), 479.

As Daley says, 'What changes in the narrative of God's "self-emptying" is not God, nor even Christ as an eternal divine person, but the "human being" in which he "formed himself" to meet the capacities of our senses.'[75] None of this is spelt out in *Life of Moses*, but the soteriological motive is clearly signalled:

> who, for our sakes, because we had been led astray from true existence by evil counsel, undertook to become like us, in order to draw back into being once again that which had become outside being.[76]

By later Chalcedonian standards, Gregory's Christology is untenable because it manages to be 'Nestorian' and 'Monophysite' at the same time. It distinguishes two persons in Jesus—Christ dwelling in a human tent; yet from the resurrection confuses the divine and human natures: 'the humanity of Jesus [being] gradually transformed by the dominant power of the divine nature, so that in the end—like a drop of vinegar in a boundless ocean—it is virtually unrecognizable, swallowed up in the greatness of God.'[77] As Daley points out, however,

> He rarely uses the vocabulary he and his fellow Cappadocians had so carefully honed for Trinitarian discussions to express what is one and what is manifold in Christ, but speaks instead in a variety of scriptural and philosophical images which were richly suggestive for him, but which were used for different purposes by both sides of the Christological conflicts a half-century later.[78]

One of those images is the tabernacle: the celestial tabernacle as a representation of the infinite Christ containing the fullness of God and the whole of creation, the earthly tabernacle as the human body within which the pre-existent Christ consents to be born.

At the incarnation, the heavenly tabernacle is, as it were, turned inside out: the infinite becomes contained within a finite 'tent'. Douglass, who discusses Gregory's understanding of language in the context of postmodern philosophy, calls this a '*metadiastemic* intrusion'. He focuses on Gregory's use of the concept of *diastēma*: 'the gap, the interval, the space, the inescapable horizontal extensions of both space and time.'[79] According to Gregory, all human existence is *diastemic*: 'all of creation moves, breathes, thinks and speaks within the receptacles of time and space.'[80] God, however, 'is completely free of any distanciation'; God is *adiastemic*.[81] It is a constitutional impossibility for human beings to reach across the gap between their created *diastemic* existence and the *adiastemic* essence of God. God, however, can choose to interact with creation through *metadiastemic* intrusions. A *metadiastemic* intrusion is

---

[75] Daley, '"Heavenly Man" and "Eternal Christ"', 480. [76] *Vit. Moys.* 2.175.
[77] Daley, 'Divine Transcendence and Human Transformation', 67–8.
[78] Daley, 'Divine Transcendence and Human Transformation', 68.
[79] Scot Douglass, *Theology of the Gap: Cappadocian Language Theory and the Trinitarian Controversy* (New York: Peter Lang, 2005), 6.
[80] Douglass, *Theology of the Gap*, 36. [81] Douglass, *Theology of the Gap*, 35.

'the *diastemic* construction of an impenetrable space within which dwells the *adiastemic* presence of God.... In such a maneuver, even though the boundary between the created and the uncreated realms remains entirely intact... there is a reversal of inside/outside, contained/uncontained and finite/infinite.'[82] Douglass argues that in developing this understanding, the Cappadocians were drawing upon the biblical 'history of impenetrable, circumscribed spaces within which dwelt the inaccessible presence of God,'[83] including the tent of meeting, the Solomonic temple, and, supremely, the incarnation:

> Moses literally constructed a physical space out of *diastemic* materials—a [*skēnē*] of skins. Once he was finished, once the space was completely enclosed, the glory of God simultaneously filled this space and made it inaccessible.... By the initiation of God, it became an impenetrable space, a dark space... within which uncreated reality resided, a space within the [*diastēma*] that transcended the [*diastēma*], a *metadiastemic intrusion*.[84]
>
> The most significant biblical *metadiastemic intrusion* is, of course, the incarnation.... With the verb [*eskēnōsen*] [John 1:14], the gospel writer embedded the incarnation within the Biblical tradition of the presence of God on earth constituted by the sacral space of the 'Holy of Holies'—a tradition which began with the wilderness [*skēnē*].[85]

The name 'tabernacle' is appropriate for Christ, because the incarnate Christ, like the tabernacle, performed the impossible feat of containing the infinite, *adiastemic* God.

8.4 *LIFE OF MOSES* 2.173-179: HEAVENLY ASCENT CONTEXT

Gregory was not the first to work Christology into an ascent to the heavenly tabernacle/temple. As Christians took over Jewish ideas and Jewish texts, they wove Christian ideas into them. But they did so in different ways, and to different extents. *2 Enoch* was transmitted in Christian circles, and yet it displays 'a total lack of a Christian Savior or scheme of salvation. On the contrary, Enoch occupies an exalted position as God's chosen and prime agent which is totally incompatible with Christian belief in Jesus as Messiah.'[86] Sometimes Christian additions made little difference to the structure of the heavenly world. *Testament of Levi* contains predictions clearly referring to Jesus Christ;[87] but,

---

[82] Douglass, *Theology of the Gap*, 132.   [83] Douglass, *Theology of the Gap*, 133.
[84] Douglass, *Theology of the Gap*, 134.   [85] Douglass, *Theology of the Gap*, 138.
[86] Francis I. Andersen, '2 (Slavonic Apocalypse of) Enoch', in James H. Charlesworth (ed.), *The Old Testament Pseudepigrapha*, vol. 1: *Apocalyptic Literature and Testaments* (New York: Doubleday, 1983), 96.
[87] See, for example, *T. Levi* 4:4, 18:6–7.

in his vision, Levi simply sees 'the Most High upon a throne of glory'.[88] Isaiah, however, in *Ascension of Isaiah*, sees two figures on either side of the Great Glory: one is 'the Beloved',[89] or 'the Lord Christ, who is to be called in the world Jesus',[90] and the other is 'the angel of the Holy Spirit'.[91] They are worshipped by the angels, while they in turn worship the Great Glory. Darrell Hannah argues that *Ascension of Isaiah* is drawing on a pre-existing Jewish Christian exegesis of Isaiah 6, although it corrects the tradition in the direction of orthodoxy, avoiding 'any implication that the Beloved is an angel'.[92]

The first attempts to fit Christ into the heavenly world come in the New Testament. The Gospel of Mark draws on Daniel 7:13–14, with Jesus predicting that 'you will see the Son of man sitting at the right hand of Power, and coming with the clouds of heaven'.[93] John 12:41, in contrast to the exegetical tradition behind *Ascension of Isaiah*, 'identifies the object of Isaiah's vision with the pre-existent Christ'.[94] Revelation deploys a variety of imagery: Christ is 'one like a son of man, clothed with a long robe and with a golden girdle round his breast...';[95] 'a Lamb standing, as though it had been slain, with seven horns and with seven eyes';[96] the Word of God riding on a white horse, 'clad in a robe dipped in blood'.[97] The dominant image in Hebrews is of Christ as the high priest in the heavenly tabernacle. This is a role taken by Michael and Metatron in Jewish works. The tradition probably has deep roots: in *1 Enoch* 9:1 Michael is listed alongside Sariel, Raphael, and Gabriel as interceding for humanity, and in Daniel he is 'the great prince who has charge of [Israel]';[98] but the texts which explicitly portray him as the heavenly priest are post-Second Temple. In *b. Ḥagigah* 12b, for example, Michael, the great prince, stands and makes offerings at the altar of the heavenly Jerusalem, situated in *Zebul*, the fourth heaven.[99] Metatron's tabernacle (*mishkan*) is referred to in the Hekhalot literature.[100] At the beginning of chapter 15B of *3 Enoch*, which exists only in a couple of manuscripts, his 'great heavenly tabernacle of light' is 'beneath the throne of glory'.[101] Boyarin argues 'that late-ancient rabbinic literature when read in the context of all contemporary and earlier texts of Judaism...affords us a fair amount of evidence for and information about a belief in (and perhaps cult of) a second divine person within, or very close to, so-called "orthodox" rabbinic circles long after the advent of Christianity'.[102] He includes

---

[88] *T. Levi* 5:1; trans. Hollander and de Jonge, 143.   [89] *Ascen. Isa.* 3:13, 7:17, 8:18.
[90] *Ascen. Isa.* 9:5; trans. Knibb, 169–70.   [91] *Ascen. Isa.* 9:36; trans. Knibb, 172.
[92] Darrell D. Hannah, 'Isaiah's Vision in the Ascension of Isaiah and the Early Church', *Journal of Theological Studies*, 50: 1 (1999), 100. Origen draws upon the same exegetical tradition, as will be discussed in 10.2.
[93] Mark 14:62.
[94] Hannah, 'Isaiah's Vision in the Ascension of Isaiah and the Early Church', 81.
[95] Rev. 1:12–18.   [96] Rev. 5:6–14.   [97] Rev. 19:11–16.
[98] Dan. 12:1, cf. 10:13, 21.   [99] Cf. *b. Menaḥot* 110a, *b. Zevaḥim* 62a.
[100] See, for example, §390.   [101] *3 En.* 15B:1; trans. Alexander, 303.
[102] Daniel Boyarin, 'Beyond Judaisms: Meṭaṭron and the Divine Polymorphy of Ancient Judaism', *Journal for the Study of Judaism*, 41 (2010), 323–4.

Logos, Memra, Sophia, Metatron, Son of Man, Son of God, and Christ among 'the various second-God theologies of Jews',[103] with the enthronement scene of Daniel 7 as 'the pumping heart of the tradition'.[104] Schäfer cautions that we need to take the late date of *3 Enoch* seriously, and therefore cannot connect Metatron directly with early traditions such as the hypostasized 'Wisdom' or 'Logos'.[105] He suggests that Enoch's transformation into Metatron is a response to the New Testament's message about Jesus Christ. But whether a continuous tradition or not, there are Jewish and Christian works with a second figure beside the divine throne. From the fourth century onwards, religious authority figures in both traditions become unhappy with these depictions. The rabbis attempt to expel 'the Two-Powers theology from within themselves by naming it as *minut*, heresy'.[106] Both *b. Ḥagigah* 15a and *3 Enoch* 16 (§20) tell the story of Aḥer ascending to heaven, seeing Metatron, and coming to the conclusion that there are 'two powers' in heaven, as a result of which both Aḥer and Metatron are punished. Despite variations in detail, the stories are obviously related, although there is disagreement as to which influenced the other. Alexander gives priority to the Talmudic version, in which Metatron is seated because of his scribal activity. He suggests that the author of *3 Enoch* seized on this and used it 'as a way of introducing material on Metatron's throne and retinue'.[107] Boyarin, on the other hand, argues that the Talmud has taken the coherent and intelligible *3 Enoch* version and muddied it on purpose, deliberately obliterating Enoch's throne. He sees the Talmudic text as 'engaged in a massive struggle, as it itself seems to understand, with such highly ancient and well-rooted elements of Jewish religiosity as the second Throne, and a second divine person who absorbs the translated Enoch':[108]

> The dual inscription of excommunication in the narrative, that of Meṭaṭron on the one hand and of his 'devotee' on the other, suggests strongly to me that it is the belief in this figure as second divine principle that is being anathematized (although somehow the Rabbis seem unable to completely dispense with him— he was just too popular, it would seem).[109]

Boyarin stresses that this 'heretical' notion is located right at the heart of the rabbinic academy, symbolized by the fact that Aḥer ('the other') is 'the pejorative nickname for this once "kosher" rabbi after his turn to "heresy"'.[110] 'Two

---

[103] Daniel Boyarin, *Border Lines: The Partition of Judaeo-Christianity* (Philadelphia: University of Pennsylvania Press, 2004), 122.
[104] Boyarin, 'Beyond Judaisms', 349.
[105] Peter Schäfer, *The Origins of Jewish Mysticism* (Tübingen: Mohr Siebeck, 2009), 323–4.
[106] Boyarin, 'Beyond Judaisms', 335.
[107] Philip Alexander, '3 Enoch and the Talmud', *Journal for the Study of Judaism in the Persian, Hellenistic and Roman Period*, 18 (1987), 65.
[108] Boyarin, 'Beyond Judaisms', 352–3.   [109] Boyarin, 'Beyond Judaisms', 350–1.
[110] Daniel Boyarin, 'Two Powers in Heaven; or, The Making of a Heresy', in Hindy Najman and Judith H. Newman (eds), *The Idea of Biblical Interpretation: Essays in Honor of James L. Kugel* (Leiden: Brill, 2004), 355.

powers' in heaven became unacceptable to the rabbis.¹¹¹ What was unacceptable to Gregory was any suggestion that the second power (and the third!) was inferior to the first. Like the rabbis, he was not dealing with a fringe 'heresy', but with ideas that were circulating at the heart of his community. Rather than expelling the Logos, however, he promoted it. In his description of the heavenly tabernacle there are no figures on thrones, only allusions to the ineffable secrets of the ark of the covenant, covered by the wings of the cherubim. The essence neither of God nor of Christ can be depicted using visual imagery.

Behind both heavenly ascent texts and Christology lurk the questions: How is the divide between heaven and earth to be bridged? Can humans have contact with the divine? They are answered in a wide variety of ways. Sometimes the divide is 'bridged' from the 'divine' side, by the Logos, wisdom, Torah, or Christ. Sometimes there is an angelic mediating figure, or a heavenly high priest. In ascent texts, exceptional human beings are apotheosized: taken into heaven. This can be an arduous and dangerous journey. In the Hekhalot texts, 'the ascending adept finds himself confronted by angels whose precise business is to keep him out':¹¹²

> If he...is not worthy to descend to the Merkavah,
> [and] if they say to him:
> Enter!
> and he [then immediately] enters,
> [then] they immediately throw pieces of iron at him.¹¹³

Even one who is worthy to gaze at God's beauty risks being torn apart and poured out like the contents of a jug.¹¹⁴ Davila argues that this is not a punishment, but a transformation, 'at least temporarily, into a fiery angel'.¹¹⁵ For 'bodily ascent into the alien, hostile, realm of heaven demands bodily transformation'.¹¹⁶ *Ascension of Isaiah* 10:17–31 depicts the opposite process: as Christ descends, he takes on the form of the angels in each of the heavens he passes

---

¹¹¹ Abrams emphasizes that what the rabbis objected to was 'an opposition or competition of wills': 'two ruling authorities' in heaven. See Daniel Abrams, 'The Boundaries of Divine Ontology: The Inclusion and Exclusion of Meṭaṭron in the Godhead', *Harvard Theological Review*, 87: 3 (1994), 298. Abrams is following Alan F. Segal, *Two Powers in Heaven: Early Rabbinic Reports about Christianity and Gnosticism* (Leiden: Brill, 1977), 7–8 n. 8.
¹¹² Philip Alexander, 'The Dualism of Heaven and Earth in Early Jewish Literature and its Implications', in Armin Lange, et al. (eds), *Light against Darkness: Dualism in Ancient Mediterranean Religion and the Contemporary World* (Göttingen: Vandenhoeck & Ruprecht, 2011), 175.
¹¹³ *Hekhalot Rabbati* §258; trans. Peter Schäfer, *The Hidden and Manifest God: Some Major Themes in Early Jewish Mysticism* (Albany: State University of New York Press, 1992), 37.
¹¹⁴ *Hekhalot Rabbati* §159.
¹¹⁵ James R. Davila, *Descenders to the Chariot: The People behind the Hekhalot Literature* (Leiden: Brill, 2001), 154.
¹¹⁶ Alexander, 'The Dualism of Heaven and Earth', 181. See 14.4.

through. Schäfer sees the rabbinic commentary on 'the work of creation' (*b. Ḥagigah* 12b–13a) as 'a polemic against the ascent apocalypses and Merkava mysticism', which 'adopts some major components of this literature but neutralizes and marginalizes them'.[117] One example is its reproduction of a midrash on the dimensions of the heavens, also found in Hekhalot material.[118] The midrash describes the exponential increases in the distances involved in crossing the seven firmaments and ascending above the *ḥayyot* (living creatures) and the throne of glory to reach the high and exalted King. In the Talmudic context, the moral drawn is that ascent 'is a presumptuous enterprise, undertaken out of sheer hubris, an act of rebellion against God'.[119] The conclusion quotes Isaiah's condemnation of King Nebuchadnezzar:

> You said: I will ascend above the heights of the clouds, I will be like the Most High! No, you shall be brought down to She'ol, to the uttermost parts of the pit![120]

The rabbis condemn any effort to ascend to heaven.

8.5 *LIFE OF MOSES* 2.173–179: CONCLUSIONS

At first sight it might seem an impossible task to compare the abstract, theological language in which Gregory expresses his Christology with the vivid imagery of the heavenly ascent texts. However, probing beneath the surface to the questions being asked yields interesting results. As Douglass points out, in calling Christ 'tabernacle' Gregory is participating in the 'Christian appropriation of Jewish conceptions of sacred space'.[121] Douglass is referring to the biblical traditions surrounding the tabernacle and Solomon's temple. But some of the paradoxes in Gregory's use of tabernacle imagery resemble later Jewish descriptions of the heavenly temple. There seem to be logical inconsistencies in Gregory's interpretation: Can a tent be infinite? Does Christ, as tabernacle, contain creation, the fullness of God, or both? How can the uncreated God fit into a created tabernacle? These are the paradoxes of Christology, and of the incarnation in particular. But they are also the paradoxes of the heavenly world, described in 7.4.

---

[117] Peter Schäfer, 'From Cosmology to Theology: The Rabbinic Appropriation of Apocalyptic Cosmology', in Rachel Elior and Peter Schäfer (eds), *Creation and Re-Creation in Jewish Thought: Festschrift in Honor of Joseph Dan on the Occasion of his Seventieth Birthday* (Tübingen: Mohr Siebeck, 2005), 56.
[118] For details of the sources see Alexander, 'The Dualism of Heaven and Earth', 175 n. 9.
[119] Schäfer, 'From Cosmology to Theology', 57.
[120] Isa. 14:14–15; *b. Ḥag.* 13a; trans. Schäfer, 'From Cosmology to Theology', 57.
[121] Douglass, *Theology of the Gap*, 26.

As a consequence of the Arian controversy, Gregory works in a theological context in which Christ as a mediator figure is no longer acceptable. He cannot, therefore, use the imagery of Hebrews and Revelation, or indeed the Logos theology of Philo and Clement. Gregory and the rabbis agree that there is no subordinate God; but whereas in *b. Ḥagigah* 15a the rabbis attempt to demote Metatron, Gregory absorbs Christ into the one God. Christ becomes fully divine. We see here religious authority figures drawing up the boundaries which will effect the parting of the ways: 'The Rabbis, by defining elements from within their own religious heritage as not Jewish, were, in effect, producing Christianity, just as Christian heresiologists were defining traditional elements of their own religious heritage as not Christian and thereby producing Judaism.'[122] Gregory superimposes upon the Platonic intelligible–sensible division an absolute ontological division between Creator and creation. Whereas in earlier pictures of the incarnation, such as Philippians 2:5–8 or *Ascension of Isaiah* 10, Christ descends from one realm into another, 'taking the form of a servant',[123] Gregory has the pre-existent Christ entering creation as *metadiastemic* intrusion. The uncreated is taken into the created unchanged. There is also no apotheosis. In the heavenly ascent texts a few exceptional individuals manage to cross the dangerous boundary between heaven and earth to glimpse the heavenly throne, becoming transformed in the process. According to Gregory, however, human beings are constrained by their created nature, and cannot apprehend the uncreated God. Christ, however, has initiated a transformation in which all can participate. In *Life of Moses*, Gregory talks of this transformation when he moves on to the priestly vestments. But it does not involve crossing the created–uncreated divide:

> By shifting the ontological opposition from the boundary between sensible and intelligible to the distinction between creator and created, he has established not a barrier that cannot be penetrated, but something like a mathematical asymptote that can be approached, but never reached.[124]

There is, therefore, in Gregory no 'absorption mysticism', but rather an endless 'straining toward those things that are still to come'.[125] Unlike the rabbis, Gregory does not condemn the desire to reach heaven; but he does redefine what is possible. Human ascent is only possible by participating in the transformation initiated by Christ; and it is an infinite journey with no possibility of crossing the created–uncreated divide.

---

[122] Boyarin, 'Two Powers in Heaven', 332.   [123] Phil. 2:7.
[124] Alden A. Mosshammer, 'Gregory's Intellectual Development: A Comparison of the *Homilies on the Beatitudes* with the *Homilies on the Song of Songs*', in H. R. Drobner and A. Viciano (eds), *Gregory of Nyssa: Homilies on the Beatitudes* (Leiden: Brill, 2000), 367.
[125] *Vit. Moys.* 1.5; trans. Malherbe and Ferguson, 30; quoting Phil. 3:13.

9

Divine Names

> If so great a good is named 'tabernacle', let the lover of Christ not be dismayed, as if the expression's literal sense could diminish the splendour of the nature of God. For neither is any other name worthy of the nature of the one designated, but all alike have fallen short of accurate designation, both those considered trivial and those in which it is assumed that lofty concepts are to be seen.[1]

9.1 *LIFE OF MOSES* 2.176–177: BIBLICAL CONTEXT

Gregory interrupts his discussion of the tabernacle as a type of Christ for a short digression on divine names. The significance of the names applied to God is a frequent theme in his writings, and key to his argument with Eunomius. Eunomius claimed that the name 'unbegotten' (ἀγέννητος) defined God's essence, and that 'as God's being is absolutely simple, every name said of God either means "unbegotten" too or is wrongly applied to the Supreme Being'.[2] In contrast, Gregory insisted that the essence of God could not be known, or named. By invoking that argument here, he implies that not even a vision of the tabernacle not made with hands gave Moses privileged access to the essence of God. Alongside this insistence on the unknowability of God, however, he developed a 'symbolic theology through which some degree of theological knowledge was made possible',[3] based on God's self-accommodation to the constraints of human expression in the language of Scripture:

> We find in each of the names a peculiar reflection (ἰδιάζουσαν ἔμφασιν) suitable to be thought and said about the divine nature, but not signifying what that nature is according to its substance (κατ' οὐσίαν).[4]

---

[1] *Vit. Moys.* 2.176.
[2] Johannes Zachhuber, 'Christological Titles—Conceptually Applied? (*CE* II 294–358)', in Lenka Karfíková, Scot Douglass, and Johannes Zachhuber (eds), *Gregory of Nyssa: Contra Eunomium II* (Leiden: Brill, 2007), 259.
[3] Frances M. Young, *Biblical Exegesis and the Formation of Christian Culture* (Cambridge: Cambridge University Press, 1997), 141.
[4] *Abl.* (GNO 3,1.43); trans. Rusch, 152.

Divine Names

Here, in *Life of Moses*, Gregory lists other scriptural names given to Christ which, like 'tabernacle', 'in keeping with what is being designated, are spoken reverently as an indication of divine power'.[5] He produces similar lists elsewhere,[6] and devotes the treatise *On Perfection* to expounding how 'the participation of one's soul and speech and activities in all of the names by which Christ is signified' leads to perfection in the Christian life.[7] Each list is slightly different, and this is the only one in which 'tabernacle' features. He also includes the Johannine names 'shepherd' (John 10:11), 'bread' (6:35), 'vine' (15:1), 'way' (14:6), 'door' (10:7), 'abode' (14:23),[8] and 'water' (4:13–14); two other names from the New Testament: 'physician' (Matt. 9:12, Mark 2:17, Luke 5:31) and 'rock' (1 Cor. 10:4); and two from the Old Testament: 'protector' (ὑπερασπιστής, frequent in the Psalms e.g. LXX Ps. 17:3) and 'spring' (πηγή, LXX Ps. 35:10). Although these two paragraphs read like a digression, written to counter any arguments against the suitability of using 'tabernacle' as a name for God, they have the effect of modifying the goal of Moses' ascent. Now it seems that the revelation vouchsafed to him was a new name for God, a name overlooked by previous biblical commentators. Like all other divine names, as will be explored further in 9.3, it only describes the 'things around God', not God's essence. But Gregory puts it on a par with the well-known Johannine Christological titles.

9.2 LIFE OF MOSES 2.176–177: ALEXANDRIAN CONTEXT

Gregory's insistence on the unknowability of God, and therefore on the impossibility of naming God definitively, has precedents in the Alexandrian tradition. Both Philo and Clement link God's transcendence with God's unnameability:

> He has no proper name, and...whatever name anyone may use of Him he will use by licence of language; for it is not the nature of Him that IS to be spoken of, but simply to be.[9]
>
> How can that be expressed which is neither genus, nor difference, nor species, nor individual, nor number; nay more, is neither an event, nor that to which an

---

[5] *Vit. Moys.* 2.177.
[6] See *Eun.* 2.294, 300, 347–349 (GNO 1.313, 314, 327); *Eun.* 3,1.127 (GNO 2.46); *Eun.* 3,8.10 (GNO 2.242); *Ref. Eun.* 124 (GNO 2.365); and *Simpl.* (GNO 3,1.62).
[7] *Perf.* (GNO 8,1.212); trans. Callahan, 121.
[8] Abode (μονή) does not occur in any other list. It seems slightly forced as a Christological title, but is perhaps included because, like tabernacle, it refers to a dwelling. There is also, however, a variant reading: 'pasture' (νομή, John 10:9). In *Eun.* 3,8.7–9 (GNO 2.240–242) Gregory talks of Christ as 'pasture', bringing in Psalm 23:2 (LXX 22.2).
[9] *Somn.* 1.230.

event happens? No one can rightly express Him wholly.... Nor are any parts to be predicated of Him. For the One is indivisible... And therefore it is without form and name.[10]

Clement makes explicit reference to Plato's declaration in *Timaeus* 28C:

> 'For both is it a difficult task to discover the Father and Maker of this universe; and having found Him, it is impossible to declare Him to all. For this is by no means capable of expression, like the other subjects of instruction,' says the truth-loving Plato.[11]

As a Christian, however, he has to reconcile this with the many names given to God in Scripture. He does so by saying that, taken together, they provide an indication of God's power:

> If we name it, we do not do so properly, even in terming it either the One, or the Good, or Mind, or Absolute Being, or Father, or God, or Creator, or Lord. We speak not as supplying His name; but out of helplessness we use good names, so that the mind has these for support and does not wander after others. For each one by itself does not express God; but all together are indicative of the power of the Omnipotent.[12]

Gregory's difficulties, therefore, in reconciling his apophaticism with the language of Scripture are not new.

In Antiquity, knowledge of the right name conferred power:

> One of the basic presuppositions of magical practice, both in Greco-Roman antiquity and elsewhere, is that there is power in names, or to be more exact, in the magician's knowledge of names.[13]

Christian texts too acknowledged the power of names, as demonstrated by Clement's commentary on the 'enigmas' of the temple. He writes:

> Furthermore there is the mystic name of four letters, which was affixed to those alone to whom the adytum was accessible; it is called Jahwe, which is interpreted as 'Who is and shall be'.[14]

The high priest had access to the holy of holies thanks to the name inscribed upon the golden *petalon* (thin plate) attached to his headdress. Later in the

---

[10] *Strom.* 5.81.5–6; trans. Wilson, 270.   [11] *Strom.* 5.78.1; trans. Wilson, 267.

[12] *Strom.* 5.82.1–2; trans. Wilson, 270, amended according to Frances M. Young, 'The God of the Greeks and the Nature of Religious Language', in William R. Schoedel and Robert L. Wilken (eds), *Early Christian Literature and the Classical Intellectual Tradition: In Honorem Robert M. Grant* (Paris: Beauchesne, 1979), 64.

[13] John M. Dillon, 'The Magical Power of Names in Origen and Later Platonism', in Richard Hanson and Henri Crouzel (eds), *Origeniana Tertia: The Third International Colloquium for Origen Studies, University of Manchester, September 7th–11th 1981* (Rome: dell'Ateneo, 1985), 203.

[14] *Strom.* 5.34.5; trans. Annewies van den Hoek, *Clement of Alexandria and His Use of Philo in the Stromateis: An Early Christian Reshaping of a Jewish Model* (Leiden: Brill, 1988), 126.

passage Clement interprets this inscribed name as the Son, in whom the invisible God becomes manifest.[15] Entry into the holy of holies, however, represents 'knowledge of the ineffable', and therefore involves 'ascending above every name that is made known by the sound of a voice'.[16] This theme of transcendence is taken further in *Excerpts from Theodotus*. There the high priest is said to remove the *petalon* before entering the holy of holies, a detail found neither in Leviticus 16 nor in *Miscellanies*:

> The priest on entering within the second veil removed the plate at the altar of incense, and entered himself in silence with the name engraved upon his heart, indicating the laying aside of the body which has become pure like the golden plate and bright through the purification of the soul and on which was stamped the luster of piety, by which he was recognized by the Principalities and Powers as having put on the Name.[17]

The Name is necessary as a password when faced with Principalities and Powers, but can now be carried in the heart. Compared with the importance given to the *petalon* in *Miscellanies* and *Excerpts from Theodotus*, Gregory's treatment of it in his section on the priestly vestments seems brief to the point of dismissal:

> The head adorned with the diadem intimates the crown laid up for those who have lived well. It is adorned by the inscription on the thin golden plate with unutterable lettering. Whoever wears an array like this does not put on sandals...[18]

He does not see the divine Name as granting access to the holy of holies, the essence of God.

Origen comments on the power of divine names. When Celsus alleges that 'Christians get the power which they seem to possess by pronouncing the names of certain daemons and incantations', Origen replies:

> They do not get the power which they seem to possess by any incantations but by the name of Jesus with the recital of the histories about him. For when these are pronounced they have often made daemons to be driven out of men, and especially when those who utter them speak with real sincerity and genuine belief. In fact the name of Jesus is so powerful against the daemons that sometimes it is effective even when pronounced by bad men.[19]

Further on, he compares Hebrew divine names with the powerful names used by Egyptian wise men and Persian magi, saying:

---

[15] *Strom.* 5.38.6–7.
[16] *Strom.* 5.34.7; trans. van den Hoek, *Clement of Alexandria and His Use of Philo*, 126.
[17] *Exc.* 27.1–2; trans. Lilla, *Clement of Alexandria*, 176. This translation follows the text of Sagnard, rather than of Casey.
[18] *Vit. Moys.* 2.201.   [19] *Cels.* 1.6; trans. Chadwick, 9–10.

The names Sabaoth, and Adonai, and all the other names that have been handed down by the Hebrews with great reverence, are not concerned with ordinary created things, but with a certain mysterious divine science that is related to the Creator of the universe.[20]

John Dillon argues that Origen 'relates the question of the efficacy of magical formulae to the philosophical debate as to the origin and nature of language'.[21] Origen follows Stoic etymological theory, derived from an interpretation of Plato's *Cratylus*, and adopted by later Platonists, in which names can be a guide to the true nature of things. In *Cratylus* 390DE Socrates remarks:

Cratylus is right in saying that names belong to things by nature (φύσει) and that not every one is an artisan of names, but only he who keeps in view the name which belongs by nature to each particular thing and is able to embody its form in the letters and syllables.

He follows this up a little later by suggesting that it is the gods who know the right names:

[Homer] distinguishes between the names by which gods and men call the same things. Do you not think he gives in those passages great and wonderful information about the correctness of names? For clearly the gods call things by the names that are naturally right.[22]

Neoplatonists commented on these remarks—as we shall have reason to discuss in 9.3, in connection with Eunomius—but Dillon suggests that 'already in Origen's time there existed in the Platonic tradition a theory of the magical efficacy of divine names', a theory with which Origen, a Christian philosopher, had no quarrel.[23] Origen generalizes from his understanding of the names used in spells to the divine origin of all language:

We say...with regard to the nature of names that they are not arbitrary conventions of those who give them, as Aristotle thinks. For the languages in use among men have not a human origin, which is clear to those able to give careful attention to the nature of spells which were adapted by the authors of the languages in accordance with each different language and different pronunciation.[24]

Gregory's lists of the names given to Christ fit into a long-standing Christian tradition,[25] and, in particular, follow Origen's delight 'in listing the fascinating array of attributes and titles which scripture gives to the Logos', best seen in the

---

[20] *Cels.* 1.24; trans. Chadwick, 24.
[21] Dillon, 'The Magical Power of Names in Origen and Later Platonism', 207.
[22] *Crat.* 391DE.
[23] Dillon, 'The Magical Power of Names in Origen and Later Platonism', 212.
[24] *Cels.* 5.45; trans. Chadwick, 299.
[25] See Abraham J. Malherbe and Everett Ferguson, *Gregory of Nyssa: The Life of Moses* (New York: Paulist Press, 1978), 180 n. 223 for examples.

*Commentary on John.*²⁶ There Origen reflects on the significance of names from John (Word, life, light, truth, way, resurrection, door, lamb, shepherd, teacher…), Paul (wisdom, power, chief cornerstone, propitiatory, great high priest…), and the prophets (sharp sword, chosen arrow, servant, rod, flower…). Occasionally he calls these names *epinoiai*—conceptions (here, translated 'aspects'):

> Although Jesus was one, he had several aspects (εἷς ὢν πλείονα τῇ ἐπινοίᾳ ἦν); and to those who saw him he did not appear alike to all. That he had many aspects (τῇ ἐπινοίᾳ πλείονα ἦν) is clear from the saying, 'I am the way, the truth, and the life', and 'I am the bread', and 'I am the door', and countless other such sayings.²⁷

Johannes Zachhuber comments,

> The point of [Origen's] elaboration is that Jesus is different things to various kinds of people.... He argues that Jesus, in his earthly life and after, appeared to people according to their capacity of recognising the divine.²⁸

Each name corresponds to a particular human experience of Christ. The variety and multiplicity of the names corresponds to the variety and multiplicity of the creation in need of salvation:

> God…is altogether one and simple. Our Savior, however, because of the many things, since God 'set' him 'forth as a propitiation' and firstfruits of all creation, becomes many things, or perhaps even all these things, as the whole creation which can be made free needs him.²⁹

A few of the names, however, seem to relate not only to Christ's saving activity, but also to his divine identity:

> He is…a 'way' for others, and so too a 'door', and a 'rod', as all would agree. But he is 'wisdom' for himself and others, and perhaps this is true also of 'Word'. And we must inquire, since there is a system of ideas in him insofar as he is 'wisdom', if there are some ideas that are incomprehensible to all begotten nature except himself, which he knows for himself.³⁰

These titles 'name both the Son's being in his turning to God and the relation to us that springs from this. "Logos", for example, signifies God's own Word before it signifies the agent of revelation.'³¹ But both in his divine identity and his saving role Christ mediates between the unity of God and the multiplicity of creation:

> [Origen's] intention…is to offer a vision in which Christ mediates between the absolute simplicity of God and the utter multiplicity of the created world. The fact

---

²⁶ Young, 'The God of the Greeks and the Nature of Religious Language', 65.
²⁷ *Cels.* 2.64; text Borret, 434; trans. Chadwick, 115.
²⁸ Zachhuber, 'Christological Titles—Conceptually Applied?', 264–5.
²⁹ *Comm. Jo.* 1.119 (GCS 10.24); trans. Heine, 1.58.
³⁰ *Comm. Jo.* 2.126 (GCS 10.75); trans. Heine, 1.127–8.
³¹ Joseph S. O'Leary, 'Logos', in John Anthony McGuckin (ed.), *The Westminster Handbook to Origen* (Louisville, Ken.: Westminster John Knox Press, 2004), 143.

that he is the redeemer is inextricably intertwined with this mediating role. He *is* one, but becomes many in his soteriological activity. Again, he *can* become many because he is not as simple as God is.[32]

Eunomius, as we shall see, picks up on this difference between the simplicity of God and the multiplicity associated with Christ. He also follows Origen in arguing for the divine origin of names. Gregory, on the other hand, will admit no difference between God and Christ, and sees language as a human construct.

9.3 LIFE OF MOSES 2.176–177: THEOLOGICAL CONTEXT

Frances Young suggests that behind Gregory's discussions of divine names is the questioning of religious language produced by the Arian controversy. Until the fourth century, the Logos had functioned as the link between the ultimate, transcendent God and the multiplicity of creation. Once the Logos as well as God was defined as transcending human comprehension, the basis of religious language was undermined. It was Gregory of Nyssa 'who more than any other, recognised that the radical distinction between creator and creature rendered the traditional accounts of religious knowledge unusable'.[33] His answer to the problem came through his theology of the divine names, forged in the conflict with Eunomius. Eunomius was

> an advocate of a representational theory of language. Things are perceived as they exist in their essences. God created intelligible concepts that correspond directly to those essences and that can be expressed unambiguously in language.[34]

He insisted on the sacred character of language, arguing that 'God has a name given by God to himself and that name is ἀγέννητος [unbegotten]'.[35] This then, of course, automatically excluded the Son, begotten by definition, from the divine nature. Eunomius further dismissed any other names given to God as mere human inventions (*epinoiai*) and of no value:

> When we say 'Unbegotten', then, we do not imagine that we ought to honour God only in name, in conformity with human invention (κατ' ἐπίνοιαν ἀνθρωπίνην);

---

[32] Zachhuber, 'Christological Titles—Conceptually Applied?', 265–6.
[33] Young, 'The God of the Greeks and the Nature of Religious Language', 66.
[34] Alden A. Mosshammer, 'Disclosing but not Disclosed: Gregory of Nyssa as Deconstructionist', in H. R. Drobner and C. Klock (eds), *Studien zu Gregor von Nyssa und der christlichen Spätantike* (Leiden: Brill, 1990), 100.
[35] Anthony Meredith, 'The Language of God and Human Language (*CE* II 195–293)', in Karfíková, Douglass, and Zachhuber (eds), *Gregory of Nyssa*, 251.

rather, in conformity with reality, we ought to repay him the debt which above all others is most due God: the acknowledgement that he is what he is. Expressions based on invention have their existence in name and utterance only, and by their nature are dissolved along with the sounds [which make them up]; but God...both was and is unbegotten.[36]

In reply, Gregory put forward four claims:

> He argues, first, that language is a human invention and therefore both arbitrary and fallible, so that the ability of language to express any reality whatsoever in its own essence is questionable. Secondly, he maintains that language is bound to an order of reality so entirely unlike the divine nature that words cannot even inadequately address the being of God. Third, Gregory argues that all apparently theological language, including the language of the Bible, can in fact only have the created order as its referent. Finally, Gregory claims that to the extent theological language expresses divine truths at all such language can have no fixed content, but must forever be reinterpreted in an endless pursuit of an ever elusive meaning.[37]

Gregory suggests that the names we apply to God come from two sources: Scripture and the human power of reasoning, but in neither case do they give access to God's essence. (Gregory, of course, unlike Eunomius, includes Christ when talking about God.) He uses the word *epinoia* positively, as 'our own reflection on the concepts we form through the reflective power we have from God'.[38] Because the power of thought and language comes from God, it produces appropriate names when used to contemplate the works of God: 'Creation and scripture guarantee that the names of God are more than a figment of the human imagination; for creation and scripture are expressive of God's will and God is truth.'[39] However, they designate God's energies/activities—whatever is 'around' the divine nature, rather than that nature itself:

> It is clear that the Divinity is given names with various connotations in accordance with the variety of his activities (πρὸς τὸ ποικίλον τῶν ἐνεργειῶν), named in such a way as we may understand.[40]

> Any name, whether discovered by human custom or transmitted by Scripture, is, we say, explicative of what we discover through thought concerning what is around the divine nature (τῶν περὶ τὴν θείαν φύσιν νοουμένων), but does not contain the significance of the nature itself.[41]

---

[36] Eunomius *Apology* 8; trans. Vaggione, 40–3.
[37] Mosshammer, 'Disclosing but not Disclosed', 100–1.
[38] Meredith, 'The Language of God and Human Language', 249.
[39] Young, 'The God of the Greeks and the Nature of Religious Language', 68.
[40] *Eun.* 2.304 (GNO 1.315); trans. Hall, 127.
[41] *Abl.* (GNO 3,1.42–43); trans. Basil Krivocheine, 'Simplicity of the Divine Nature and the Distinctions in God, according to St. Gregory of Nyssa', *St. Vladimir's Theological Quarterly*, 21 (1977), 88.

We build up our understanding by producing a whole variety of names:

> Since no one title (ὄνομα) has been discovered to embrace the divine Nature by applying directly to the subject itself, we therefore use many titles (πολλοῖς ὀνόμασι), each person in accordance with various interests achieving some particular idea about him, to name the Divinity, as we hunt amid the pluriform variety of terms applying to him for sparks to light up our understanding of the object of our quest.[42]

In this debate between Gregory and Eunomius, the meaning of *epinoia* changes in emphasis from its use in Origen. As Daniélou says, for Origen *epinoia* has a particular meaning: 'celui d'une diversité de notions relatives à une réalité unique'.[43] Eunomius, while insisting that the Father is absolutely simple, and can only be named 'unbegotten', is happy to assign a certain multiplicity to the Only-begotten:

> It is reasonable, [Eunomius] says, to suppose that the Only-begotten God is in various ways subject to concepts because of the variety of his actions and certain analogies and relationships: he spells out at length these titles applied to him.[44]

This is in line with Origen's understanding. Daniélou comments:

> ...si le Monogène peut être désigné par diverses appellations, c'est qu'il y a en lui une diversité réelle: ces diversités sont les ἐπίνοιαι. Et par conséquent les noms qui désignent le Monogène ne sont pas des synonymes, empruntés à des analogies diverses, mais des termes propres qui désignent des réalités diverses.[45]

Gregory, on the other hand, sees multiplicity not in Christ, but in human notions about Christ. The essence of both Father and Son, to which human beings have no access, is simple; the variety of *epinoiai* reflects the impossibility of talking about God in human language. Gregory accuses Eunomius of having borrowed his ideas from Plato's *Cratylus*, '[stitching] together his own nonsense with the rubbish he found there'.[46] Daniélou sees this as a clue that Eunomius has been influenced by ideas from contemporary neoplatonist circles. The disciples of Iamblichus in particular seem to have drawn both on Socrates' remarks in *Cratylus* 390DE and 391DE, and on material from the

---

[42] *Eun.* 2.145 (GNO 1.267); trans. Hall, 90.
[43] 'that of a variety of concepts related to a single reality'. Jean Daniélou, 'Eunome l'Arien et l'éxégèse néo-platonicienne du Cratyle', *Revue des études grecques*, 69 (1956), 417.
[44] *Eun.* 2.363 (GNO 1.332); trans. Hall, 140.
[45] 'if the Only-begotten may be designated by various names, it is because there is in him a real diversity: this diversity is the *epinoiai*. And therefore the names that designate the begotten are not synonymous, borrowed from various analogies, but specific terms that refer to the multiplicity of his being.' Daniélou, 'Eunome l'Arien et l'éxégèse néo-platonicienne du Cratyle', 418.
[46] *Eun.* 2.403–404 (GNO 1.344); trans. Hall, 150.

Chaldean Oracles, such as Fr. 150: 'Do not change the *nomina barbara*,'[47] to produce an understanding of efficacious divinely revealed names:

> In those names for which we have received scientific analysis, we possess a knowledge of the whole divine essence, power, and order (θείας οὐσίας καὶ δυνάμεως καὶ τάξεως), comprehended in the name.[48]

Whether influenced by neoplatonist interest in theurgy or not, Eunomius' understanding of language picks up on the widespread belief in the power of divine names found not only in magical texts and on amulets but also in Origen.

In *Life of Moses*, Gregory says that no name is 'worthy of the nature of the one designated, but all alike have fallen short of accurate designation, both those considered trivial and those in which it is assumed that lofty concepts are to be seen',[49] implying that there is a hierarchy among divine names. Young argues that

> Gregory does make distinctions among the 'names' offered by scripture...Some are to be referred to God absolutely, others are relative....The terms used 'relatively' are invariably those that relate to the *oikonomia*, to God's relationship with the world, to the divine activity in creation, providence and salvation, whether one speaks of Father or Son. The terms used 'absolutely' are those that refer to the Being of God, especially the eternal being in relationship which is the absolute nature of Father and Son.[50]

As she observes, this distinction 'easily slips into a traditional Christological pattern' with 'absolute' terms assigned to Christ's Godhead and 'relative' ones to his humanity.[51] Where does 'tabernacle' fit? By placing it alongside the Johannine names, Gregory seems to be assigning it to the 'relative' category. Certainly, as a designation for the incarnation, it would fit there. And when he talks of 'the power which encloses all existence' and 'the common shelter of all, enclosing everything within himself', he would seem to be talking of Christ's role in creation, again part of the *oikonomia*.[52] But 'in whom dwells the whole fullness of divinity' is a comment on the full divinity of Christ, which would be part of his 'absolute' nature.[53]

Gregory is trying to maintain a balancing act: neither agreeing with Eunomius that names are God-given and correspond to the essence of things, nor asserting that they are completely arbitrary. In the words of Young,

> Through the names and attributes revealed by God's will, some grasp of and advance in understanding is made possible. The biblical narratives, read

---

[47] Trans. Ruth Majercik, *The Chaldean Oracles: Text, Translation, and Commentary* (Leiden: Brill, 1989), 107.
[48] Iamblichus *On the Mysteries* 7.4; text Des Places, 192; trans. Taylor, 292–3.
[49] *Vit. Moys.* 2.176.
[50] Young, *Biblical Exegesis and the Formation of Christian Culture*, 143.
[51] Young, 'The God of the Greeks and the Nature of Religious Language', 69.
[52] *Vit. Moys.* 2.177.   [53] *Vit. Moys.* 2.177.

imaginatively rather than literally, but accorded an authority greater than the merely metaphorical, can become luminous of a divine reality beyond human expression. This is not so much allegorical as sacramental.[54]

Mosshammer draws attention to the way in which Gregory 'describes the text of Scripture as a "veil" for hidden meanings':[55]

> The divine intention is hidden under the surface of the text, as it were by a screen (παραπετάσματί), as some commandment or story is set before the intelligent student. This is exactly the reason why the Apostle says that those who look to the bodily aspect of scripture have a veil (κάλυμμα) over their hearts, and are unable to see through to the glory of the spiritual law, being restrained by the veil covering the facial aspect of the lawgiver (*2 Cor* 3.13).[56]

Mosshammer comments,

> This veil is not merely a cloak behind which deeper meanings hide, but the indispensable verbal medium through which unspeakable truths are spoken. This veil is the 'body' of Scripture. Gregory uses the same language in reference to the flesh of Christ—His earthly body is a veil for the Godhead dwelling therein.[57]

He refers to *Against Eunomius* 3,9.13, which talks of the rich young man coming to Jesus (Matt. 19:16–22):

> He was not a person able to open the curtains (*katapetasma*) of the flesh and discern the hidden depth (*aduton*) of his godhead.[58]

This is tabernacle language. In the New Testament, *katapetasma* always refers to the inner veil of the temple or tabernacle.[59] In *Life of Moses*, Gregory tends to use it in the plural:[60]

> Near these were variegated veils (*katapetasmata*), lovingly crafted of woven fabric, the different colours intertwined with each other to produce the elegance of the weave. By these were separated that part of the tabernacle which was visible and accessible to some of those conducting ceremonies from that which was secret (*aduton*) and inaccessible.[61]

Douglass too 'stresses the parallel in Gregory's thought between Christ's incarnation in the flesh and his incarnation/expression in language'.[62] Having described the Cappadocian understanding of the incarnation in terms of a

---

[54] Young, *Biblical Exegesis and the Formation of Christian Culture*, 143–4.
[55] Mosshammer, 'Disclosing but not Disclosed', 111.
[56] *Eun.* 3,5.9 (GNO 2.163); trans. Hall.
[57] Mosshammer, 'Disclosing but not Disclosed', 111.   [58] GNO 2.268; trans. Hall.
[59] Matt. 27:51; Mark 15:38; Luke 23:45; Heb. 6:19, 9:3, 10:20.
[60] Except when alluding to Hebrews 10:20 at 2.178.   [61] *Vit. Moys.* 2.172.
[62] Morwenna Ludlow, *Gregory of Nyssa, Ancient and (Post)modern* (Oxford: Oxford University Press, 2007), 238.

metadiastemic intrusion,⁶³ he uses the same concept to illuminate their understanding of language: 'What the reconstitution of the *metadiastemic* intrusion provided for the Cappadocians was the possibility that God could simultaneously inhabit language and still remain Other to language.'⁶⁴ The same paradoxes recur: 'Dimensional man's ability to build a temple remains in tension with his inability to enter it. Language's ability to reconstitute the *metadiastemic* intrusion of Christ stands in tension with its inability to speak into its silence.'⁶⁵ Douglass emphasizes this silence:

> Language's *diastemic* ability to reconstitute the *metadiastemic* intrusion of Christ set in motion for the Cappadocians a disseminated discourse indelibly marked by its *epinoetic* genesis. Never more than tangential to an impenetrable space, a place of silence, a saturated absence, an entirely other world of inaccessible essence, theological discourse extended language to its uttermost limit.⁶⁶

That discourse can only proceed by producing a collection of names:

> The infinite and eternal silence, epiphanically inhabiting the *diasteme* while remaining other to it, generated in each of its visitations an infinite number of *diastemic* names—(non)names that could not name essentially. Since no single name could reconstitute the space of a *metadiastemic* intrusion, let alone enter it, the Cappadocians recognized the necessity of adapting a multiplicity of (in)appropriate names to Christ in order to gain, like Moses, an indirect glimpse of God.⁶⁷

'Tabernacle' does not feature in Gregory's other lists of divine names, nor is it among the many names discussed by Origen in *Commentary on John*. It is included in *Life of Moses* 2.177, with biblical support from John 1 and Colossians 1, in order to bolster Gregory's argument that the heavenly and earthly tabernacles were types of Christ. Mosshammer and Douglass, however, show that 'tabernacle' is more than another Johannine name alongside 'shepherd', 'bread', 'vine', 'way', and so on. It encapsulates Gregory's understanding both of the incarnation and of theological language. The tabernacle's holy of holies, the incarnation, and theological discourse all contain the uncontainable—the fullness of divinity, yet without giving human beings access to the essence of that fullness. 'Tabernacle' is both a divine name, and a metaphor for all divine names. As such it relates to the *oikonomia*, to the ways in which the *adiastemic* God enters into relationship with creation. I would therefore suggest that Gregory's use of the phrase 'in whom dwells the whole fullness of divinity' in *Life of Moses* 2.177 is a reference to the fullness out of which we have all received (John 1:16), the fullness present, yet inaccessible, in the tabernacle, the incarnation, and theological speech.

---

⁶³ See 8.3.
⁶⁴ Scot Douglass, *Theology of the Gap: Cappadocian Language Theory and the Trinitarian Controversy* (New York: Peter Lang, 2005), 163.
⁶⁵ Douglass, *Theology of the Gap*, 159.   ⁶⁶ Douglass, *Theology of the Gap*, 161.
⁶⁷ Douglass, *Theology of the Gap*, 174.

9.4 *LIFE OF MOSES* 2.176–177: HEAVENLY ASCENT CONTEXT

Divine names are a prominent feature of the Hekhalot texts. As Rachel Elior writes,

> Hekhalot literature conceives of the Divinity as a system of Holy Names woven about the Ineffable Name; the Ineffable Name itself is seen as inexplicable units of sound, embodying a supreme concentration of the divine power that created the Universe. In other words, the Ineffable Name transcends any linguistically defined meaning; it is the source of the essence, vitality and unity of Creation, the pivot of the mystical–theurgical knowledge associated with the being and oneness of Creation.[68]

Schäfer characterizes Hekhalot literature as moving 'between the two poles of the heavenly journey and the magical–theurgic adjuration',[69] with names playing a part in both 'poles': knowledge of divine names enables both ascent/descent to the *merkavah*, and the conjuration of angels. 'Through the names revealed by God, man has God at his disposal, as a result he has been given precisely the means by which he becomes master of the earth and heaven.'[70] *Hekhalot Rabbati* describes Neḥuniah ben ha-Qannah performing a heavenly ascent in front of his fellow scholars. He tells them:

> When a man wants to descend to the Merkavah, he should call Suriya, the Prince of the Countenance, and conjure him a hundred and twelve times in the name of Tetrasii, Lord God...He should neither add nor subtract from that number of a hundred and twelve, for if he does, he fatally endangers himself. His mouth should utter the names and his fingers should count a hundred and twelve, and he immediately descends and masters the Merkavah.[71]

On the dangerous journey, divine names are the passwords needed to overcome the fearsome angelic doorkeepers. As Michael Swartz writes,

> The secret to success is to possess elaborate divine names, often known as 'seals', which the traveller presents to the angelic guard, and to have esoteric knowledge of the heavenly topography and the names and characteristics of specific angels. If he presents these names successfully, the traveller is reassured that he has been expected and will be honoured by the heavenly hosts.[72]

---

[68] Rachel Elior, 'From Earthly Temple to Heavenly Shrines: Prayer and Sacred Song in the Hekhalot Literature and Its Relation to Temple Traditions', *Jewish Studies Quarterly*, 4 (1997), 250.
[69] Peter Schäfer, *The Hidden and Manifest God: Some Major Themes in Early Jewish Mysticism* (Albany: State University of New York Press, 1992), 150.
[70] Schäfer, *The Hidden and Manifest God*, 150.
[71] §204–5; trans. Ithamar Gruenwald, *Apocalyptic and Merkavah Mysticism* (Leiden: Brill, 1980), 105.
[72] Michael D. Swartz, 'Mystical Texts', in Shmuel Safrai et al. (eds), *The Literature of the Sages, second part: Midrash and Targum, Liturgy, Poetry, Mysticism, Contracts, Inscriptions, Ancient Science and the Languages of Rabbinic Literature* (Assen: Royal Van Gorcum, 2006), 405.

But the divine name is highly dangerous, it is 'enveloped in fire, flames of fire and hail', and must not fall into the wrong hands.[73] A text in *Hekhalot Zutarti* reworks Hillel's dictum in *m. Avot* 1:13 against ambition, and the improper use of Torah knowledge,[74] turning it into a warning against the unwarranted transmission of God's name:

> [R. Aqiva] used to say:
> Who spreads [his] name, loses his name,
> and who does not learn, deserves death.
> Who makes use of the crown, vanishes.
> Who does not know QYNTMYS', shall be put to death,
> and who knows QYNTMYS', will be desired in the world to come.[75]

QYNTMYS' has no obvious meaning, and yet here 'the knowledge or ignorance of this particular name decides the mystic's life or death'.[76] In *Hekhalot Zutarti*, Moses and Aqiva perform ascents in order to obtain divine names which enable instant learning:

> When Moses ascended on high to God, the Holy One, blessed be he, taught him:
> Anyone, whose heart goes astray,
> recite over him these names, in the name of… [*nomina barbara* follow],
> so that everything that I see and hear will be grasped by my heart,
> [namely] Bible, Mishnah, Talmud, Halakhot, and Haggadot,
> so that I will never forget,
> [not] in this world and not in the world to come….
> This is the name, which was revealed to R. 'Aqiva
> when he observed the working of the Merkavah.
> 'Aqiva [again] descended and taught it to his students.
>
> He said to them:
>
> My sons, handle this name carefully,
> [for] it is a [great] name,
> it is a holy name,
> it is a pure name.
> Because each one, who makes use of it in fright, in fear,
> in purity, in holiness, in humility,

---

[73] *Ma'aseh Merkavah* §552; trans. Michael D. Swartz, *Mystical Prayer in Ancient Judaism: An Analysis of Ma'aseh Merkavah* (Tübingen: Mohr Siebeck, 1992), 230.

[74] 'Who spreads his name, loses his name, and one who does not add, perishes. Who does not study, deserves death, and who makes use of the crown, vanishes'; trans. Peter Schäfer, *The Origins of Jewish Mysticism* (Tübingen: Mohr Siebeck, 2009), 292.

[75] §360; trans. Schäfer, *The Hidden and Manifest God*, 71.

[76] Schäfer, *The Origins of Jewish Mysticism*, 292.

> will multiply the seeds,
> be successful in all his endeavours,
> and his days shall be long.[77]

Just as the climax of the liturgy in the temple had been the enunciation of the divine name,[78] so too in heaven 'the angelic hosts pronounce the names of God in their daily recitation of hymns and praises, and the pronouncement of The Name seems to be a central aspect of their devotions'.[79] A particularly dramatic ceremony is described in one manuscript of *Hekhalot Zutarti*:

> And that youth whose name is Metatron brings whispering fire and places it in the ears of the Hayyot, so that they should not hear the voice of the Holy One, blessed be He, speaking, and the Ineffable Name that the youth whose name is Metatron pronounces at that time in seven voices in the name of the Living and Pure and Venerated and Awesome.... YHWH, I am that I am, the Living, YHWH, YWAY, HKH HH WH HWH WHW HH HY HH HH YHY HYH YHY YHWH...this shall be my Name for ever, my appellation for all eternity.[80]

Ma'aseh Merkavah is largely a collection of prayers with 'a distinctly liturgical quality',[81] some of which centre around the divine name:

> Your name is holy in the highest heavens;
> high and exalted over all of the Cherubim.
> Let your name be sanctified in Your holiness,
> let it be magnified in Your greatness,
> let it be strengthened in might,
> and Your dominion to the end of all generations.
> For Your might is forever and ever.
> Blessed are You, YY, magnificent in strength, great in power.[82]

Schäfer comments that this and similar texts 'often read like an explication of the liturgical response to the uttering of the tetragram: "Blessed be the name of the glory of his kingdom forever and ever."'[83] This signals the links between Hekhalot mysticism and not only temple liturgy, but also the ongoing synagogue liturgy. In talking of God in Hekhalot literature, Schäfer argues that 'it is still the same God of Rabbinic Judaism who is the object of desire of the Merkavah mystic, but this God consists, so to speak, of names'. He says that 'what Scholem has said on later manifestations of Jewish mysticism equally applies to Merkavah

---

[77] §336–7; trans. Schäfer, *The Hidden and Manifest God*, 67–8.
[78] See *m. Yoma* 3:8, 6:2.
[79] Rachel Elior, 'The Concept of God in Hekhalot Literature', in Joseph Dan (ed.), *Studies in Jewish Thought* (New York: Praeger, 1989), 104.
[80] §390; trans. Elior, 'From Earthly Temple to Heavenly Shrines', 249.
[81] Swartz, 'Mystical Texts', 409.
[82] §590; trans. Swartz, *Mystical Prayer in Ancient Judaism*, 246.
[83] Schäfer, *The Hidden and Manifest God*, 78–9.

mysticism: "As such, the revelation is one of the name or names of God, which are perhaps the various modi of his active being. The language of God has no grammar. It consists only of names."[84]

Karl Grözinger insists that 'name' in the context of the Hekhalot texts 'has a totally different connotation from what we mean by a "name" in the modern social and legal sense':[85]

> A name within the scope of Hekhalot-texts is not a simple appelation, nor a convention for the purpose of naming and recognizing persons, but...a name itself is a venerable bearer of power, indeed, it is a hypostasis of inherent power and function.[86]

Divine names are assumed to have power, because they give access to the being of God. In this, there are parallels between 'glory' and 'name'. Just as 'glory' is a visible manifestation of God, so the 'name' of God is an aural manifestation. These parallels go back to the Bible: when Moses asks to see the glory of God, God replies, 'I will make all my goodness pass before you, and will proclaim before you my name "The LORD (יהוה)".... But you cannot see my face...'[87] In Exodus the tabernacle is the place of God's glory, in Deuteronomy the central sanctuary is the place of God's name.[88] Moshe Weinfeld argues that 'the difference in terminology reflects a conceptual difference. P thought of God in a more corporeal way...Deuteronomy thinks of God more abstractly.' He admits, however, that 'both *šēm* [name] and *kābôḏ* [glory] express semantically the majesty of sovereign divine power.'[89] Turning back to the Hekhalot texts, there seems to be 'a real resemblance, if not an identity, of God and His Name':[90]

> He is His name, and His name is He;
> He is in Him, and His name is in His name;
> Song is His name and His name is Song.[91]

Grözinger goes as far as to suggest that 'the God of these mystics is strictly speaking nothing else than the hypostasis of His own Name. He and His Name

---

[84] Peter Schäfer, 'Merkavah Mysticism and Magic', in Peter Schäfer and Joseph Dan (eds), *Gershom Scholem's Major Trends in Jewish Mysticism 50 Years After: Proceedings of the Sixth International Conference on the History of Jewish Mysticism* (Tübingen: Mohr Siebeck, 1993), 76.
[85] Karl Erich Grözinger, 'The Names of God and the Celestial Powers: Their Function and Meaning in the Hekhalot Literature', in Joseph Dan (ed.), *Early Jewish Mysticism: Proceedings of the First International Conference on the History of Jewish Mysticism (Jerusalem, February 1984)* (Jerusalem: Hamakor, 1987), 54.
[86] Grözinger, 'The Names of God and the Celestial Powers', 58.   [87] Exod. 33:19–20.
[88] Compare Exod. 40:34 with Deut. 12:11.
[89] Moshe Weinfeld, 'כָּבוֹד', in G. Johannes Botterweck, Helmer Ringgren, and Heinz-Josef Fabry (eds), *Theological Dictionary of the Old Testament* (Grand Rapids, Mich.: Eerdmans, 1995), 7.37.
[90] Grözinger, 'The Names of God and the Celestial Powers', 60.
[91] *Ma'aseh Merkavah* §588; trans. Swartz, *Mystical Prayer in Ancient Judaism*, 244.

are one.'⁹² Just like glory, however, names can be dangerous, and they hide as well as reveal. Names promise access, yet the long lists of unpronounceable, nonsensical combinations of letters seem to indicate rather the ungraspability of the divine.

9.5 *LIFE OF MOSES* 2.176–177: CONCLUSIONS

The Hekhalot texts seem worlds away from Gregory. But maybe the distance is not as great as we think. Christians knew of Jewish scruples about pronouncing the divine name, hence Clement's reference to the 'mystic name of four letters'.⁹³ Young argues that Christian understandings of God were influenced by Jewish ideas, particularly as transmitted by Hellenistic writers such as Philo and Josephus:

> It is the congruence of Platonic and Hellenistic–Jewish motifs which contributed to the Christian understanding of God. The fact that Jews never pronounced God's name, never made images of him, and used scriptures which asserted that the greatest prophet of all had no direct confrontation with God, 'for no one can see God and live', undoubtedly contributed to this 'negative' Jewish theology. Words emphasizing God's otherness and incomparability seem to have been particularly characteristic of Hellenistic Judaism, and so entered Christian tradition: God is unapproachable (ἀπρόσιτος), untraceable (ἀνεξιχνίαστος) and inscrutable (ἀνεξερεύνητος); so he is incomprehensible (ἀκατάληπτος). Not surprisingly many of the terms of Hellenistic Judaism and of philosophy overlapped, and in Christian tradition they tended to be amalgamated, as previously in Philo, so as to point to a more ultimate transcendence than the mainstream Platonist tradition suggested. Thus God came to be regarded as beyond human understanding, as well as beyond human language.⁹⁴

This puts the emphasis on the positive influence of Hellenistic Jews who wrote using apophatic philosophical terms. Was Gregory also reacting to, and guarding against, suggestions that God could be reached by the use of the right names? He will not have known the Hekhalot texts, but he must have been familiar with the power widely attributed to divine names, commented on, after all, in Origen. Daniélou posits a link between Eunomius and contemporary neoplatonists via Aetius, and it is not far-fetched to suggest that Gregory knew something of the ideas of Iamblichus and his disciples.⁹⁵ But there is no need to argue that he was countering any one particular text or

---

⁹² Grözinger, 'The Names of God and the Celestial Powers', 61.
⁹³ *Strom.* 5.34.5, see 9.2.
⁹⁴ Young, 'The God of the Greeks and the Nature of Religious Language', 53.
⁹⁵ Daniélou, 'Eunome l'Arien et l'exégèse néo-platonicienne du Cratyle', 428.

set of ideas. This chapter has highlighted the importance of names in the Late Antique world, and therefore placed Gregory's debates with Eunomius into a much wider context. In some Hekhalot texts the goal of heavenly ascent is to obtain divine names. And Gregory has turned Moses' vision of the heavenly tabernacle into an understanding of a new name for God: 'tabernacle'. But he insists that this is only one name among many, none of which give access to the essence of God. He accordingly plays down the importance of the high priest's *petalon*: there is no one name which gives access to the holy of holies. Hekhalot literature, by contrast, ascribes great power to divine names, hinting that they provide access to the innermost chambers of heaven, and to the secrets of creation. And yet the multiplication of those names undercuts this suggestion of power. There clearly is no one all-powerful divine name to which human beings have access. Frenzied attempts are made to reach it, but the longer the lists of unintelligible letters become, the further away the goal seems. Paradoxically, the Hekhalot texts illustrate Gregory's thesis: progress towards the divine is infinite, an ever-receding horizon.

10

Heavenly Powers

> Surely then the pillars bright with silver and plated with gold, the carrying-poles and rings, and those cherubim, covering the ark with their wings, and all the other elements which the description of the tabernacle's construction contains, if one examines them by looking to things above, are the supercosmic powers (ὑπερκόσμιοι δυνάμεις), which are contemplated in the tabernacle, and which undergird everything in keeping with the divine will.[1]

10.1 *LIFE OF MOSES* 2.178–183: BIBLICAL CONTEXT

Having designated the heavenly tabernacle a type of Christ, Gregory argues that not only does Moses' vision as a whole correspond to the name 'tabernacle', but each element of furniture leads 'to the contemplation of a concept fitting to God'.[2] In order to decipher the meaning of the furniture, he turns to Colossians 1:16:

> For [the apostle] says somewhere about the Only-begotten, who, we have perceived, corresponds to the tabernacle, that 'in him all things were created, visible and invisible, whether thrones (θρόνοι) or authorities (ἐξουσίαι) or principalities (ἀρχαί) or dominions (κυριότητες)' or powers (δυνάμεις).[3]

This enables him to interpret the contents of the tabernacle not cosmologically, or Christologically, but 'angelologically'. Daniélou points out that this personalizes the Platonic world of Forms:

> Les objets contenus dans le Tabernacle sont les réalités du monde céleste. Mais ce monde céleste n'est pas le monde des idées impersonnelles, des archétypes, mais celui des anges personnels.[4]

---

[1] *Vit. Moys.* 2.179.   [2] *Vit. Moys.* 2.178.   [3] *Vit. Moys.* 2.179.
[4] 'The objects within the Tabernacle are the realities of the heavenly world. This heavenly world, however, is not the world of impersonal ideas, of archetypes, but that of personal angels.' Jean Daniélou, *Grégoire de Nysse: La Vie de Moïse, ou Traité de la perfection en matière de vertu* (Paris: Cerf, 2000), 225 n. 2.

Since Gregory goes on to interpret the earthly tabernacle ecclesiologically, we are presented with a picture of Christ's celestial tabernacle/body consisting of angels, and his earthly tabernacle/body consisting of the church. Gregory, however, does not draw attention to this parallelism. And he is not totally consistent in his angelological interpretation, correlating some of the furniture with angels, but some with Christ or the Spirit. He does not here maintain the strict boundary between uncreated and created one might expect from his doctrinal position.

Having made his general statement, Gregory goes on to examine some of the details. He characterizes the heavenly powers as supporting the universe (τὸ πᾶν ὑπερείδουσαι), thus relating them to pillars. He moves on to the bearing poles and rings (ἀναφορεῖς καὶ δακτύλιοι). He has not mentioned these in either of his general tabernacle descriptions.[5] He is referring to the carrying-poles which were slipped through the rings attached to the sides of ark, and left there permanently,[6] interpreting them as follows:

> There are found our true carrying-poles, 'sent forth to serve for the sake of those who are to obtain salvation', which are inserted, as though through rings, through the souls of us who are being saved, and thereby carry those lying on the earth up to the height of virtue.[7]

He is quoting Hebrews 1:14, which speaks of ministering spirits being sent forth to serve. Earlier in the treatise, in the context of the brotherly assistance given to Moses by Aaron, he has said that God appoints 'an angel with an incorporeal nature to help in the life of each person'.[8] This good angel 'by rational demonstration shows the benefits of virtue which are seen in hope by those who live aright'.[9]

From the poles and rings of the ark, Gregory moves to the cherubim above it, saying that 'we have learnt that this is the name of the powers envisaged around the divine nature (τῶν περὶ τὴν θείαν φύσιν θεωρουμένων δυνάμεων), as Isaiah and Ezekiel observed'.[10] In *To Theophilus, Against the Apollinarians*, Gregory places Moses' vision of the heavenly tabernacle in parallel to Elijah's fiery ascent, Isaiah and Ezekiel's visions, and Paul's entry into Paradise:

> If everyone had the ability to come, as Moses did, inside the cloud, where Moses saw what may not be seen, or to be raised above three heavens as Paul was and to be instructed in Paradise about ineffable things that lie above reason, or to be taken up in fire to the ethereal region, as zealous Elijah was, and not to be weighed down by the body's baggage, or to see on the throne of glory, as Ezekiel and Isaiah did, the one who is raised above the Cherubim and glorified by the

---

[5] *Vit. Moys.* 1.49–50 and 2.170–172.   [6] Exod. 25:12–15.   [7] *Vit. Moys.* 2.180.
[8] *Vit. Moys.* 2.45; trans. Malherbe and Ferguson, 45.
[9] *Vit. Moys.* 2.46; trans. Malherbe and Ferguson, 45.   [10] *Vit. Moys.* 2.180.

Seraphim—then surely if all were like this, there would be no need for the appearance of our God in flesh.[11]

In all these ascents, human beings glimpse the heavenly world and its angelic powers. This understanding enables Gregory to conflate the cherubim of Exodus and Ezekiel with the seraphim of Isaiah. Such conflation was commonplace, especially in liturgy, as Jerome testifies with a complaint:

> The mistake—although a pious one—of those also is to be reprehended who in their prayers and oblations venture to say: 'Thou that sittest above the cherubim and the seraphim.' For it is written that God sits above the cherubim…but no Scripture states that God sits above the seraphim…[12]

Indeed the conflation starts in the New Testament: the living creatures of Revelation 4:6–11 fuse Isaiah's seraphim with Ezekiel's cherubim. Gregory includes the cherubim/seraphim amongst the heavenly powers. In *Against Eunomius* 1 he argues against those who suggest that they are to be reckoned above creation, or on a par with the Holy Spirit, saying that in Colossians 1:16 Paul includes the cherubim under 'thrones', and the seraphim under 'powers'.[13] But elsewhere in his works the phrase 'around the divine nature' (περὶ τὴν θείαν φύσιν) denotes 'all that is manifest in God, all his potentially self disclosing attributes, that is the fullness of his positive perfections'.[14] In other words, it designates God's energies/activities/operations (ἐνέργειαι). For example, in *On the Beatitudes*, he says,

> [God] who is by nature invisible becomes visible in his operations (ἐνεργείαις), being seen in certain cases by the properties he possesses (ἔν τισι τοῖς περὶ αὐτὸν ἰδιώμασι καθορώμενος).[15]

In *Life of Moses*, the word 'powers' has been added to the phrase 'around the divine nature'; but, even so, the impression is given that the cherubim have become symbols of those things about the divine which can be known. They represent God's visible properties. In Exodus 25:18–22, the cherubim cover

---

[11] GNO 3,1.123–124; trans. Gary A. Anderson, 'Towards a Theology of the Tabernacle and Its Furniture', in Ruth A. Clements and Daniel R. Schwartz (eds), *Text, Thought, and Practice in Qumran and Early Christianity: Proceedings of the Ninth International Symposium of the Orion Center for the Study of the Dead Sea Scrolls and Associated Literature, Jointly Sponsored by the Hebrew University Center for the Study of Christianity, 11–13 January, 2004* (Leiden: Brill, 2009), 187.

[12] *Epist*. 18B 1.4; trans. Mierow, 97–8.

[13] *Eun*. 1.306–313 (GNO 1.117–119); cf. *Ref. Eun*. 196 (GNO 2.395). The list in Col. 1:16 does not, in fact, include 'powers'. In *Eun*. 1.307 Gregory gives the contents of that list correctly (although in a different order); but in *Eun*. 1.313 and *Ref. Eun*. 196, as in *Vit. Moys*. 2.179, he adds 'powers', presumably on the basis of Eph. 1:21: '…above all rule (ἀρχῆς) and authority (ἐξουσίας) and power (δυνάμεως) and dominion (κυριότητος)…'

[14] Verna E. F. Harrison, *Grace and Human Freedom according to St. Gregory of Nyssa* (Lewiston, NY: Edwin Mellen, 1992), 47.

[15] *Beat*. 6 (GNO 7,2.141.25–27); trans. Hall, 69.

the ark of the testimony with their wings. The LXX translates Isaiah 6:2, with its description of the seraphim's wings, as:

> ... with two they covered the face (τὸ πρόσωπον), and with two they covered the feet (τοὺς πόδας), and with two they flew.[16]

Whose face and feet are being referred to? Early Christian writers assumed that the face and feet of God were being shielded from view.[17] Gregory is thus able to equate the ark with the face of God:

> For the same thing is called 'ark of the covenant' in one place, and 'face' (*prosōpon*) in the other; and in the one it is the ark which is covered by wings, and in the other it is the face; as though what is being apprehended in both cases is the one symbolic representation, so it seems to me, of the impossibility of understanding ineffable things.[18]

The word *prosōpon*, however, is not only the Greek for 'face', an accurate translation of the Hebrew *panim*, it also carries theological resonance. The Cappadocians developed a Trinitarian terminology (which became the orthodox norm) of one divine *ousia* and three *hypostases* or *prosōpa*. Gregory writes:

> Thus, inasmuch as the Father is different from the Son and from the Holy Spirit, we profess the three Persons (*prosōpa*) of the Father and of the Son and of the Holy Spirit. In the same way, because the Father does not differ from the Son and the Holy Spirit according to essence, we say that there is one essence (*ousia*) of the Father and of the Son and of the Holy Spirit.[19]

So the ark/face—the ineffable things (τῶν ἀπορρήτων)—covered by the wings of the cherubim/seraphim, represents the person of Christ. In *Refutation of the Confession of Faith of Eunomius*, however, Gregory insists that Isaiah's vision, along with 'every specially divine vision, every theophany, every word uttered in the Person of God, is to be understood to refer to the Father, the Son, and the Holy Spirit.'[20] So although his interpretation of the ark focuses on the person of Christ, in line with the heavenly tabernacle as a type of Christ, the ineffable things are common to all three divine persons.

Exodus 25:31–39 contains a detailed, if somewhat obscure, description of the seven-branched lampstand which was to stand in the holy place, just outside the holy of holies (Exod. 26:35). Nowhere does Gregory mention its placement; but he describes it as solid gold, 'a lampstand with a single base stem

---

[16] My translation.   [17] See Origen *Cels.* 6.18, or Jerome *Epist.* 18A 7.1–2.
[18] *Vit. Moys.* 2.180 (Daniélou) or 2.181 (Malherbe and Ferguson).
[19] *Graec.* (GNO 3,1.21); trans. Stramara, 382–3.
[20] *Ref. Eun.* 193 (GNO 2.394); trans. NPNF² 5.129. Gregory interprets Isaiah 6 in the light of John 12:41 and Acts 28:25–27. Didymus the Blind was the first to bring these passages together in order to prove that the seraphim were worshipping the Trinity. This was to counter Origen's interpretation of the seraphim as Christ and the Holy Spirit. See Lucien Chavoutier, 'Querelle origeniste et controverses trinitaires à propos du *Tractatus contra Origenem de visione Isaiae*', *Vigiliae christianae*, 14 (1960), 11–12.

which divided into seven branches at the top, holding up an equal number of lights on the branches'.[21] He interprets it in terms of the Holy Spirit:

> And should you hear about lamps being held up by many branches stemming from one lampstand, so that ample intense light is projected all around, you would not be wrong to interpret them as the varied sparks of the Spirit shining conspicuously in this tabernacle; as Isaiah says, when he divides into seven the lights of the Spirit.[22]

He has turned the 'seven eyes' of Zechariah 4:10, and the 'seven spirits' of Revelation 4:5 and 5:6, into attributes of the one Spirit, thanks to LXX Isaiah 11:2–3—'And the spirit of God shall rest on him, the spirit of wisdom and understanding, the spirit of counsel and might, the spirit of knowledge and godliness. The spirit of the fear of God will fill him.'[23] Malherbe and Ferguson comment:

> In view of Gregory's role in establishing the deity of the Holy Spirit in the doctrinal controversies of the time, it is striking that the Holy Spirit appears so seldom [in *Life of Moses*] and then never in a strictly theological context. The Holy Spirit was the means of the incarnation (II, 216), and now 'grace...flourishes through the Spirit' (II, 187). Gregory commends those before him who interpreted the cloud that led the Israelites as the Holy Spirit (II, 121), and he considers the lamps in the tabernacle to represent the rays of the Spirit (II, 181).[24]

If the ark represents the person of Christ, then to make the lampstand, which stands outside the holy of holies, represent the Holy Spirit seems to contradict Gregory's insistence on equality between the persons of the Trinity. But the equation of the Holy Spirit with light does tie in with his Trinitarian theology:

> For since it is said *their angels always behold the face of my Father who is in heaven* (Mt 18.10) and it is not possible to behold the *hypostasis* of the Father otherwise than by fixing the gaze upon it through his impress, and *the impress of the hypostasis* (Heb 1.3) of the Father is the Only-begotten (Jn 1.14,18), and again to him no-one can draw near whose mind has not been illumined (καταυγασθείς) by the Holy Spirit...[25]

It is by the light of the Spirit that Christians draw near to God.

From the lampstand, Gregory moves on to the mercy seat (כפרת; ἱλαστήριον). Here Romans 3:25 supplies the interpretation:

> The mercy seat, I think, needs no interpretation, since the apostle exposed what is hidden when he said, 'whom God put forward as a mercy seat' for our souls.[26]

---

[21] *Vit. Moys.* 2.171.   [22] *Vit. Moys.* 2.181.   [23] Trans. NETS.
[24] Abraham J. Malherbe and Everett Ferguson, *Gregory of Nyssa: The Life of Moses* (New York: Paulist Press, 1978), 15–16.
[25] *Eust.* (GNO 3,1.13); trans. Silvas, 243.
[26] *Vit. Moys.* 2.182. Unlike English translations, Gregory takes ἱλαστήριον not as an abstract noun (propitiation, expiation, sacrifice for atonement...), but in its invariable LXX sense of 'mercy seat' (cf. Heb. 9:5).

Gregory does not expand further. If the ark represents Christ, then it makes sense that its cover should represent the reconciliation he effected on humanity's behalf. But, as with his earlier allusion to Hebrews 1:14, one gets the impression that Gregory is trying to shoehorn New Testament verses, and their traditional interpretations, into his new interpretation of the tabernacle. It means that the passion becomes part of the incomprehensible, ineffable mystery, shielded by the cherubim's wings.

The altar of offering (θυσιαστήριον) and the altar of incense (θυμιατήριον) suggest to Gregory 'the adoration by heavenly beings which is continuously performed in this tabernacle'.²⁷ This will be looked at further in Chapter 12.

Gregory's last section on the heavenly tabernacle concerns 'skin dipped in red dye and woven hairs'.²⁸ The materials for the construction of the tabernacle, listed in Exodus 25:3–7, include goats' hair (עזים; τρίχας αἰγείας) and rams' skins dyed red (ערת אילם מאדמים; δέρματα κριῶν ἠρυθροδανωμένα). The tabernacle was to have three or four coverings: the first made of multicoloured cloth with cherubim woven into it (Exod. 26:1), the second of goats' hair (Exod. 26:7), and the third of red rams' skins, together with the enigmatic ערת תחשים (RSV: goatskins; NJPS: dolphin skins), which the LXX translates as blue skins (δέρματα ὑακίνθινα) (Exod. 26:14). Gregory interprets the red skins and woven hair as a foretelling of the saving passion:

> ...the redness representing blood, and the hair death. For hair on the body is without sensation, therefore it rightly becomes a symbol of death.²⁹

He has thus made the passion part of the eternal, heavenly Christ. It is not entirely clear, however, how this fits either with the angelological interpretation of the tabernacle, or with the redemption symbolized by the mercy seat.

10.2 *LIFE OF MOSES* 2.178–183: ALEXANDRIAN CONTEXT

Within his overall cosmological interpretation of the tabernacle, Philo distinguishes between the realm of sense (αἰσθητά) and the realm of mind (νοητά), although he is not altogether consistent about where the dividing line comes. Sometimes he interprets the tabernacle tent (comprising both the holy of holies and its forecourt) as the realm of mind, with the outside court as the realm of sense;³⁰ and sometimes only the holy of holies, or the ark within it, is the incorporeal, intelligible world.³¹ As Koester notes, 'in *Mos.* 2.101–108, the

---

²⁷ *Vit. Moys.* 2.182.   ²⁸ *Vit. Moys.* 2.183.   ²⁹ *Vit. Moys.* 2.183.
³⁰ *Mos.* 2.81, cf. *Ebr.* 134.   ³¹ *Q.E.* 2.69, 83, 94.

furnishings of the forecourt correspond to heaven, earth, and sea, which are presumably in the realm of sense'.[32] It is with his interpretation of the contents of the holy of holies that Philo indulges in speculation on the heavenly powers. He is particularly interested in cherubim, discussing them in seven of his treatises.[33] He offers an etymology of the word 'cherubim'—recognition and full knowledge (ἐπίγνωσις καὶ ἐπιστήμη πολλή)[34]—and several alternative explanations of their symbolism. In *On Moses* 2.98 he interprets them cosmologically as 'symbols of the two hemispheres, one above the earth and one under it, for the whole heaven has wings'. He goes on to say,

> I should myself say that they are allegorical representations of the two most august and highest potencies (δυνάμεις) of Him that is, the creative and the kingly (ποιητικὴν καὶ βασιλικήν).[35]

In *Questions on Exodus* 2.68 and *On Flight and Finding* 100–101 he comments on LXX Exodus 25:21—'I will speak to you (λαλήσω σοι) from above the mercy seat between the two cherubim'—introducing a whole hierarchy of powers into the holy of holies, which bridge the gap between God (ὁ ὤν or τὸ ὄν) and the world of Platonic Forms:

> ...if you make the beginning from the upper end, (you will find) the Speaker (τὸν λέγοντα) first, and the Logos (τὸν λόγον) second, and the creative power (τὴν ποιητικὴν δύναμιν) third, and the ruling (power) (τὴν ἀρχήν) fourth, and then, below the creative, the beneficent (power) (τὴν εὐεργέτιν) fifth, and, below the royal, the punitive (power) (τὴν κολαστήριον) sixth, and the world of ideas (τὸν ἐκ τῶν ἰδεῶν κόσμον) seventh.[36]

He describes these powers in terms of a chariot, alluding both to the chariot in Plato's *Phaedrus* and to the biblical imagery of the cherubim as God's chariot. He interprets 'I will speak to you' as referring to God's communication with the Logos:

> ...while the Word is the charioteer of the Powers (ἡνίοχον τῶν δυνάμεων), He who talks is seated in the chariot, giving directions to the charioteer for the right wielding of the reins of the Universe.[37]

As described in 8.2, the Logos appears in a variety of guises in Philo's allegorization of the tabernacle, including as the central branch of the lampstand.[38] But since the holy of holies represents God's presence, and human access to that presence, it makes sense that the ark, the cherubim, and God speaking from

---

[32] Craig R. Koester, *The Dwelling of God: The Tabernacle in the Old Testament, Intertestamental Jewish Literature, and the New Testament* (Washington, DC: Catholic Biblical Association of America, 1989), 61.
[33] *Cher.* 21–29, *Her.* 166, *Fug.* 100–101, *Mos.* 2.97–100, *QG* 1.57, *QE* 2.62–68, *Deo* 4–9.
[34] *Mos.* 2.97. [35] *Mos.* 2.99, cf. *Cher.* 27–28. [36] *QE* 2.68; cf. *Fug.* 100–101.
[37] *Fug.* 101. [38] *Her.* 216, 225.

above them, enable Philo to set out his vision of how the Logos and its powers mediate between the transcendent God and the created world. For, as he says,

> The most lucid and most prophetic mind receives the knowledge and science of the Existent One not from the Existent One Himself, for it will not contain His greatness, but from his chief and ministering powers.[39]

Like Philo, Clement correlates the layout of the temple/tabernacle with the division between the sensible and the intelligible worlds. For him this also symbolizes the different categories of Christian believer.[40] He gives a couple of interpretations of the intermediate space, accessible to priests, between the outer covering and the veil:

> ...they say that this is the middlemost point of heaven and earth. But others say it is the symbol of the intellectual and sensible world.[41]

Of the lampstand standing in this intermediate space, he starts off by saying that it shows 'the motions of the seven light-bearing stars (φωσφόρων),'[42] but then adds:

> The golden candlestick has another enigma of the sign of Christ, not only by its form but also by its casting light at many times and in many ways on those who believe and hope in him and look at him through the service of the first-created beings (τῶν πρωτοκτίστων). And they say that the seven eyes of the Lord are the seven spirits resting on the rod that springs from the root of Jesse.[43]

The seven first-created beings also appear in *Excerpts from Theodotus* 10–12, chapters attributed to Clement:[44]

> [The Seven] have received perfection from the beginning, at the time of the first creation from God through the Son.... they 'always behold the face of the Father' and the face of the Father is the Son, through whom the Father is known.... they see not with an eye of sense, but with the eye of mind, such as the Father provided.[45]

In the *Miscellanies* they are linked to the lampstand thanks to the 'seven eyes' of Zechariah 4:10, the 'seven spirits' from Revelation 4:5 and 5:6, and 'the rod that springs from the root of Jesse' from Isaiah 11:1. Their presence in the intermediate space is probably best seen as a foretaste of what is behind the veil. For there is the 'intellectual world' (*noētos kosmos*), which is also the

---

[39] *QE* 2.67.   [40] See 4.2.
[41] *Strom.* 5.33.2; trans. Annewies van den Hoek, *Clement of Alexandria and His Use of Philo in the Stromateis: An Early Christian Reshaping of a Jewish Model* (Leiden: Brill, 1988), 122.
[42] *Strom.* 5.34.8–9; trans. van den Hoek, *Clement of Alexandria and His Use of Philo*, 128; cf. Philo *Mos.* 2.102.
[43] *Strom.* 5.35.1–2; trans. van den Hoek, *Clement of Alexandria and His Use of Philo*, 128.
[44] On the attribution to Clement, see F. Sagnard, *Clément d'Alexandrie: Extraits de Théodote* (Paris: Cerf, 1948), 8, 12.
[45] *Exc.* 10; trans. Casey, 49.

angelic world.⁴⁶ According to *Excerpts from Theodotus* 27, it is when the soul enters behind the veil that it 'passes into the spiritual realm and becomes now truly rational and high priestly, so that it might now be animated, so to speak, directly by the Logos, just as the archangels became the high-priests of the angels, and the First-Created the high-priests of the archangels'.⁴⁷

In the holy of holies are the ark and the cherubim. Clement gives several interpretations for each of these, reflecting a variety of source material. The ark might signify 'the eighth region and the world of thought (*noētos kosmos*)', or 'God, all-embracing, and without shape, and invisible', or 'the repose which dwells with the adoring spirits, which are meant by the cherubim'.⁴⁸ These at least are not mutually incompatible. When it comes to the cherubim, he 'chops his [picture] up with manifold alternative interpretations, sometimes contradicting himself in the process'.⁴⁹ In *Miscellanies* 5.35.6–7 he connects them with the world of sense:

> Indeed, those golden figures, each of them with six wings, signify either the constellations of the two Bears, as some will have it, or rather the two hemispheres. And the name cherubim meant 'much knowledge'. But both together have twelve wings and by zodiac and by time, which moves on it, point to the world of sense.⁵⁰

In the next paragraph they are identified with the intelligible realm:

> But the face is a symbol of the rational soul, and the wings are the lofty ministers and energies of powers right and left; and the voice is delightsome glory in ceaseless contemplation.⁵¹

We see the influence of Philo in the mention of the two hemispheres and in the etymology. But Clement obviously has other sources of cosmological information. He goes on to quote from a tragedy he attributes to Euripides (now reattributed to Critias), which mentions the twin bears.⁵² When it comes to the intelligible realm, the wings of the cherubim represent the service and activities of 'powers right and left'. These are not Philo's two chief powers, representing divine activity in the cosmos. On the basis of an Armenian fragment, Alain Le Boulluec identifies them as angels of judgement: those on the left expel people who persevere in doing evil, while those on the right embrace the penitent.⁵³ Runia points out, however, that

> The basic opposition between punishment and beneficence is the same as we find in the Philonic doctrine of the powers, especially in *QE* 2.68, where the merciful

---

⁴⁶ *Strom.* 5.34.7. ⁴⁷ *Exc.* 27.3; trans. Casey, 61.
⁴⁸ *Strom.* 5.36.3; text Le Boulluec, 1.85; trans. Wilson, 242.
⁴⁹ Van den Hoek, *Clement of Alexandria and His Use of Philo*, 133.
⁵⁰ Trans. van den Hoek, *Clement of Alexandria and His Use of Philo*, 130.
⁵¹ *Strom.* 5.36.4; trans. Wilson, 242–3.
⁵² See Alain Le Boulluec, *Clément d'Alexandrie: Les Stromates, Stromate V*, 2 vols (Paris: Cerf, 1981), 2.147–8.
⁵³ Le Boulluec, *Clément d'Alexandrie: Les Stromates, Stromate V*, 2.151.

power is introduced as subordinate to the beneficent power and the punitive power as subordinate to the ruling power.⁵⁴

Despite the confusion, and the piling up of interpretations, the key phrases in Clement's interpretation of the ark and the cherubim would seem to be 'the repose which dwells with the adoring spirits' and 'delightsome glory in ceaseless contemplation'. These tie in with his description of the high priest entering the holy of holies.

Heavenly powers do not play a major role in Origen's interpretations of the tabernacle. In *Homilies on Numbers* 5, in the context of the tabernacle being carried on the shoulders (Num. 7:9), he refers to both Hebrews 1:14 and LXX Psalm 90:11–12—'Since he commanded his angels concerning you that they should lift you up in their hands, lest you strike your foot against a stone'—in order to justify his interpretation that those who are truly holy are being carried by angels towards the promised land.⁵⁵ In *Commentary on Romans*, whilst dealing with Romans 3:25, he interprets the mercy seat as the soul of Jesus. It is made of pure gold because Jesus 'committed no sin nor was deceit found in his mouth';⁵⁶ and its measurements are 2.5 by 1.5 cubits because 'this holy soul was a certain mid-point between the divinity of the Trinity and the frailty of humanity'.⁵⁷ The cherubim signify 'that the Word of God, who is the only begotten Son, and his Holy Spirit always dwell in the propitiatory, that is, in the soul of Jesus'.⁵⁸ The ark of the covenant 'can be understood of his holy flesh in which this blessed soul is placed', or else as 'the heavenly powers (*uirtutes caelestes*)'. For 'they too are capable of containing the Word of God and the Holy Spirit; but the soul of Jesus is placed before them, and by his mediation, as it were, they receive the divinely bestowed grace'.⁵⁹ God speaks from between the cherubim (Exod. 25:22) because it is only through the Son and the Spirit that God becomes known.⁶⁰ Elsewhere, Origen interprets the seraphim of Isaiah 6 along similar lines, saying that he learnt this from his Hebrew teacher.⁶¹ Hannah argues that although Origen regarded the seraphim and cherubim as symbols of the Son and the Holy Spirit, he 'did not deduce from the use of these symbols the conclusion that the Son and the Spirit belonged to the angelic realm'.⁶² Origen was drawing on a Jewish Christian exegetical tradition going back to the end of the first century or, at the latest, the opening decades of the second, in which Isaiah's vision of the Lord flanked by seraphim was

---

⁵⁴ David T. Runia, 'Clement of Alexandria and the Philonic Doctrine of the Divine Power(s)', *Vigiliae christianae*, 58: 3 (2004), 263.
⁵⁵ *Hom. Num.* 5.3.3; trans. Scheck, 19–20.
⁵⁶ *Comm. Rom.* 3.8.3; trans. Scheck, 218. Cf. LXX Isa. 53:9, 1 Pet. 2:22.
⁵⁷ *Comm. Rom.* 3.8.4; trans. Scheck, 219.   ⁵⁸ *Comm. Rom.* 3.8.5; trans. Scheck, 220.
⁵⁹ *Comm. Rom.* 3.8.7; text Hammond Bammel, 1.241–2; trans. Scheck, 221.
⁶⁰ *Comm. Rom.* 3.8.8; trans. Scheck, 221.   ⁶¹ *Princ.* 1.3.4, 4.3.14; *Hom. Isa.* 1.2, 4.1.
⁶² Darrell D. Hannah, 'Isaiah's Vision in the Ascension of Isaiah and the Early Church', *Journal of Theological Studies*, 50: 1 (1999), 91.

interpreted as a vision of the Trinity.[63] Origen's interpretation was to become quite unacceptable: Jerome refers to it as 'this hateful explanation'.[64]

Gregory, therefore, was not the first interpreter to think of the tabernacle furniture as representing heavenly powers. The correlation of the layout of the tabernacle with the cosmos naturally led to the holy of holies being seen as symbolic of the intelligible world. It was also an obvious move to correlate the cherubim of the tabernacle with other biblical cherubim, and with the seraphim of Isaiah. However, the term 'powers' is imprecise. It means different things to different writers. For Philo, the creative and kingly powers (with the gracious and punitive powers below them) are a way of describing God's action in the world. Clement talks of powers which seem to be angels of judgement. Gregory himself uses 'powers' as a collective term for all heavenly beings, but also adds them to the list from Colossians 1:16, implying that they are one particular kind of spiritual being. He uses 'power', in the singular, to refer to Christ.[65] There are also inconsistencies in the interpretations of the layout of the tabernacle. The symbolism of the seven-branched lampstand, which was in the holy place, not the holy of holies, fluctuates, even within the same author, between a representation of the physical universe, and an intimation of something higher. Thus, for Philo it is both 'a copy of the march of the choir of the seven planets'[66] and a representation of the soul, in which the main branch represents 'the holy and divine Word, the All-severer'.[67] Clement brings in the seven planets, the shape of the cross, the light of Christ, and the seven 'first-created beings'. The cherubim too, within the holy of holies, are subjected to multiple interpretations: they are the two hemispheres of the cosmos (Philo, Clement), powers representing divine activity (Philo), angelic powers engaged in ceaseless adoration (Clement), and symbols of the Son and the Spirit (Origen). Gregory has, therefore, inherited a number of traditions relating the tabernacle to heavenly powers, but with no consistency between them. Some of his interpretations bear some relationship to those of his predecessors: like Origen, he quotes Hebrews 1:14, referring to the support given by angelic spirits, and uses Romans 3:25 in interpreting the mercy seat. He refers to the same biblical texts as Clement (Zech. 4:10; Rev. 4:5, 5:6; Isa. 11:1–3) when discussing the lampstand. He may have been influenced by these predecessors, or he may have arrived at his supporting biblical references independently. He himself shows a lack of consistency, especially in interpreting the lampstand as the Holy Spirit, and in referring to the cherubim as 'around the divine nature', a phrase he usually reserves for divine attributes. Where he is original is in using

---

[63] Hannah, 'Isaiah's Vision in the Ascension of Isaiah and the Early Church', 99–101. The earliest witness to this tradition is *Ascension of Isaiah*.
[64] *Epist.* 84; trans. NPNF² 6.176.   [65] *Vit. Moys.* 2.174, 177.
[66] *Her.* 221, cf. *Mos.* 2.102–103.   [67] *Her.* 225.

Colossians 1:16 to tie together a Christological interpretation of the tabernacle as a whole with an angelological interpretation of some its furniture.

Gregory's image of a heavenly tabernacle composed of angels, when placed in its Christological context, creates a parallelism between an angelic body of Christ and the church—the earthly body of Christ. Others before him had produced heavenly/earthly church dualisms. The Valentinians made 'Church' one of the eight aeons of the 'principal Ogdoad'.[68] Origen speaks disparagingly of 'some who speak of a certain heavenly Church, and say that the church on earth is an emanation from a higher world'.[69] But he himself develops the idea of two churches. In *Homilies on Numbers* 3.3 he quotes Hebrews 12:22–23—'you have come to Mount Zion and to the city of the living God, the heavenly Jerusalem, and to innumerable angels in festal gathering, and to the assembly of the first-born who are enrolled in heaven…'—giving the impression that the heavenly church is an angelic one. Elsewhere he identifies the heavenly church with the elect of the earthly church: 'The empirical church includes many who are not truly members of the church, but the heavenly church is comprised only of the perfect believers, those who are truly united with the Logos.'[70] This church has existed 'from the beginning of the human race and from the very foundation of the world—indeed, if I may look for the origin of this high mystery under Paul's guidance, even *before* the foundation of the world (Eph 1:4)'.[71] With its background in 'heretical' groups such as the Valentinians, it is not surprising that Gregory does not make explicit reference to a heavenly church. But the parallelism he creates between earthly and heavenly worship will be explored further in Chapter 12.

10.3 *LIFE OF MOSES* 2.178–183: THEOLOGICAL CONTEXT

Where do angels fit into Gregory's thinking? Daniélou argues that Gregory's cosmology consists of three heavens: the realm of air, containing wind, clouds and birds; the realm of ether, including the stars (together these make up the sense-perceptible heavens); and the noetic world, beyond which lies the darkness of the incomprehensible God.[72] Gregory, however, replaces the Platonic *kosmos noētos* with the world of angels:

> Le monde réel pour Grégoire, c'est [le plérôme des créatures spirituelles], composé des cent mondes angéliques. C'est cela qui remplace chez lui le monde intelligible

---

[68] Irenaeus *Haer.* 1.1.1.   [69] *Cels.* 6.35; trans. Chadwick, 351.
[70] William G. Rusch, 'Church', in John Anthony McGuckin (ed.), *The Westminster Handbook to Origen* (Louisville, Ken.: Westminster John Knox Press, 2004), 79.
[71] *Comm. Cant.* 2.8; trans. Lawson, 149.
[72] Jean Daniélou, *Platonisme et théologie mystique: Doctrine spirituelle de Saint Grégoire de Nysse*, 2nd edn (Paris: Aubier, 1954), 156.

de Platon, comme constituent le monde réel, par opposition à l'illusion cosmique, mais en même temps come un monde créé qui s'oppose radicalement à Dieu.[73]

David Balás agrees: 'In Gregory of Nyssa the "intelligible" or "intellectual beings" do not designate divine ideas—of which there are only a very few traces in his writings—but spiritual subjects, especially the angels and human souls.'[74] Angels are intelligible, immaterial, spiritual beings,[75] but they are created and, like human beings, have no access to the essence of God:

> God…can be grasped neither by any name nor by any thought nor any other conception, remaining loftier than the grasp of not only human beings, but even angelic and every supramundane being.[76]

Hans Urs von Balthasar analyses Gregory's appropriation of his Platonic heritage slightly differently, arguing that he splits the Platonic realm of *nous* (the mind) into three: 'Its formally divine aspect is linked to its true proprietor, God himself', 'its psychological aspect returns to the soul', and 'its existential aspect is absorbed into the realm of the angels, which Gregory readily calls the spiritual world (κόσμος νοητός)'.[77] According to Daniélou,

> Toutes les expressions cosmologiques sont allégorisées chez Grégoire. Elles sont les symboles des étapes d'une ascension intérieure, qui est profondément réelle, qui fait traverser à l'âme des mondes objectifs distincts, mais qui ne sont pas localisables spatialement.[78]

Our true home is in the third heaven (2 Cor. 12:2). Daniélou picks up on von Balthasar's analysis when he says, 'c'est une même chose pour Grégoire que de rentrer dans la société des Anges, de restaurer en soi l'image de Dieu, de connaître Dieu par participation'.[79] The third heaven has an angelic aspect, a psychological aspect, and a divine aspect. Gregory talks of his sister Macrina both as having 'nourished secretly in the inmost recesses of her soul' a 'divine

---

[73] 'The real world, for Gregory, is [the pleroma of spiritual creatures], made up of the one hundred angelic worlds. This is what replaces for him Plato's intelligible world, as the real world, in contrast to the illusion of the cosmos; but it is at the same time a created world, radically unlike God.' Daniélou, *Platonisme et théologie mystique*, 162.

[74] David L. Balás, ΜΕΤΟΥΣΙΑ ΘΕΟΥ: *Man's Participation in God's Perfections according to Saint Gregory of Nyssa* (Rome: Herder, 1966), 35–6.

[75] See *Infant.* (GNO 3,2.78–79); trans. NPNF² 5.375.

[76] *Eun.* 1.683 (GNO 1.222); trans. Richard Lim, *Public Disputation, Power, and Social Order in Late Antiquity* (Berkeley: University of California Press, 1995), 157.

[77] Hans Urs von Balthasar, *Présence et pensée: Essai sur la philosophie religieuse de Grégoire de Nysse* (Paris: Beauchesne, 1942); trans. Mark Sebanc as *Presence and Thought: An Essay on the Religious Philosophy of Gregory of Nyssa* (San Francisco: Ignatius Press, 1995), 20.

[78] 'All cosmological expressions are allegorised in Gregory. They become symbols of the stages of an inner ascent, which is profoundly real, making the soul travel through distinct objective worlds; but they cannot be located spatially.' Daniélou, *Platonisme et théologie mystique*, 157.

[79] 'For Gregory, joining the angelic company, restoring the image of God within oneself, and knowing God through participation, are one and the same.' Daniélou, *Platonisme et théologie mystique*, 161.

and pure love of the unseen Bridegroom', and as living an 'angelic and heavenly life'.[80] Daniélou is keen to stress, however, the distinction between God's incommunicable essence and God's energies/activities (ἐνέργειαι), within which human beings can participate:

> Or le κόσμος νοητός, par opposition à l'οὐσία, c'est précisément le domaine de la participation de Dieu par la grâce déifiante, qui est identique avec l'image de Dieu dans l'âme et qui constitue l'état angélique.[81]

In his three-stage analysis of Gregory's mysticism (light, cloud, darkness), it is stage two, *theōria*, which involves entering into the angelic world. Darkness is a stage further:

> Au delà, nous entrons, hors des voies de la contemplation, dans la quête de l'âme à la recherche de son Bien-Aimé. Elle dépasse alors la sphère des anges et s'enfonce dans les profondeurs de la participation à la vie divine. C'est l'ordre de l'amour, la ténèbre au sens fort…[82]

Daniélou assigns the vision of the tabernacle to *theōria*, because it represents the pleroma of spiritual creatures surrounding the Logos.[83] When Gregory talks of the power which encloses 'all existence', or more literally 'the things that are' or 'the beings' (τὰ ὄντα),[84] Daniélou interprets those 'beings' as angels, personalized Platonic Forms.[85] The heavenly powers make up the celestial world: 'Ils forment le sanctuaire de Dieu.'[86] This still leaves it unclear exactly how Gregory understands the words he quotes from Colossians: that the heavenly powers were created *in Christ*. Is there a remnant here of the Middle Platonist conception of the Ideas existing in the divine mind?[87] Daniélou firmly places the tabernacle within his *theōria* stage, and yet Gregory characterizes it as the *aduta*, containing within it the *aduton* of the holy of holies. This is the vocabulary of Daniélou's third stage:

> Normalement l'ἄδυτον apparaîtra-t-il avec la troisième voie, comme le lieu où se consomme l'union de l'âme avec Dieu et où l'âme contemple Dieu dans la ténèbre.[88]

---

[80] *Macr.* (GNO 8,1.396, 387); trans. Silvas, 132–3, 126.

[81] 'The *kosmos noētos*, as opposed to the *ousia*, is precisely the domain of participation in God by deifying grace, which is identical to the image of God in the soul, and which constitutes the angelic state.' Daniélou, *Platonisme et théologie mystique*, 161.

[82] 'Beyond the paths of contemplation, we enter into the soul's quest to find her Beloved. She goes beyond the angelic sphere and plunges herself into the depths of participation in divine life. It is about love, darkness in the strongest sense.' Daniélou, *Platonisme et théologie mystique*, 161.

[83] Daniélou, *Platonisme et théologie mystique*, 163. [84] *Vit. Moys.* 2.177.

[85] Daniélou, *Platonisme et théologie mystique*, 164 n. 1.

[86] 'They constitute God's sanctuary.' Daniélou, *Platonisme et théologie mystique*, 164.

[87] Cf. Philo *Opif.* 20, 36.

[88] 'Normally the *aduton* will appear with the third stage, as the place where the union of the soul with God is consumated, and where the soul contemplates God in the darkness.' Daniélou, *Platonisme et théologie mystique*, 185.

Although Gregory is known for placing an unbridgeable gap between the Creator and creation, he brings the two together in his tabernacle interpretation, and the gap is not always clear. In trying to reconcile his new understanding of the tabernacle as a type of Christ with an older tradition of interpreting the individual pieces of furniture he produces inconsistencies.

10.4 *LIFE OF MOSES* 2.178–183: HEAVENLY ASCENT CONTEXT

Gregory relates the furniture of the tabernacle to heavenly powers. Are there any parallels in heavenly ascent texts? The place to start is Ezekiel 1, the prophet's vision of God's mobile throne. The bearers of the throne are termed *hayyot* (living creatures); but later (Ezek. 10:20) they are identified as cherubim, thus connecting the inanimate cherubim of the temple with the living carriers of God's throne. Jon Levenson detects a similar move in Isaiah 6:

> Isaiah witnesses the transformation of glyptic symbols into full reality; the art of the Temple comes alive.[89]

Associated with the living creatures of Ezekiel 1 are *'ophannim*: mysterious wheels, their rims covered in eyes. These too come to be seen as alive. In later texts *hayyot*, cherubim, and *'ophannim* are independent orders of angels:

> ...from the sound of the harp playing of his *hayyot*,
> from the rejoicing sound of the tambourine of his Ophannim
> [and] from the sound of the cymbal playing of his Keruvim
> there rises a sound...[90]

Halperin suggests that this process of angelification begins in Ezekiel 10:9–17. He argues that the subject of verses 11 and 12 is not, as usually assumed, the *hayyot*-cherubim, but the *'ophannim*, and therefore that they have been equipped with heads, flesh, arms, and wings.[91] The *merkavah* is a living structure, composed of angels.

Songs of the Sabbath Sacrifice features the living, moving *merkavah* participating in the worship:

> In the tabernac[le...] knowledge, the [cheru]bim fal[l] before him and b[le]ss as they rise. A sound of divine stillness

---

[89] Jon D. Levenson, 'The Temple and the World', *The Journal of Religion*, 64: 3 (1984), 289.
[90] *Hekhalot Rabbati* §161; trans. Peter Schäfer, *The Hidden and Manifest God: Some Major Themes in Early Jewish Mysticism* (Albany: State University of New York Press, 1992), 25.
[91] David J. Halperin, *The Faces of the Chariot: Early Jewish Responses to Ezekiel's Vision* (Tübingen: Mohr Siebeck, 1988), 45–6.

[is heard] and (there is) a tumult of exultation as their wings lift up, the
  sound of divine [stillne]ss. The form of the chariot throne do they
  bless, (which is) above the firmament of the cherubim.
[And (in) the maje]sty of the luminous firmament do they exult,
  (which is) beneath his glorious seat. And when the ophannim move,
  the holy angels return. They go out < > from between
its glorious [h]ubs.[92]

In the Hekhalot literature too, God's throne comes to life and joins in the praise:

> Rejoice, rejoice, supernal dwelling!
> Shout, shout for joy, precious vessel!
> Made marvelously and a marvel!
> Gladden, gladden the king who sits upon you![93]

Sabbath Songs seems to extend this idea of a living structure to the whole heavenly temple. In Song 7, after exhorting the angels to praise, the text turns to architectural elements:

> With these let all fo[undations of…]° holies praise, the uplifting pillars of the supremely lofty abode, and all the corners of its structure.[94]

A little further on we find:

> And all the decorations of the inner room make haste with wondrous
>   psalms in the inner ro[om…]
> wonder, inner room (*devir*) to inner room with the sound of holy
>   tumult. And all their decorations […]
> And the chariots (*markavot*) of his inner room give praise together,
>   and their cherubim and thei[r] ophannim bless wondrously […][95]

Once again the building is participating in praise. There are a plurality of *markavot*, in line with the plurality of *devirim*. Maybe there is one *merkavah* in each *devir*, or maybe the *markavot* 'have become a class of heavenly beings present in large numbers in each of the [*devirim*]'.[96] Morray-Jones suggests that the author of *Sabbath Songs* has associated *devir* with the verb 'to speak' (*dāvar*), which is formed of the same consonants, so that the phrase 'inner room to inner room with the sound of holy tumult' 'implies that the courts or sanctuaries of the temple are formed by the "utterances" of the angels and the

---

[92] Song 12.2–5 (4Q405 20–22 ii 7–10); trans. Charlesworth and Newsom, 183.
[93] *Hekhalot Rabbati* §94; trans. Schäfer, *The Hidden and Manifest God*, 13.
[94] Song 7.12 (4Q403 1 i 41); trans. Charlesworth and Newsom, 163.
[95] Song 7.36–38 (4Q403 1 ii 13–15); trans. Charlesworth and Newsom, 167.
[96] Carol A. Newsom, *Songs of the Sabbath Sacrifice: A Critical Edition* (Atlanta: Scholars Press, 1985), 237.

worshipping community and that the heavenly temple is conceived as a structure composed of living sound'.[97]

Ra'anan Boustan points out that 'the "angelification" of the celestial Temple' is achieved not only by transferring 'the verbs of praise so central to the liturgical framework from angelic host to celestial architecture', but also by portraying 'the angelic creatures in material terms as images inscribed, carved, or woven into the Temple's walls, furnishings and tapestries',[98] as in this fragment, assigned to Song 9:

> [And the likene]ss of the living godlike beings is engraved in the vestibules where the king enters, figures of luminous spirit [. .. k]ing, figures of glorious li[ght,] spirits of
> [. . . in the] midst of spirits of splendour, works of wondrous mingled colors, figures of living godlike beings °[. . .] glorious [in]ner rooms, the structure of
> [the sanctuary of ho]liest holiness in the inner rooms of the king, figure[s of god]lik[e beings; and from] the likeness of °[. . .] holiest holiness.[99]

Alexander says of Song 9:

> Though the language is concrete (note the reference to the 'glorious brickwork' at 11Q17 6–8 5), the architectural features are spiritualized. Engraved on them are images of angels. The motif is borrowed from Ezekiel's visionary temple (Ezek. 41.15–26), and ultimately from Solomon's temple (1 Kgs 6.29–35). The difference is that here the figures are not mere decoration: the images of the angels are animate and praise God.[100]

In Song 7, the animate temple not only participates in the praise, it also seems to become its object:

> Sin[g-praise]
> (to) Go[d who is dr]eadful (in) power [. . .] knowledge and light to lift up together the splendidly shining firmament of [his] holy sanctuary.
> [. . .]° god[like] spirits, to confe[ss] forever (and) ever the firmament of the uppermost heights, all [its] b[eams] and its walls, a[l]l
> its [struct]ure, the works of [its] fo[rm.] The spirits of holiest holiness, the living godlike beings (*'elohim*), spirits of eternal holiness, above.[101]

---

[97] Christopher R. A. Morray-Jones, 'The Temple Within', in April D. DeConick (ed.), *Paradise Now: Essays on Early Jewish and Christian Mysticism* (Atlanta: Society of Biblical Literature, 2006), 167.

[98] Ra'anan S. Boustan, 'Angels in the Architecture: Temple Art and the Poetics of Praise in the Songs of the Sabbath Sacrifice', in Ra'anan S. Boustan and Annette Yoshiko Reed (eds), *Heavenly Realms and Earthly Realities in Late Antique Religions* (Cambridge: Cambridge University Press, 2004), 196–7.

[99] Song 9.14–16 (4Q405 14–15 i 5–7); trans. Charlesworth and Newsom, 175.

[100] Philip Alexander, *The Mystical Texts: Songs of the Sabbath Sacrifice and Related Manuscripts* (London: T&T Clark, 2006), 34.

[101] Song 7.12–15 (4Q403 1 i 41–44, 4Q405 6 2–5); trans. Charlesworth and Newsom, 163.

Alexander understands 'to lift up' (למשא) as 'to bear up', so that 'the praises create the temple': 'The purpose of the angelic liturgy is to "raise" the temple of God.'[102] This is in line with Morray-Jones' suggestion of a structure composed of living sound. But if 'to lift up' is taken in the metaphorical sense of 'to exalt', the temple becomes the object of praise. Anderson argues that just as there is confusion between the angelic beings, regularly called *'elohim*, and God, so the temple is ascribed divine qualities:

> Hebrew constructions such as *elohim hayyím* ('the living God') that one would normally construe as divine titles now become attributes of the supernal temple ('a living pulsating godlike [building]').[103]

This is part of a wider proposal: that 'the furniture of the temple was treated as quasi-divine in Second Temple Jewish sources of both a literary and iconographic nature'.[104] However, he pushes the evidence too far, both in the case of *Songs of the Sabbath Sacrifice*, which describes the heavenly temple, and in the case of his other examples, which deal with the earthly temple. It is one thing to say that temple furniture shares in the holiness of God, and therefore should be treated with the utmost reverence (cf. Num. 4:20), or even that the cherubim 'are, in some real sense, representations of God's true presence in the temple', and quite another to say that 'seeing the furniture is analogous to seeing the very being of God', or 'it is not possible to divide or separate fully the being of God from the objects he inhabits'.[105] As regards *Sabbath Songs*, Alexander is adamant that despite the use of *'elohim* for both, the 'authors evince a deep consciousness of the difference between God and the angels': 'God is the source of all knowledge; the angels know only what he chooses to reveal to them'.[106] *Sabbath Songs* preserves 'a profound sense of the ultimate transcendence and mystery of God',[107] as shown by its strategy of displacement: there is no direct visualization of God; attention is transferred instead to the angels and the heavenly temple.

Anderson's analysis, however, does illustrate what a fine line is trod when associating God's presence with the temple/tabernacle and its furniture. Texts which describe the earthly temple have to negotiate the relationship between God's immanence and God's transcendence. Texts which deal with the heavenly temple have to maintain a boundary between God and angels. But sometimes the language slips. It does so in the Hekhalot literature, as Rebecca Lesses notes:

> The ascent account in *Hekhalot Zutarti*, which gives instructions for the journey through the seven Hekhalot to the lap of God, reveals in a particularly acute way the confusion between God and the highest angelic princes that one often finds

---

[102] Alexander, *The Mystical Texts*, 30.
[103] Anderson, 'Towards a Theology of the Tabernacle and Its Furniture', 170.
[104] Anderson, 'Towards a Theology of the Tabernacle and Its Furniture', 162.
[105] Anderson, 'Towards a Theology of the Tabernacle and Its Furniture', 177, 166, 188.
[106] Alexander, *The Mystical Texts*, 105.   [107] Alexander, *The Mystical Texts*, 106.

in the hekhalot texts. This text elides the differences between God and the angels, both by giving God multiple names, and by compounding the names of God and the angels with the tetragrammaton.[108]

10.5 *LIFE OF MOSES* 2.178–183: CONCLUSIONS

In both *Life of Moses* and *Songs of the Sabbath Sacrifice* the heavenly temple is not a material entity. Gregory, with his Platonic background, sees it as an ideal Form, an archetype. That makes it not less real but more so: the reality of which material things are but a copy. And he links it with Christ, again giving it more presence not less. But if the heavenly tabernacle is not material, what is it made of? Both *Life of Moses* and *Sabbath Songs* seem to suggest that it is made of angels, of heavenly powers. They arrive at this conclusion, however, by different routes. Gregory uses Colossians 1:16 to personalize Platonic Ideas. *Sabbath Songs* extends the idea of a living, angelic *merkavah* to the whole heavenly temple. According to Gregory, Moses gets a glimpse of the heavenly realms—of the powers which undergird everything, which raise humanity to the height of virtue, which cover the ineffable mysteries. The only way these can be described is in material terms—as silver and gold pillars, as bearing poles and rings, as cherubim. Other writers in the Alexandrian tradition interpret individual elements of the heavenly temple in terms of heavenly powers, but none lays down a general rule for doing so in the way that Gregory does. By using Colossians 1:16 he creates a picture of an angelic body of Christ which parallels Christ's earthly body, the church. But when working through the details he is not consistent. This is partly because he shoehorns in older traditions, such as the association between the mercy seat and Christ's redemptive action, or between the seven lights of the lampstand and the seven characteristics of the Spirit in Isaiah 11:2–3. His interpretations oscillate between the angelological and the Christological. Particularly problematic is his use of the phrase 'around the divine nature' with reference to the cherubim/seraphim, as elsewhere in his works this is reserved for divine attributes. Such oscillation, the lack of a clear-cut distinction between the divine and the angelic, can also be found in *Sabbath Songs* and the Hekhalot texts. This needn't imply that Gregory, the Qumran community, or the authors of the Hekhalot literature were confused about the difference between God and angels. Alexander argues that, in the case of *Sabbath Songs*, the angelic

---

[108] Rebecca Macy Lesses, *Ritual Practices to Gain Power: Angels, Incantations, and Revelation in Early Jewish Mysticism* (Harrisburg, Penn.: Trinity Press International, 1998), 257.

liturgies, with their dramatic setting, 'only make sense if we postulate an eternal distinction between the worshipping community and the divine object of its adoration'.[109] In Gregory's case, the gap between Creator and creation is certainly firmly established. This then allows language to be used freely, with occasional logical inconsistencies.

---

[109] Alexander, *The Mystical Texts*, 105.

11

The Earthly Tabernacle

> Whenever, therefore, the prophet looks to the tabernacle above, he sees these concepts by means of its components. If one should contemplate the tabernacle below, then, seeing that the church is called Christ by Paul in many places, it would be good to consider these terms to refer to the servants of the divine mystery, the apostles, teachers and prophets, whom the word indeed calls 'pillars' of the church.[1]

11.1 *LIFE OF MOSES* 2.184–187: BIBLICAL CONTEXT

From the saving passion, Gregory turns his attention to the earthly tabernacle. He has previously described it as a type of the incarnate Christ, but here he does not elaborate further on its relationship to the incarnation. Instead, relying on Paul's portrayal of the church as the body of Christ (Rom. 12:4–5; 1 Cor. 12:12–13; Eph. 1:22–23), he uses the earthly tabernacle to depict the church. Gregory does not mention it, but there is also precedent in Paul for both individual Christians and the church being described as God's temple (1 Cor. 3:16; 2 Cor. 6:16; Eph. 2:19–22). Christopher Rowland writes, 'The imagery of the Temple was in the theological bloodstream of early Christians and through them became part of Christian identity.'[2] As we shall see in 11.2, Clement comments on the relationship between the temple, the incarnation, and the church; and Origen develops elaborate allegorical interpretations of the tabernacle in terms of the church. Gregory is not, therefore, being particularly original in seeing the earthly tabernacle as a type of the church; but in expounding it here, in parallel with Moses' vision of the heavenly tabernacle, he is making a statement about where Christians should view themselves in relationship to the 'mysteries' of which he has been speaking.[3]

---

[1] *Vit. Moys.* 2.184.

[2] Christopher Rowland, 'The Temple in the New Testament', in John Day (ed.), *Temple and Worship in Biblical Israel: Proceedings of the Oxford Old Testament Seminar* (London: T&T Clark, 2007), 479.

[3] *Vit. Moys.* 2.173, 178.

Gregory does not systematically interpret all the furniture of the earthly tabernacle, only picking out a few features. He starts with 'pillars' and 'lights', assembling a medley of New Testament passages:

> It would be good to consider these terms to refer to the servants of the divine mystery, the apostles, teachers and prophets [cf. 1 Cor 12:28], whom the word indeed calls 'pillars' of the church [Gal 2:9]. For not only Peter and James and John are pillars of the church, nor was John the Baptist the only 'burning lamp' [John 5:35], but all those who themselves support the church and become 'luminaries' [Phil 2:15] by their own works are called 'pillars' and 'lamps'. 'You are the light of the world' says the Lord to the apostles [Matt 5:14]. And again, the divine apostle exhorts others to be pillars, saying, 'Be steadfast and immovable' [1 Cor 15:58]. He built Timothy into a good pillar, making him, as he says in his own words, 'a pillar and foundation of the truth' [1 Tim 3:15].[4]

He has presented the pillars as an important feature of the tabernacle:

> There were golden pillars fixed into silver bases and adorned with similar silver heads; yet other pillars with heads and bases made of bronze, but with silver between the extremities; and the interior of all these was wood not prone to rot, while visibly the radiance of such materials shone out all around.[5]

In the MT of Exodus, the tabernacle is constructed using planks or possibly frames (קְרָשִׁים), overlaid with gold.[6] There are then four pillars (עַמּוּדִים) overlaid with gold at the entrance to the holy of holies, and five at the door of the tent.[7] The hangings around the courtyard are hung on a further sixty pillars which have hooks (וָוִים) and fillets (חֲשֻׁקִים) made of silver.[8] The LXX uses 'pillars' (στῦλοι) for both 'planks' and 'pillars', and describes the courtyard pillars as 'silverplated with silver' (κατηργυρωμένοι ἀργυρίῳ).[9] The details of the bases and capitals (not to mention tenons, rings, bars, hooks, and fillets) become highly complicated, especially as the LXX translation gives the impression of being 'often inconsistent and sometimes inexact'.[10] The small solid gold hooks (וָוִים) of the tent pillars in the MT, for example, become implausible solid gold capitals (κεφαλίδες) in the LXX.[11] Gregory, in turn, provides a simplified account of the LXX. His interest in the pillars is no doubt fuelled by their allegorical possibilities. He also refers to them in *On the Song of Songs*, in the context of LXX Song of Songs 5:15—'His legs are marble pillars, founded upon golden bases.'[12] Alluding to Proverbs 9:1, he says,

---

[4] *Vit. Moys.* 2.184.   [5] *Vit. Moys.* 2.170; cf. 1.49.   [6] Exod. 26:15, 29.
[7] Exod. 26:32, 37.   [8] Exod. 27:10–18.   [9] LXX Exod. 27:17.
[10] D. W. Gooding, *The Account of the Tabernacle: Translation and Textual Problems of the Greek Exodus* (Cambridge: Cambridge University Press, 1959), 20. Wade is more understanding of the translators' dilemmas and priorities. For her discussion of 'Pillars and Related Items' see Martha Lynn Wade, *Consistency of Translation Techniques in the Tabernacle Accounts of Exodus in the Old Greek* (Atlanta: Society of Biblical Literature, 2003), 92–7.
[11] Exod. 26:32, 37.   [12] Trans. NETS.

> The house that Wisdom 'built for herself' has many pillars; and many too are the pillars, decorated with a variety of materials, that uphold the tent of witness, whose capitals and pedestals are of gold, while their central portions are embellished with a covering of silver.[13]

This does not correspond to anything in either the MT or the LXX of Exodus: nowhere are there any pedestals made of gold. Gregory has been too eager to reconcile the Song of Songs' verse with the pillars of the tabernacle. He goes on to refer to Galatians 2:9,[14] and 1 Timothy 3:15,[15] as in *Life of Moses*. The 'lights' of *Life of Moses* 2.184 presumably refer to the golden 'lampstand with a single base stem which divided into seven branches at the top, holding up an equal number of lights on the branches'.[16] Heine contends that there is 'a repeated emphasis on the leadership of the church throughout the treatise' and, specifically, that Gregory 'thinks of the leaders of the church when he considers the earthly tabernacle'.[17] But having mentioned prominent figures of the New Testament, Gregory holds out the possibility that all Christians can become 'pillars' and 'lights', so long as they support the church and shine through their works. Similarly, in *On the Song of Songs*, he says that the bridegroom's legs are 'those who by their shining life and healthful speech bear up the common body of the church and support it and by whose work the pedestal of faith retains its steadfast character, and virtue's race is completed, and the whole body, in its leaps of a divine hope, touches the heavens'.[18] There is no reference to hierarchy or leadership.

Gregory moves on to the worship of the earthly tabernacle, turning physical sacrifices into praise and prayer. We shall examine his comments in Chapter 12, comparing them with his description of heavenly worship.

The washbasin (כיור; λουτήρ) is not mentioned in connection with the heavenly tabernacle, either in Exodus 25–27 or by Gregory. In Exodus, the earthly tabernacle contains a single one,[19] but Gregory seems to think that there are several,[20] and makes them a symbol of baptism:

> Anyone hearing of the washbasins will no doubt understand them as those who wash away the defilement of sins with sacramental water. John was a washbasin, washing in the Jordan with the baptism of repentance; Peter was a washbasin, leading three thousand down into the water at the same time [Acts 2:41]; Philip was the washbasin of Candace's man [Acts 8:27–39]; as are all those who administer the grace to all partaking of the gift.[21]

---

[13] *Cant.* 14 (GNO 6.415.15–19); trans. Norris, 441.
[14] GNO 6.416.13–15; 419.9–10.   [15] GNO 6.415.21–22; 416.18; 419. 12–13.
[16] *Vit. Moys.* 2.171.
[17] Ronald E. Heine, *Perfection in the Virtuous Life: A Study in the Relationship Between Edification and Polemical Theology in Gregory of Nyssa's De Vita Moysis* (Cambridge, Mass.: Philadelphia Patristic Foundation, 1975), 24.
[18] *Cant.* 14 (GNO 6.417.3–7); trans. Norris, 443.   [19] Exod. 30:18.
[20] *Vit. Moys.* 2.172.   [21] *Vit. Moys.* 2.185.

It is interesting that nowhere in this tabernacle interpretation does Gregory mention the Eucharist, especially as one would have thought that the table and showbread would have provided an obvious 'type'.

Gregory's next paragraph, on 'the curtains (τὰς αὐλαίας), which by being joined to one another (διὰ τῆς μετ' ἀλλήλων συμβολῆς) encircle the tabernacle' seems to have caused some confusion for previous translators of *Life of Moses* into English. Both Malherbe and Ferguson, and Herbert Musurillo, have not 'curtains' but 'courts'.[22] The tabernacle only had one court. A comparison with LXX Exodus 26:1–6 shows that Gregory is referring to the ten curtains (δέκα αὐλαίας) which made up the first layer of the tent covering. Exodus 26:4, 5 talks of the coupling (ἡ συμβολή) between the two sets of five curtains. Gregory, therefore, is echoing the LXX vocabulary. In *Life of Moses* 2.172 he lists the layers of the tent, talking of 'the outer covering of curtains (ἡ ἔξωθεν τῶν αὐλαίων περιβολή), hairy hides and skins coloured red'.[23] The curtains symbolize for Gregory the 'harmony, love and peace of believers'.[24] He quotes a verse from the psalms: 'For such is David's interpretation, when he says, "he who made your borders peace"'.[25] One can hear here the voice of the bishop concerned about the detrimental effect of contemporary theological controversies.

According to the instructions given to Moses, the tabernacle curtains were to be covered with an outer tent made of goat's hair.[26] A further layer was to include rams' skins dyed red.[27] In the context of the heavenly tabernacle, Gregory has interpreted the skin dyed red and the coverings made of hair as the saving passion. In the earthly tabernacle they become 'the death (νέκρωσις) of sinful flesh ... and the severe life of self-control (ἡ τραχεῖα διαγωγὴ κατ' ἐγκράτειαν)'.[28] Christ's passion is to be imitated by the believer's mortification of the flesh. Gregory places particular importance on this, saying that by these qualities 'the tabernacle of the church is especially beautified'. He then interprets the red dye as 'the grace which flourishes through the Spirit' in people who have thus made themselves 'dead to sin'. This is his second mention of the Holy Spirit, again not 'in a strictly theological context'.[29] He tentatively offers

---

[22] Abraham J. Malherbe and Everett Ferguson, *Gregory of Nyssa: The Life of Moses* (New York: Paulist Press, 1978), 102; Herbert Musurillo, *From Glory to Glory: Texts from Gregory of Nyssa's Mystical Writings* (New York: Scribner, 1961; repr., Crestwood, NY: St Vladimir's Seminary Press, 2001), 136.

[23] Musurillo has here 'a circuit of outer courts' (Musurillo, *From Glory to Glory*, 131), and Malherbe and Ferguson 'hangings around the outer court' (Malherbe and Ferguson, *The Life of Moses*, 98). There were hangings around the outer court, but the LXX generally refers to them as ἱστία (e.g. LXX Exod. 27:9). So both from the evidence of the LXX vocabulary, and from their presence in a list with the other layers of the tent, it seems unlikely that Gregory is referring to the hangings around the court.

[24] *Vit. Moys.* 2.186. [25] *Vit. Moys.* 2.186, cf. LXX Ps. 147:3.
[26] Exod. 26:7, cf. 25:4. [27] Exod. 26:14, cf. Exod. 25:5. [28] *Vit. Moys.* 2.187.
[29] Malherbe and Ferguson, *The Life of Moses*, 16. The first reference is in *Vit. Moys.* 2.181, see 10.1.

another possible interpretation of the dye, which alludes to the root meaning 'blush' of the Greek word he is using for redness (ἐρύθημα): 'Whether chaste modesty is signified by the word with the dipping in red dye, I leave for whoever wishes to judge.' In his interpretation of the hairs, Gregory refers specifically to virginity:

> The intertwining of hairs, which produces a rough and rigid fabric, alludes to this severe self-control which reduces habitual passions. The life of virginity demonstrates all such things in itself, pummelling (ὑπωπιάζουσα) the flesh of those who live this way.[30]

The verb 'pummel' alludes to 1 Corinthians 9:26–27, where Paul says, 'Well, I do not run aimlessly, I do not box as one beating the air; but I pommel (ὑπωπιάζω) my body and subdue it, lest after preaching to others I myself should be disqualified.'

The final paragraph in Gregory's exposition of the earthly tabernacle, concerning the holy of holies, will be examined in Chapter 13.

11.2 *LIFE OF MOSES* 2.184–187: ALEXANDRIAN CONTEXT

Paul depicts the church as both the body of Christ and a temple. Ephesians' use of temple language (2:19–22) and body terminology (1:22–23; 4:12) yields 'a complex mix of imagery concerning organic and structural growth'.[31] 1 Peter 2:5 also uses temple language metaphorically to refer to the community of the Christian elect. John 2:21, meanwhile, describes Jesus' body as a temple. In a fragment said to come from Clement's *Canon of the Church* or *Against the Judaisers* (a work otherwise lost), these New Testament precedents enable the temple to become a type both of the incarnation and the church. The passage takes as its point of departure Solomon's remark in LXX 1 Kings 8:27—'For will God indeed dwell with people on the earth?'[32] Clement comments,

> In the book of Kings, Solomon, the son of David, understood that the construction of the true temple was not only a heavenly and spiritual matter, but concerned already the flesh which the Son and Lord of David was destined to build, not only by his presence, which he decided to establish as an animate image, but also by the church, raised up in the assembly of faith. He said, word for word, 'Will then God truly dwell with people on earth?' He dwells on earth, clothed in flesh, and the union and harmony among the righteous, making and building a holy temple, becomes his dwelling with people. For the righteous are earth while still clad in

---

[30] *Vit. Moys.* 2.187. [31] Rowland, 'The Temple in the New Testament', 475.
[32] Trans. NETS.

earth, and earth when compared to the greatness of the Lord. About these indeed the blessed Peter did not hesitate to say, 'And like living stones be yourselves built into a spiritual house, a holy priesthood, to offer spiritual sacrifices acceptable to God through Jesus Christ.' About his body, which, as a circumscribed space filled with divinity, he himself consecrated on earth, the Lord said, ' "Destroy this temple, and in three days I will raise it up." The Jews said, "It has taken forty-six years to build this temple, and will you raise it up in three days?" But he spoke of the temple of his body.'[33]

The first Jerusalem temple was not only a copy of the heavenly temple, but also a prefiguration of the body of Christ—the incarnate Christ, the church, and the individual members within it. (The element in Gregory which is missing in Clement is the heavenly temple as a type of the pre-existent Christ.) As Claude Mondésert writes,

> On peut admirer d'abord, dans ces quelques lignes, l'amplitude de la vision spirituelle, qui parcourt toute la Bible, de l'Ancien au Nouveau Testament, du temple de pierre de Salomon au temple de la Jérusalem céleste, en passant par ce temple admirable que fut le Christ vivant sur terre, et qui est maintenant continué par le corps de l'Église, rassemblement des hommes encore plongés dans la vie d'ici-bas. Et d'ailleurs chacun d'eux, s'il est juste, est aussi un lieu saint, plein de la divinité.[34]

The same combination of ideas is taken up by Origen when commenting on John 2:18–21:

> The Saviour, however, by joining as one the saying about his own body with that about that temple, answers the question, 'What sign do you show us, seeing that you do these things?' with 'Destroy this temple, and in three days I will raise it up.'...Both, however, (I mean the temple and Jesus' body) according to one interpretation, appear to me to be a type of the Church, in that the Church, being called a 'temple', is built of living stones, becoming a spiritual house 'for a holy priesthood', built 'upon the foundation of the apostles and prophets, Christ Jesus being the chief corner stone.'[35]

Thanks to the macrocosm–microcosm relationship, Philo's elaborate cosmological interpretation of the tabernacle and its furniture leads into an anthropological deciphering of tabernacle symbolism, although Philo does not develop

---

[33] GCS 3.218–219; my translation. For a French translation and commentary on this fragment, see Claude Mondésert, 'A propos du signe du temple: Un texte de Clément d'Alexandrie', *Recherches de science religieuse*, 36 (1949).

[34] 'One can first admire, in these few lines, the breadth of the spiritual vison, which encompasses the whole Bible, from the Old to the New Testament, from Solomon's stone temple to the temple of the heavenly Jerusalem, by way of the wonderful temple of Christ living on earth, which is continued by the body of the church, the gathering of those still immersed in life here below. And each member, if righteous, is also a holy place, filled with divinity.' Mondésert, 'A propos du signe du temple', 581.

[35] *Comm. Jo.* 10.226, 228; trans. Heine, 305.

this in as much detail as he does with the cosmology. Origen picks up on Philo's presentation of the relationship between cosmology and anthropology:

> For if, as some before us have said, this tabernacle represents the whole world, and each individual also can contain an image of the world, why can not each one also complete a form of the tabernacle in himself?[36]

But Origen links his anthropological interpretation to the tabernacle as symbolic of the church. The virtues he sees represented there are not those of human beings in general, but of the believers who constitute the church. In *Homilies on Exodus* (9 and 13) and *Homilies on Numbers* (5) he analyses the elements of the tabernacle with as much care as Philo, but with cosmology and anthropology turned into ecclesiology. *Homilies on Numbers* 5 deals with Numbers 4, which enumerates the duties of the Levites when packing up the tent of meeting. Origen interprets 'the tabernacle of testimony to refer to all the saints who are assessed under God's covenant'. Its furniture represents those 'more exalted in their merits and superior in grace': the lampstand is identified with the apostles, who 'illuminate those who draw near to God'; the holy table with those who refresh and feed souls hungry for justice; the incense altar with those who pray for the entire people; the ark with those to whom God has entrusted the secret mysteries; the mercy seat with those who intercede for the sins of the people; and the cherubim with those who abound in the wealth of the knowledge of God.[37] The biblical context of packing up and moving on allows him to talk of the people represented by these symbols being carried on the shoulders of angels to the place of promise.[38] In *Homilies on Exodus* he focuses on the materials which go into making the tabernacle. They represent, he says, 'those things by which the Church is adorned': gold is faith; silver is the word of preaching; bronze is patience; incorruptible wood is either the knowledge which comes through the wood (presumably the cross) or the incorruptibility of purity; linen is virginity.[39] Like Gregory, he associates pillars with Galatians 2:9, and so allegorizes them in terms of teachers and ministers. He adds further detail: the interposed bars are the right hand of fellowship; the silver overlay is the words of the Lord, 'pure words, silver proved by fire' (LXX Psalm 11:7); the bases are the prophets and their testimonies; and the capitals of the pillars are Christ.[40] He takes notice of the peculiarities of the biblical text: in 13.4–5 he picks up on the 'scarlet doubled' (κόκκινον διπλοῦν) and the 'twisted linen' (βύσσον κεκλωσμένην) of the LXX text of Exodus 35:6. The 'scarlet doubled' he associates with two kinds of fire: the fire that enlightens, and the fire that burns; and he finds biblical verses relating to each. The 'twisted linen' he sees as symbolic of weakening the flesh 'by abstinence, by vigils, and by the exertion of meditations'.[41]

---

[36] *Hom. Exod.* 9.4; trans. Heine, 340–1. [37] *Hom. Num.* 5.3.2; trans. Scheck, 19.
[38] *Hom. Num.* 5.3.3. [39] *Hom. Exod.* 9.3; trans. Heine, 340. Cf. *Hom. Exod.* 13.2.
[40] *Hom. Exod.* 9.3; trans. Heine, 338–9. [41] *Hom. Exod.* 13.5; trans. Heine, 383.

Although Gregory, like Origen, interprets the earthly tabernacle as symbolic of the church, there seem to be few correlations between their accounts, although it is difficult to make precise comparisons as we only have Origen's homilies in Rufinus' Latin translation. They both use Galatians 2:9 to connect the apostles with the pillars, but Gregory adds other NT verses, and widens his interpretation to include all supportive church members. Gregory's comments on lights, sacrifices, washbasins, and interconnecting curtains seem to have no parallel in Origen. (Rufinus' translation, however, does reflect the confusion between curtains and courts: the word 'court' (*atrium*) occurs in contexts where 'curtain' (*cortina*) would be expected. Heine is unsure whether the confusion originates with Rufinus or Origen.[42]) Origen comments that 'hair is a dead, bloodless, soulless form', and therefore that the person who offered this material towards the building of the tabernacle 'shows that the disposition to sin is already dead in himself, nor does sin further live or rule in his members.[43] In the context of the skins and hair coverings, Gregory also mentions becoming dead to sin. But he adds an emphasis on asceticism, talking of self-control and virginity. Origen does quote 1 Corinthians 9:27, with its reference to chastising and subduing the body, but in the context of the 'twisted linen' rather than the coverings of skin.[44] He mentions virginity in passing:

> This...is the sanctuary which the Lord orders to be constructed, which the Apostle also wishes to be present in virgins 'that they may be holy in body and spirit', [cf. 1 Cor. 7:34] knowing without doubt that he who makes a sanctuary for the Lord by the purity of his own heart and body will himself see God. Let us, therefore, also make a sanctuary for the Lord both collectively and individually.[45]

11.3 *LIFE OF MOSES* 2.184–187: THEOLOGICAL CONTEXT

Gregory's interpretation of the tabernacle, unlike Clement's passage in *Miscellanies* 5.32–40, does not end with an entry into the heavenly holy of holies. It turns from the heavenly to the earthly tabernacle. Is this simply a reflection of the Exodus narrative, or does it serve a purpose for Gregory? The first question to ask is 'For whom did Gregory write *Life of Moses*?' Towards the beginning of the work, he declares, 'Let us put forth Moses as our example for life.'[46] To whom does the 'our' refer? Is Gregory writing for all Christians,

---

[42] Ronald E. Heine, *Origen: Homilies on Genesis and Exodus* (Washington, DC: Catholic University of America Press, 1982), 339–40 n. 26.
[43] *Hom. Exod.* 13.5; trans. Heine, 383. [44] *Hom. Exod.* 13.5; trans. Heine, 383.
[45] *Hom. Exod.* 9.3; trans. Heine, 338.
[46] *Vit. Moys.* 1.15; trans. Malherbe and Ferguson, 33.

or only for a select minority? It is often assumed that he presents Moses as 'a model of the soul's spiritual journey to God';[47] but are all souls expected to imitate Moses equally?

Gregory tells us that the treatise was written in response to a letter requesting 'some counsel concerning the perfect life'.[48] In some manuscripts, the name Caesarius is found in the concluding paragraphs. Daniélou includes it in his edition (2.319), Musurillo does not. In any case, it does not get us any further, as Caesarius is 'otherwise unknown'.[49] Gregory tells his recipient, 'Although there may be nothing useful for you in my words, perhaps this example of ready obedience will not be wholly unprofitable to you.'[50] Daniélou concludes, 'Ceci indique que le destinataire est moine.'[51] The same conclusion was reached much earlier: a fourteenth-century manuscript (codex Vaticanus graecus 444) adds 'to Caesarius the monk (πρὸς Καισάριον μόναχον)' to the title. Malherbe and Ferguson argue that 'the treatise...takes its place as part of Gregory's program to provide an ideological undergirding for the monastic movement organized by Basil'.[52] Heine, however, puts forward the view that the treatise was directed not to a monk, but a priest.[53] He bases his argument on Gregory's interpretation of the blossoming of the rod of Aaron.[54] Gregory calls it 'the rod of priesthood', and makes reference to 'your office (ἀξίωμα)'. According to Heine, this rod of priesthood 'seems to have special significance for the person to whom the treatise is dedicated', and this person 'appears to hold an office which can be compared in some way to that of Moses'.[55] Malherbe and Ferguson, however, translate ἀξίωμα not as 'office' but as 'worth', which weakens the force of Heine's argument. As already mentioned, Heine also says that there is 'a repeated emphasis on the leadership of the church throughout the treatise'.[56] He includes among the passages with this emphasis the earthly tabernacle, as a representation of the church, and the priestly vestments, symbolically teaching about 'priestly virtue'.[57] This virtue is twofold, involving faith and conduct,[58] which Heine sees as appropriate for a work addressed to a priest:

> Virtue, for a man who led and taught in the church, had to be carefully regulated by the rule of orthodoxy. Both his belief and his life had to be correct by this standard.[59]

---

[47] Bernard McGinn, *The Foundations of Mysticism: Origins to the Fifth Century* (New York: Crossroad, 1991), 140.
[48] *Vit. Moys.* 1.2; trans. Malherbe and Ferguson, 29.
[49] Malherbe and Ferguson, *The Life of Moses*, 3.
[50] *Vit. Moys.* 1.2; trans. Malherbe and Ferguson, 29.
[51] 'This indicates that the addressee is a monk.' Jean Daniélou, *Grégoire de Nysse: La Vie de Moïse, ou Traité de la perfection en matière de vertu* (Paris: Cerf, 2000), 47 n. 1.
[52] Malherbe and Ferguson, *The Life of Moses*, 3.
[53] Heine, *Perfection in the Virtuous Life*, 22. [54] Num. 17; *Vit. Moys.* 2.316.
[55] Heine, *Perfection in the Virtuous Life*, 22–3.
[56] Heine, *Perfection in the Virtuous Life*, 23. [57] *Vit. Moys.* 1.55.
[58] See *Vit. Moys.* 2.192, 198. [59] Heine, *Perfection in the Virtuous Life*, 25.

In some of Gregory's statements about Moses' virtuous example, there seems to be no reason why he should not be imitated by all Christians:

> The lives of honoured men [are] set forth as a pattern of virtue for those who come after them. Those who emulate their lives, however, cannot experience the identical literal events.... [Therefore] one might substitute a moral teaching for the literal sequence in those things which admit of such an approach. In this way those who have been striving toward virtue may find aid in living the virtuous life.[60]

In other passages, however, Moses is clearly a leader, and not to be imitated by all:

> The person who has crossed the sea...believes in God...and is obedient to his servant Moses. We see this happening even now with those who truly cross the water, who dedicate themselves to God and are obedient and submissive, as the Apostle says, to those who serve the Divine in the priesthood.[61]
>
> The multitude was not capable of hearing the voice from above but relied on Moses to learn by himself the secrets and to teach the people whatever doctrine he might learn through instruction from above. This is also true of the arrangement in the Church: Not all thrust themselves toward the apprehension of the mysteries, but, choosing from among themselves someone who is able to hear things divine, they give ear gratefully to him, considering trustworthy whatever they might hear from someone initiated into the divine mysteries.[62]

Life of Moses is not the only work in which Gregory cites Moses as an example. In *Life of Gregory the Wonderworker* and *On Basil* he compares the two bishops to Moses. Andrea Sterk outlines the way in which, in both works, Gregory uses 'the three stages of Moses' life as a paradigm for the episcopate':[63]

> Ideally the episcopal candidate should be educated in profane learning, would abandon academic and all other ambitions for the contemplative life, and should finally sacrifice even the bliss of monastic solitude in order actively to serve the people of God.[64]

Life of Moses is not structured in the same way, but it is interesting to note that Gregory had been reflecting on the figure of Moses for some time (assuming the traditional dating). His previous use of Moses in connection with two outstanding Cappadocian bishops may well have influenced *Life of Moses*. Sterk argues that both Gregory of Nyssa and Gregory of Nazianzus 'managed to

---

[60] *Vit. Moys.* 2.48–49; trans. Malherbe and Ferguson, 65.
[61] *Vit. Moys.* 2.130; trans. Malherbe and Ferguson, 85.
[62] *Vit. Moys.* 2.160; trans. Malherbe and Ferguson, 94.
[63] Andrea Sterk, 'On Basil, Moses, and the Model Bishop: The Cappadocian Legacy of Leadership', *Church History*, 67: 2 (1998), 228.
[64] Sterk, 'On Basil, Moses, and the Model Bishop', 250.

harmonize monastic ideals and practices with active service to the church'.[65] The vision of the tabernacle played a crucial role in their self-understanding:

> [Moses'] encounter with God on Mount Sinai and consequent 'instruction from above' or 'initiation into the mysteries' was indispensable preparation for the task of instructing the multitudes. Indeed the vision of God epitomized by the Sinai theophany was the ultimate goal of monastic withdrawal and the mark of the true theologian. To teach or lead the Christian people without such a revelation was for both Gregorys the height of presumption.[66]

This suggests that Gregory did not see Moses as a model to be imitated by all, or even by all priests. *Life of Moses* implies that, in being granted a vision of the heavenly tabernacle, Moses joined the elite company of David, Paul, and John. Everyone else should aspire to becoming a pillar or light in the earthly tabernacle. Whether the historical addressee was a monk or a priest, the message of the treatise is not about aspiring to a vision of heavenly mysteries, but belonging to the worshipping community on earth.

In that worshipping community, asceticism was clearly to take pride of place. Heine may be right to argue that Gregory was targeting priests, including possibly Eunomius, who did not put enough emphasis on right living. But could Gregory also have been guarding against those whose asceticism was distancing them from the Christian community? That he was quite capable of attacking two opposite extremes at once can be illustrated from *On Virginity*:

> Who could enumerate all such deviations into which one is carried because of not wishing to associate himself with those esteemed in the sight of God? Of these, we know also those who starve themselves to death on the grounds that such a sacrifice is pleasing to God, and again, others, completely opposite to these, who practice celibacy in name, but who do not refrain from social life, not only enjoying the pleasures of the stomach, but living openly with women...[67]

The idea that Gregory was concerned to prevent individualistic asceticism ties in with Malherbe and Ferguson's argument that he provided an ideological undergirding for Basil's monastic movement. Basil, a disciple of Eustathius of Sebaste,[68] was 'in contact with the incipient "wild-man" element of early monasticism', but encouraged its integration into ecclesial structures.[69] According to Marcus Plested, 'he set a pattern whereby the charismatic and eschatological vision of monasticism might be integrated within an ecclesiastical framework'.[70] And 'Gregory of Nyssa's irenic and sympathetic approach

---

[65] Sterk, 'On Basil, Moses, and the Model Bishop', 228.
[66] Sterk, 'On Basil, Moses, and the Model Bishop', 250.
[67] *Virg.* 23 (GNO 8,1.337–338); trans. Callahan, 71.
[68] Basil broke with Eustathius in the early 370s, over the divinity of the Holy Spirit.
[69] Marcus Plested, *The Macarian Legacy: The Place of Macarius–Symeon in the Eastern Christian Tradition* (Oxford: Oxford University Press, 2004), 47.
[70] Plested, *The Macarian Legacy*, 48.

to aberrant forms of monasticism perfectly accords with that of Basil.[71] Jean Gribomont summarizes Basil and Gregory's attitude to the Eustathian monks and their successors as follows:

> Le meilleur moyen de tirer parti de ces forces impétueuses était de les discipliner de l'intérieur, de les purifier en leur faisant méditer le Nouveau Testament, de les mettre au service de l'Eglise et de les unir à la hiérarchie, non sans plaider leur cause devant le public cultivé en dissertant avec art sur leurs antécédents philosophiques.[72]

This is illustrated by Gregory's use of the *Great Letter* of Pseudo-Macarius as the model for his treatise *On the Christian Mode of Life* (*De Instituto Christiano*). The *Great Letter* itself has been seen as exercising a moderating influence on radical ascetic tendencies,[73] and 'Gregory's respect for his model was such as to allow him to incorporate the positive aspects of ascetic enthusiasm within his own teaching.'[74] There are some interesting parallels between *On the Christian Mode of Life* and the short commentary on the earthly tabernacle in *Life of Moses*. The themes of baptism, harmony amongst believers, the grace of the Holy Spirit, and the hardships of the virtuous life, which Gregory sees in the earthly tabernacle, also appear in *On the Christian Mode of Life*. This background may explain why he allegorizes the washbasins as baptisers, but does not take the opportunity to make the showbread, for example, a symbol of the Eucharist. In *On the Christian Mode of Life* Gregory emphasizes that 'holy Baptism is important, important for the things perceptible to the mind of those who receive it with fear; for the rich and ungrudging Spirit is always flowing into those accepting grace, filled with which the holy apostle reaped a full harvest for the churches of Christ.'[75] The Eucharist does not feature in the same way.

---

[71] Plested, *The Macarian Legacy*, 57.

[72] 'The best way to take advantage of these impetuous forces was to discipline them from inside, purifying them by imposing New Testament meditations, putting them at the service of the Church, and uniting them to the hierarchy, not without pleading their case to the cultivated public by discoursing eloquently on their philosophical antecedants.' J. Gribomont, 'Le De Instituto Christiano et le Messalianisme de Grégoire de Nysse', in F. L. Cross (ed.), *Papers Presented to the Third International Conference on Patristic Studies Held at Christ Church, Oxford, 1959, Part 3* (Berlin: Akademie-Verlag, 1962), 321.

[73] These tendencies are usually labelled 'Messalian', and identified with the Messalian heretics who were condemned by a series of synods and councils, starting with synods held during the 380s or 390s at Antioch in Syria and Side in Pamphylia. But there are problems with this identification. 'None of our immediate sources are able to provide a convincing picture of the nature of Messalianism. We know *that* Messalianism was; we do not know *what* it was. We are led to the conclusion that "Messalianism" was little more than a sobriquet for a radical ascetic tendency stemming from the Syrian East, and...little welcomed or understood by the Greek bishops who confronted it.' Plested, *The Macarian Legacy*, 21. For more details see also Columba Stewart, '*Working the Earth of the Heart*': *The Messalian Controversy in History, Texts, and Language to AD 431* (Oxford: Clarendon, 1991).

[74] Plested, *The Macarian Legacy*, 57.   [75] GNO 8,1.44; trans. Callahan, 129.

Gregory's commentary on the earthly tabernacle illustrates the high value he places on ascetic observance. But it is significant that he places this observance within the church. He is not encouraging individualistic attempts to imitate Moses. The benefits of the vision that Moses received—an understanding of the heavenly and earthly Christ—are available to all through the earthly body of Christ, the church.

11.4 LIFE OF MOSES 2.184-187: HEAVENLY ASCENT CONTEXT

Exodus presents the earthly tabernacle as a copy of a heavenly model. Thus, the tabernacle and temple were provided with heavenly endorsement. But by Second Temple times, not everyone was convinced that the endorsement still stood. Heavenly ascent texts witness to unease over whether the earthly temple was still a faithful copy of the heavenly original. Himmelfarb writes,

> The Book of the Watchers' interest in a heavenly Temple reflects a certain discontent with the earthly Temple and its personnel. The author uses the story of the fall of the watchers to criticize the corrupt priests of the Jerusalem Temple. As angels fail to perform their duties in heaven, these priests fail to fulfill their responsibilities in the earthly Temple, and for some of the same reasons, like inappropriate marriages.[76]

Schäfer detects not mild condemnation, but a devastating critique, since Enoch's vision could imply

> that God in fact can no longer be found in the Temple on earth: the Holy of Holies in the earthly Temple is indeed empty; the missing Ark signals that God is gone, that he has withdrawn himself to his Temple in heaven.[77]

He also draws attention to the temple-critical motif in *Testament of Levi*:

> Levi is invested with the insignia of the priesthood, yet unfortunately, his successors will not live up to the task. They will corrupt the priesthood until God appoints a new eschatological priest whose priesthood will endure forever.[78]

Once the Jerusalem temple had been destroyed, there no longer was an earthly copy of God's heavenly dwelling. Elior suggests that the Hekhalot texts involve

---

[76] Martha Himmelfarb, 'The Temple and the Garden of Eden in Ezekiel, the Book of the Watchers, and the Wisdom of ben Sira', in Jamie Scott and Paul Simpson-Housley (eds), *Sacred Places and Profane Spaces: Essays in the Geographics of Judaism, Christianity, and Islam* (New York: Greenwood, 1991), 67–8.

[77] Peter Schäfer, *The Origins of Jewish Mysticism* (Tübingen: Mohr Siebeck, 2009), 66.

[78] Schäfer, *The Origins of Jewish Mysticism*, 28.

'a transferal and elevation of the priestly and Levitical traditions of Temple worship to the supernal regions.'[79] As we shall see in 12.4, Schäfer argues that they validate synagogue worship. But the synagogue is not confused with the temple. Rabbinic Judaism transfers temple language not so much over to congregational gatherings, as to the Torah: 'The skin-covered tabernacle of the Israelites grows into the skin-made parchment of the Torah scrolls.'[80] The church, on the other hand, starting with Paul, appropriates temple imagery to describe its community life. There is a Jewish parallel in the literature from Qumran.[81]

The Qumran text *4QFlorilegium* (4Q174) has already been mentioned in 7.1, when discussing the tabernacle not made with hands. It refers not only to the temple of Israel, now defiled, and to the eschatological temple to be built by God, but also to a 'temple of man':

> And he commanded to build for himself a temple of man (מקדש אדם), to offer (מקטירים) him in it, before him, the works of thanksgiving (מעשי תודה).[82]

According to George Brooke,

> This highly descriptive phrase means literally 'sanctuary of Adam' or 'sanctuary of man' which can also be taken collectively as 'sanctuary of men'. The purpose of the sanctuary is to make smoking sacrifices which are appositionally described as 'deeds of thanksgiving', thank-offerings.[83]

He argues that the phrase is deliberately polyvalent:

---

[79] Rachel Elior, 'From Earthly Temple to Heavenly Shrines: Prayer and Sacred Song in the Hekhalot Literature and Its Relation to Temple Traditions', *Jewish Studies Quarterly*, 4 (1997), 222.

[80] Risa Levitt Kohn and Rebecca Moore, *A Portable God: The Origin of Judaism and Christianity* (Lanham: Rowman & Littlefield, 2007), 129.

[81] Gärtner writes, 'The resemblance between Qumran and the New Testament on [the] point of temple symbolism is sufficiently detailed to suggest that there must have existed some form of common tradition.' Bertil Gärtner, *The Temple and the Community in Qumran and the New Testament: A Comparative Study in the Temple Symbolism of the Qumran Texts and the New Testament* (Cambridge: Cambridge University Press, 1965), 100–1. Hogeterp questions many of Gärtner's presuppositions, and denies any 'direct relation between early Christian and Qumranite traditions about the temple', but does argue that 'Paul relied on Palestinian Jewish temple-theological traditions'. Albert L. A. Hogeterp, 'Paul's Judaism Reconsidered: The Issue of Cultic Imagery in the Corinthian Correspondence', *Ephemerides theologicae lovanienses*, 81: 1 (2005), 91, 108. The question of the relationship, if any, between Qumran traditions and Christianity need not be settled for the purposes of this study, which is an exercise in heuristic comparison.

[82] 4Q174 1 i 6–7; trans. Martínez and Tigchelaar, 1.353. Dimant prefers the reading מעשי תורה —'works of Torah': Devorah Dimant, '4QFlorilegium and the Idea of the Community as Temple', in A. Caquot, M. Hadas-Lebel, and J. Riaud (eds), *Hellenica et Judaica: Hommage à Valentin Nikiprowetzky* (Leuven: Peeters, 1986), 169.

[83] George J. Brooke, 'Miqdash Adam, Eden and the Qumran Community', in Beate Ego, Armin Lange, and Peter Pilhofer (eds), *Gemeinde ohne Tempel, Community without Temple: Zur Substituierung und Transformation des Jerusalemer Tempels und seines Kults im Alten Testament, antiken Judentum und frühen Christentum* (Tübingen: Mohr Siebeck, 1999), 288.

The two principal meanings would seem to be that of 'sanctuary of man/men', namely a reference to the community to whom the commentary is addressed as if they are formed to be a sanctuary proleptically, and 'sanctuary of Adam', that is a reference to how both the proleptic last days community-sanctuary and the divinely constructed eschatological sanctuary would be places where the intention of God in creating Eden would be restored.[84]

Devorah Dimant comments further on the Qumran community's self-perception, arguing that 'the community, or, in fact, its core of full members, functioned analogously to a community of priestly angels, officiating in the innermost sanctuary of the heavenly temple'.[85] In support of this, she draws up a comparison between the angelic activities depicted in *Songs of the Sabbath Sacrifice* and the main activities of the Qumran community as described in such documents as *Rule of the Community* (1QS), *Thanksgiving Hymns* (1QH), and the *Damascus Document* (CD), and concludes that 'a striking resemblance' is revealed.[86] 'In spite of the keenly felt abyss separating men from angels, the community aimed at creating on earth a replica of the heavenly world. Thus, the notorious communion of the Qumranites with the angels, referred to by several scrolls, should be understood as a communion by analogy rather than an actual one.'[87] Fletcher-Louis disagrees with the idea of a 'keenly felt abyss separating men from angels', and a communion by analogy. He argues that *Songs of the Sabbath Sacrifice* does not describe angelic worship in heaven but the worship of the community, with the community members taking on 'a heavenly, angelic and divine identity':[88]

> The cosmology which can describe the cultic space in terms of the heavenly world is one which believes that the true temple is a microcosm of the universe. And the place where all this liturgy and a communion between angels and men takes place will then be the human community's own, concrete, earthly cultic space.[89]

He questions, in other words, the presence at Qumran of what he sees as a dualistic 'Temple-above and Temple-below idea'.[90] Alexander thinks that Fletcher-Louis has taken realized eschatology too far:

---

[84] Brooke, 'Miqdash Adam, Eden and the Qumran Community', 288–9. Wise disagrees with Brooke (and Dimant), arguing that מקדש אדם is another name for the temple of the Lord: an actual physical temple, 'which Israel is to build for the first stage of the eschaton, the End of Days'. Michael O. Wise, '4QFlorilegium and the Temple of Adam', *Revue de Qumran*, 15: 57–8 (1991), 131.

[85] Devorah Dimant, 'Men as Angels: The Self-Image of the Qumran Community', in Adele Berlin (ed.), *Religion and Politics in the Ancient Near East* (Bethesda, MD: University Press of Maryland, 1996), 98.

[86] Dimant, 'Men as Angels', 100.   [87] Dimant, 'Men as Angels', 101.

[88] Crispin H. T. Fletcher-Louis, 'Heavenly Ascent or Incarnational Presence? A Revisionist Reading of the *Songs of the Sabbath Sacrifice*', *Society of Biblical Literature Seminar Papers*, 37 (1998), 369.

[89] Crispin H. T. Fletcher-Louis, *All the Glory of Adam: Liturgical Anthropology in the Dead Sea Scrolls* (Leiden: Brill, 2002), 274.

[90] Fletcher-Louis, *All the Glory of Adam*, 273.

The extent to which he envisages the community as a whole, or at least its priesthood, as having already transcended its humanity, and achieved immortality, amounts almost to a totally realized eschatology, which does not sit easily either with common sense (had the community completely lost touch with reality?), or with its continued experience of the trials and tribulations of the world, the burdens of the flesh and the struggle with sin (which are vividly described all over their literature), or with its sharp longing for an *eschatological* deliverance.[91]

He agrees with Dimant and Brooke that 'the living community at Qumran...constituted God's temple on earth' and that the aim of their worship was to 'commune with the angels in the heavenly sanctuary'.[92] Although there may be disagreement over the extent to which the community members identified themselves with angels, and whether there was one temple or two, there is no doubt about the pervasive use of temple imagery in the community's self-understanding.

There are many similarities between *Songs of the Sabbath Sacrifice* and the later Hekhalot texts, particularly in their descriptions of the heavenly world.[93] But there is no parallel to the Qumran community's self-designation as a temple. Like Christianity, rabbinic Judaism had to adapt to the loss of the temple. Both the synagogue and the home took on temple characteristics, but there was no wholesale appropriation of priestly temple theology to designate the people of God. *B. Ḥagigah* witnesses to rabbinic unease about *merkavah* speculation. Using dramatic examples, it conveys the message that exposition of the *merkavah* is for the select few, everyone else is to steer clear. The approved alternative to attempting to penetrate the heavenly mysteries is spelt out by the wider rabbinic corpus. *Halakhah* (Jewish law) focuses on the details of daily living. That is where the *mitsvot* (commandments) are to be carried out—not in heaven. No link is made between daily living and the tradition of heavenly ascent. Gregory too is concerned that not everyone should attempt to follow Moses up the mountain, thinking that they can glimpse the 'tabernacle not made with hands'. Most people are to reap the benefit of Moses' vision by participating in the church, and clothing themselves with faith and virtue. But Gregory is able to draw on pre-existing Christian imagery of the church as body and temple. There is no need to speculate about the divine essence, because the worshipping community is the body of Christ. The mystery of the incarnation is embodied in the earthly tabernacle, the church. In their different ways, both Gregory and the rabbis argue that there is no escape from the difficult business of human living, no fast lane to heaven. Only Gregory, however, is able to tie his argument to an earthly copy of the heavenly tabernacle.

---

[91] Philip Alexander, 'The Qumran *Songs of the Sabbath Sacrifice* and the *Celestial Hierarchy* of Dionysius the Areopagite: A Comparative Approach', *Revue de Qumran*, 22: 87 (2006), 47.
[92] Alexander, '*Songs of the Sabbath Sacrifice* and the *Celestial Hierarchy*', 100.
[93] See Alexander, '*Songs of the Sabbath Sacrifice* and the *Celestial Hierarchy*', 125–7.

11.5 *LIFE OF MOSES* 2.184–187: CONCLUSIONS

One way in which Gregory undermines the dangerous potential of heavenly ascent traditions is by his use of the earthly tabernacle. Moses was granted a vision of the heavenly tabernacle so that the Israelites could build a copy of it. It is to this earthly tabernacle that the people in general, as opposed to a few privileged figures, are to relate. Gregory first allegorizes the earthly tabernacle as the incarnation, and then as the church. His prescription for Christian life is not a solitary ascent to the divine world, but participation in the orthodox Christian community on earth. He stresses the value of asceticism to this community. His identification of the earthly tabernacle as the church taps into long-standing Christian traditions, going back to Paul, both of the church as the body of Christ, and of the church community as a temple. There is a Jewish parallel in the Qumran literature. There, as in Gregory, we find a heavenly temple composed of angels, and an earthly one made up of human beings. The relationship between them, however, is depicted differently. At Qumran angels and humans mingle, particularly in liturgy, as we shall see in 12.4. The community was critical of the temple cult in Jerusalem, and therefore participated in the heavenly cult instead. Gregory keeps the heavenly and earthly tabernacles separate. The heavenly model validates the earthly church, so that the need for ascent is obviated.

12

Heavenly and Earthly Worship

Hearing 'altar' (θυσιαστήριον) and 'incense altar' (θυμιατήριον), I understand the adoration by heavenly beings which is continuously performed in this tabernacle. For he says that not only the tongues of those 'on earth' and 'under the earth' but also of 'heavenly beings' offer praise to the Origin of all things (τῇ τῶν πάντων ἀρχῇ). This is the sacrifice pleasing to God, the 'fruit of lips' (τὸ κάρπωμα τῶν χειλέων), as the apostle says, and the fragrance of prayers (τῶν προσευχῶν ἡ εὐωδία).[1]

In this tabernacle both a 'sacrifice of praise' and an incense of prayer are seen being offered continually at daybreak and at nightfall. Great David also allows us to understand these things, directing the incense of prayer as 'a fragrant offering' (ὀσμὴν εὐδίας) to God and performing the sacrifice by the stretching out (ἐκτάσεως) of hands.[2]

12.1 *LIFE OF MOSES* 2.182, 185: BIBLICAL CONTEXT

In Gregory's interpretation of the heavenly tabernacle furniture, the two altars suggest to him the adoration of the heavenly beings. He comments on this adoration with a medley of New Testament verses. The first allusion is to Philippians 2:10–11—'at the name of Jesus every knee should bow, in heaven and on earth and under the earth, and every tongue confess...'—which attests to the existence of heavenly worship. In Philippians, the worship is triggered by the name of Jesus. Gregory draws on Colossians 1:15–18, itself probably a reflection on the characterization of wisdom as 'the beginning' in Proverbs 8:22, for his description of Christ as 'the Origin of all things'. In his Trinitarian theology, however, he insists that 'the Persons of the Divinity are not separated from one another either by time or place',[3] so that adoration is always directed to all three.[4] Philippians uses the physical language

---

[1] *Vit. Moys.* 2.182. [2] *Vit. Moys.* 2.185.
[3] *Graec.* (GNO 3,1.25.8–10); trans. Stramara, 385. [4] *Maced.* (GNO 3,1.110–111).

of knees bowing, and Gregory too creates a picture of angelic movement. The word he uses for 'adoration' (προσκύνησις) strictly speaking refers to making obeisance. Eleven times in the New Testament the cognate verb (προσκυνέω) is preceded by 'to fall down' (πίπτω).[5] Gregory himself comments that, in common parlance, the 'self-prostration (ἐπίκλισιν) of inferiors upon the ground which they practise when they salute their betters is termed worship (προσκύνησιν)'.[6] In philosophical moments he may argue that angels have no bodies—'for inasmuch as human nature is compounded of body and soul and the angelic nature has for its portion the bodiless life...'[7]—but when writing more poetically, he talks of the angelic choral dance (ἡ ἀγγελικὴ χορεία).[8] Here in *Life of Moses* his language recalls the scene in Revelation in which angels and elders fall on their faces and worship before the throne.[9]

After Philippians comes a reference to Hebrews 13:15—'through him then let us continually offer up a sacrifice of praise to God, that is, the fruit of lips (καρπὸν χειλέων) that acknowledge his name'. Hebrews has taken the phrase 'the fruit of lips' from the LXX version of Hosea 14:3. In both Hebrews and Hosea the phrase refers to human praises. The final significant words, 'the fragrance of prayers', recall three New Testament verses:

> For we are the aroma (εὐωδία) of Christ to God... [2 Cor 2:15]

> And walk in love, as Christ loved us and gave himself up for us, a fragrant offering and sacrifice to God (προσφορὰν καὶ θυσίαν τῷ θεῷ εἰς ὀσμὴν εὐωδίας). [Eph 5:2]

> I am filled, having received from Epaphroditus the gifts you sent, a fragrant offering (ὀσμὴν εὐωδίας), a sacrifice acceptable and pleasing to God. [Phil 4:18]

Here too 'fragrance' refers to human activities. The verses from Ephesians and Philippians contain the phrase 'a fragrant offering', or more literally 'the smell of sweetness'.[10] A phrase that initially referred to the smell of animal sacrifices came to denote a variety of activities pleasing to God. Gregory is drawing on a long tradition, not confined to Christian circles, of reinterpreting the sacrifices of the tabernacle/temple as verbal offerings of prayer. And then he is arguing that such verbal offerings are made not only by humans, but also by angels. In his description of angelic praise, he can but use physical, pictorial language. Since this is the heavenly tabernacle, there are altars and sacrifices. Even though the sacrifices are of prayer and praise, they are described in terms of doing obeisance, tongues, lips, and fragrance. There is, however, no specification of the content of the praise. No words are put into the angels' mouths.

---

[5] Matt. 2:11; 4:9; 18:26; Acts 10:25; 1 Cor. 14:25; Rev. 5:14; 7:11; 11:16; 19:4; 19:10; 22:8.
[6] *Maced.* (GNO 3,1.111.2–5); trans. NPNF² 5.324.
[7] *Eust.* (GNO 3,1.12.21–23); trans. Silvas, 242.
[8] *Inscr.* 2.6 (GNO 5.86–87); trans. Heine, 138–9.   [9] Rev. 7:11.
[10] ὀσμὴ εὐδίας is the LXX translation of ריח ניחוח (cf. Exod. 29:18, 25, 41).

In 2.184–188 Gregory turns to the earthly tabernacle. As with the heavenly tabernacle, physical sacrifices are reinterpreted spiritually: the two altars become the 'sacrifice of praise' (θυσία τῆς αἰνέσεως) and the 'incense of prayer' (θυμίαμα τῆς προσευχῆς). The first phrase occurs in Hebrews 13:15. It comes from the LXX, where it translates 'thank offering' (זבח התודה).[11] In the Hebrew Bible this refers to a particular kind of sacrifice, which may or may not be a subset of peace offerings.[12] Hebrews reinterprets it, using the LXX version of Hosea 14:3, as 'the fruit of lips'. The second phrase, the conjunction of incense and prayer, Gregory traces to LXX Psalm 140:2—'Let my prayer succeed as incense before you, a lifting up of my hands be an evening sacrifice.'[13] There is also possibly an allusion to Revelation 5:8 in which 'golden bowls full of incense' are 'the prayers of the saints'. In 2.181 Gregory talked of the fragrance of prayers, here he uses the whole LXX phrase 'a fragrant offering' (ὀσμὴ εὐωδίας). Sacrifice and incense have become praise and prayer, which are offered in both the heavenly and the earthly tabernacles: in the angelic world and in the church. The psalm refers to the lifting up (ἔπαρσις) of hands. A similar phrase occurs in 1 Timothy 2:8: 'I desire then that in every place the men should pray, lifting (ἐπαίροντας) holy hands…' Gregory, however, does not refer to lifting up, but, instead, to stretching out (ἐκτάσεως). Why make the change? The verb 'to stretch out' (ἐπεκτείνω), taken from Philippians 3:13, is highly significant in *Life of Moses*:

> Ce texte de *Phil.* 3, 13, est le leit-motiv de tout le traité. Il exprime la thèse essentielle de Grégoire, que la perfection est un continuel progrès.[14]

But the noun used here is derived from a very slightly different verb (from ἐκτείνω rather than ἐπεκτείνω). Elsewhere in *Life of Moses* it refers to Moses stretching out his hands, either to destroy the plague of frogs (2.78, 84) or to enable victory over the Amalekites (2.150, 153, 229), as a type of the cross. Therefore, it is more likely that Gregory is referring to the liturgical practice of stretching out arms in the form of a cross. The reference to praise and prayer being offered 'continually at morning and evening' would certainly seem to be an allusion to the church's liturgical observance of morning and evening prayer. The expression 'day and night', used to refer to continuous worship, occurs in the New Testament (Luke 2:37; Rev. 4:8); but Gregory's text seems to be referring to particular points in the day.

---

[11] See Lev. 7:12 (LXX 7:2); Ps. 107:22 (LXX 106:22); Ps. 116:17 (LXX 115:17).
[12] Compare Lev. 7:11–12 with Lev. 22:21, 29.   [13] Trans. NETS.
[14] 'This text of Phil 3:13 is the leitmotif of the whole treatise. It expresses Gregory's essential thesis, that perfection is continual progress.' Jean Daniélou, *Grégoire de Nysse: La Vie de Moïse, ou Traité de la perfection en matière de vertu* (Paris: Cerf, 2000), 49 n. 1.

12.2 *LIFE OF MOSES* 2.182, 185: ALEXANDRIAN CONTEXT

Liturgy, whether earthly or heavenly, does not feature prominently in Alexandrian tabernacle interpretations. Philo does once describe angels as priests:

> The highest, and in the truest sense the holy, temple of God is...the whole universe, having for its sanctuary the most sacred part of all existence, even heaven, for its votive ornaments the stars, for its priests the angels who are servitors to His powers, unbodied souls...with the irrational eliminated...pure intelligences...[15]

He does not, however, elaborate on this identification. In his cosmological and anthropological allegorizations of the tabernacle furniture there is no mention of priests or worship. Clement interprets the ark as 'the repose which dwells with the adoring spirits' and the voice of the cherubim as 'delightsome glory in ceaseless contemplation'.[16] Thus, the delights of the 'ineffable inheritance' available to the 'spiritual and perfect man' include participation in angelic worship, but Clement's interests lie elsewhere. Origen brings prayer into his tabernacle interpretations, but only in the context of the earthly tabernacle, not the heavenly one. His interpretation of the incense altar has similarities to Gregory's:

> Others are the 'altar of incense', whosoever 'by means of prayers and fasting day and night does not leave the temple' of God, who pray not only for themselves, but also for the entire people.[17]

Origen, however, alludes to Anna in the temple (Luke 2:37); whereas Gregory relies on LXX Psalm 140:2. Origen also interprets the mercy seat in terms of the prayers of the church:

> And still more are those ones to be named the 'propitiatory', who with all confidence propitiate God to men by means of the sacrifices of prayers and the victims of supplications, and those who intercede for the transgressions of the people.[18]

Although Origen's interpretation of the earthly tabernacle could possibly have provided a starting point for Gregory, the two accounts differ in detail. And Origen does not present an earthly–heavenly parallelism.

---

[15] *Spec.* 1.66. [16] *Strom.* 5.36.3, 4; trans. Wilson, 242–3.
[17] *Hom. Num.* 5.3.2; trans. Scheck, 19. [18] *Hom. Num.* 5.3.2; trans. Scheck, 19.

12.3 *LIFE OF MOSES* 2.182, 185: THEOLOGICAL CONTEXT

In *Life of Moses*, the heavenly and earthly tabernacles offer their praises in parallel. In *On the Titles of the Psalms*, Gregory explains that 'there was a time when the dance (ἡ χοροστασία) of the rational nature was one, and looked to the one leader of the chorus (τὸν τοῦ χοροῦ κορυφαῖον)'. But sin 'put an end to that divine concord of the chorus, when it poured the slipperiness of deceit at the feet of the first humans who used to sing in chorus (συγχορευόντων) with the angelic powers and caused the fall, wherefore man was separated from connection with the angels'.[19] At the end of time, however, there will be a reunion of humanity with the angels, when 'through one another and with one another they will sing a hymn of thanksgiving to God for his love for humanity which will be heard throughout the universe'.[20] One of Gregory's images for this reunion involves the feast of Tabernacles. In *On the Soul and Resurrection*, and also in his sermon *On the Nativity of Christ*, Gregory designates the celebration at the end of time as a *skēnopēgia* (a pitching of tents, i.e. the feast of Tabernacles). The LXX translates both 'tabernacle' (משכן) and 'booth' (סכה) by *skēnē*, thus introducing a linguistic connection between the tabernacle as precursor of the temple and the feast of Tabernacles (חג הסכות Lev. 23:34) which is absent in the Hebrew. Gregory says that in LXX Psalm 117:27—'The Lord is God, and he showed us light (ἐπέφανεν ἡμῖν). Arrange a feast with the thick ones (πυκάζουσιν), up to the horns of the altar'[21]—the word 'thick ones' signifies 'the feast of tabernacle-fixing (τὴν τῶν σκηνοπηγίων ἑορτήν) which was instituted of old in the tradition of Moses...prophetically announcing beforehand the things which are to come'.[22] Tabernacles represents both the incarnation:

> In this feast, the human tabernacle was built up (σκηνοπηγεῖται τὸ ἀνθρώπινον σκήνωμα) by Him who put on human nature because of us. Our tabernacles (σκηνώματα), which were struck down by death, are raised up again by Him Who built our dwelling from the beginning.... It is He, Our Lord, who has appeared (ἐπέφανεν) to make the solemn feast day in thick branches of foliage up to the horns of the altar.[23]

and the end of time:

> The words of life have sounded in the ears that were shut, so that one feast of harmony is made by the reunion in one cluster in the feast of Tabernacles (διὰ

---

[19] *Inscr.* 2.6 (GNO 5.86); trans. Heine, 138.
[20] *Inscr.* 1.9 (GNO 5.66); trans. Heine, 121.
[21] Trans. NETS. A footnote suggests that 'thick ones' might refer to garlands.
[22] *An. et res.* (PG 46.132B); trans. Silvas, 231.
[23] *Diem nat.* (GNO 10,2.236); trans. Jean Daniélou, *The Bible and the Liturgy* (Notre Dame, Ind.: University of Notre Dame Press, 1956), 345.

τοῦ πυκασμοῦ τῆς σκηνοπηγίας), of the creation below with the sublime powers around the heavenly altar. Indeed, the horns of the altar are the sublime and eminent powers of spiritual nature, the Principalities, the Powers, the Thrones and the Dominations to which human nature is reunited by the *Scenopegia* in a common feast.[24]

In *Life of Moses*, Gregory uses the word *skēnopēgia* once:

> The pillars... and all the other elements which the description of the tabernacle's construction (ἡ τῆς σκηνοπηγίας ὑπογραγή) contains, if one examines them by looking to things above, are the supercosmic powers...[25]

Daniélou comments, 'Pour Grégoire ce tabernacle céleste contient la totalité de la création spirituelle, puisque les hommes en feront partie à l'apocatastase.'[26] The heavenly tabernacle, therefore, is perhaps a vision of what the church will become at the end of time, when humanity will rejoin its older kin, the angels. In the meanwhile, the task is to build an exact replica on earth.

12.4 *LIFE OF MOSES* 2.182, 185: HEAVENLY ASCENT CONTEXT

Through his allegorization of the heavenly altars, Gregory depicts the heavenly powers as priests. This is nothing new. The picture of ministering angels standing around the throne of God goes back to *1 Enoch* 14 and Daniel 7. Himmelfarb and George Nickelsburg argue that the verb 'draw near' (ἤγγιζω) used in *1 Enoch* 14:23 of certain holy ones of the angelic corps, indicates priestly service.[27] In *Songs of the Sabbath Sacrifice*, the heavenly beings are designated priests of the inner sanctum (כוהני קורב) or priests of the highest heights (כוהני מרומי רום).[28]

Another indication of the link between angels and priests is the experience of the human characters who ascend to heaven. Himmelfarb argues that in *1 Enoch* 14 Enoch acts as a priest: he ascends to the heavenly temple in order to intercede for the sins of the watchers, gains access to the sanctuary, and looks into the holy of holies, where God speaks to him with his own mouth.[29] Levi

---

[24] *Diem nat.* (GNO 10,2.237–238); trans. Daniélou, *The Bible and the Liturgy*, 346.
[25] *Vit. Moys.* 2.179.
[26] 'For Gregory this celestial tabernacle contains the whole spiritual creation, since human beings will join at the apocatastasis.' Daniélou, *La Vie de Moïse*, 225 n. 2.
[27] Martha Himmelfarb, *Ascent to Heaven in Jewish and Christian Apocalypses* (Oxford: Oxford University Press, 1993), 20; George W. E. Nickelsburg, *1 Enoch 1: A Commentary on the Book of 1 Enoch, Chapters 1–36; 81–108* (Minneapolis: Fortress, 2001), 265.
[28] For example Song 1:19–20 (4Q400 1 i 19–20).
[29] Himmelfarb, *Ascent to Heaven*, 25.

ascends to heaven in order to be consecrated as a priest. In the *Aramaic Levi Document* this is deduced from the reference to anointing, although the same word (רבות) could also be translated as 'greatness'. In *Testament of Levi* there is no ambiguity: God says, 'Levi, I have given to you the blessings of the priesthood';[30] and in Chapter 8 Levi undergoes a robing and anointing ceremony. The transformation of Enoch into 'one of the glorious ones' in *2 Enoch* 22:8–10 would also seem to be a priestly investiture, although Enoch is never explicitly called a priest, as his descendents are.[31]

If angels are heavenly priests, one would presume that they offer heavenly sacrifices, and/or burn heavenly incense. However, as Newsom remarks, 'Explicit references to a heavenly sacrificial cult are less common than one might think.'[32] In *Testament of Levi*, 'the angels of the presence of the Lord... minister and make propitiation to the Lord for all the sins of ignorance of the righteous, and they offer to the Lord a pleasant odour (ὀσμὴν εὐωδίας), a reasonable and bloodless offering (λογικὴν καὶ ἀναίμακτον προσφοράν)'.[33] Here, as in Gregory, we have the Greek translation of 'a fragrant offering' (ריח ניחוח). Himmelfarb comments,

> I am inclined to see the 'sweet savor' of the Testament of Levi as a cultic term intended to suggest that heavenly sacrifices are at once like and unlike earthly. The sweet savor is the most ethereal product of the sacrifices performed on earth; in heaven it becomes the sacrifice itself.[34]

The wording of *Testament of Levi* 3:6 is reminiscent of Romans 12:1, suggesting that the phrase 'reasonable and bloodless offering' may have come from a Christian redactor. Alexander cautions that this is not necessarily so: there were Jewish attempts to spiritualize the Jerusalem cult, set against the background of 'a wider philosophical unease about animal sacrifice'.[35] 'Reasonable' (*logikos*) might better be translated as 'made up of words (*logoi*)': 'The adjective is simply calling attention to the fact that the offerings in heaven are "offerings of the lips".'[36] Schäfer goes further than Himmelfarb and Alexander, suggesting the 'the angels perform a sacrifice that is radically different from the sacrifice in the earthly Temple': 'it is bloodless and *therefore* gives off a sweet odor; its odor is truly sweet *because* it is bloodless.'[37] In Revelation, the four living creatures and twenty-four elders hold 'golden bowls full of incense',

---

[30] *T. Levi* 5:2; trans. Hollander and de Jonge, 143.
[31] For the descendants, see *2 En.* 69:15, 70:26, 71:19.
[32] Carol A. Newsom, *Songs of the Sabbath Sacrifice: A Critical Edition* (Atlanta: Scholars Press, 1985), 372.
[33] *T. Levi* 3:5–6; trans. Hollander and de Jonge, 136.
[34] Himmelfarb, *Ascent to Heaven*, 35.
[35] Philip Alexander, *The Mystical Texts: Songs of the Sabbath Sacrifice and Related Manuscripts* (London: T&T Clark, 2006), 81 n. 2.
[36] Alexander, *The Mystical Texts*, 81.
[37] Peter Schäfer, *The Origins of Jewish Mysticism* (Tübingen: Mohr Siebeck, 2009), 69.

said to be the prayers of the saints.³⁸ A little further on, another angel stands at the altar with a golden censor, and 'either the incense is mingled with the prayers of the saints or the incense is the prayers'.³⁹ Once again we have an association between scent and words. There is some ambiguity about whether there is one altar or two in the heavenly world of Revelation. An altar is mentioned seven times.⁴⁰ The golden altar of 8:3b is clearly the heavenly equivalent of the incense altar; and most of the other references could also be alluding to the incense altar. However, 6:9 describes the souls of the martyrs as being under the altar, suggesting that the martyrs' 'untimely deaths on earth are from God's perspective a sacrifice on the altar of heaven', which fits the altar of burnt offering.⁴¹ Charles insisted that Revelation conforms to the general pattern of Jewish apocalyptic, in which there is only one altar in heaven on which 'only bloodless sacrifices and incense could be offered'.⁴² This altar 'has the characteristics of the earthly altar of incense, and in part those of the earthly altar of burnt-offering'.⁴³ The souls of the martyrs are a living sacrifice, even if their bodies have been slain on earth. Song 13 of *Songs of the Sabbath Sacrifice*, of which there are only fragments, hints at an angelic cult:

> ...for the sacrifices of the Holy Ones (לזבחי קדושים)...the odor of their offerings (ריח מנחותם)...and the o[do]r of their drink offerings (ור[י]ח נסכיהם)...⁴⁴

Fletcher-Louis, who denies that the text refers to a heavenly temple, sees this sacrificial language as referring to the cultic activity of the human worshippers, whether used metaphorically of praise and prayer, or providing evidence that animal sacrifices were conducted at Qumran.⁴⁵ Schäfer, however, argues that these sacrifices 'only make sense as substitutes for the sacrifices in the polluted earthly Temple':⁴⁶

---

³⁸ Rev. 5:8.
³⁹ Rev. 8:3–4. The translation depends on how the dative ταῖς προσευξαῖς is understood. Robert H. Mounce, *The Book of Revelation* (Grand Rapids, Mich.: Eerdmans, 1977), 182.
⁴⁰ Rev. 6:9; 8:3 (twice), 5; 9:13; 14:18; 16:7.
⁴¹ Mounce, *The Book of Revelation*, 157.
⁴² R. H. Charles, *A Critical and Exegetical Commentary on the Revelation of St. John*, 2 vols (Edinburgh: T&T Clark, 1920), 1.228.
⁴³ Charles, *A Commentary on the Revelation of St. John*, 1.229.
⁴⁴ Song 13:5–6 (11Q17 21–22 4–5); text and trans. Charlesworth and Newsom, 186–7.
⁴⁵ Crispin H. T. Fletcher-Louis, *All the Glory of Adam: Liturgical Anthropology in the Dead Sea Scrolls* (Leiden: Brill, 2002), 361.
⁴⁶ Schäfer, *The Origins of Jewish Mysticism*, 141–2. The question of whether the Qumran community still offered sacrifices at the Jerusalem temple is disputed. See Joseph M. Baumgarten, *Studies in Qumran Law* (Leiden: Brill, 1977), 39–74; Lawrence H. Schiffman, 'Community without Temple: The Qumran Community's Withdrawal from the Jerusalem Temple', in Beate Ego, Armin Lange, and Peter Pilhofer (eds), *Gemeinde ohne Tempel, Community without Temple: Zur Substituierung und Transformation des Jerusalemer Tempels und seines Kults im Alten Testament, antiken Judentum und frühen Christentum* (Tübingen: Mohr Siebeck, 1999), 267–84; and Martin Goodman, 'The Qumran Sectarians and the Temple in Jerusalem', in Charlotte Hempel (ed.), *The Dead Sea Scrolls: Text and Context* (Leiden: Brill, 2010), 263–73.

Whereas the members of the community can participate, to some degree, in the angelic praise by reciting the songs in their worship, they can no longer offer the expiatory sacrifice. The sacrifice on earth has become corrupt, and it is only the angels in heaven who are still able to perform this ritual so crucial to the existence and well-being of the earthly community (until it becomes fully united with the angels).[47]

Song 1 does indeed mention propitiation:

> ...By these all the eternally Holy Ones sanctify themselves. And he purifies the pure ones of
> [...] for all who pervert the way. And they propitiate (ויכפרו) his goodwill for all who repent of transgression.[48]

Finally, in *b. Ḥagigah* 12b Michael brings offerings (מקריב קרבן) to the altar of the heavenly Jerusalem, situated in *Zebul*, the fourth heaven. Of these texts, therefore, only *Songs of the Sabbath Sacrifice* explicitly mentions sacrifices in heaven. *Testament of Levi* refers to 'sweet savour', but emphasizes that heavenly offerings are 'bloodless'. Revelation talks of incense, the most evanescent of material offerings. *B. Ḥagigah* mentions heavenly offerings, but does not specify what they are, although commentators assume that Michael is offering human petitions. The only text, Jewish or Christian, which refers to sacrificial blood in heaven is Hebrews 9:12: '[Christ] entered once for all into the Holy Place, taking not the blood of goats and calves but his own blood, thus securing an eternal redemption'. In all these texts, the reason that there is incense, or other offerings, in heaven is not for the sake of the angels, but because of human sin and need.

Since blood is not seen as appropriate to heaven, the worship of heavenly beings is praise. *Songs of the Sabbath Sacrifice* gives long exhortations to heavenly praise. Praise was a component of temple worship in the form of Levitical singing, and Elior argues that it was this, rather than sacrificial rites or priestly laws, which the authors of the Hekhalot literature wanted to preserve:

> They considered it necessary to preserve all the vocally and orally expressed ceremonial and numinous elements that had been denied written documentation because of their esoteric nature: the musical and vocal tradition of the Temple, on the one hand, and the tradition of Names and benedictions accompanying the Temple rites, on the other.[49]

---

[47] Schäfer, *The Origins of Jewish Mysticism*, 145–6.
[48] Song 1:15–16 (4Q400 1 i 15–16); text and trans. Charlesworth and Newsom, 138–9.
[49] Rachel Elior, 'From Earthly Temple to Heavenly Shrines: Prayer and Sacred Song in the Hekhalot Literature and Its Relation to Temple Traditions', *Jewish Studies Quarterly*, 4 (1997), 231.

Some texts put the words from Isaiah 6:3, the *Qedushah*/Sanctus, into angelic mouths, sometimes with the addition of Ezekiel 3:12. One of the earliest texts to do so is Revelation 4:8, with a slightly altered version:

> And the four living creatures... day and night never cease to sing,
> Holy, holy, holy, is the Lord God Almighty, who was and is and is to come.

2 Enoch specifies the song of the cherubim and seraphim only in the longer recension.[50] *3 Enoch* gives a dramatic description of the recitation of the heavenly *Qedushah*:

> When the ministering angels utter the 'Holy', all the pillars of the heavens and their bases shake, and the gates of the palaces of the heaven of 'Arabot quiver; the foundations of the earth and of Šeḥaqim shudder; the chambers of Ma'on and the chambers of Makon writhe, and all the orders of Raqia', the constellations and the stars, are alarmed; the orb of the sun and the orb of the moon hurry from their paths in flight...[51]

3 Enoch is unusual amongst Hekhalot texts in that it focuses exclusively on the *Qedushah*, and does not contain elaborate hymns. The tradition of including other hymns alongside the *Qedushah* starts with Revelation:

> The twenty-four elders fall down before him who is seated on the
> throne and worship him... singing,
> 'Worthy art thou, our Lord and God,
> to receive glory and honour and power,
> for thou didst create all things,
> and by thy will they existed and were created.'[52]

By the time of the Hekhalot texts, these hymns include variations on the divine name:

> And I shall sanctify Your great, mighty, and awesome name:
> Holy, Holy, Holy is YHWH of Hosts, Great, mighty, and awesome,
> beautiful, magnificent, wondrous, and honored:
> HDYRYRWM steadfast, great, pure, explicit,
> Your name is carved in flames of fire
> HY YH YHW, holy and awesome.
> Blessed are You YWY, magnificent in the chambers of song.[53]

In *Songs of the Sabbath Sacrifice*, heavenly beings are exhorted to praise, but no words are specified. The text seems to suggest that angels worship silently. Part of Song 12 reads:

---

[50] *2 En.* 21:1.   [51] *3 En.* 38:1; §56; trans. Alexander, 290.   [52] Rev. 4:11.
[53] *Ma'aseh Merkavah* §551; trans. Michael D. Swartz, *Mystical Prayer in Ancient Judaism: An Analysis of Ma'aseh Merkavah* (Tübingen: Mohr Siebeck, 1992), 230.

... In the tabernac[le...] knowledge, the [cheru]bim fal[l] before him and b[le]ss as they rise. A sound of divine stillness (קול דממת אלוהים) [is heard] and (there is) a tumult of exultation (והמון רנה) as their wings lift up, the sound of divine [stillne]ss....
(And there is) a still sound of blessing in the tumult of their movement, and holy <> praise as they return on their ways. As they rise, they rise wondrously; and when they settle,
they [stand] still. The sound of exultant rejoicing falls silent, and (there is) a stilln[ess] of divine blessing in all the camps of the godlike beings; [and] the sound of lau[ding].[54]

The implication is that the heavenly beings use their wings as organs of song. Halperin argues that this idea derives from Ezekiel 3:12–13, which can be read as an antiphonal performance of blessing, in which the wings of the *ḥayyot* are answered by the voice of the *'ophannim*:[55]

> I heard a great roaring sound: 'Blessed is the Presence of the Lord, in His place', with the sound of the wings of the creatures beating against one another, and the sound of the wheels (*'ophannim*) beside them—a great roaring sound.[56]

Sabbath Songs combines this tumult with 'the still small voice' (קול דממה דקה) of 1 Kings 19:12. Dale Allison suggests that the allusions to silence indicate 'an awareness that the words of this world cannot plumb the depths of Godhead'.[57] Israel Knohl points out that the meaning of 'stillness' (דממה) is not absolute silence but a very quiet voice: 'We must therefore conclude that the angels are not silent but sing in a quiet voice.'[58] He links this quiet voice to the angels' priestly role, since the temple priestly cult was conducted in silence: 'The compromise between the conflicting elements of the voice of song of the angels and the silence of the cult of the Priestly Temple appears in the description of the angels, who bless their Creator with a still and silent voice.'[59] A tradition of silent angelic worship may also be reflected in the 'gentle voice' of *2 Enoch* 21:1 (longer recension). And allusions to 1 Kings 19:12 are also to be found in the Hekhalot literature:

> And [the holy *ḥayyot*] open their mouth
> in a great hymn,

---

[54] Song 12:2–3, 7–8 (4Q405 20–22 ii 7–8, 12–13); text and trans. Charlesworth and Newsom, 182–3.
[55] David J. Halperin, *The Faces of the Chariot: Early Jewish Responses to Ezekiel's Vision* (Tübingen: Mohr Siebeck, 1988), 45.
[56] NJPS translation.
[57] Dale C. Allison, 'The Silence of Angels: Reflections on the Songs of the Sabbath Sacrifice', *Revue de Qumran*, 13: 49–52 (1988), 194.
[58] Israel Knohl, 'Between Voice and Silence: The Relationship between Prayer and Temple Cult', *Journal of Biblical Literature*, 115: 1 (1996), 25.
[59] Knohl, 'Between Voice and Silence', 25.

with fright,
with trembling and shuddering,
with fear and terror,
in purity and holiness
and with the soft murmuring sound,
as it is written:
after the earthquake [came the] soft murmuring sound.[60]

What is the relationship between angelic praise in heaven and the worship of the human community on earth? In the ascent apocalypses, privileged human beings join the angelic priestly ranks. Newsom suggests that the effect of the poetry of *Songs of the Sabbath Sacrifice* was to enable a communal ascent:

> Although the Sabbath Shirot make no mention of actual translation of the human worshippers to the heavenly sphere, the vivid description of the heavenly realia create a virtual experience of presence in the heavenly temple. Consequently, those who experience the description of the merkabah share in an experience comparable in sacrality to the highly restricted entry of the high priest into the holy of holies on the Day of Atonement.[61]

She cautiously adds in a footnote, 'Whether the cultivation of actual mystical experience lies behind the literary description of the celestial holy of holies is more difficult to say.'[62] Morray-Jones is less cautious:

> By performing the liturgical cycle, the worshippers undertake a 'ritual journey', which involves an 'ascent' through the seven *debirim* (songs 1–7), followed by a detailed tour of the celestial temple, moving inwards towards the center, where the Glory manifests upon the throne.... The sacred structure within which this manifestation occurs has been constructed by means of [the] extended ritual performance. The worship of the holy community and its celestial, angelic counterpart is, so to speak, the substance of which the temple is composed.[63]

According to Esther Chazon, the human worshippers 'pray like the angels to a certain, but not a full, extent': they maintain 'the proper distinction between the two choirs, the one human and the other angelic'.[64] But Alexander suggests 'that she is underestimating the degree of progression in Sabbath Songs: while the choirs remain distinct at the beginning, by the end of the liturgy, on the

---

[60] *Hekhalot Rabbati* §187; trans. Peter Schäfer, *The Hidden and Manifest God: Some Major Themes in Early Jewish Mysticism* (Albany: State University of New York Press, 1992), 28.

[61] Carol A. Newsom, 'Merkabah Exegesis in the Qumran Sabbath Shirot', *Journal of Jewish Studies*, 38: 1 (1987), 14–15.

[62] Newsom, 'Merkabah Exegesis in the Qumran Sabbath Shirot', 15 n. 12.

[63] Christopher R. A. Morray-Jones, 'The Temple Within', in April D. DeConick (ed.), *Paradise Now: Essays on Early Jewish and Christian Mysticism* (Atlanta: Society of Biblical Literature, 2006), 166–7.

[64] Esther G. Chazon, 'Human and Angelic Prayer in Light of the Dead Sea Scrolls', in Esther G. Chazon (ed.), *Liturgical Perspectives: Prayer and Poetry in Light of the Dead Sea Scrolls* (Leiden: Brill, 2003), 43.

twelfth and thirteenth Sabbaths, perhaps, they have merged'.[65] Fletcher-Louis objects to Newsom's dualistic paradigm, arguing that 'the place where all this liturgy and a communion between angels and men' took place was 'the human community's own, concrete, earthly cultic space'.[66] He sees 'the references to angels, elohim, elim, and so on' as referring 'to the sectarians themselves'.[67] But he then uses ascent language himself:

> Like the apocalypses and the Hekhalot texts the *Sabbath Songs* do envisage the possibility of a human ascent from earth to heaven, and it is within this context that a human transformation and a sharing of the life of the angels and of that of God himself takes place.... In the *Sabbath Songs* ascent is a ritualised and communal experience...[68]

Schäfer criticizes Morray-Jones for interpreting Qumran literature in the light of the Hekhalot texts, saying that he 'improperly confuses the textual level (the heavenly ritual) and the performative level (the enacting of the text in the worship of the sectarians)'.[69] He insists that 'the Qumran literature describes an experience sui generis', but concludes:

> We definitely and most conspicuously do find the idea of the *unio liturgica*—the liturgical union or, better, the communion of humans and angels. This feature connects the Qumran evidence with the ascent apocalypses and the Hekhalot literature.[70]

One way in which the liturgical communion between humans and angels is expressed is by the recital of the *Qedushah*/Sanctus. This started as a heavenly song (Isa. 6:3, cf. Rev. 4:8), but made its way into earthly liturgies, as human communities sought to imitate angelic worship. The origins of the use of the *Qedushah*/Sanctus in earthly liturgies, whether Jewish or Christian, are difficult to uncover.[71] The earliest Jewish reference to the *Qedushah* in synagogue worship comes in the Tosephta (*t. Berakhot* 1:9), usually dated to around 400.[72] There is reliable evidence for Christian use of the Sanctus, in the context of the

---

[65] Alexander, *The Mystical Texts*, 104.
[66] Fletcher-Louis, *All the Glory of Adam*, 274.
[67] Crispin H. T. Fletcher-Louis, 'Heavenly Ascent or Incarnational Presence? A Revisionist Reading of the *Songs of the Sabbath Sacrifice*', *Society of Biblical Literature Seminar Papers*, 37 (1998), 372.
[68] Fletcher-Louis, *All the Glory of Adam*, 392.
[69] Schäfer, *The Origins of Jewish Mysticism*, 144.
[70] Schäfer, *The Origins of Jewish Mysticism*, 348–9.
[71] See Bryan D. Spinks, *The Sanctus in the Eucharistic Prayer* (Cambridge: Cambridge University Press, 1991); Robert Taft, 'The Interpolation of the Sanctus into the Anaphora: When and Where? A Review of the Dossier', *Orientalia christiana periodica*, 57: 2, 58:1 (1991–1992); and R. M. M. Tuschling, *Angels and Orthodoxy: A Study in their Development in Syria and Palestine from the Qumran Texts to Ephrem the Syrian* (Tübingen: Mohr Siebeck, 2007), 177–96.
[72] For the dating see Jacob Neusner and Richard S. Sarason, *The Tosefta Translated from the Hebrew* (Hoboken, NJ: Ktav, 1977–1986), 1.ix.

Eucharistic prayer, from the fourth century onwards. Gregory contributes to this with his sermon *Against Those Who Defer Baptism*:

> Join with the mystical [i.e. baptized] people and learn secret words. Say with us those things that also the six-winged Seraphim say, singing a hymn of praise with the initiated Christians.[73]

There are other clear references in Cyril/John of Jerusalem, the *Apostolic Constitutions*, and John Chrysostom.[74] Earlier Christian texts alluding to the Sanctus describe the heavenly choir, without unequivocal reference to earthly liturgy.[75] Thus, the evidence for the use of the *Qedushah*/Sanctus in both synagogue and church is roughly contemporaneous, although in both cases the texts may well be reflecting practices which had been established for some time. In the fourth century Christians were building monumental churches, and developing elaborate rituals performed by a priestly caste. Ruth Langer argues that 'in response, Jews looked for a similar religious leadership, a heightened liturgical experience, and a sanctified setting in which this could all take place.... The two institutions were in direct competition.'[76] Claiming to worship with the angels was part of that competition.

In *3 Enoch*, Enoch ascends to heaven and joins in the heavenly *Qedushah*:

> The Holy One, blessed be he, opened to me gates of Šekinah... He enlightened by eyes and my heart to utter psalm, praise, jubilation, thanksgiving, song, glory, majesty, laud, and strength. And when I opened my mouth and sang praises before the throne of glory the holy creatures below the throne of glory and above the throne responded after me, saying, 'Holy, holy, holy', and, 'Blessed be the glory of the Lord in his dwelling place.'[77]

Schäfer argues that although ostensibly this is about Enoch worshipping in heaven, the text is in fact validating earthly synagogue worship:

> The Merkavah mystic participates in the liturgy of the heavenly court. Significantly, it is not he who joins the singing of the angels. Rather, the angels answer his singing, which is infused in him by God, with the Trisagion of Isaiah 6:3 and with Ezekiel 3:12, thus with nothing but the liturgy which is performed on earth in synagogues.[78]

---

[73] GNO 10,2.362.15–17; trans. Taft, 'The Interpolation of the Sanctus into the Anaphora', 2.104.

[74] Cyril/John of Jerusalem *Myst. Cat.* 5.6; *Apos. Con.* 8.12.27; Chrysostom *Hom. Eph.* 14.4.

[75] See 1 Clement 34:6–7; the *Martyrdom of Perpetua and Felicitas* 12.2; Tertullian *Prayer* 3.3.

[76] Ruth Langer, 'Early Rabbinic Liturgy in Its Palestinian Milieu: Did Non-Rabbis Know the 'Amidah?', in Alan J. Avery-Peck, Daniel Harrington, and Jacob Neusner (eds), *When Judaism and Christianity Began: Essays in Memory of Anthony J. Saldarini*, vol. 2: *Judaism and Christianity in the Beginning* (Leiden: Brill, 2004), 433.

[77] *3 En.* 1:11–12; §2; trans. Alexander, 256.

[78] Peter Schäfer, 'The Aim and Purpose of Early Jewish Mysticism', in *Hekhalot-Studien* (Tübingen: Mohr Siebeck, 1988), 287.

Other passages in Hekhalot literature stress the importance of the earthly *Qedushah*:

> Blessed are you [pl.] unto heaven and earth,
> you who ascend to the Chariot,
> when you tell and proclaim to my sons
> what I do at the morning, afternoon, and evening prayer,
> on every day and at every hour,
> when Israel speaks the 'Holy, [holy, holy]' before me.
> Teach them and tell them:
> Raise your eyes to heaven opposite your house of prayer
> when you speak the 'Holy, [holy, holy]' before me.
> For I have no joy in my world,
> which I created,
> except at the hour in which your eyes are raised to my eyes,
> and my eyes to your eyes,
> [namely] in the hour in which you speak before me
> the 'Holy, [holy, holy]!'[79]

And so Schäfer concludes:

> The Merkavah mystic represents in his person the participation of Israel in the heavenly liturgy and simultaneously confirms for the earthly congregation that it stands in direct contact with God in its synagogue liturgy, a contact which God needs just as much as Israel does.[80]

Elior too stresses the mediating role of the elite 'descenders to the *merkavah*'. They see 'themselves as the people's mystical messengers, maintaining the link between the terrestrial and celestial worlds after the destruction [of the temple]'.[81]

Schäfer interprets much of the Bavli's exposition of 'the work of creation' (*b. Ḥagigah* 11b–13a) as 'a polemic against the ascent apocalypses and Merkavah mysticism in the technical sense of the word—the attempt to actually ascend to heaven and see God on his throne'.[82] In its inventory of the heavens, the description of the fifth heaven, *Maʿon*, which contains companies of ministering angels, is interrupted. The ministering angels are said to utter song by night but remain silent during the day 'for the sake of Israel's glory',[83] based on Psalm 42:9 (RSV 42:8)—'By day the Lord commands his steadfast love; and at night his song is with me.' A series of rabbinic comments are added in which the 'song' of the biblical verse becomes 'the Torah, the epitome of the

---

[79] *Hekhalot Rabbati* §163; trans. Schäfer, 'The Aim and Purpose of Early Jewish Mysticism', 287–8.
[80] Schäfer, 'The Aim and Purpose of Early Jewish Mysticism', 287.
[81] Elior, 'From Earthly Temple to Heavenly Shrines', 267.
[82] Schäfer, *The Origins of Jewish Mysticism*, 224.   [83] *B. Ḥag.* 12b.

rabbinic value system, and God's mercy upon Israel during the day is the result of the righteous' Torah study at night'.[84] Whereas in the Hekhalot texts, human beings ascend to heaven and join the angelic liturgy, in the Bavli, angels and humans worship in parallel, in their separate spheres:

> Moreover, Israel is even more important to God than the angels who dwell with him in heaven. Or, to put it differently and more pungently, Torah study and praise of God are Israel's *only* task, not the attempt to equal the angels and aspire to be like them in the heavens.[85]

Gregory too depicts the earthly and heavenly communities worshipping in parallel. Like the Bavli, he is concerned with validating mainstream community worship. Heavenly worship is described not as an incentive for individuals to try and ascend to heaven, but as the model for earthly worship. Unlike the Bavli, however, Gregory sees heavenly worship as superior, and looks forward to the time when angels and humans will be reunited.

12.5 *LIFE OF MOSES* 2.182, 185: CONCLUSIONS

Gregory presents the altars of the heavenly tabernacle as representing the adoration of the angelic priests. In depicting the heavenly powers as priests, he is doing nothing new: it is a long-standing tradition going back to *1 Enoch* 14 and Daniel 7. In allocating two altars to the heavenly tabernacle, and talking of heavenly sacrifice, however, Gregory is unusual. The two altars come about because he is following the Exodus account of the tabernacle. Other heavenly ascent texts do not draw so close a parallel with the earthly tabernacle/temple. They imply that there is only one heavenly altar, with some of the characteristics of the earthly incense altar. Other than in Hebrews, sacrifices, and their association with blood, are not deemed appropriate to heaven. Gregory is able to draw on the Pauline reinterpretation of sacrifice, itself with Jewish roots, as prayer and righteous deeds. The angelic beings offer praise and prayer. Gregory never quotes from Revelation, and does not even seem to be alluding to it, yet its picture of heaven, with the adoring elders falling down before the throne, and the offering of prayers as incense, is there in the background. Gregory does not specify the content of the angelic song, which seems strange, as we know that he is aware of the Sanctus, sung before the

---

[84] Peter Schäfer, 'From Cosmology to Theology: The Rabbinic Appropriation of Apocalyptic Cosmology', in Rachel Elior and Peter Schäfer (eds), *Creation and Re-Creation in Jewish Thought: Festschrift in Honor of Joseph Dan on the Occasion of his Seventieth Birthday* (Tübingen: Mohr Siebeck, 2005), 45.

[85] Schäfer, 'From Cosmology to Theology', 56.

Eucharist, as the song of the seraphim. Although he describes both heavenly and earthly worship, each in the context of their respective tabernacle, he keeps the two strictly separate. There are few verbal links between the two descriptions, the most obvious being 'fragrance' (εὐωδία). He applies the second half of Hebrews 13:15, the 'fruit of lips', to heavenly worship, and the first half, the 'sacrifice of praise', to earthly worship. This separation is in contrast to other heavenly ascent texts. In Revelation the incense offered in heaven is the prayer of the righteous, whereas in *Life of Moses* the heavenly incense seems to be the prayer and praise of the angels themselves. In the ascent apocalypses and the Hekhalot texts human beings join the worship of heaven; *Songs of the Sabbath Sacrifice* gives the impression that the earthly community feels itself to be in the presence of the praising angels. In *Life of Moses*, however, there is no suggestion that Moses becomes involved with the heavenly worship. He sees the heavenly tabernacle, and realizes that it consists of heavenly powers, but is not drawn into it. The closest parallel is with the Babylonian Talmud: there too heaven and earth worship separately. The Talmud implies that Israel's worship takes priority, whereas there is no doubt that for Gregory, angelic worship is superior. He mentions morning and evening prayer in connection with earthly worship, but gives the impression that angelic worship is timeless. There is no eschatological thrust in the Bavli. Gregory, on the other hand, envisages a reunion at the end of time when angels and human will worship together. In the meanwhile, there is the earthly tabernacle, the church. Gregory uses his description of the heavenly tabernacle not to encourage others to follow Moses, but to validate earthly worship.

13

The Holy of Holies

If the interior, which is called the holy of holies, is not accessible to the multitude (τοῖς πολλοῖς), let us not consider this out of tune with the sequence of ideas. For the truth of all existence is truly a holy matter, a holy of holies, incomprehensible and unapproachable for the multitude. Since it is set in the secret and ineffable spaces of the tabernacle of mystery, the understanding of realities beyond apprehension must not be meddled with, for we believe that what is sought exists, and yet is not set before the eyes of all, but remains ineffable in the secret spaces of the mind.[1]

13.1 *LIFE OF MOSES* 2.188: BIBLICAL CONTEXT

According to the instructions given to Moses on Mount Sinai, the tabernacle tent was to be divided by a veil, creating the holy place (הקדש; τὸ ἅγιον) and the holy of holies (קדש הקדשים; τὸ ἅγιον τῶν ἁγίων).[2] The dimensions of the tent are unclear; they have to be estimated from the measurements of the 'planks'/'frames' (קרשים) and curtains. Most scholars settle on dimensions of 30 cubits in length, 10 in width, and 10 in height for the tent as a whole (1 cubit being about 45 cm), making the holy of holies a cube 10 cubits in each direction.[3] The high priest was to enter the holy of holies only once a year, on the Day of Atonement, as set out in Leviticus 16. Inside it would have been pitch dark. Victor Hurowitz argues that the same was true of the *devir* in Solomon's

---

[1] *Vit. Moys.* 2.188.

[2] Exod. 26:33. In the biblical text, הקדש and קדש הקדשים do not serve as consistent technical terms. In the description of the Day of Atonement in Leviticus 16, for example, the inner sanctum is designated הקדש (Lev. 16:2–3, 16, 20, 23). See Menahem Haran, 'The Priestly Image of the Tabernacle', *Hebrew Union College Annual*, 36 (1965), 213 n. 52.

[3] See, for example, Frank M. Cross, 'The Tabernacle: A Study from an Archaeological and Historical Approach', *The Biblical Archaeologist*, 10: 3 (1947), 62; Haran, 'The Priestly Image of the Tabernacle', 193–4; or Nahum M. Sarna, *The JPS Torah Commentary: Exodus* (Philadelphia: Jewish Publication Society, 1991), 169–71. Friedman disagrees, suggesting instead that the tent is 20 cubits long, 8 wide, and 10 high. He also doubts whether the *parokhet* is a hanging veil, arguing that it is a canopy over the ark. See Richard E. Friedman, 'The Tabernacle in the Temple', *The Biblical Archaeologist*, 43: 4 (1980), 243–4.

temple, as indicated by Solomon's declaration in his dedication prayer: 'The Lord has said that he would dwell in thick darkness (בערפל).'[4] He comments that this 'resembles statements in Mesopotamian texts describing temples as dark inside'.[5] To this darkness, Knohl adds silence, arguing that

> The Temple may...be described as a series of concentric circles. The inner circle is that of the priests, in which the sacred service is conducted in absolute silence; the outer circle is that of the folk prayers of the people; while in the middle is the circle of the song of the Levites.[6]

In the dark, silent holy of holies of the tabernacle stood the ark, with two golden cherubim adorning its cover. God promises Moses, 'There I will meet with you, and from above the mercy seat, from between the two cherubim that are upon the ark of the testimony, I will speak with you...'[7] The *devir* of Solomon's temple contained two gigantic olive-wood cherubim overlaid with gold; the ark stood under their outstretched wings.[8] 1 Chronicles 28:18 refers to 'the golden chariot of the cherubim'. By the time of the second temple, the ark had disappeared, leaving the holy of holies empty.[9]

The imagery of the holy of holies plays a significant part in Gregory's thought, appearing in several of his works. He says of the seventh beatitude:

> All the Beatitudes previously made known to us upon this mountain...are sacred and holy every one, but...the unentered sanctuary (*aduton*) which is now the subject of our study is very truly also a holy of holies.[10]

and of Song of Songs:

> Let us come within the holy of holies, that is, the Song of Songs. For we are taught by this superlative form of expression that there is a superabundant concentration of holiness within the holy of holies, and in the same way the exalted Word promises to teach us mysteries of mysteries by the agency of the Song of Songs.[11]

He is particularly fond of the term *aduton*: the innermost shrine, not to be entered. As set out in 6.1, he uses it to refer to the darkness of Mount Sinai and the tabernacle as a whole (in the plural), as well as to the holy of holies. *On the Lord's Prayer* treats the entrance of the high priest into the holy of holies

---

[4] 1 Kgs 8:12.
[5] Victor Avigdor Hurowitz, 'YHWH's Exalted House—Aspects of the Design and Symbolism of Solomon's Temple', in John Day (ed.), *Temple and Worship in Biblical Israel: Proceedings of the Oxford Old Testament Seminar* (London: T&T Clark, 2007), 77.
[6] Israel Knohl, 'Between Voice and Silence: The Relationship between Prayer and Temple Cult', *Journal of Biblical Literature*, 115: 1 (1996), 23.
[7] Exod. 25:22.   [8] 1 Kgs 6:23–28; 8:6–7.
[9] See Josephus *B.J.* 5.219. Speculation on what might have happened to the ark can be found in John Day, 'Whatever Happened to the Ark of the Covenant?', in Day (ed.), *Temple and Worship in Biblical Israel*, 250–70.
[10] *Beat.* 7 (GNO 7,2.149); trans. Hall, 75.
[11] *Cant.* 1 (GNO 6.26.11–12); trans. Norris, 29.

as an allegory of prayer. Here the *aduton* is 'the hidden inner chamber of our heart'; and the Lord's Prayer is the petition 'which the person within the sanctuary (*aduton*) has been ordered to offer to God'.[12] Gregory interprets *aduton* as meaning 'impenetrable to evil and inaccessible to vile thoughts'.[13] *On the Lord's Prayer* is thought to be one of Gregory's early works,[14] and *aduton* does not have the same connotation of mystery there as in *Life of Moses* or *On the Song of Songs*. In *Life of Moses*, Gregory's commentary on the heavenly tabernacle does not refer to the holy of holies, only to the cherubim covering the mysteries in the ark with their wings; but it plays a significant role in his interpretation of the earthly tabernacle. There it represents 'the truth of all existence': 'realities beyond apprehension', which are not accessible to the multitude (*hoi polloi*).

Is it possible to enter the *aduton*? When talking of Moses entering the darkness, Gregory uses a paradoxical expression which literally means 'he enters into the unenterable' (ἄδυτον παραδύεται).[15] He says that David 'was initiated into ineffable mysteries in the same secret place (*aduton*)' and that Paul spent time in 'the supercelestial secret places (*aduta*)'.[16] In his *Funeral Oration on Meletius* he declares, 'The priest is within the holy place (*aduta*). He is entered into that within the veil (*katapetasma*), whither our forerunner Christ has entered for us.'[17] In *On the Song of Songs* he invites each person to 'get beyond the material cosmos and ascend somehow, by way of impassibility, into paradise', and 'journey to the inner shrine (*aduton*) of the mysteries manifested to us in this book'.[18] As all these examples show, the *aduton* is not impenetrable: it is the summit of spiritual achievement. Moses enters the *aduton* of the darkness, where he sees the *aduta* of the heavenly tabernacle. There are, however, mysteries in the ark, covered by the cherubim's wings; even he does not have access to everything. But the message of *Life of Moses* 2.188 is different: here the emphasis is on the inaccessibility of the holy of holies to the multitude.

13.2 LIFE OF MOSES 2.188: ALEXANDRIAN CONTEXT

Philo saw the holy of holies as symbolic of the intelligible world, and placed within it his hierarchy of divine powers. Like Gregory, he refers to it as an

---

[12] *Or. dom.* 3 (GNO 7,2.32, 33); trans. Graef, 46, 47.
[13] *Or. dom.* 3 (GNO 7,2.32); trans. Graef, 46.
[14] See Jean Daniélou, 'La chronologie des oeuvres de Grégoire de Nysse', in F. L. Cross (ed.), *Papers Presented to the Fourth International Conference on Patristic Studies Held at Christ Church, Oxford, 1963, Part 1* (Berlin: Akademie-Verlag, 1966), 162.
[15] *Vit. Moys* 2.167, cf. 1.46. I have translated it as 'he steals into the secret place'.
[16] *Vit. Moys.* 2.164, 178.   [17] GNO 9.454; trans. NPNF² 5.516.
[18] *Cant.* 1 (GNO 6.25.6–10); trans. Norris, 27.

aduton;[19] he also uses *aduta* with reference to both rooms within the tabernacle tent.[20] In his description of Moses' ascent into darkness in *On the Posterity of Cain*, he describes that darkness as representing 'conceptions regarding the Existent Being that belong to the unapproachable region (*aduta*) where there are no material forms'.[21] But he does not make as much use of the symbolism of the holy of holies as does Gregory.

Clement maps heavenly ascent onto the floor plan of the tabernacle/temple. The goal of the gnostic, therefore, is to enter the holy of holies. His first reference to this entrance suffers from textual variation. William Wilson translates *Miscellanies* 5.34.7 as:

> Now the Lord, having come alone into the intellectual world, enters by His sufferings (διὰ τῶν παθῶν), introduced into the knowledge of the Ineffable, ascending above every name which is known by sound.[22]

Van den Hoek, using a text which omits the preposition 'by' (διά), produces:

> He alone will come (εἴσεισι) into the intellectual world (τὸν νοητὸν κόσμον) who has become lord over his emotions (ὁ κύριος γενόμενος ... τῶν παθῶν), reaching the knowledge of the ineffable (εἰς τὴν τοῦ ἀρρήτου γνῶσιν) and ascending above every name that is made known by the sound of a voice.[23]

Le Boulluec comments:

> Comme le montre l'allusion à *Phil.* 2,9, 'au-dessus de tout nom', cette entrée mystique est celle du Christ; mais il sert de modèle, et de moteur, à l'entrée du croyant dans la 'gnose', comme l'indique l'emploi du futur, εἴσεισι.[24]

This is confirmed by the ending of Clement's tabernacle interpretation, which introduces Leviticus 16. The high priest becomes a symbol of the perfect, gnostic Christian:

> ...distinguishing the objects of the intellect from the things of sense, rising above the other priests, hasting to the entrance of the noetic realm, to wash himself from the things here below, not in water as formerly one was cleansed on being enrolled in the tribe of Levi, but already by the gnostic Word.[25]

---

[19] E.g. *Mos.* 2.87.   [20] E.g. *Mos.* 2.82   [21] *Post.* 14.   [22] Wilson, 241.

[23] Annewies van den Hoek, *Clement of Alexandria and His Use of Philo in the Stromateis: An Early Christian Reshaping of a Jewish Model* (Leiden: Brill, 1988), 126. Le Boulluec's French translation is similar.

[24] 'As the reference to Phil 2:9 —"above every name"—shows, this is the mystical entrance of Christ; but it serves as model and driving force to the believer's entrance into "gnosis", as indicated by the use of the future "will come".' Alain Le Boulluec, *Clément d'Alexandrie: Les Stromates, Stromate V*, 2 vols (Paris: Cerf, 1981), 2.142.

[25] *Strom.* 5.39.4; trans. van den Hoek, *Clement of Alexandria and His Use of Philo*, 141. See 4.2 n. 34.

Once 'sanctified both in word and life', the 'spiritual and perfect man' receives 'the ineffable inheritance' 'which eye has not seen and ear has not heard and which has not entered into the heart of man [1 Cor. 2:9]'. He becomes son and friend and is replenished 'with insatiable contemplation face to face'.[26] Paragraph 40.3 makes clear the connection between the gnostic's ascent and Christ's descent:

> But in one way, as I think, the Lord puts off and puts on by descending into the realm of sense, and in another, he who through Him has believed puts off and puts on, as the apostle intimated, the consecrated stole.[27]

Another description of the entrance of the high priest into the holy of holies is to be found in section 27 of *Excerpts from Theodotus*. There it is used to describe the ascent of the gnostic soul to the highest level of the celestial hierarchy:

> Now the soul, stripped by the power of him who has knowledge, as if it had become a body of the power, passes into the spiritual realm and becomes now truly rational and high priestly, so that it might now be animated, so to speak, directly by the Logos, just as the archangels become the high-priests of the angels and the First-Created the high-priests of the archangels.[28]

Not only is the soul animated by the Logos, it becomes a Logos:

> ...having transcended the angelic teaching and the Name taught in Scripture, it comes to the knowledge and comprehension of the facts. It is no longer a bride but has become a Logos and rests with the bridegroom together with the First-Called and First-Created...[29]

Lilla suggests that when Clement wrote *Miscellanies* 5.39.3–40.1 'he had still in mind paragraph 27 of the *Excerpta* as well as other passages of Gnostic writings dealing with the topic of the entry of the High Priest into the Holy of Holies', and, as a result, his exegesis 'plunges directly into Gnosticism'.[30] Kovacs agrees that 'this part of the *Stromateis* betrays strong Gnostic influence', but argues that Lilla 'has misconstrued the relation of the two exegeses to each other'.[31] She suggests that the treatment of the high priest in *Excerpts from Theodotus* 27 supplements Clement's earlier exegesis in *Miscellanies* 5,

---

[26] *Strom.* 5.40.1; trans. van den Hoek, *Clement of Alexandria and His Use of Philo*, 141.
[27] *Strom.* 5.40.3; trans. van den Hoek, *Clement of Alexandria and His Use of Philo*, 141.
[28] *Exc.* 27.3; trans. Casey, 61.   [29] *Exc.* 27.3; trans. Casey, 61.
[30] Salvatore R. C. Lilla, *Clement of Alexandria: A Study in Christian Platonism and Gnosticism* (Oxford: Oxford University Press, 1971), 180, 181.
[31] Judith L. Kovacs, 'Concealment and Gnostic Exegesis: Clement of Alexandria's Interpretation of the Tabernacle', in Elizabeth A. Livingstone (ed.), *Papers Presented at the Twelfth International Conference on Patristic Studies Held in Oxford 1995*, part 3: *Preaching, Second Century, Tertullian to Arnobious, Egypt before Nicaea* (Leuven: Peeters, 1997), 433. Lilla assigns *Excerpts from Theodotus* 27 to a Valentinian writer, Kovacs to Clement—see 4.3.

'by providing a picture of the last stage of the soul's ascent, after it has been fully instructed and purified and ascended through the angelic ranks'.[32] In *Miscellanies* Clement stresses 'the importance of the incarnation and of the other modes of divine revelation in creation and the history of salvation'; but once the gnostic soul has entered within the veil of the noetic world, into the very depths of God, it 'has passed beyond the revelation given in the incarnation and even beyond the superior teaching of the angels to become one with the Logos, the "face" of God'.[33] Whether *Excerpts* 27 represents Clement's own thoughts or not, there is no doubt that he 'unambiguously proposes a sharp distinction between Christians at different levels of understanding'.[34] Entry into the holy of holies is only for the enlightened gnostic, not for ordinary believers, although this 'distinction between the different kinds of believer is certainly not fixed permanently. The gnostic's task is to make more gnostics.'[35]

In *Homilies on Exodus*, Origen develops an elaborate anthropological interpretation of the tabernacle, in which each believer is expected to 'complete a form of the tabernacle in himself'.[36] He sees the furniture of the tabernacle and the high priest's vestments as symbolic of Christian virtues. The aim of adorning the inner person as a high priest to God is so as to be able 'to enter not only the sanctuary (*sancta*), but also the Holy of Holies (*sancta sanctorum*)':

> The sanctuary can be those things which a holy way of life can have in the present world. But the Holy of Holies, which is entered only once, is, I think, the passage to heaven, where the mercy seat and the cherubim are located and where God will be able to appear to the pure in heart...[37]

For Origen, the holy of holies is the vision of God after death.

13.3 *LIFE OF MOSES* 2.188: THEOLOGICAL CONTEXT

When commenting on Gregory's use of holy of holies imagery, modern scholars tend to apply the definition of the *aduton* as 'the hidden inner chamber of our heart' from *On the Lord's Prayer* to all other texts in which Gregory mentions it. So Daniélou writes:

> Les ἄδυτα représentent l'intérieur, τὸ ἐνδότατον. Mais ici ce n'est pas le lieu le plus retiré du Temple, mais le plus profond de l'âme, la chambre secrète....C'est...la

---

[32] Kovacs, 'Concealment and Gnostic Exegesis', 437.
[33] Kovacs, 'Concealment and Gnostic Exegesis', 437.
[34] Rowan Williams, *The Wound of Knowledge: Christian Spirituality from the New Testament to St. John of the Cross* (London: DLT, 1979), 34.
[35] Williams, *The Wound of Knowledge*, 35.   [36] *Hom. Exod.* 9.4; trans. Heine, 341.
[37] *Hom. Exod.* 9.4; trans. Heine, 344.

réalité mystique du sanctuaire de l'âme où Dieu habite et où l'âme doit pénétrer pour le trouver et vivre dans sa familiarité.[38]

Although he places the tabernacle within the second stage of his outline of Gregory's mysticism, he makes *aduton* one of the significant words characterizing the third stage: 'comme le lieu où se consomme l'union de l'âme avec Dieu et où l'âme contemple Dieu dans la ténèbre.'[39] He draws attention to the accumulation of negative terms in *Life of Moses* 2.188, seeing them as designating transcendence. But he insists that this transcendence is to be linked with interiority: 'C'est l'union de l'un et de l'autre qui characterise précisément la vie mystique.'[40] Laird draws attention to the way in which Gregory prioritizes faith over comprehension:

> The function of grasping the Beloved in union, that is to say, the faculty which bridges the gap between intelligence and God, is reserved by Gregory of Nyssa for faith.[41]

And he illustrates this with two passages from *Life of Moses* describing Moses' experience on Mount Sinai:

> whoever intends to be with God must go beyond all appearances and, lifting up his mind to the invisible and incomprehensible as to a mountain peak, must *believe* that the divine is there where the understanding cannot reach.[42]

> ...in the impenetrable darkness draw near to God by your *faith*...[43]

Laird goes on to comment on Gregory's sixth homily in *On the Song of Songs*. There Gregory is interpreting Song of Songs 3:1–4, in which the bride rises from her bed at night and wanders about in the city searching for the one whom her soul loves. When she finds him, she will not let him go until she has brought him into her mother's house. Gregory equates the night with the darkness of Mount Sinai, also quoting LXX Psalm 17:12.[44] He paraphrases the bride's words as follows:

> Even when, as one judged worthy of perfection, I am taking my rest as upon some *bed* of the comprehension of what I have known; when I have entered into the

---

[38] 'The *aduta* represent the interior. Not here the innermost room of the temple, but the depths of the soul, its secret chamber. It is the mystical reality of the soul's sanctuary, God's dwelling place, which the soul must discover in order to find God and live in his intimacy.' Jean Daniélou, *Platonisme et théologie mystique: Doctrine spirituelle de Saint Grégoire de Nysse*, 2nd edn (Paris: Aubier, 1954), 184.

[39] 'as the place where the union of the soul with God is consummated and where the soul contemplates God in the darkness'. Daniélou, *Platonisme et théologie mystique*, 185.

[40] 'It is precisely the union of the one with the other which characterises mystical life.' Daniélou, *Platonisme et théologie mystique*, 187.

[41] Martin Laird, *Gregory of Nyssa and the Grasp of Faith: Union, Knowledge, and Divine Presence* (Oxford: Oxford University Press, 2004), 62.

[42] *Vit. Moys.* 1.46. For Laird's commentary see *Gregory of Nyssa and the Grasp of Faith*, 78–81.

[43] *Vit. Moys.* 2.315; trans. Malherbe and Ferguson, 135. For Laird's commentary see *Gregory of Nyssa and the Grasp of Faith*, 83–5.

[44] *Cant.* 6 (GNO 6.181.7–8).

Invisible, with the world of sense left behind me; when, surrounded by the divine night, I am seeking what is hidden in the darkness—that is when I have indeed laid hold on love for the one I desire, but the object of my love has flown from the net of my thoughts (τῶν λογισμῶν τὴν λαβήν).[45]

She rises again, and 'in her understanding moves about the intelligible and supracosmic nature'; but it is only when she leaves behind 'every conceptual approach' that she finds her Beloved by faith:

> And holding on by faith's grasp (τῇ τῆς πίστεως λαβῇ) to the one I have found, I will not let go until he is within my *chamber*. Now the *chamber* is surely the heart, which at that moment became receptive of his divine indwelling...[46]

Laird comments, 'The Beloved is ungraspable on the level of mind but is clearly graspable on the level of faith.'[47] His interpretation of *Life of Moses* 2.188 follows similar lines: 'The mind itself is the temple, comprehension is the multitude which cannot enter the sanctuary.'[48] Laird is equating the holy of holies with 'the secret chamber of the heart' thanks to *On the Lord's Prayer*;[49] and assuming that, because Gregory identifies Song of Songs with the holy of holies, the philosophy presented in *On the Song of Songs* of abandoning 'noetic–erotic control in order to enter the hidden sanctuary' can be applied to the holy of holies in *Life of Moses*.[50] This ignores the context of *Life of Moses* 2.188: Gregory is talking of the earthly tabernacle, not the heavenly one. Does he really intend 'the multitude', *hoi polloi*, to be taken allegorically, as comprehension? Is it not rather to be taken literally, as the common people?

Richard Lim is interested in Gregory's political agenda. He argues that more was at stake between Gregory and Eunomius than theology alone. Gregory not only criticized Eunomius' use of 'unbegotten' to describe the essence of God, he also launched vituperative personal attacks upon him, saying that he 'found a fat living in the simplicity of those deceived', so that 'the meanness and obscurity of [his] former life was lost to sight'.[51] He even went as far as to associate him with the Antichrist.[52] Eunomius was from an undistinguished family of 'farmers, craftsmen, and small entrepreneurs'.[53] Gregory, on the other

---

[45] *Cant.* 6 (GNO 6.181.10–16); trans. Norris, 193.
[46] *Cant.* 6 (GNO 6.182–183); trans. Norris, 195.
[47] Laird, *Gregory of Nyssa and the Grasp of Faith*, 90.
[48] Laird, *Gregory of Nyssa and the Grasp of Faith*, 82.
[49] Martin Laird, 'Under Solomon's Tutelage: The Education of Desire in the Homilies on the Song of Songs', in Sarah Coakley (ed.), *Re-Thinking Gregory of Nyssa* (Oxford: Blackwell, 2003), 84.
[50] Laird, 'Under Solomon's Tutelage', 85.
[51] *Eun.* 1.55–56 (GNO 1.41); trans. Hall, 43.   [52] *Eun.* 3,9.64 (GNO 2.288).
[53] Raymond Van Dam, *Becoming Christian: The Conversion of Roman Cappadocia* (Philadelphia: University of Pennsylvania Press, 2003), 18.

hand, came from a wealthy landed family, probably of the curial class.[54] 'It is arguable that this social gulf separated the Cappadocians and Eunomius more effectively and irreconcilably than any amount of theological and philosophical disagreement.'[55] Lim argues that 'before Constantine, many Christian apologists had taken pride in the fact that even uneducated and nearly illiterate Christians were able to discuss supramundane topics, hitherto the exclusive preserve of upper-class philosophers'. Now, however, 'the *via universalis* had become problematic for many Christians'.[56] In particular, bishops did not take kindly to having their doctrines questioned by social upstarts.

A key word in *Life of Moses* 2.188 is the adjective *apolupragmonētos*—'not to be meddled with'. Gregory can use *polupragmosunē*—'curiosity'—in a positive sense. He does so in *Life of Moses* 2.163:

> For leaving behind everything visible, not only what the senses grasp but also what the mind seems to see, he yearns to go ever further in, until, thanks to the mind's curiosity (*polupragmosunē*), he slips into the unseen and incomprehensible, and there sees God.

Here it describes 'the dynamic quality of the mind that allows it to penetrate into the incomprehensible where God is seen.'[57] However, in commenting on the departure from Egypt, when the Israelites were to burn any leftovers from the Passover lambs, Gregory writes,

> The food placed before us...I call the warm and fervent faith which we receive without having given thought to it. We devour as much of it as is easily eaten, but we leave aside the doctrine concealed in the thoughts which are hard and tough without investigating it thoroughly or seeking to know more about it (*apolupragmonēton*). Instead we consign this food to the fire.[58]

Here, as in the paragraph on the holy of holies in the earthly tabernacle, there is reference to not displaying *polupragmosunē*, now 'meddlesome curiosity'. Gregory continues,

> Such thoughts as are beyond our understanding—like the questions, What is the essence of God? What was there before the creation? What is there outside the visible world? Why do things which happen happen? and other such things as are sought out by inquiring minds—these things we concede to know only by the Holy Spirit, who reaches the depths of God, as the Apostle says.[59]

---

[54] See Thomas A. Kopecek, 'The Social Class of the Cappadocian Fathers', *Church History*, 42: 4 (1973); and Claudia Rapp, 'The Elite Status of Bishops in Late Antiquity in Ecclesiastical, Spiritual, and Social Contexts', *Arethusa*, 33: 3 (2000).
[55] Richard Lim, *Public Disputation, Power, and Social Order in Late Antiquity* (Berkeley: University of California Press, 1995), 142.
[56] Lim, *Public Disputation, Power, and Social Order in Late Antiquity*, 151.
[57] Laird, 'Under Solomon's Tutelage', 92 n. 30.
[58] *Vit. Moys.* 2.109; trans. Malherbe and Ferguson, 79.
[59] *Vit. Moys.* 2.110; trans. Malherbe and Ferguson, 79–80.

Like Origen before him, Gregory often appeals to 1 Corinthians 2:10. But, according to Heine, whereas 'Origen believes his own interpretation of Scripture [to be] guided by the Spirit', Gregory is more circumspect and 'disclaims such guidance for himself'.[60] Instead he justifies his interpretations by reference to Paul, who had the necessary spiritual understanding. This reference to Paul is particularly prominent in Gregory's tabernacle interpretation, because he believes that Paul had a vision of the tabernacle. Those who have not had such a vision, and who are not guided by the Holy Spirit, should not presume to discuss abstruse thoughts. Lim argues that 'idle curiosity and a spirit of meddling' caused deep concern to fourth-century bishops such as the Cappadocians and John Chrysostom.[61] They

> opposed those who acquired for themselves, and who also helped others to acquire, the ability to ask acute theological questions not through a systematic training in philosophy but through the use of manuals and other shortcuts. They circumvented a system of long and difficult apprenticeship that cultivated a student's sense of social responsibility.[62]

It was in order to muzzle people who challenged episcopal authority by engaging in public theological disputations that the nature of the divine essence was represented as 'a mystery ringed by taboos'.[63] Gregory is not always as negative about *polupragmosunē*, as Lim implies. But his references to 'the multitude' in 2.188 are not allegorical. Gregory's sense of the mystery and incomprehensibility surrounding God had social consequences.

Patrick O'Connell notes that there are 'two distinct yet interrelated spiritual journeys' described in *Life of Moses*: that of the people of Israel and that of Moses.[64] Initially, in the sections leading up to Sinai, they are complementary, but after Moses' ascent they diverge. The people are aiming for the Promised Land, the reward for virtuous living, but Moses 'is beyond the need for a hope of reward as a motivation for virtue'.[65] His 'goal is nothing other than God Himself'.[66] Unlike Lim, O'Connell does not correlate the difference with socio-political realities:

> This distinction was based not on any rigid classification of two types of Christian, but on Gregory's pragmatic observation that those who aspire to the perfect life are relatively rare: all had the same preparation, but not all ascended the mountain.

---

[60] Ronald E. Heine, 'Gregory of Nyssa's Apology for Allegory', *Vigiliae christianae*, 38: 4 (1984), 362.
[61] Lim, *Public Disputation, Power, and Social Order in Late Antiquity*, 163.
[62] Lim, *Public Disputation, Power, and Social Order in Late Antiquity*, 164.
[63] Lim, *Public Disputation, Power, and Social Order in Late Antiquity*, 169.
[64] Patrick F. O'Connell, 'The Double Journey in Saint Gregory of Nyssa: *The Life of Moses*', *Greek Orthodox Theological Review*, 28: 4 (1983), 302.
[65] O'Connell, 'The Double Journey', 321. [66] O'Connell, 'The Double Journey', 322.

The reader is encouraged to identify with and imitate the journey of Moses, who did aspire to perfection.[67]

He does, however, stress that Moses' elevation above the Israelites confers responsibility: 'Contemplation is no privatized, individualistic accomplishment, but the God-given insight and ability to teach, heal and lead others.'[68] This is nowhere better illustrated than by Moses' experience on Mount Sinai. Once he emerged out of the darkness,

> [Moses] descended to his people in order to share with them the wonders shown to him in the theophany, to hand over the laws, and to establish for the people the temple and the priesthood according to the pattern shown to him on the mountain.[69]

Gregory sees this as the typology which was imitated by such model bishops as Gregory Thaumaturgus and Basil:

> [Gregory Thaumaturgus] was filled with a certain boldness and confidence through that vision, like an athlete who, since he has enough experience through competition and strength from training, strips confidently for the race and prepares for combat against his competitors.[70]

> Many times we perceived that [Basil] also was in the dark cloud wherein was God. For what was invisible to others, to him [was] the initiation into the mysteries of the Spirit made visible, so that he seemed to be within the compass of the dark cloud in which knowledge about God was concealed. Many times he arrayed himself against the Amalecites, using prayer as his shield. And when he raised his hands, the true Jesus conquered His enemy.[71]

Leaders, however, by definition, are in a minority. Gregory clearly does not expect the majority to gain access to the holy of holies.

13.4 *LIFE OF MOSES* 2.188: HEAVENLY ASCENT CONTEXT

In heavenly ascent texts, the equivalent to the holy of holies—the epicentre of holiness, where the glory of God is to be found—is the *merkavah*. It is usually assumed that the goal of heavenly ascent was to obtain a vision of the divine glory upon the *merkavah* throne. However, in *Songs of the Sabbath Sacrifice*, as in the Hekalot texts, this vision fails to materialize:

> The whole thrust of the Songs is towards the climactic vision of God: as each song moves ever closer to the ultimate mystery, anticipation mounts, but when the

---

[67] O'Connell, 'The Double Journey', 323.   [68] O'Connell, 'The Double Journey', 323.
[69] *Vit. Moys.* 1.56.   [70] *Thaum.* (GNO 10,1.19–20); trans. Slusser, 55.
[71] *Bas.* (GNO 10,1.129); trans. Stein, 47–9.

climax is reached the description seems to have been astonishingly perfunctory. Because of the damaged state of the text, the final vision of God is, unfortunately, missing, but reconstruction suggests that it cannot have been elaborate.[72]

Schäfer comments on the way in which terms used by Ezekiel to describe the divine human-like figure on the throne, such as *hashmal* and 'brightness'/'radiance' (נגה), are assigned to the angelic spirits in Song 12:

> ...Like the appearance of fire (are) the spirits of holiest holiness round about, the appearance of streams of fire like electrum (בדמות חשמל). And (there are) works of
> [ra]diance (ומעשי [נ]וגה) with glorious mingled colors...[73]

As he says,

> What Ezekiel encounters as a vision of God has been transferred to the angels in Song XII. The angels move to center-stage; God's physical appearance recedes into the background and is hardly mentioned at all. That which remains important is only his praise, not the vision of his shape.[74]

When it comes to the Hekhalot literature, Schäfer disagrees with Scholem:

> What is the aim of this heavenly journey [the ascent of the Merkavah mystic]? Is it, as Scholem presumes, exclusively or at least primarily the vision of God on his throne?...The first surprising result of an examination of the texts is that the ascent accounts say almost nothing at all about what the mystic actually sees when he finally arrives at the goal of his wishes. The reader, who has followed the adept in his dangerous and toilsome ascent through the seven palaces, and whose expectations have been greatly raised is rather disappointed.[75]

Even Aḥer does '*not* see God but an angel (albeit the highest angel in heaven)'.[76] This diffidence over describing God is already there in earlier texts. Ezekiel only sees the figure on the chariot at three removes: 'Such was the appearance of the likeness of the glory of the Lord (מראה דמות כבוד־יהוה)' (Ezek. 1:28). In *1 Enoch* 14, Enoch 'does not see much of God: the narrative moves immediately from the Glory of the Great One seated on the throne to his garment'.[77]

B. Ḥagigah 14b–15b relates the story of the four who entered *pardes*:

> Our masters taught: Four entered a garden, and these are they: Ben Azzai, Ben Zoma, Aher, and R. Akiba. R. Akiba said to them, When you draw near the stones

---

[72] Philip Alexander, 'The Qumran *Songs of the Sabbath Sacrifice* and the *Celestial Hierarchy* of Dionysius the Areopagite: A Comparative Approach', *Revue de Qumran*, 22: 87 (2006), 358.
[73] Song 12.5–6 (4Q405 20–22 ii 10–11); text and trans. Charlesworth and Newsom, 182–3.
[74] Peter Schäfer, *The Origins of Jewish Mysticism* (Tübingen: Mohr Siebeck, 2009), 138.
[75] Peter Schäfer, 'The Aim and Purpose of Early Jewish Mysticism', in *Hekhalot-Studien* (Tübingen: Mohr Siebeck, 1988), 285.
[76] Schäfer, *The Origins of Jewish Mysticism*, 235.
[77] Schäfer, *The Origins of Jewish Mysticism*, 61.

of pure marble, do not say, Water, water; for it is said, *The speaker of lies shall not be established in My sight*. Ben Azzai looked and died.... Ben Zoma looked and was smitten.... Aher cut the shoots.... R. Akiba ascended safely and descended safely.[78]

The same story also appears, with variations, in the Tosephta, the Palestinian Talmud, and the Hekhalot literature.[79] As Halperin points out, 'there is no evidence specifically linking [the *pardes* story] with the *merkabah*, or suggesting that it originally referred to ecstatic mysticism of the *Hekhalot* type'.[80] Schäfer suggests that the story started out referring to the rabbis being 'initiated by God into the innermost mysteries of the Torah'.[81] Already in the Tosephta, however, it appears as part of a 'mystical collection' attached to *m. Ḥagigah* 2:1,[82] suggesting that the editors understood it as 'referring to the *exegesis* of the *Merkavah*'.[83] The enigmatic sentence about the stones of pure marble does not appear in the Tosephta or the Yerushalmi. Schäfer argues that it is a truncated version of the 'water episode' in the Hekhalot literature, which the Bavli imported in order 'to turn the *pardes* narrative into an ascent account' and 'ensure that the reader would understand the entrance of the four rabbis into the "garden" as an ascent to the Merkavah in heaven'.[84] As such, it becomes a warning of the dangers of ascent. The restriction in *m. Ḥagigah* 2:1 states that the chariot may not be expounded 'in the presence of one, unless he is a sage (*hakham*) and understands of his own knowledge'. Morray-Jones points out that, of the four who entered *pardes*, only Aqiva was an ordained rabbi, a *hakham* according to rabbinic terminology: 'The others, in spite of their great learning, were merely *talmidei hakhamim* [students of rabbis] and so their involvement in *maase merkava* resulted in disaster'.[85] Unlike Elisha b. Avuyah, who came to be known as Aḥer, the archetypal 'other', Ben Azzai and Ben Zoma have a good press in rabbinic literature; all that they have done wrong is not to be ordained rabbis.[86] The Bavli reports that in response to the second

---

[78] Trans. David J. Halperin, *The Merkabah in Rabbinic Literature* (New Haven: American Oriental Society, 1980), 75–6.
[79] For details of the parallel versions see Halperin, *The Merkabah in Rabbinic Literature*, 86–8.
[80] Halperin, *The Merkabah in Rabbinic Literature*, 91.
[81] Schäfer, *The Origins of Jewish Mysticism*, 201.
[82] The term 'mystical collection' is coined by Halperin. See Halperin, *The Merkabah in Rabbinic Literature*, 65.
[83] Schäfer, *The Origins of Jewish Mysticism*, 201.
[84] Schäfer, *The Origins of Jewish Mysticism*, 202–3.
[85] Christopher Rowland and Christopher R. A. Morray-Jones, *The Mystery of God: Early Jewish Mysticism and the New Testament* (Leiden: Brill, 2009), 364–5.
[86] Sweeney's alternative explanation is that Ben Azzai was punished because he failed to produce children. Ben Zoma's shortcoming was his errant biblical interpretation. Marvin A. Sweeney, 'Pardes Revisited Once Again: A Reassessment of the Rabbinic Legend concerning the Four Who Entered Pardes', in *Form and Intertextuality in Prophetic and Apocalyptic Literature* (Tübingen: Mohr Siebeck, 2005), 278–9. Schäfer argues, on the basis of the biblical verse quoted—'Precious in the sight of the Lord is the death of his saints' (Ps. 116:15)—that Ben Azzai was not punished at all: 'God took him to heaven because he liked him so much and approved of what he did'. Schäfer, *The Origins of Jewish Mysticism*, 199.

story of a child understanding *hashmal* and being burnt up, it was suggested that the book of Ezekiel should be consigned to a Genizah. But R. Joshua b. Gamala retorts, 'If this one is a scholar (*hakham*), all are scholars!',[87] meaning that just because 'a child (who is not a scholar) was burned does not mean that the book of Ezekiel is off limits for (real) scholars'.[88] The holiest mysteries are to be kept for those in authority.

13.5 *LIFE OF MOSES* 2.188: CONCLUSIONS

The holy of holies of the earthly tabernacle represents for Gregory the same mystery as climbing Mount Sinai to see the heavenly tabernacle—the ultimate mystery of God, and the coming of the believer into the presence of that mystery. He is drawing on the Alexandrian tradition of the holy of holies as the *kosmos noētos*. Whereas for Clement knowledge (*gnōsis*) is superior to faith, and it is the gnostic who reaches the holy of holies, for Gregory the opposite is true: one encounters God by faith, not knowledge. In *On the Lord's Prayer* he is happy to use the entrance of the high priest into the holy of holies as an allegory of prayer; but by *Life of Moses* he has become more reticent. Only the 'superheroes' of the faith—Moses, Isaiah, Ezekiel, Paul, John—are able to enter the unenterable. And even Moses cannot see the mysteries shielded by the cherubim's wings. For Origen the holy of holies is a symbol of the vision of God after death, and for the Valentinians entry into the Pleroma is the ultimate stage of salvation for the 'spiritual'.[89] Gregory too uses this symbolism for life after death in the *Funeral Oration on Meletius*. And one of his descriptions of the eschaton is of the dividing veil being removed.[90] But in *Life of Moses* he is anxious to stress the never-ending nature of the quest to find God. The holy of holies, like the heavenly tabernacle, participates in the infinity of God. Therefore Gregory, unlike Clement, does not make use of Leviticus 16. The holy of holies does not provide an endpoint to the spiritual journey. The heavenly ascent texts also frustrate expectations. The promised *merkavah* never clearly appears. They do not have Gregory's philosophical language, but they too imply that God is beyond human vision.

Theological mysteries have social consequences. The imagery of the holy of holies had already been used in the Alexandrian tradition to make distinctions between believers: witness Clement and the Valentinians. But with Gregory

---

[87] B. Ḥag. 13a; trans. Halperin, *The Merkabah in Rabbinic Literature*, 156. There are some textual variants, set out by Halperin in a footnote.
[88] Schäfer, *The Origins of Jewish Mysticism*, 228 n. 61.   [89] See 4.3.
[90] *An. et res.* (PG 46.133C); trans. Silvas, 233.

those distinctions became a matter of ecclesial authority. Lim demonstrates how, in a situation in which theological arguments were threatening to split the church, fourth-century bishops became determined to cut off debate. They wanted the elucidation of the highest mysteries to be left to those in authority. Everyone else was to take them on faith. This comes out clearly in Gregory's description of the place of the holy of holies within the earthly tabernacle. Hoi polloi are to keep out. Despite the differences in genre, there is a parallel with the treatment of the 'work of creation' and the 'work of the chariot' in *b. Ḥagigah* 11b–16a. Just as Gregory turns the tabernacle into a manual of orthodoxy, so the rabbis 'rabbinized' *ma'aseh merkavah*. For Gregory, ascent becomes theology, for the rabbis, exegesis. And both restrict access to 'higher' matters to those in positions of religious authority: Gregory stresses the inaccessibility of the holy of holies; the rabbis depict the dangers of trying to ascend to the *merkavah*.

14

The Priestly Vestments

> Most people are prevented from correctly understanding these [garments] by the very names of the clothing. For what sort of name for bodily attire is 'disclosure' or 'oracle' or 'truth'? These clearly show that it is not this perceptible clothing that is described for us by the history, but a certain adornment of the soul woven by virtuous pursuits.[1]

14.1 *LIFE OF MOSES* 2.189–201: BIBLICAL CONTEXT

After being shown the pattern of the tabernacle, Moses is given instructions concerning Aaron's vestments.[2] Gregory devotes considerable space to these garments: five paragraphs in the *historia* and thirteen paragraphs in the *theōria*.[3] His descriptions do not entirely tally with the LXX. Some of the technical terms he uses are different: neither the 'clasps' (πορπαί) securing the shoulder pieces nor the 'straps' (τελαμῶνες) tying the breastpiece to the arms appear in the LXX.[4] Whereas the LXX refers to the high priest's headpiece as a 'turban' (κίδαρις) or 'headdress' (μίτρα—*mitra*), Gregory uses the words 'headband' (ταινία) and 'diadem' (διάδημα).[5] The descriptions of the way in which the breastpiece is attached to the ephod, in the MT, the LXX, and *Life of Moses*, are particularly obscure; and the three accounts do not correlate.[6] Gregory does not simply reproduce the LXX, or indeed Origen's revised version. He is either summarizing and interpreting the data in his own words, or he knows other traditions about the priestly garments. Philo's account of the vestments in *On Moses* 2.109–135 does not account for the 'clasps', 'straps', 'headband', or the

---

[1] *Vit. Moys.* 2.190.   [2] Exod. 28.   [3] *Vit. Moys.* 1.51–55, 2.189–201.
[4] *Vit. Moys.* 1.52, 53; 2.200. At 36:13 the LXX does employ the hapax legomenon συμπεπορπημένους ('fastened'), whose root is based on πόρπη ('brooch, clasp'); and Josephus uses the verb πορπάω in his description of the stones on the shoulders (*A.J.* 3.165).
[5] Compare LXX Exod. 28:4, 28:33 with *Vit. Moys.* 1.55, 2.189, 2.201.
[6] MT: Exod. 28:13–14, 22–28; 39:15–21. LXX: Exod. 28:13–14, 22–25; 36:22–29. *Vit. Moys.* 1.53; 2.197. In his hexaplaric revision, Origen added a translation of Exod. 28:23–28 from Theodotion.

description in *Life of Moses* 1.53 of 'plaited cords, which were interlaced through each other crosswise in a net-like pattern'. The word Gregory uses for 'cords' (σειραί), which does not occur in LXX Exodus or Philo's descriptions of the priestly vestments, is found in Josephus *Jewish Antiquities* 3.170, but Josephus' account of the breastpiece's fixings does not otherwise tally with Gregory's.

Gregory gives another allegorical interpretation of the priestly vestments in the third homily of *On the Lord's Prayer*. Some of his vocabulary there differs again. The LXX once refers to the breastpiece (MT חֹשֶׁן) as the *peristēthion*,[7] which literally means 'round the chest/breast', elsewhere it uses *logion* (oracle). In *Life of Moses*, Gregory calls it the *prostēthion* ('before the chest/breast').[8] In *On the Lord's Prayer*, he talks of the band (*mitra*) placed around the chest (*peristēthios*) of the priest,[9] despite the fact that the LXX uses *mitra* for the headpiece.[10] *On the Lord's Prayer* refers to the three decorations on the hem of the robe using the LXX's terminology: pomegranates, bells, and flowers (ἄνθινα).[11] *Life of Moses* does not use the word 'flower', although Gregory does refer to the fabric pomegranates in 1.54. Both there and in 2.194 he seems to be conflating them with the tassels of the tunic. It suits his purpose of extolling the dual aspect of virtue only to refer to pomegranates and bells in 2.192.

Gregory interprets the priestly clothing in terms of virtue. He has interpreted the heavenly tabernacle Christologically, the earthly tabernacle ecclesiologically, and now he turns to the theme of ethical living. He first lists the clothing (2.189), and then proceeds to a detailed interpretation, beginning with the full-length robe. As with his interpretation of the tabernacle, quotations from the New Testament play an important role. His interpretation in *On the Lord's Prayer*, which also equates the priestly vestments with 'the graces of virtue',[12] can be seen as a preliminary version which he has revised and expanded, particularly by the addition of New Testament proof texts.

In 2.191 Gregory focuses on the full-length robe (מְעִיל; ποδήρης/ὑποδύτης). The high priest wore this underneath the ephod and the breastpiece, but over the tunic (כְּתֹנֶת; χιτών).[13] The robe was blue (תְּכֵלֶת; ὑάκινθος). As part of his elaborate cosmological interpretation of the vestments, Philo declares it to be 'an image of the air'.[14] Gregory clearly was aware of this: 'Certain of those who have previously

---

[7] Exod. 28:4.   [8] *Vit. Moys.* 2.189.   [9] *Or. dom.* 3 (GNO 7,2.31.9).

[10] This has confused Hilda Graef: she translates GNO 7,2.32.1 as 'the diadem (*mitra*) with the rays coming from precious stones' (Graef, *The Lord's Prayer, The Beatitudes*, 45). There are no precious stones on the headpiece; *mitra* here refers to the band around the chest, i.e. the breastpiece.

[11] For the flowers see LXX Exod. 28:30, Philo *Mos.* 2.119. Graef's translation of *On the Lord's Prayer* was made before the GNO edition had been published. In the edition by Krabinger that she used, the flowers are twice omitted, although the third reference is there. See J. G. Krabinger, *S. Gregorii, Episcopi Nysseni: De precatione orationes v, graece et latine* (Landshut: Attenhofer, 1840), 46.7, 46.33, 48.3; cf. GNO 7,2.31.11, 32.7–8, 32.13–14.

[12] *Or. dom.* 3 (GNO 7,2.31.24); trans. Graef, 45.

[13] Malherbe and Ferguson confuse matters by translating ὑποδύτης, ποδήρης, and χιτών as 'tunic' (cf. 2.189, 191, 194).

[14] *Mos.* 2.118.

examined the word say that the dye signifies the air.'[15] Gregory is not here concerned with cosmology, but this interpretation proves useful, as it enables him to talk of an airy tunic, in contrast to the thick and fleshy clothing of ordinary living. In 2.185 Gregory talked of the church offering 'a sacrifice of praise and an incense of prayer' in the earthly tabernacle. Here, the sacrifice required becomes purity of life. He quotes Romans 12:1—'a living sacrifice and rational service'—and brings in 1 Thessalonians 4:17, which describes a meeting with the Lord in the air:

> One who intends to become a priest of God... should not damage the soul with the thick and fleshy clothing of ordinary living, but by purity of life should make all his pursuits as delicate as the thread of a spider's web, and come close to that which ascends and is light and airy. He should respin this bodily nature, in order that when we hear the last trumpet, and are found weightless and light in responding to the voice of the one who urges us on, we may be carried on high through the air together with the Lord, with no weight dragging us back to earth.[16]

References to the upward-bearing (ἀνωφερής) and light (κοῦφος) nature of the virtuous soul, recalling the upward flight of the soul in Plato's *Phaedrus* (246C), are frequent in Gregory's work,[17] as are allusions to 1 Thessalonians 4:17.[18] That verse is eschatological, and Gregory uses it as such, but he argues that if on the last day we wish to 'be carried on high through the air', then we need to don an 'airy tunic' in life. In *Life of Macrina*, he presents his sister and her community as having fulfilled this ideal:

> Their life was lived on the border between the human and the incorporeal nature.... they were not weighed down by the drag of the body, so that their life was borne aloft to the skies and trod on high with the heavenly powers.[19]

They were 'divorced from all earthly vanities and attuned to the imitation of the angelic life'.[20] In *Life of Moses*, Gregory brings together virtue with the light, airy garment of the priestly robe without explicitly mentioning angels. In *Life of Macrina*, however, he makes the equation virtuous = light = angelic. And in *On the Soul and Resurrection* he puts the following words into Macrina's mouth, as she explains the resurrection:

> You will see this bodily covering which is now dissolved in death, woven again from the same elements, not according to its present dense and heavy texture, but with its fibre spun again into something more subtle and ethereal, so that you will

---

[15] Wisdom, Josephus, and Clement all give cosmological interpretations of the robe, but only Philo equates it with the air. See Albert Geljon, *Philonic Exegesis in Gregory of Nyssa's De Vita Moysis* (Providence: Brown Judaic Studies, 2002), 140.
[16] *Vit. Moys.* 2.191.
[17] See *Virg.* 18 (GNO 8,1.322.10–11); *Beat.* 1 (GNO 7,2.89.4–5); *Bas.* (GNO 10,1.122.9).
[18] See *Eun.* 3,10 (GNO 2.295.1–2); *Beat* 1 (GNO 7,2.89.2–3); *Beat* 2 (GNO 7,2.93.2–3); *Or. dom.* 4 (GNO 7,2.49.9–10); *Mort.* (GNO 9.62.23–24).
[19] GNO 8,1.382.20–383.5; trans. Silvas, 122.
[20] GNO 8,1.382.5–6; trans. Silvas, 121.

not only have with you that which you love, but it will be restored to you with a brighter and more captivating beauty.[21]

The light and airy 'clothing' represented by the priestly robe is the resurrection body, of which believers can have a foretaste by living a virtuous life. Twice in *Life of Moses* 2.191 Gregory compares this robe to a spider's web, the second time quoting Psalm LXX 38:12. A word in MT Psalm 39:12 (RSV 39:11), which probably refers to a moth (עָשׁ), is translated by the LXX as 'spider' (ἀράχνης), thus giving Gregory a biblical proof text.[22] He interprets the length of the robe as referring to the fullness of virtue. Elsewhere in his writings he argues both that in order to be virtuous it is necessary to 'remain aloof from every evil',[23] and that all the virtues are 'attached and dependent on each other'.[24] According to Daniélou, this thesis of Gregory's that it is necessary to have all the virtues comes from Basil.[25]

From the colour and length of the robe, Gregory moves on to the bells and pomegranates attached to its hem. These represent 'the sparkle of noble feats'.[26] In the MT, two objects are attached to the robe's hem: pomegranates of blue, purple, and scarlet, and golden bells.[27] The LXX turns these into three decorations: multicoloured pomegranates, golden pomegranates, and bells. The fabric pomegranates then become designated 'flower-work' or 'blossom' (ἄνθιν ον), and as such are mentioned by both Philo and Gregory.[28] Here in *Life of Moses*, however, at first Gregory only mentions two ornaments—golden bells and pomegranates—which suits his interpretative purpose. When Moses first arrived in the darkness, he was taught that 'religious virtue is divided into two: into the divine and the correct ordering of behaviour'.[29] Gregory is referring there to the Ten Commandments, but the same twofold structure returns here. Virtue is acquired through 'faith as regards the divine, and conscience as regards life': 'These pomegranates and bells the great Paul bestows upon Timothy's garment, saying that he must have "faith and a good conscience" [1 Tim 1:19]'.[30] There then follows the only reference to the Trinity in Gregory's tabernacle interpretation:

> So, on the one hand, let faith ring out loud and clear by the proclamation of the holy Trinity, and, on the other, let life imitate the nature of the pomegranate's fruit.[31]

---

[21] *An. et res.* (PG 46.108A); trans. Silvas, 217.
[22] Malherbe and Ferguson use the Jerusalem Bible translation of the psalm, which, in line with the MT, refers to a moth, making Gregory's proof text incomprehensible.
[23] *Virg.* 16 (GNO 8,1.313); trans. Callahan, 53.
[24] *Inst.* (GNO 8,1.78.4–5); trans. Callahan, 151.
[25] Jean Daniélou, *Grégoire de Nysse: La Vie de Moïse, ou Traité de la perfection en matière de vertu* (Paris: Cerf, 2000), 237 n. 2.
[26] *Vit. Moys.* 2.192.   [27] Exod. 28:33.
[28] LXX Exod. 28:29–30; *Mos.* 2.119; *Or. Dom.* 3 (GNO 7,2.31.11, 32.7–8, 32.14).
[29] *Vit. Moys.* 2.166.   [30] *Vit. Moys.* 2.192.   [31] *Vit. Moys.* 2.192.

Gregory allegorizes pomegranates in terms of the philosophical life, which, although 'hard to accept and disagreeable to the senses, is yet full of good hopes, and ripens in its own time'.[32] He produces the same image three times in *On the Song of Songs*, thanks to the three references to pomegranates in Song of Songs.[33] In *Life of Moses*, he links the interpretation with Hebrews 12:11:

> For the divine Apostle also says somewhere that 'for the moment all discipline seems painful rather than pleasant (that is the impression on first encountering the pomegranate), later it yields the peaceful fruit'. This is the sweetness of the food inside.[34]

In both Hebrews and *Life of Moses*, the Greek word translated as 'discipline' is *paideia*. Malherbe and Ferguson follow the Jerusalem Bible in translating it as 'punishment', which is misleading. Education may well involve painful discipline, but, as Gregory is pointing out, that is not its primary purpose. As well as drawing on biblical imagery, he is reinterpreting the Hellenistic ideals of *paideia* and the philosophical life in terms of Christian virtue.

Underneath the robe, the high priest was to wear a tunic (כתנת; χιτών).[35] The description of this tunic in the MT (תשבץ) is usually translated 'of chequer work', although the NJPS has 'fringed'. The LXX translation is 'tasseled' (κοσυμβωτόν). Here at 2.194 Gregory refers to the 'tunic', but the evidence of 1.54 suggests that he conflates the tunic with the robe, which presumably involves equating the tassels of the tunic with the fabric pomegranates of the robe. Gregory says that 'the tassels are spherical ornaments attached to [the tunic] for the sake of decoration, not need'. Therefore, 'virtue is not to be measured by commandment alone', 'we should find something for ourselves, through original invention, so that extra decoration might be added to the garment'.[36] He illustrates this by reference to Paul's lifestyle, weaving together 1 Corinthians 9:13–14, 1 Corinthians 9:18, and 1 Corinthians 4:11:

> Whereas the law directs that 'those attending the altar receive a share from the altar' and 'those proclaiming the gospel make their living' from it, he makes the gospel 'free of charge', undergoing hunger, thirst and nakedness. These are the tassels, which by their addition adorn the tunic of the commandments.[37]

From the tunic, Gregory moves on to the ephod, although he doesn't call it by that name. In 2.189 he refers to it as the 'overgarment' (ἐπενδύτης).[38] In 2.195 he describes it as two pieces of cloth (δύο πέπλοι) 'coming down from the shoulders as far as the chest and the back', 'joined to each other by two clasps, one on each shoulder'. This might explain why he seems to conflate the ephod (אפוד; ἐπωμίς) and its shoulder pieces (כתפת; ἐπωμίδες). The MT refers to these

---

[32] *Vit. Moys.* 2.193.
[33] Song 4:3, 13, 6:7; *Cant.* 7 (GNO 6.229–231), 9 (GNO 6.282–283), 15 (GNO 6.455–456).
[34] *Vit. Moys.* 2.193.   [35] Exod. 28:4.   [36] *Vit. Moys.* 2.194.
[37] *Vit. Moys.* 2.194.   [38] This is similar to Aquila's translation ἐπένδυμα.

using distinct words, but the LXX uses the same word for both: singular for the ephod, and plural for the shoulder pieces. Gregory only uses the plural form, seemingly for the ephod itself.[39] He lists the colours of the ephod, which are the same as those of the veil (and tabernacle curtains) with the addition of gold thread. In 2.178 he has mentioned the cosmological interpretation of those colours;[40] here he allegorizes them in terms of virtues:

> The blue is woven with the purple. For royalty is partnered by purity of life. Scarlet mingles with flax, because the radiance and purity of life somehow grow naturally together with the blush of modesty. The gold shining among these colours hints at the treasure laid up for such a life.[41]

The clasps, with their engraved stones, enable Gregory to acknowledge the virtues of Old Testament figures:

> The patriarchs written on the shoulder pieces contribute in no small way to such an embellishment for us. Human life is enriched all the more by the models of goodness received from the past.[42]

'There is another decoration set over the decoration provided by these cloths.'[43] Gregory is here referring to the breastpiece. The one Hebrew word for 'breastpiece' in the MT (חשן) is translated by the LXX as *peristēthion* (something around the chest) at Exodus 28:4, and as *logion* (oracle) elsewhere. One manuscript tradition has *logeion* (a speaking place), which is the word used by Philo.[44] Clement seems to have misunderstood the LXX, not realizing that *logion* and *peristēthion* refer to the same object.[45] Gregory may have suffered from a similar confusion: in his list of vestments in 2.189 he refers both to 'that breastpiece (*prostēthion*), sparkling with the varied glints of precious stones' and to 'the "oracle" (*logion*), the "disclosure", and, contemplated in both, the "truth". 'Disclosure' (δήλωσις) and 'truth' (ἀλήθεια) are the LXX's translation of the Urim and the Thummim of Exodus 28:30. In 2.197 Gregory does not refer to either *logion* or *prostēthion*, but simply to a 'decoration' (κόσμος). The LXX description of the breastpiece, and its attachment to the ephod, is complicated and difficult to visualize. Here in 2.197 Gregory simplifies it into two golden shields, one hanging from each shoulder piece, to which is attached a rectangular golden object decorated with twelve stones arranged in four rows, no two of which are alike. 'Golden object' (χρυσότευκτον) gives the impression that he takes the breastpiece to be a metal breastplate, but a little further on (2.199) he refers to it as 'the cloth (πέπλος) of virtue', showing that he is aware that it is made of woven material. In the *historia*, he also talks of 'plaited cords, which were interlaced through each other crosswise in a net-like

---

[39] *Vit. Moys.* 1.52, 2.189, 196.
[40] Cf. Philo *Mos.* 2.88; Josephus *A.J.* 3.183; Clement *Strom.* 5.32.3; Origen *Hom. Exod.* 13.3.
[41] *Vit. Moys.* 2.196.   [42] *Vit. Moys.* 2.196.   [43] *Vit. Moys.* 2.197.
[44] E.g. *Mos.* 2.112.   [45] See *Strom.* 5.38.2.

pattern, suspended on each side from the clasp above the shields', but they do not reappear here.[46] The shields (ἀσπίδες) correspond to the 'small shields' (ἀσπιδίσκαι) of the LXX, themselves a substitution for the 'settings' (מִשְׁבְּצֹת) of the stones on the shoulders in the MT.[47] Gregory highlights these shields, seeing their meaning (*dianoia*) as 'the twofold nature of the armour against the adversary'.[48] This further reference to the twofold way of virtue is backed up by a quotation from 2 Corinthians 6:7: 'by means of the weapons of righteousness for the right hand and for the left'.[49] The four-cornered shape is 'a sign to you of steadfastness in the good. For such a shape is hard to alter, fixed firm thanks to the right-angled corners based on the straight sides'.[50] With the twelve stones, Gregory returns to the virtues of the patriarchs:

> The word teaches us through this design that the one who drives away the evil archer with these two shields will adorn his own soul with all the virtues of the patriarchs, each shining on the cloth of virtue in its own way.[51]

Gregory turns next to the 'straps by which these ornaments are tied to the arms'. They teach that 'it is necessary to unite practical philosophy with the work of contemplation', since the heart symbolizes contemplation, while the arms symbolize works.[52] Here is yet another variation on his theme of the twofold nature of virtue.

In his preliminary list of priestly garments, Gregory includes 'the headband and on it the thin plate (*petalon*)'.[53] The word 'headband' (ταινία) is not in the LXX. The MT distinguishes between the 'turban' (מִצְנֶפֶת) worn by Aaron, the high priest, and the 'caps' (מִגְבָּעוֹת) worn by Aaron's sons, the other priests.[54] The LXX sometimes translates 'turban' (מִצְנֶפֶת) as 'headdress' (μίτρα—*mitra*),[55] but uses 'turban' (κίδαρις) indiscriminately for both the high priest's and the other priests' headgear.[56] Here, in this concluding section, Gregory does not refer to the headband, only to the 'diadem' (διάδημα), which he says 'intimates the crown laid up for those who have lived well'.[57] Since he refers to the *petalon* straight afterwards, it would seem that he is using 'diadem' for the headdress. But he is less concerned about accurate description than alluding to the many New Testament verses which promise a crown to the righteous.[58] He mentions the inscription in 'unutterable lettering', but makes no comment upon it.

No footwear is prescribed in Exodus for the high priest. Gregory explains that he 'does not put on sandals, so as not to be weighed down for the race and

---

[46] *Vit. Moys.* 1.53.
[47] Exod. 28:13, 14, 25; *Vit. Moys.* 1.53; 2.197, 198, 199.
[48] *Vit. Moys.* 2.198.   [49] *Vit. Moys.* 2.198.   [50] *Vit. Moys.* 2.199.
[51] *Vit. Moys.* 2.199.   [52] *Vit. Moys.* 2.200.   [53] *Vit. Moys.* 2.189.
[54] Compare Exod. 28:4 with 28:40.   [55] E.g. LXX Exod. 28:33, 29:6.
[56] E.g. LXX Exod. 28:4, 35, 36; 29:9.   [57] *Vit. Moys.* 2.201.
[58] 1 Cor. 9:25; 2 Tim. 4:8; Jas. 1:12; 1 Pet. 5:4; Rev. 2:10, 3:11, 4:4.

hindered by the covering of dead skins'.[59] He has already interpreted God's command to Moses to remove his shoes along the same lines:

> Sandaled feet cannot ascend that height where the light of truth is seen, but the dead and earthly covering of skins, which was placed around our nature at the beginning when we were found naked because of the disobedience to the divine will, must be removed from the feet of the soul.[60]

The 'covering of dead skins', a reference to the clothing of Adam and Eve in Genesis 3:21, corresponds to the 'thick and fleshy clothing of ordinary living'.[61] As Malherbe and Ferguson explain,

> The 'garments of skin' are not bodily existence *per se*, for man has a body in Paradise, but animality or biological existence. The garments include the passions, sexuality, and especially mortality, which are added to the human nature made in the image of God.[62]

They are to be cast off, as they constitute an 'impediment to the ascent'.[63]

14.2 *LIFE OF MOSES* 2.189–201: ALEXANDRIAN CONTEXT

All the Alexandrian writers assume that the details of the high priest's vestments carry symbolic meanings, although they differ as to the framework within which those meanings are to be deciphered. Philo describes the high priest's apparel as 'a likeness and copy of the universe',[64] and provides a detailed cosmological interpretation: the robe is an image of the air, with its flowers representing the earth, its pomegranates water, its bells the harmonious alliance of the two; the two stones on the shoulders of the ephod symbolize the sun and moon; the twelve stones on the breastpiece are the signs of the zodiac; the four letters on the gold plate are related to geometrical categories and musical harmonies.[65] In a discussion of the *logeion* (breastpiece), which, according to Exodus 28:16, was to be doubled over, he refers to the Stoic distinction between the indwelling (ἐνδιάθετος) and the uttered (προφορικός) logos, comparing it to the difference between 'the incorporeal and archetypal ideas' and 'the visible objects which are the copies and likenesses of those ideas'.[66] He says that the holy vestments were so designed that 'in performing his holy office

---

[59] *Vit. Moys.* 2.201.   [60] *Vit. Moys.* 2.22; trans. Malherbe and Ferguson, 59.
[61] *Vit. Moys.* 2.191.
[62] Abraham J. Malherbe and Everett Ferguson, *Gregory of Nyssa: The Life of Moses* (New York: Paulist Press, 1978), 160 n. 29.
[63] *Vit. Moys.* 2.201.   [64] *Spec.* 1.84.   [65] *Mos.* 2.117–135; *Spec.* 1.84–97.
[66] *Mos.* 2.127.

[the high priest] should have the whole universe as his fellow-ministrant'.[67] As in the case of the tabernacle, this cosmological interpretation is not unique, since it can also be found in Josephus, with some variation in the details.[68] In a move not found in Josephus, Philo relates cosmology to anthropology. The high priest is to represent the universe not only by his clothes, but by his whole self. He is to 'be in himself a little world, a microcosm'.[69] In some places, Philo designates him as the Logos:

> We say, then, that the High Priest is not a man, but a Divine Word and immune from all unrighteousness whether intentional or unintentional.[70]

He develops his anthropological allegorization in less detail than the cosmological one, but *Questions on Exodus* provides anthropological interpretations of some individual elements of the garments. The shoulder pieces, for example, 'designate serious labours', and the twelve stones on the breastplate are related to the four virtues, each virtue with three aspects.[71]

Clement's allegorization of the priestly garments is influenced by Philo's. He says that their 'multicolored symbols allude to celestial phenomena'.[72] But he also imports ideas from other sources, some of which cannot now be identified. He talks, for example, of 'the five stones and two carbuncles (ἄνθρακες)' representing the seven planets, which have no equivalent in either the LXX or Philo.[73] No other known writer numbers the bells suspended from the robe at 360. The main thrust of his interpretation is Christological: the 360 bells proclaim 'the magnificent epiphany of the Saviour';[74] the gold cap 'indicates the regal power of the Lord, since "the head of the church" is the Saviour';[75] the *logion* 'signifies the prophecy which cries by the Word and proclaims the judgement that is to come'.[76] Clement refers to different grades of Christian, saying that the stones 'might be the various phases of salvation; some occupying the upper, some the lower parts of the entire saved body'.[77] And he exploits Leviticus 16: the high priest, 'the spiritual and perfect man', puts off his consecrated robe, which 'prophesied the ministry in the flesh by which [the Word] was made visible to the world directly', 'washes himself and puts on the other tunic, a holy-of-holies one, so to speak, which is to accompany him into the adytum'.[78] On re-emerging he does the opposite. This putting on and off of clothes represents both the ascent of the gnostic to the noetic realm wearing 'the

---

[67] *Spec.* 1.96. [68] *A.J.* 3.183–187. [69] *Mos.* 2.135.
[70] *Fug.* 108; cf. *Migr.* 102. [71] *QE* 2.108, 112.
[72] *Strom.* 5.32.2; trans. Annewies van den Hoek, *Clement of Alexandria and His Use of Philo in the Stromateis: An Early Christian Reshaping of a Jewish Model* (Leiden: Brill, 1988), 118.
[73] *Strom.* 5.37.1; trans. van den Hoek, *Clement of Alexandria and His Use of Philo*, 134.
[74] *Strom.* 5.37.4; trans. van den Hoek, *Clement of Alexandria and His Use of Philo*, 134.
[75] *Strom.* 5.37.5; trans. van den Hoek, *Clement of Alexandria and His Use of Philo*, 134.
[76] *Strom.* 5.39.2; trans. van den Hoek, *Clement of Alexandria and His Use of Philo*, 140.
[77] *Strom.* 5.37.3; trans. van den Hoek, *Clement of Alexandria and His Use of Philo*, 134.
[78] *Strom.* 5.39.2–3; trans. van den Hoek, *Clement of Alexandria and His Use of Philo*, 140.

bright array of glory', and the Lord 'descending into the realm of sense'.[79] The interpretation of the high priest's entry into the holy of holies is taken further in *Excerpts from Theodotus* 27. There he is said to remove the golden plate at the altar of incense, 'indicating the laying aside of the body which has become pure like the golden plate'.[80] Kovacs argues that 'this seems to refer not to the physical body but to a further purification of the soul by shedding everything that is not essential to it'.[81] Divested of its inferior parts, the soul of the high priest 'passes into the spiritual realm and becomes now truly rational and high priestly'.[82] This involves 'being controlled directly by the Lord and becoming, as it were, his body'.[83] The golden plate is also associated with 'the pursuit of knowledge'.[84] Kovacs, who argues that *Excerpts from Theodotus* 27 stems from Clement himself, puts this together with *Miscellanies* 5.32–40:

> The gnostic high priest, who has earlier exchanged the garment of faith for the bright array of [*gnōsis*] (*Str.* V 6, 40.1), now removes the vestment of [*gnōsis*] and enters into direct contemplation of God.[85]

Origen tackles the priestly garments in *Homilies on Exodus* (with reference to Exodus 28) and *Homilies on Leviticus* (with reference to Leviticus 8:7–9). He departs from both the predominantly cosmological interpretation of Philo and the predominantly Christological interpretation of Clement, instead allegorizing the garments in terms of virtues. He uses LXX Psalm 131:9 and Colossians 3:12 to designate the priestly clothing as garments of justice and mercy.[86] And whereas for Philo the high priest represents the Logos, and for Clement an elite category of Christian, Origen argues that, at least in theory, anyone can wear these clothes: 'that part which is the most precious in man can hold the office of high priest'; 'you too can function as a high priest before God within the temple of your spirit if you would prepare your garments with zeal and vigilance'.[87] His interpretation of the vestments is not the same in the two series of sermons, partly because he notices details in the biblical texts, such as that LXX Leviticus 8:7–8 talks about girding Aaron twice.[88] Leviticus 8:7 also mentions both the tunic (χιτών) and the robe (ὑποδύτης), which is why in *Homilies on Leviticus* he talks

---

[79] *Strom.* 5.40.1, 3; trans. van den Hoek, *Clement of Alexandria and His Use of Philo*, 141.
[80] *Exc.* 27.2; trans. Casey, 61.
[81] Judith L. Kovacs, 'Concealment and Gnostic Exegesis: Clement of Alexandria's Interpretation of the Tabernacle', in Elizabeth A. Livingstone (ed.), *Papers Presented at the Twelfth International Conference on Patristic Studies Held in Oxford 1995, part 3: Preaching, Second Century, Tertullian to Arnobious, Egypt before Nicaea* (Leuven: Peeters, 1997), 435.
[82] *Exc.* 27.3; trans. Casey, 61.   [83] *Exc.* 27.6; trans. Casey, 63.
[84] *Exc.* 27.6; trans. Casey, 63.
[85] Kovacs, 'Concealment and Gnostic Exegesis', 437. See 4.2 n. 34.
[86] *Hom. Exod.* 9.3.
[87] *Hom. Exod.* 9.4; trans. Heine, 343; *Hom. Lev.* 6.5.2; trans. Barkley, 125.
[88] This arises because the MT has two different 'girdles': the אבנט (Exod. 28:4, 39; Lev. 8:7) and the חשב אפדתו (Exod. 28:8; Lev. 8:7). Haran interprets חשב as the upper part of the ephod. Menahem Haran, *Temples and Temple-Service in Ancient Israel: An Inquiry into the Character of*

of two tunics: 'one of the ministry of the flesh; another of spiritual understanding'.[89] The interpretations do not contradict each other, but, as far as can be ascertained from the Latin translations, the wording is different. In *Homilies on Exodus* the *logion* 'represents the rational understanding which is in us', in *Homilies on Leviticus* it 'is a sign of wisdom because wisdom is founded on reason'.[90] 'Truth' (*ueritas*) and 'manifestation'/'communication' (*manifestatio*)—the Urim and the Thummim—are placed on the *logion*, either so that we might 'perceive the message of the Gospel which, in its fourfold order, sets out to us the truth of the faith and the manifestation of the Trinity', or because the high priest must 'communicate what he knows to the people' and never depart from the truth.[91] The length of the robe (which signifies that the whole person should be clothed with chastity) and the bells ('that you might never keep silent about the last times') feature in *Homilies on Exodus*,[92] but not in *Homilies on Leviticus*. The latter, on the other hand, reflects on the differences in clothing between 'minor priests and major priests', arguing that not everyone reaches the required standards:

> For anyone can perform the religious ministry, but few there are who are adorned with morals, instructed in doctrine, educated in wisdom, very well adapted to communicate the truth of things and who expound the wisdom of the faith, not omitting the ornament of understandings and the splendor of assertions which is represented by the ornament 'of gold plate' placed on his head.[93]

Geljon argues that Gregory's reference to the robe representing the air adds to the evidence that he had read Philo's *On Moses*.[94] There are a few other details in Gregory's interpretation, not mentioned by Geljon, which also have a Philonic ring to them. He connects the twelve stones of the breastpiece with the virtues of the patriarchs, as does Philo.[95] Philo does so, however, as part of a complex interpretation which includes the cosmological understanding of the twelve stones as the twelve signs of the zodiac, with the patriarchs becoming constellations. Gregory says that the four-cornered shape of the breastpiece should be 'a sign to you of steadfastness in the good'.[96] A similar interpretation appears in Philo:

> The master did well also in assigning a four-square shape to the reason-seat (τῷ λογείῳ), thereby shewing in a figure that the rational principle (λόγος), both in nature and in man, must everywhere stand firm and never be shaken in any respect at all.[97]

Cult Phenomena and the Historical Setting of the Priestly School (Oxford: Clarendon, 1978), 167 n. 39.

[89] *Hom. Lev.* 6.3.5; trans. Barkley, 122.
[90] *Hom. Ex.* 13.7; trans. Heine, 385; *Hom. Lev.* 6.4.2; trans. Barkley, 123.
[91] *Hom. Exod.* 9.4; trans. Heine, 343; *Hom. Lev.* 6.4.3; trans. Barkley, 123.
[92] *Hom. Exod.* 9.4; trans. Heine, 343–4.   [93] *Hom. Lev.* 6.6.1; trans. Barkley, 126.
[94] Geljon, *Philonic Exegesis in Gregory of Nyssa's De Vita Moysis*, 138–40.
[95] *Vit. Moys.* 2.199 cf. QE 2.114.   [96] *Vit. Moys.* 2.199.   [97] *Mos.* 2.128.

Shoulders consistently represent work in the Alexandrian tradition, and so, therefore, do both the ephod (אפוד; ἐπωμίς) and the shoulder pieces (כתפת; ἐπωμίδες).[98] Although Gregory transfers work from shoulders to arms, and then associates the heart with philosophy, his twofold interpretation of the 'straps' echoes Philo's comment on the two shoulder pieces:

> There are two form of labour: one is the desire of pleasing God, and of piety; the other is being beneficent to men, which is called kindness and love of man.[99]

Gregory's overall purpose, however, is very different to Philo's. He is not interested in cosmological parallels. Neither is he interested in the kind of Christological interpretation given by Clement, who connects the *logion* to the Logos. Gregory's avoidance of *logion* in his detailed interpretation may be a deliberate move, so as not to become drawn into Christological subordinationism. His interpretative framework is much closer to Origen's. His rhetorical question: 'What sort of name for bodily attire is "disclosure" or "oracle" or "truth"?'[100] resembles Origen's remark:

> If anyone ever saw, if anyone ever heard of the vestments called 'communication and truth', let them tell us who the women are who wove these, or in what shop they were woven. But if you want to hear the truth, it is wisdom that makes garments like this.[101]

He does not, however, borrow Origen's wording (always allowing that Origen is only available in translation). Both interpret the garments in terms of virtue, but the details differ, as illustrated by the colours of the ephod. Origen interprets blue/violet (ὑάκινθος) as the hope of the kingdom of heaven, purple (πορφύρα) as the splendour of love, scarlet (κόκκος) as the glory of suffering, and linen (βύσσος) as virginity.[102] There is no overlap with Gregory's list in 2.196. Origen's interpretation, with its inclusion of suffering and virginity, seems more 'ascetic' than Gregory's. Did Gregory take over the general idea from Origen, but then develop his own variations? He does not use the garments to develop a list of Christian virtues; the allegorization of the four colours is the only place where he mentions individual virtues. Instead, we learn that virtue should not be truncated; that the philosophical life, although outwardly disagreeable, is yet full of good hopes; that we should add to virtue by our own invention; that human life is enriched by models of goodness from the past; and so on. The 'refrain' is that virtue is twofold. Despite the wealth of detail, the message of the clothing is simple: that 'practical philosophy' should be united to 'the work of contemplation'.[103] Gregory is not arguing for particular virtues, but that Christian virtue is to be measured by the extent to which theory and practice synchronize. There

---

[98] See Philo *Mos.* 2.130, *QE* 2.108; Clement *Strom.* 5.38.2; Origen *Hom. Lev.* 6.3.6.
[99] *QE* 2.108. [100] *Vit Moys.* 2.190. [101] *Hom. Lev.* 6.4.3; trans. Barkley, 124.
[102] *Hom. Exod.* 9.3; trans. Heine, 340.
[103] *Vit. Moys.* 2.200.

14.3 LIFE OF MOSES 2.189-201: THEOLOGICAL CONTEXT

In Heine's view, not only is Gregory's theological insistence on the incomprehensibility of God's essence aimed at Eunomius, but so too is his emphasis on virtue: 'Gregory seems to have had Eunomius' disregard for asceticism in mind in his interpretation of the color of the priestly robe'.[104] He sets Gregory's interpretation of the blue robe alongside an extract from *Against Eunomius* in which Gregory compares his brother Basil—'who decrees alike for himself and for his circle sobriety and decency and absolute purity of soul and body through strictest chastity'—with Eunomius—'who forbids us to make difficulties for the character which is advancing as it chooses through the appetites of the body, nor to oppose pleasures'.[105] Heine comments,

> The two key elements in the *De vita Moysis* passage can be found in Gregory's depiction of Basil and Eunomius. The *De vita Moysis* passage implies that negligence in respect to the flesh can harm the soul, and, therefore, one must guard against this by purity of living. In the *Contra Eunomium* passage Gregory represents Basil as a man who was concerned about purity of soul and body. Eunomius, however, plays this down saying that the soul cannot be harmed by indulging the flesh. Here, again, the teaching of the *De vita Moysis* opposes a view that Eunomius had championed and which Gregory had attacked.[106]

However, the imagery used in *Life of Moses* is widespread in Gregory's work, and cannot be pinned down simply to his conflict with Eunomius. And it is striking how little emphasis there is on asceticism in his interpretation of the priestly garments. He talks about 'virtue' without specifying which particular virtues he has in mind. The philosophical life is 'hard to accept and disagreeable to the senses', and he talks about Paul undergoing 'hunger, thirst and nakedness'; but his interpretation of the four colours is milder than Origen's—there is no 'glory of suffering'.[107] The references to 'the death of sinful flesh', 'the severe life of self-control', and 'virginity' come earlier, in the description of the earthly tabernacle.[108] The exegesis of the priestly vestments is a series of

---

[104] Ronald E. Heine, *Perfection in the Virtuous Life: A Study in the Relationship Between Edification and Polemical Theology in Gregory of Nyssa's De Vita Moysis* (Cambridge, Mass.: Philadelphia Patristic Foundation, 1975), 184.
[105] *Eun.* 1.99 (GNO 1.55–56); trans. Hall, 50.
[106] Heine, *Perfection in the Virtuous Life*, 185.
[107] *Vit. Moys.* 193, 194; *Hom. Exod.* 9.3.   [108] *Vit. Moys.* 2.187.

variations on the theme of the twofold nature of virtue. Gregory returns to this again and again: the bells and pomegranates, the two shields, the breastpiece joined to the arms. The interest of his interpretation is not in the details, but in the overall picture. Gregory explains in *To Call Oneself a Christian* that heaven is not 'some remote habitation of God', but a result of human choice: 'a heavenly sojourn is easy for anyone who wants it even on earth...by our thinking heavenly thoughts and depositing in the treasury there a wealth of virtue'.[109] As Sterk says,

> For Gregory virtue is not a step on the pathway to perfection, a stage that must be surpassed and superceded by the mystical or unitive experience. Virtuous action must flow from contemplation and knowledge of God for it is part of a continuous process of perfection.[110]

Nowhere does Gregory mention that these are garments of the high priest, and only twice does he link them to priests.[111] The impression given is that these are garments anyone can aspire to wear. What he is most keen to stress is that virtue and doctrine are intertwined. He may have been fighting on two fronts: against people like Eunomius who, in Gregory's mind, emphasized doctrine and neglected virtue; and against radical ascetics, who claimed authority for themselves from their lifestyle, bypassing the structures of the church.[112] Henry Chadwick comments on Basil's emphasis on restraint, saying that he prescribed severe penalties 'for monks who set themselves austere fasts without leave'.[113] Elsewhere in *Life of Moses* Gregory says that 'virtue is discerned in the mean'.[114] In his interpretation of the priestly garments he stresses not heroic individual feats of asceticism, but that virtue cannot be disengaged from orthodoxy, and therefore from the church.

Alongside participation in virtue, does the transformation from the heavy garments of flesh to the light angelic robe also involve an ontological change? It was argued in 8.3 that the heavenly tabernacle represents the eternal Christ, and therefore the *adiastemic* existence of God. And it was suggested in 8.5 that human beings can only approach this *adiastemic* existence asymptotically, never crossing the Creator–created divide. Boersma, however, has recently argued (on the basis of *On the Three Day Period, On the Sixth Psalm*, and *On the Beatitudes*) that Gregory understands light, angelic garments to represent the non-*diastemic* life of the resurrection, and that 'the moral (virtuous)

---

[109] GNO 8,1.138.25, 140.11–14; trans. Callahan, 87, 88.
[110] Andrea Sterk, 'On Basil, Moses, and the Model Bishop: The Cappadocian Legacy of Leadership', *Church History*, 67: 2 (1998), 248 n. 101.
[111] *Vit. Moys.* 2.189, 191.   [112] Cf. Chapter 11.
[113] Henry Chadwick, *The Early Church* (Harmondsworth: Penguin, 1967), 179.
[114] *Vit. Moys.* 2.288; trans Malherbe and Ferguson, 128.

and the ontological (bodily) transformations go hand in hand'.[115] Ascent to the heavenly tabernacle involves getting beyond the limitations of space and time found in earthly existence, although 'God's being will infinitely outdistance human ascent'.[116] Boersma acknowledges 'a tension in Gregory's thought', which he insists is not 'a blatant inconsistency'.[117] He maintains that he is not negating Gregory's doctrine of eternal progress into the infinite divine life, but leaves unclear what it is that constitutes the ontological divide between Creator and creation in Gregory's thinking, if not the presence or lack of *diastēma*. And he accounts for non-*diastemic* heavenly bodies by suggesting that, for Gregory, materiality is a fluid configuration of intelligible properties: 'This fluidity allows the body either to become heavy through association with the passions and so to be dragged down to earth or to become light through a life of virtue and so to ascend to the heavenly Paradise.'[118] In the face of all the inconsistencies, however, Boersma is forced to resort to Gregory's well-known sense of paradox:

> In the resurrection life, the ordinary boundaries and measurements of life on earth will no longer apply. As a result, Gregory struggles to describe this paradisal life. After all, how does one give expression to an existence that will be drastically different from the sensible objects characterized by the spatial and temporal dimensions of this life? As his frequent use of paradox makes clear, however, for Nyssen this struggle is an exhilarating joy rather than a burden. The joy lies in the otherness of the eschatological future.[119]

14.4 *LIFE OF MOSES* 2.189-201: HEAVENLY ASCENT CONTEXT

Garments feature prominently in heavenly ascent texts. There are four categories of beings who wear distinctive clothing: transformed ascending heroes, such as Enoch or Levi; the righteous dead; angels; and God, or, perhaps more accurately, the glory of God. They do not each have distinct clothing: there are correlations between their garments. Depicting angels, and even God,

---

[115] Hans Boersma, *Embodiment and Virtue in Gregory of Nyssa: An Anagogical Approach* (Oxford: Oxford University Press, 2013), 50.
[116] Boersma, *Embodiment and Virtue*, 44.
[117] Boersma, *Embodiment and Virtue*, 44.
[118] Boersma, *Embodiment and Virtue*, 50. A further problem is caused by Gregory's references, in *On the Making of Humankind*, to human embodiment and gender before the Fall: 'how is it possible to have gendered bodies in an adiastemic angelic-like existence in Paradise?' This, says Boersma, is not a question with which Gregory deals. Boersma, *Embodiment and Virtue*, 49 n. 134.
[119] Boersma, *Embodiment and Virtue*, 52.

as wearing clothes, is clearly anthropomorphic. Viewed from another angle, however, these garments are metaphors for the absence of flesh and blood in heaven. There is interplay between angelic dress and the divine glory, with neither understood as earthly.

Heavenly clothing is sometimes white, sometimes multicoloured. Each of these traditions may relate to priestly vestments. Mysterious angelic figures wearing plain linen (בד) appear in Ezekiel and Daniel.[120] The garments of the Ancient of Days in Daniel 7:9, and of the Great Glory in *1 Enoch* 14:20,[121] are compared to white snow.[122] Himmelfarb suggests that the plain linen garment worn by the high priest for his yearly entry into the holy of holies, 'the earthly counterpart of the spot where God sits enthroned in the heavenly temple', may have contributed to the whiteness of the divine robe in *1 Enoch* 14.[123] Following on from these early texts, there emerged a more generalized picture of white clothing in heaven. The elders in Revelation and the 'men' in *Testament of Levi* wear white, as do the righteous dead in Revelation.[124] This whiteness was also associated with luminosity. The garment of the Great Glory in *1 Enoch* 14:20 shines more brightly than the sun.[125] Halperin sees here the influence of the phrase 'you wrap yourself with light as with a garment' from Psalm 104:2.[126] Alexander points out that 'the description of the raiment baffles visualization; it is like the glare of the sun's orb, or of a snow-field, both of which overwhelm and "whiteout" human vision'.[127] The luminous quality of other heavenly garments is symbolic of participation in this divine glory.

One source for multicoloured clothing in heaven is the rainbow brightness surrounding the figure on the mobile throne in Ezekiel 1:26–28. A rainbow appears, for example, in the description of the allusive figure on the throne in Revelation 4:2–4; and the description of the angelic spirits who surround and

---

[120] Ezek. 9:2–3, 11; 10:2, 6, 7; Dan. 10:5; 12:6–7.

[121] *1 En.* 14:20: 'His apparel was like the appearance of the sun and whiter than much snow (τὸ περιβόλαιον αὐτου ὡς εἶδος ἡλίου λαμπρότερον καὶ λευκότερον πάσης χιόνος, cf. 4QEn^c 1 vii 2: [א]לגאראב[ת]).' Greek text Black, 29; Aramaic text Milik, 199; trans. Nickelsburg and VanderKam, 35.

[122] The Ancient of Days in Daniel 7 also has hair like pure wool, which is presumably white. That imagery is widely attributed to Canaanite influence; see J. A. Emerton, 'The Origin of the Son of Man Imagery', *Journal of Theological Studies*, 9 (1958). There is, however, no mention of hair in *1 Enoch* 14.

[123] Martha Himmelfarb, *Ascent to Heaven in Jewish and Christian Apocalypses* (Oxford: Oxford University Press, 1993), 18. For the plain linen garment see Lev. 16:14.

[124] Rev. 4:4; *T. Levi* 8:2; Rev. 3:5; 6:11; 7:9, 13–14.

[125] The syntax of the phrase is awkward. See Nickelsburg, *1 Enoch 1*, 258 n. 20a.

[126] David J. Halperin, *The Faces of the Chariot: Early Jewish Responses to Ezekiel's Vision* (Tübingen: Mohr Siebeck, 1988), 83.

[127] Philip Alexander, 'The Qumran *Songs of the Sabbath Sacrifice* and the *Celestial Hierarchy* of Dionysius the Areopagite: A Comparative Approach', *Revue de Qumran*, 22: 87 (2006), 358 n. 15.

move with the *merkavah* in Song 12 of *Songs of the Sabbath Sacrifice* draws on Ezekiel 1:27–28:[128]

> ... Like the appearance of fire (כמראי אש) (are) the spirits of holiest holiness round about, the appearance of streams of fire like electrum (חשמל). And (there are) works of
> [ra]diance with glorious mingled colors (ומעשי נוגה ברוקמת כבוד), wondrously hued (צבעי פלא), bright<ly> blended (ממולח טוהר), spirits of living [g]odlike beings moving continuously with the glory of [the] wondrous chariots.[129]

This language also resembles the evocation of the angelic priestly garments in Song 13, which, in turn, uses vocabulary from Exodus 28:[130]

> their holy places. In their wondrous station (are) spirits of mingled colors like woven work (רוחות רוקמה כמעשי אורג), engraved (פתוחי) with images of splendor.
> In the midst of the glorious appearance of scarlet (שני) are (garments) dyed with a light of a spirit of holiest holiness, those who stand fast (in) their holy station before
> (the) [k]ing, spirits of [brightly] dyed (צבעי) stuffs in the midst of the appearance of whiteness. And the likeness of (the) glorious spirit (is) like fine gold work, shedding
> [ligh]t. And all their decoration is brightly blended (ממולח טוהר), an artistry like woven works (חשב כמעשי אורג). These are the chiefs of those wondrously arrayed for service,[131]

In the much later *3 Enoch*, the influence of both high priestly apparel and Ezekiel's rainbow brightness can be seen in the description of Metatron's clothing:

> The Holy One, blessed be he, fashioned for me a majestic robe (לבוש של גאה), in which all kinds of luminaries were set, and he clothed me in it. He fashioned for me a glorious cloak (מעיל כבוד) in which brightness, brilliance, splendor, and luster of every kind were fixed, and he wrapped me in it. He fashioned for me a kingly crown in which 49 refulgent stones were placed, each like the sun's orb, and its brilliance shone into the four quarters of the heaven of 'Arabot, into the seven heavens, and into the four quarters of the world.[132]

Testament of Levi contains an even clearer reference to priestly vestments: during his second ascent Levi undergoes an investiture ceremony whose seven items of clothing are clearly intended to be high priestly, even if the terminology does not entirely conform to that of Exodus 28:

---

[128] Note כמראי אש; חשמל; נוגה.
[129] Song 12.5–6 (4Q405 20–22 ii 10–11); text and trans. Charlesworth and Newsom, 182–3.
[130] Cf. מעשה רקם (Exod. 28:39; 39:29); מעשה אורג (Exod. 28:32; 39:22, 27); חשב (Exod. 28:8); תפתח (Exod. 28:11); שני (Exod. 28:5).
[131] Song 13.18–21 (4Q405 23 ii 7–10); text and trans. Charlesworth and Newsom, 186–9.
[132] *3 En* 12:1–5; §15; trans. Alexander, 265.

And I saw seven men in white clothing, saying to me:

> Arise, put on the robe (τὴν στολὴν) of the priesthood
> and the crown (τὸν στέφανον) of righteousness
> and the breastplate (τὸ λόγιον) of understanding
> and the garment (τὸν ποδήρη) of truth
> and the plate (τὸ πέταλον) of faith
> and the turban (τὴν μίτραν) of (giving) a sign
> and the ephod (τὸ ἐφοὺδ) of prophecy.[133]

This is the only heavenly ascent text which, like Gregory, makes the priestly garments symbolic of virtue. There is no correspondence, however, between the symbolism given to each item in *Testament of Levi* and Gregory's allegorization. *Testament of Levi*'s interpretation could well be the work of Christian editors, influenced by Ephesians 6:13–17, which allegorizes armour. Quotations from the New Testament play an important role in Gregory's interpretation of the garments, but he does not allude to Ephesians 6. Despite the superficial resemblance, therefore, there is no link between the texts. In *Testament of Levi* the high priestly vestments are handed over in heaven, to one privileged individual, in order to validate his earthly ministry; in *Life of Moses* they represent the virtuous behaviour of all believers.

The elaborate multicoloured clothing of Exodus 28, including stones engraved with the name of the twelve tribes, encapsulates the high priest's representative function. Later interpretations, such as those contained in *Wisdom of Solomon*, Philo, and Josephus, declare the priestly clothing to be 'a likeness and copy of the universe'.[134] A vestige of this tradition survives in the Hekhalot literature, which refers to a divine garment (using the term *ḥaluq*—a shirtlike robe) with a cosmic function:

> Constellations and stars and zodiacal signs
> Flow and issue forth from the garment of Him
> Who is crowned and [shrouded] in it...[135]

The plain garments of Leviticus 16, by contrast, strip the high priest of his representative function, and bring him 'naked' before God.[136] So too in heaven, the multicoloured clothing seems to be given to those with ritual or representative

---

[133] *T. Levi* 8:2–10; trans. Hollander and de Jonge, 149.

[134] *Spec.* 1.84; cf. Wis. 18:24; *A.J.* 3.180.

[135] *Hekhalot Rabbati* §105; trans. Gershom G. Scholem, *Jewish Gnosticism, Merkabah Mysticism, and Talmudic Tradition* (New York: Jewish Theological Seminary of America, 1960), 61.

[136] This is explored in Deborah W. Rooke, 'The Day of Atonement as a Ritual of Validation for the High Priest', in John Day (ed.), *Temple and Worship in Biblical Israel: Proceedings of the Oxford Old Testament Seminar* (London: T&T Clark, 2007), 350–5.

functions, those closest to the glory of God. Messenger angels and the multitude of righteous dead wear white.

Human beings who make it to heaven after death shed their material bodies and, like angels, wear 'clothes' which partake of the divine glory. In *Ascension of Isaiah*, Isaiah sees 'the righteous from the time of Adam onwards... stripped of (their) robes of the flesh; and... in their robes of above, and they [are] like the angels who stand there in great glory'.[137] There is an angel in *3 Enoch* named 'Azbogah who 'girds men with garments of life (בגדי חיים) and in time to come he will wrap the righteous and pious of the world in robes of life (מעיל חיים), so that clad in them they may enjoy eternal life'.[138] Alexander comments, 'The "garments of life" and the "robes of life" are the immortal bodies which the righteous receive in heaven.'[139] Privileged individuals who ascend before death also have to be transformed. As Alexander writes,

> Bodily ascent to the alien environment of heaven has huge theological implications, and demands the transformation of flesh and blood into a more spiritual substance. The material body in its present terrestrial form cannot endure the fiery celestial regions.[140]

Not all ascent texts describe a bodily ascent: in *1 Enoch* Enoch sees heaven in a vision;[141] and Alexander argues that in *3 Enoch* Ishmael 'seems to make a soul excursion into heaven'.[142] But *2 Enoch* reports that Enoch was taken bodily into heaven by two huge men,[143] hence the need for a transformation and change of clothing:

> The LORD said to Michael, 'Take Enoch, and extract (him) from the earthly clothing. And anoint him with the delightful oil, and put (him) into the clothes of glory.' And Michael extracted me from my clothes. He anointed me with the delightful oil... And I gazed at all of myself, and I had become like one of the glorious ones, and there was no observable difference.[144]

For his descent back to earth his face has to be chilled, otherwise 'no human being would be able to look at [it]'.[145] Isaiah's transformation seems to take place gradually: 'the glory of my face was being transformed as I went up

---

[137] *Ascen. Isa.* 9:7–9; trans. Knibb, 170.   [138] *3 En.* 18:22; §27; trans. Alexander, 274.

[139] Philip Alexander, '3 (Hebrew Apocalypse of) Enoch', in James H. Charlesworth (ed.), *The Old Testament Pseudepigrapha, vol. 1: Apocalyptic Literature and Testaments* (New York: Doubleday, 1983), 274 n. i2.

[140] Philip Alexander, *The Mystical Texts: Songs of the Sabbath Sacrifice and Related Manuscripts* (London: T&T Clark, 2006), 77.

[141] *1 En.* 14:1, 2, 4, 8.

[142] Philip Alexander, 'The Dualism of Heaven and Earth in Early Jewish Literature and its Implications', in Armin Lange, et al. (eds), *Light against Darkness: Dualism in Ancient Mediterranean Religion and the Contemporary World* (Göttingen: Vandenhoeck & Ruprecht, 2011), 181.

[143] *2 En.* 1:4–9.   [144] *2 En.* 22:8–10; trans. Andersen, 139.

[145] *2 En.* 37:2 in the longer recension; trans. Andersen, 160.

from heaven to heaven.'[146] When he arrives at the seventh heaven, a voice asks, 'How far is he who dwells among aliens to go up?'; but another voice, that of Christ, answers, 'The holy Isaiah is permitted to come up here, for his robe is here.'[147] When Enoch is transformed into Metatron, he is first enlarged until he matches the world in length and breadth,[148] and then, as he tells Ishmael:

> My flesh turned to flame, my sinews to blazing fire, my bones to juniper coals, my eyelashes to lightning flashes, my eyeballs to fiery torches, the hairs of my head to hot flames, all my limbs to wings of burning fire, and the substance of my body to blazing fire.[149]

This is reminiscent of the fate of any human being who dares look at the divine *ḥaluq*:

> Of no creature are the eyes able to behold it...
> And as for him who does behold it, or sees or glimpses it,
> Whirling gyrations grip the balls of his eyes.
> And the balls of his eyes cast out and send forth torches of fire
> And these enkindle him and these burn him.[150]

As Scholem points out,

> This is not...a description of dangers confronting the mystic, but of a mystical transfiguration taking place within him. What is a permanent transfiguration in the case of Enoch, however, is only a temporary experience in the case of the Merkabah mystic.[151]

And, as Morray-Jones adds, the process 'is terrifyingly dangerous, even fatal, should he prove unworthy'.[152] Morray-Jones has designated this process 'transformational mysticism', arguing that in a wide range of texts 'the vision of the Glory entailed the transformation of the visionary into an angelic likeness of that divine image'.[153]

14.5 *LIFE OF MOSES* 2.189–201: CONCLUSIONS

What light does the comparison with heavenly ascent texts shed on Gregory's work? In equating the high priestly robe with an airy tunic—a heavenly

---

[146] *Ascen. Isa.* 7:25; trans. Knibb, 167.   [147] *Ascen. Isa.* 9:1–2; trans. Knibb, 169.
[148] *3 En.* 9:2; §12.   [149] *3 En.* 15:1; §19; trans. Alexander, 267.
[150] *Hekhalot Rabbati* §102; trans. Scholem, *Jewish Gnosticism, Merkabah Mysticism, and Talmudic Tradition*, 60.
[151] Scholem, *Jewish Gnosticism, Merkabah Mysticism, and Talmudic Tradition*, 60.
[152] Christopher R. A. Morray-Jones, 'Transformational Mysticism in the Apocalyptic–Merkabah Tradition', *Journal of Jewish Studies*, 43 (1992), 25.
[153] Christopher Rowland and Christopher R. A. Morray-Jones, *The Mystery of God: Early Jewish Mysticism and the New Testament* (Leiden: Brill, 2009), 334.

garment—he is tapping into a widespread tradition. Angelic clothing in ascent texts also mirrors priestly vestments. Like the authors of those texts, Gregory believes that ascending to heaven involves shedding the heavy garments of earthly existence and donning new 'clothing', similar to angelic garb. The heavenly ascent texts, with their 'transformational mysticism', hold out the hope that, for a few exceptional individuals, it is possible to undergo the necessary transformation and ascend to heaven before death. Gregory also states that it is possible to wear an airy tunic in this life—his sister Macrina provides a contemporary example. There are, however, also clear differences. On a minor point, Gregory's interpretation of the robe starts out from Philo's allegorization of its blue colour. Ascent texts pick up either on the white of the priestly garments in Leviticus 16, or on the multicoloured nature of the ephod and breastpiece in Exodus 28. More important is Gregory's emphasis on virtue. Heavenly ascent texts assume that anyone ascending to heaven before death must be righteous. Virtue is a precondition. Gregory makes it the journey: the process of donning priestly garments is the process of becoming virtuous. The garments he allegorizes belonged to the high priest—the representative of Israel and the one person allowed into the holy of holies. But he calls them 'the apparel of the priesthood (τὸν στολισμὸν τῆς ἱερωσύνης)', never mentioning the high priest.[154] Neither does he refer to Leviticus 16. In 2.188 he has said that the holy of holies is inaccessible, representing the incomprehensible essence of God. The one high priest has been replaced by the company of the virtuous. These cannot grasp the essence of God with the mind, but, by living a modest and pure life, they participate in the divine glory, replacing their earthly bodies with heavenly robes. Heaven is not a place, not 'some remote habitation of God',[155] but a result of how we live here and now. According to Williams,

> Gregory determinedly revises the notion [of participation in the divine] so as to direct attention to participation not in what God is, but in what he *does*.[156]

As Gregory himself says, 'whoever pursues true virtue participates in nothing other than God'.[157] In his interpretation of the priestly robe, therefore, he agrees with the heavenly ascent texts that the ultimate goal is to become like an angel, with the angelic state symbolized by a garment; but in his 'transformational mysticism', the transformation involved is an ethical one. Does this transformation also involve ontological change? Maybe the contradictions highlighted by Boersma's work are a result of Gregory's use of the imagery of angelic garments, inherited from Jewish apocalyptic and amply attested to

---

[154] *Vit. Moys.* 2.189.   [155] *Prof.* (GNO 8,1.138.25); trans. Callahan, 87.
[156] Rowan Williams, *The Wound of Knowledge: Christian Spirituality from the New Testament to St. John of the Cross* (London: DLT, 1979), 53.
[157] *Vit. Moys.* 1.7; trans. Malherbe and Ferguson, 31.

in heavenly ascent texts. Lightweight robes symbolizing participation in the divine glory cannot easily be reconciled either with the Platonic distinction between sensible and intelligible, or with the clear divide Gregory draws in *Against Eunomius* between *diastemic* human reality and the *adiastemic* existence of God.

15

The Value of Heuristic Comparison

This study has set out to explore Gregory of Nyssa's tabernacle imagery. The methodology it has employed of heuristic comparison with heavenly ascent texts from the Hellenistic and Late Antique worlds is innovative. Has the exercise been worthwhile? Has it yielded results? In other words, have we gained insights into Gregory's tabernacle interpretation? The heavenly ascent texts used have been of very different genres to *Life of Moses*, including pseudepigraphic apocalypses, liturgical material, and rabbinic debates. They often employ vivid imagery, rather than philosophical argumentation. And yet it has been shown that they wrestle with some of the same issues as those faced by Gregory. The same questions recur, albeit posed in different ways:

- How can God be described or talked about when God cannot be seen or even named?
- If 'heaven' is different to 'earth', can anyone cross from one to the other? And if so, how?
- Who is allowed access to holy mysteries?

Different texts come to different solutions. The inaccessibility of God can be conveyed with imagery either of blinding light/glory or of impenetrable darkness. The fact that no name is capable of encompassing the essence of God may be set out with rational arguments, or it can transpire through the longer and longer lists of gobbledygook which never fulfil their promise. The uninitiated can be kept away from holy mysteries either by statements of prohibition, or with graphic descriptions of supernatural punishments. Sometimes different texts arrive at similar solutions quite independently. Both Gregory and the rabbis of the Babylonian Talmud quote Psalm 18:12 (LXX 17:12; RSV 18:11), with its talk of darkness surrounding God. Both *Life of Moses* and *Songs of the Sabbath Sacrifice* describe a heavenly tabernacle/temple constituted of angelic powers; yet Gregory comes to that conclusion thanks to Colossians 1:16, whereas *Sabbath Songs* draws on Ezekiel 1.

Gregory's ideas are usually discussed in relation either to the theology of other church fathers, or to Platonist philosophy. They are not related to 'fringe texts' such as ascent apocalypses. Yet works such as *1 Enoch, Testament of Levi*, and *Ascension of Isaiah*, even if they preserve some Jewish traditions, were edited, copied, and transmitted by Christians. *1 Enoch* is quoted as a work of prophecy by Jude, *Barnabas*, and Clement of Alexandria.[1] Origen refers to it in four of his writings, cautioning that 'the books entitled Enoch are not generally held to be divine by the churches'.[2] Therefore, Gregory may well have been familiar with some of its content, even if, like Jerome,[3] he gave it little credence. He certainly seems familiar with the tradition in *Ascension of Isaiah* about Christ taking on the form of the angels in each of the heavens through which he descends, although his use of LXX Psalm 23 (MT 24) indicates that he was not drawing directly on the text of *Ascension of Isaiah* as we now have it. It has not been necessary for the purposes of this study to prove that Gregory was influenced by any particular text; but it is important to point out that ideas about heavenly ascent were circulating in fourth-century Christian circles. Although the comparison undertaken has been heuristic, the possibility of interaction between 'orthodox' theologians and ascent traditions should not be ruled out. However, it is comparisons with texts where there is no possibility of influence—*Songs of the Sabbath Sacrifice*, the Babylonian Talmud, and the Hekhalot literature—which have proved particularly striking. Gregory will not have read any of the Dead Sea Scrolls, nor had any contact with the rabbinic world in Babylonia. But the exploration of similarities and differences between these texts and *Life of Moses* has sharpened the deliniation of Gregory's use of tabernacle imagery.

15.1 *LIFE OF MOSES* AND *SONGS OF THE SABBATH SACRIFICE*

Both *Life of Moses* and *Songs of the Sabbath Sacrifice* evoke a celestial tabernacle/temple composed of heavenly powers. They both recognize that God's heavenly sanctuary is not a material building, but a 'spiritual' one. *Sabbath Songs* employs language from Ezekiel—cherubim, *'ophannim, ḥashmal*—and seems to be extending Ezekiel's depiction of God's throne as a living, moving angelic structure to the whole heavenly temple. The pillars and corners join

---

[1] James C. VanderKam, '1 Enoch, Enochic Motifs, and Enoch in Early Christian Literature', in James C. VanderKam and William Adler (eds), *The Jewish Apocalyptic Heritage in Early Christianity* (Assen: Van Gorcum, 1996), 35–47.

[2] *Cels.* 5.54; trans. VanderKam, '1 Enoch, Enochic Motifs, and Enoch in Early Christian Literature', 59.

[3] See William Adler, 'Introduction', in VanderKam and Adler (eds), *The Jewish Apocalyptic Heritage in Early Christianity*, 23.

in the praise. The elusive language may even be suggesting that it is the praise itself which creates the temple—'a structure composed of living sound'.[4] Gregory, on the other hand, starts with the heavenly tabernacle as a type of Christ. He then makes use of Colossians 1:16, which talks of heavenly powers being created in Christ. He draws on the Alexandrian tradition of allegorizing the tabernacle furniture, and equates the different elements of the tabernacle with the features of angelic beings. He goes on to draw on the Pauline tradition of the church as the body of Christ to allegorize the earthly tabernacle in terms of the members of the church. Thus, he creates a parallelism between an earthly body of Christ and a heavenly angelic one. At Qumran too, 'the community aimed at creating on earth a replica of the heavenly world'.[5] This surfaces not in *Sabbath Songs*, but in some of the other Dead Sea Scrolls, such as *4QFlorilegium* (4Q174), *Rule of the Community* (1QS), *Thanksgiving Hymns* (1QH), and the *Damascus Document* (CD). However, this parallelism is exploited in very different ways in the two contexts. Whether or not they boycotted the Jerusalem temple completely, the Qumran community was at odds with its leadership. They therefore turned instead to the worship of the heavenly temple. In *Songs of the Sabbath Sacrifice* human beings observe, and perhaps thereby feel themselves to be participating in, angelic worship. This was presumably regarded as a foretaste of what earthly liturgy would be like once the Jerusalem temple was returned to its true vocation. Gregory, on the other hand, is not criticizing contemporary earthly worship, but validating it. He is discouraging attempts to ascend to heaven, by pointing out that all that is needful can be found in the earthly tabernacle, the church. The reunion with angelic worship will only happen at the end of time, as he describes in *On the Titles of the Psalms*, *On the Soul and Resurrection*, and *On the Nativity of Christ*.

15.2 *LIFE OF MOSES* AND B. ḤAGIGAH

Gregory's allegorical interpretation of Moses' vision of the tabernacle not made with hands and the Bavli's discussions about the exegesis of the first chapter of Ezekiel both draw on pre-existing heavenly ascent traditions. They embrace and celebrate those traditions, but then ring them around

---

[4] Christopher R. A. Morray-Jones, 'The Temple Within', in April D. DeConick (ed.), *Paradise Now: Essays on Early Jewish and Christian Mysticism* (Atlanta: Society of Biblical Literature, 2006), 167.

[5] Devorah Dimant, 'Men as Angels: The Self-Image of the Qumran Community', in Adele Berlin (ed.), *Religion and Politics in the Ancient Near East* (Bethesda, MD: University Press of Maryland, 1996), 101.

with taboos. The epicentre of holiness and power, whether conceptualized as the holy of holies of the heavenly tabernacle or as the *merkavah*, is not open to all. God's privacy must be safeguarded, and religious authority channelled through appropriate people. Both texts independently turn to the biblical imagery of darkness to symbolize God's inaccessibility and incomprehensibility to the human mind. But they also present an elite—high priests as it were—who can venture into the darkness. Moses ascends Mount Sinai and sees a vision of the heavenly tabernacle. A few in the church—monks, priests, bishops?—are called to follow him. Most people, however, are to remain at the foot of the mountain. Hoi polloi are not allowed in the holy of holies: they are to worship in the outer room of the earthly tabernacle. Similarly, heroic rabbis of old performed an exegesis of Ezekiel 1 which dissolved the boundaries between heaven and earth. Aqiva safely negotiated all the dangers and was able to enter *pardes*. Contemporary rabbis draw from their authority, but everyone else is to steer clear of such dangerous mysteries. The righteous of Israel are to praise God by day and study Torah by night, not ascend to heaven, or speculate on matters too high for them. There is no *unio mystica* in these texts—no one is united to the divine. There are possibly hints of a *unio liturgica*: parts of Moses' vision symbolize angelic liturgy; correctly performed *ma'aseh merkabah* calls forth the ministering angels. For most people, however, earthly and heavenly worship are strictly in parallel. Gregory is able to exploit the imagery of the earthly tabernacle: since it is an exact copy of the heavenly one, there is no need to aspire to heaven. Only at the end of time will the curtain in front of the holy of holies be destroyed, so that humans and angels will worship together. The Bavli makes Israel's worship superior to that of the angels; here too, heavenly ascent is declared unnecessary.

These similarities exist not because of influence, but because in Late Antiquity both Jewish and Christian religious authorities had to deal with the challenge of heavenly ascent texts. Traditions which interpreted biblical texts such as Exodus 25 and Ezekiel 1 in terms of heavenly ascent were too widespread to be ignored, and may indeed have been taken for granted by Gregory and the rabbis. But this apocalyptic legacy opened the door to the possibility of fresh revelation, and to bids for leadership based on knowledge of heavenly secrets. Bishops and rabbis both had a vested interest in the institutionalization of authority, and needed to keep a lid on prophetic, charismatic outbursts. Their leadership was based on their skill in interpreting their respective religious traditions. In both cases, exegesis had a political agenda. They could not ignore heavenly ascent traditions, and therefore commandeered them, claiming their authority for themselves. Religious authority figures are represented as making the ascent, and thus as having access to the fountainhead of religious power. Everyone else is firmly told that the holy of holies is out of bounds to the hoi polloi.

15.3 *LIFE OF MOSES* AND THE HEKHALOT LITERATURE

Life of Moses and the Hekhalot literature seem poles apart. One is a carefully argued allegorical exegesis of Exodus by a known author; the other is a collection of fluid texts, whose history is debateable, containing a potpourri of hymns, incantations, fragments of narrative, and lists of names resembling gibberish. However, this study has shown that, despite the differences of genre, they address some of the same questions, the most important being 'what can human beings know of God?' Gregory argues that God's essence cannot be known, and sees both darkness and the holy of holies as symbols of that incomprehensibility. The Hekhalot texts stress the dangers of trying to see God, from terrifying guardian angels to the consuming fire emanating from the divine garment. This garment seems to be a protective measure against even greater danger. Despite the risks, the texts imply that a vision of the King in his beauty, on his throne of glory, is possible. However, as Schäfer points out, they promise more than they deliver, saying 'almost nothing at all about what the mystic actually sees when he finally arrives at the goal of his wishes'.[6] A similar scenario occurs with regard to names. Gregory argues that Moses' vision reveals a new name for God—tabernacle—but he is clear about the limitations of that name. The Hekhalot texts promise that the names they reveal will accomplish wonders, from giving access to the heavenly palaces to enabling instant learning; but the longer the lists of names become, the more unconvincing the promises seem. Unwittingly, these texts illustrate Gregory's argument that no name gives access to the divine essence. Schäfer argues that the goal of the *yored merkavah* is not to see the divine throne, but to participate in the heavenly liturgy as a representative of Israel, thereby confirming 'for the earthly congregation that it stands in direct contact with God in its synagogue liturgy'.[7] Gregory sees Moses' vision as validating earthly worship: it confirms that the church's liturgy is in parallel with the angelic one. In the Hekhalot texts, the *yored merkavah* undergoes a fiery transformation. Gregory too draws on the theme of transformation, but with quite a different purpose. He emphasizes that a believer's transformation takes place not by ascending to heaven, but by embracing a life of virtue.

---

[6] Peter Schäfer, 'The Aim and Purpose of Early Jewish Mysticism', in *Hekhalot-Studien* (Tübingen: Mohr Siebeck, 1988), 285.
[7] Schäfer, 'The Aim and Purpose of Early Jewish Mysticism', 288.

15.4 *LIFE OF MOSES* AND SCHOLARSHIP ON JEWISH MYSTICISM

This study has not only involved examining heavenly ascent texts; it has also drawn on the scholarship engendered by them. The discussions surrounding heavenly ascent texts have helped to frame the questions to be asked of *Life of Moses*. As pointed out in 1.4, there are parallels between the 'mysticism' versus 'theology' debates in Gregorian scholarship, and the 'experience' versus 'exegesis' divide among scholars of both pseudepigraphic ascent apocalypses and Jewish mysticism. More will be said on this topic in 16.2. Two concepts developed by scholars of Jewish mysticism have proved particularly useful in analysing Gregory's tabernacle imagery. The first is the distinction between *unio mystica* and *unio liturgica*. Schäfer argues that only in Philo, with his division between body and soul, and individualistic agenda, is there anything which could be described as *unio mystica*.[8] In the ascent apocalypses, *Songs of the Sabbath Sacrifice*, and the Hekhalot literature, there is but a *unio liturgica*—a liturgical communion of the mystic with the angels.[9] He insists that the rabbis of the Bavli, by contrast, were preoccupied with exegesis, not with mystical experiences of any kind. *B. Ḥagigah* 12b does, however, mention liturgy—both that of the angels and that of Israel. These are to occur in parallel, in separate spheres and at separate times. The Bavli even indicates that Israel's worship is superior to that of the angels. This analysis helps to clarify Gregory's mysticism: parts of Moses' vision symbolize angelic liturgy, but with no suggestion that Moses joins in; the rest of the people are expected to worship in the earthly tabernacle. This is much more like the Bavli than heavenly ascent texts proper. In other works Gregory does talk of a *unio liturgica*, but one which is to occur at the end of time, when humanity will be reunited with the angels. The other concept which has proved useful is that of 'transformational mysticism'. Morray-Jones argues that, in a wide range of heavenly ascent texts, 'the vision of the Glory entailed the transformation of the visionary into an angelic likeness of that Divine Image'.[10] Wolfson suggests that this angelification, found in Jewish sources, may provide an alternative model to the typology of mystical experience rooted in neoplatonic ontology and epistemology, in which 'contemplation of God results in a form of union whereby the soul separates from the body and returns to its ontological source in the One'.[11] Wolfson seems

---

[8] Peter Schäfer, *The Origins of Jewish Mysticism* (Tübingen: Mohr Siebeck, 2009), 352–3.
[9] Schäfer, *The Origins of Jewish Mysticism*, 341, 349.
[10] Christopher Rowland and Christopher R. A. Morray-Jones, *The Mystery of God: Early Jewish Mysticism and the New Testament* (Leiden: Brill, 2009), 334.
[11] Elliot R. Wolfson, 'Mysticism and the Poetic-Liturgical Compositions from Qumran: A Response to Bilhah Nitzan', *Jewish Quarterly Review*, 85: 1–2 (1994), 186.

to equate becoming angelic with becoming divine,[12] whereas Schäfer cautions that 'the transformed seer, in his angelicized state, at no time enters into a union with his God'.[13] As shown in 14.4, this transformation is often described in terms of a change of clothing. It was argued there that Gregory too connects heavenly ascent with the shedding of the heavy garments of earthly existence in order to don airy, angelic clothing. For Gregory, however, this transformation is linked to virtue. It is by living a life of asceticism, within the community of the church, that it becomes possible to participate in the divine glory, and replace one's earthly body with a heavenly robe.

Without the heuristic comparison with heavenly ascent texts, and the stimulus provided by their accompanying scholarship, this study would have been much poorer. Many of the themes explored stem from the biblical text, and occur in Gregory's Alexandrian predecessors, but the richness of possibilities they provide, and therefore the choices made by Gregory, whether consciously or unconsciously, only become apparent when a wide range of interpretations is on display. Ascent to heaven as the ascent to the heavenly tabernacle/temple, in particular, comes from Christianity's Jewish heritage, not from Platonism. And Jewish sources have provided the wherewithal to draw out the intricacies of Gregory's tabernacle interpretation.

---

[12] Wolfson, 'Mysticism and the Poetic-Liturgical Compositions from Qumran', 187.
[13] Schäfer, *The Origins of Jewish Mysticism*, 337.

Conclusions

C.1 GREGORY'S TABERNACLE INTERPRETATION

As a result not only of the heuristic comparison with heavenly ascent texts, but also of the thorough exploration of its biblical, Alexandrian, and theological contexts, what has been learnt about Gregory's tabernacle interpretation? These are the key ideas which have emerged:

- Gregory is drawing on long-standing traditions about heavenly ascent, going back to *1 Enoch* 14, in which heaven is depicted as a temple, with God enthroned upon an angelic chariot in the holy of holies.
- As do his Alexandrian predecessors, he weaves Platonic assumptions into the biblical narrative.
- Following Philo, he uses the darkness of Exodus 20:21 as a symbol of the incomprehensibility of God. However, faithful to Exodus, he describes how, within that darkness, Moses had a vision of 'the tabernacle not made with hands'—there is 'content' to the darkness. But this is not an abandonment of apophaticism: within the *aduton* of the darkness is the tabernacle (*aduta*), within which is the *aduton* of the holy of holies. And within the holy of holies are the cherubim who 'cover with their wings the mysteries lying in the ark of the covenant'.[1]
- There is no mention in *Life of Moses* of a 'sense of presence', a phrase which scholars import from *On the Song of Songs*.[2] Here the imagery is of ascent to a place, not a person. The tabernacle not made with hands is not, however, an earthly, material building. In the Platonic tradition it represents the *kosmos noētos*—the realm of Ideas. The heavenly ascent texts present a paradoxical place in which ice and fire coexist, larger rooms can fit inside smaller ones, or the temple is a living angelic structure. Gregory describes a multifaceted experience: Moses sees a vision, in which each element has a symbolic meaning; but it is also a theophany, and reveals a new name for Christ.[3]

---

[1] *Vit. Moys.* 2.180.
[2] See Martin Laird, *Gregory of Nyssa and the Grasp of Faith: Union, Knowledge, and Divine Presence* (Oxford: Oxford University Press, 2004), 199; Verna E. F. Harrison, *Grace and Human Freedom according to St. Gregory of Nyssa* (Lewiston, NY: Edwin Mellen, 1992), 77.
[3] *Vit. Moys.* 1.56; 2.176.

- Gregory uses the heavenly and earthly tabernacles to lay out his theological 'manifesto', exploring the incomprehensibility of God, the divinity of Christ, the incarnation, the use of divine names, the angelic world, the church community and its worship, and virtuous living. The summit of the ascent is Christian doctrine.

- Gregory is influenced by the interpretations of his Alexandrian predecessors, but has to make major changes in the light of the new orthodoxy. Christ is no longer one element of the tabernacle, but the tabernacle as a whole. And since Christ participates in the infinity of God, he ends up with the paradoxical picture of an infinite tent.

- At the incarnation, the heavenly tabernacle is, as it were, turned inside out: the infinite becomes contained within a finite 'tent'. Douglass call this a '*metadiastemic* intrusion', and argues that in using it as a way of solving the gap between God and creation, Gregory is drawing upon the biblical 'history of impenetrable, circumscribed spaces within which dwelt the inaccessible presence of God'.[4]

- Gregory's tabernacle imagery could not survive the fifth century Christological controversies because it implied too extrinsic a relationship between the divinity and humanity of Christ. It was not, therefore, picked up by later patristic authors.

- Gregory argues that the name 'tabernacle' is appropriate for Christ because the incarnate Christ, like the tabernacle, performed the impossible feat of containing the infinite, *adiastemic* God. It is, however, only one name among many, and does not give access to the essence of God. In sharp distinction from Clement, Gregory plays down the importance of the high priest's *petalon*: no name gives access to the holy of holies.

- Thanks to Colossians 1:16, the heavenly tabernacle can represent both the pre-existent Christ, and the angelic powers created in Christ. Gregory attempts to map these powers onto the furniture of the tabernacle, in a style reminiscent of Philo's cosmological interpretation. But, in accommodating biblical verses such as Isaiah 11:1–3 and Romans 3:25, his interpretation loses consistency, and blurs the boundary between the angelic and the divine.

- By his use of the earthly tabernacle, Gregory subverts the framework of heavenly ascent. In 2.160 he makes it clear that not all are to aspire to follow Moses up the mountain. Heavenly ascent is not, for him, a 'democratic' ideal. It is reserved for the superheroes of the faith—Moses, David, Paul, and John. Others should aspire to becoming a pillar or light in the

---

[4] Scot Douglass, *Theology of the Gap: Cappadocian Language Theory and the Trinitarian Controversy* (New York: Peter Lang, 2005), 133.

earthly tabernacle. The message of the treatise is not about aspiring to a vision of heavenly mysteries, but belonging to the worshipping community on earth.

- The holy of holies of the earthly tabernacle represents the same mystery as climbing Mount Sinai to see the heavenly tabernacle. It symbolizes the incomprehensibility and inaccessibility of God. Gregory uses it to issue a warning that the hoi polloi should refrain from theological discussion. Holiness has social consequences, and the aristocratic bishop wishes to keep that which is most sacred away from the common people.

- The heavenly and earthly tabernacles symbolize two communities: angelic and human, which will remain separate until the eschaton. Only then will the *unio liturgica* occur. Meanwhile, however, the worship of the earthly community is a reflection of angelic activity.

- Gregory interprets the priestly garments in terms of virtue. He is particularly anxious to stress the twofold nature of virtue: 'faith as regards the divine, and conscience as regards life'.[5]

- He describes the priestly robe as a light and airy garment, which contrasts with the thick and fleshy clothing of ordinary living. He is drawing on traditions of angelic priestly robes. He agrees with the heavenly ascent texts that the ultimate goal is to become like an angel, with the angelic state symbolized by a garment; but, in his 'transformational mysticism', the transformation involved is an ethical one.

- Neither the darkness nor the vision of the tabernacle are the end of Moses' journey. He comes down the mountain to face the incident of the golden calf. Heavenly ascent is a preparation for pastoral responsibilities.

C.2 MYSTICISM, THEOLOGY, AND POLITICS

Scholars tend to favour one way of viewing Gregory's works over others. According to Daniélou, *Life of Moses* 'retrace les étapes de la vie spirituelle depuis ses origines jusqu'à la vie mystique'.[6] He ties this understanding of the text to Gregory's personal experience:

> Once freed from administrative burdens and the heat of theological controversy, Gregory now turned himself wholly towards the life of the spirit. It was a change

---

[5] *Vit. Moys.* 2.192.
[6] 'retraces the steps of the spiritual life from its beginnings to the mystical life'. Jean Daniélou, *Platonisme et théologie mystique: Doctrine spirituelle de Saint Grégoire de Nysse*, 2nd edn (Paris: Aubier, 1954), 10.

which reflected the interior evolution which he had been undergoing. The writings that come from this period reveal an extraordinary originality and mastery of his subject.⁷

Similarly, Silvas concludes that, in his later writings, 'Gregory himself has moved to another spiritual echelon. His words are lit up from within by a profound spiritual élan. He is deeply, personally engaged in the ultimate truths and beauties of which he speaks so eloquently.'⁸ As noted in 2.2, not everyone agrees. Heine, for example, argues that *Life of Moses* reflects Gregory's polemical debates with Origenism and Eunomianism. He objects to a mystical interpretation of the treatise, both because *Life of Moses* does not set out clear-cut stages for the ascent of the soul, following rather the biblical chronology of Moses' life, and because it 'lacks any clear indication of the concept of attaining "union" with God.'⁹ Lim, meanwhile, as explored in 13.3, points out the social and political factors behind Cappadocian apophaticism. Belief in a transcendent God shrouded in mystery

> helped to preserve social solidarity and order by undermining the legitimacy of any differential claim to precise knowledge about the divine essence... Henceforth, claims to virtue and consideration within Christian communities were to be based on the hierarchical factors of birth and ecclesiastical rank.¹⁰

Are these interpretations mutually exclusive? Or is it possible to develop a more rounded, nuanced perspective on the treatise, which integrates 'mysticism', 'theology', and 'politics'?

The heavenly ascent texts used in this study combine psychology, theology, science, and politics. In *1 Enoch*, Enoch dreams—a psychological state—of ascending to heaven, where he learns both about God—theology—and about rivers, mountains, rocks, winds, and stars—cosmology. Embedded in the text is a polemic against the priests of the Jerusalem temple—politics. There has been much debate over the rival claims of 'exegesis' and 'experience'. Are heavenly ascent texts literary, reflective creations taking the biblical text as their starting point, or are they descriptions of personal experience? Himmelfarb argues that the ascent apocalypses 'are literary documents in which the depiction of the hero's experience needs to be understood as an act of imagination, with its specifics determined by the author's manipulation of conventions'.¹¹

---

⁷ Jean Daniélou, 'Introduction', in Herbert Musurillo, *From Glory to Glory: Texts from Gregory of Nyssa's Mystical Writings* (New York: Scribner, 1961; repr., Crestwood, NY: St Vladimir's Seminary Press, 2001), 9–10.

⁸ Anna M. Silvas, *Gregory of Nyssa: The Letters: Introduction, Translation and Commentary* (Leiden: Brill, 2007), 56.

⁹ Ronald E. Heine, *Perfection in the Virtuous Life: A Study in the Relationship Between Edification and Polemical Theology in Gregory of Nyssa's De Vita Moysis* (Cambridge, Mass.: Philadelphia Patristic Foundation, 1975), 109.

¹⁰ Richard Lim, *Public Disputation, Power, and Social Order in Late Antiquity* (Berkeley: University of California Press, 1995), 179.

¹¹ Martha Himmelfarb, *Ascent to Heaven in Jewish and Christian Apocalypses* (Oxford: Oxford University Press, 1993), 98.

Stone objects: 'Religious experience always stood in the background, whether at first, second, or third remove.'[12] He admits, however, that recognizing the influence of experience only produces the challenge of 'how to assess it and how to integrate it into our understanding of ancient literature'.[13] No text is a clear window onto the experience of its author. Rowland has pointed out that 'early Christianity emerged in a world where contact with the divine by dreams, visions, divination and other related forms of extraordinary insight was common'.[14] He sees dreams—'that tantalizing and inventive part of the human intellect'—as the nearest we can get to the visionary state, 'in which the conscious experience merges in the unconscious in forms which are unpredictable and often highly charged'.[15] Some texts talk explicitly in terms of dreams: in the Book of the Watchers, Enoch reports, 'I saw in my dream what I now speak with a human tongue'.[16] Other texts indicate some form of ecstatic experience: in Revelation, John declares that he 'was in the spirit'.[17] Davila sees the 'descender to the chariot' in the Hekhalot texts 'as a magico-religious practitioner with striking similarities to the cross-cultural practitioner known as the "shaman/healer"'.[18] Experience, however, does not have to be dramatic. It can simply be a case of the heart being strangely warmed. Writers in the Alexandrian tradition seem to use heavenly ascent language of a noetic, rather than an emotional, experience. For Clement, becoming high priest involves 'distinguishing the objects of the intellect from the things of sense'.[19] For Origen, ascent to God is achieved through biblical interpretation: to 'seek the spiritual meaning of the word of God' is to 'ride through the most spacious places of the mystical and spiritual understanding'.[20] This has not been a study of the phenomenology of mysticism; there has been no attempt to define the experiences lying behind either *Life of Moses* or any of the heavenly ascent texts. There is no doubt, however, that authors of heavenly ascent texts claim a religious experience, either for themselves, or, more often, for their pseudepigraphic heroes. But this is not seen as simply a private, subjective experience. The throne of God is the epicentre of holiness and power. To claim knowledge of an ascent to that throne is to claim authority. As Rowland says of the apocalypses,

---

[12] Michael E. Stone, 'A Reconsideration of Apocalyptic Visions', *Harvard Theological Review*, 96: 2 (2003), 180.

[13] Stone, 'A Reconsideration of Apocalyptic Visions', 180.

[14] Christopher Rowland and Christopher R. A. Morray-Jones, *The Mystery of God: Early Jewish Mysticism and the New Testament* (Leiden: Brill, 2009), 213.

[15] Rowland and Morray-Jones, *The Mystery of God*, 209.

[16] *1 En.* 14:2; trans. Nickelsburg and VanderKam, 33.   [17] Rev. 1:10.

[18] James R. Davila, 'The Ancient Jewish Apocalypses and the *Hekhalot* Literature', in April D. DeConick (ed.), *Paradise Now: Essays on Early Jewish and Christian Mysticism* (Atlanta: Society of Biblical Literature, 2006), 106.

[19] *Strom.* 5.39.4; trans. Annewies van den Hoek, *Clement of Alexandria and His Use of Philo in the Stromateis: An Early Christian Reshaping of a Jewish Model* (Leiden: Brill, 1988), 141.

[20] *Comm. Rom.* 7.11.3; trans. Scheck, 97.

Unless we grasp the high view of authority inherent in these texts, we shall not fully appreciate the potentially exclusive view of the value and content of the revelations. After all, what the apocalypses purport to offer is not the mere opinion of the expositor but a divine revelation emanating either from the throne of God or from an angelic intermediary commissioned by God for that purpose.[21]

The authors of heavenly ascent texts were involved in the power politics of their day, and a vision of heaven was seen as a trump card, used both by disaffected minorities and by religious authorities trying to curb unruly enthusiasm: 'The claim to direct revelation is used just as much by those who control the levers of religious power as those who do not.'[22] The Qumran community, estranged from the Jerusalem temple, maintained its identity and self-belief by turning instead to the heavenly temple: 'The community... functioned analogically to a community of priestly angels, officiating in the innermost sanctuary of the heavenly temple.'[23] This was a temporary measure:

> The sectarians expected that at some point in the future they would come to control the Jerusalem Temple and to be able to operate it according to their legal rulings and sacrificial procedures.[24]

But claims of heavenly ascent were not only produced and treasured within rebellious prophetic movements. The rabbis appropriated *ma'aseh merkavah*, issuing warnings of dire consequences to keep everyone else away. Heavenly ascent texts are not disinterested descriptions of personal experiences, they are bids for religious power, attempts to give divine authority to the knowledge they present. But that is not to negate their spiritual dimension. Lesses criticizes Halperin for 'reducing the religious goal of the Hekhalot texts to nothing more than a search for power and [refusing] to acknowledge that the framers of these texts sought in some of their rituals to attain a vision of the transcendent God'.[25] Personal spiritual experience, scientific curiosity, and political agenda were all motors of heavenly ascent texts.

---

[21] Christopher Rowland, 'Apocalyptic Literature', in D. A. Carson and H. G. M. Williamson (eds), *It Is Written: Scripture Citing Scripture: Essays in Honour of Barnabas Lindars* (Cambridge: Cambridge University Press, 1988), 181.
[22] Rowland, 'Apocalyptic Literature', 184.
[23] Devorah Dimant, 'Men as Angels: The Self-Image of the Qumran Community', in Adele Berlin (ed.), *Religion and Politics in the Ancient Near East* (Bethesda, MD: University Press of Maryland, 1996), 98.
[24] Lawrence H. Schiffman, 'Community without Temple: The Qumran Community's Withdrawal from the Jerusalem Temple', in Beate Ego, Armin Lange, and Peter Pilhofer (eds), *Gemeinde ohne Tempel, Community without Temple: Zur Substituierung und Transformation des Jerusalemer Tempels und seines Kults im Alten Testament, antiken Judentum und frühen Christentum* (Tübingen: Mohr Siebeck, 1999), 276.
[25] Rebecca Macy Lesses, *Ritual Practices to Gain Power: Angels, Incantations, and Revelation in Early Jewish Mysticism* (Harrisburg, Penn.: Trinity Press International, 1998), 32.

Can this multifaceted understanding of heavenly ascent texts help to shape a rounded view of Gregory's tabernacle imagery? The first point to stress is that *Life of Moses* is a work of exegesis. Heine is right that 'the stages Gregory sets forth are based on the chronology of Moses' life, and what he discusses in each stage is controlled by what the imagery of the Biblical text suggests'.[26] As pointed out by Laird, the ascent of Moses 'is described as a movement from light to dark, a description rife with apophatic terminology and motifs, because the vocabulary and imagery of the scriptural text lends itself to this'.[27] Exegesis, however, can still engage the imagination, and there are many choices to be made. McGinn, who sees mysticism 'as the ongoing search for a heightened consciousness, or awareness, of the presence of the living God', argues that for both Jews and Christians this search 'is inherently biblical'. The mystical use of the Bible attempts 'to find in the depths of the text a direct encounter with the divine presence'.[28] As Steven Katz points out, 'mystics across traditions and cultures have always assumed that the sacred texts of their traditions are authentic centers of divine, transcendental, ultimate truth'.[29] To what extent, in Gregory's case, his exegetical choices were guided by personal religious experience is impossible to ascertain. But it is possible to examine his elaborations of the biblical imagery, and discuss the extent to which they have been informed by mysticism, theology, or politics.

This has not been a study of Gregory's mysticism in general, but of his tabernacle imagery. Whereas Daniélou brings together imagery from *Life of Moses* and *On Song of Songs* to develop a unified understanding of Gregory's mysticism, here the focus has been solely on *Life of Moses* 2.160–201. It has, therefore, been possible to use 'heavenly ascent' as a heuristic category, rather than 'mysticism', thus sidestepping the need for a precise definition of 'mysticism'. Certainly, in regard to this second theophany in *Life of Moses*, Heine is right that there is no imagery of union with God. Schäfer cautions that 'we should take seriously the possibility that the history of research on mysticism—Jewish and non-Jewish alike—is deeply imbued with Christian theological assumptions and biases'.[30] One of those biases is a tendency to define mysticism in terms of *unio mystica*. Scholars of Jewish mysticism have developed alternative categories to *unio mystica*, such as *unio liturgica* or angelification. *Life of Moses*, paradoxically, is a Christian text which is closer to these 'Jewish' paradigms

---

[26] Heine, *Perfection in the Virtuous Life*, 107.
[27] Laird, *Gregory of Nyssa and the Grasp of Faith*, 200.
[28] Bernard McGinn, 'Selective Affinities: Reflections on Jewish and Christian Mystical Exegesis', in Rachel Elior and Peter Schäfer (eds), *Creation and Re-Creation in Jewish Thought: Festschrift in Honor of Joseph Dan on the Occasion of his Seventieth Birthday* (Tübingen: Mohr Siebeck, 2005), 86.
[29] Steven T. Katz, 'Mysticism and the Interpretation of Sacred Scripture', in Steven T. Katz (ed.), *Mysticism and Sacred Scripture* (Oxford: Oxford University Press, 2000), 14.
[30] Schäfer, *The Origins of Jewish Mysticism*, 355.

than to notions of union with God. Gregory describes Moses being initiated into the divine mysteries by ascending to the tabernacle not made with hands—the heavenly sanctuary, laid out along the same lines as the earthly tabernacle/temple. This vision, with its paradoxes and logical inconsistencies, has the dream-like quality written of by Rowland. A vision of a tabernacle—pillars, curtains, lampstand, altars...—is somehow also a vision of the pre-existent Christ, and is equated with a name. The vision of Christ then morphs into a vision of the heavenly powers, with the ultimate mystery hidden by cherubim and seraphim. Moses is observing this, rather than becoming involved. There is no comment on his emotional reaction—emotions were left behind once he detached himself from the people.[31] Gregory is drawing on ancient imagery, the same imagery that fed Jewish mysticism. He manipulates it, however, to fit new theological norms. In the background of his interpretation are also theological debates spiralling out of control, the growth of elaborate liturgies, and the need to contain ascetic movements within the church. He briefly refers to the colours of the veil representing the four elements, and to Philo's interpretation of the blue robe as signifying the air, but he is not interested here in the science of cosmology.[32] He makes the vision explicitly Christian, and does so differently to predecessors such as Clement and Origen, because he believes that Christ is fully God. Tabernacle imagery serves him particularly well because of its previous uses by Paul (Col. 1:15–20, 2:9) and John (1:14) to convey the paradoxes of the incarnation. Just as the transcendent God was somehow to be found in the holy of holies of the tabernacle/temple, so the infinite God is fully present in both the earthly and heavenly Christ. It is when Gregory moves on to the earthly tabernacle and the priestly vestments that his political agenda becomes apparent. He has used the imagery of heavenly ascent only to undercut it. In *To Theophilus, Against the Apollinarians* he argues that had we all had a similar experience to Moses, Paul, Elijah, Ezekiel, or Isaiah there would be no need for the incarnation.[33] Here the logic is reversed: given the incarnation, there is no need to ascend to heaven. Heavenly ascent is reserved for the superheroes of the faith, and Gregory never explicitly spells out who, if anyone, in the contemporary church is entitled to follow them. Moses, however, is a figure who does not rest in contemplation, but rather descends Mount Sinai to take responsibility for a people 'carried along into disorderliness by uncontrolled impulses'.[34] The common people—*hoi polloi*—are to become part of the body of Christ by participating in the earthly tabernacle. In his commentary

---

[31] *Vit. Moys.* 1.45–46.

[32] Schäfer shows that the Babylonian Talmud too, in its commentary on the 'work of creation', leaves behind the 'almost scientific curiosity' of the ascent apocalypses, because it 'is not really interested in the cosmological makeup of the world'. Peter Schäfer, 'From Cosmology to Theology: The Rabbinic Appropriation of Apocalyptic Cosmology', in Elior and Schäfer (eds), *Creation and Re-Creation in Jewish Thought*, 39, 42.

[33] See 10.1.   [34] *Vit Moys.* 1.58; trans. Malherbe and Ferguson, 46.

on the priestly vestments Gregory once again draws on a theme which occurs in Jewish mysticism, that of angelification. By putting on the light and airy priestly robe, believers aspire to become like the angels. He ties this angelification, however, to virtue. Participation in the divine is participation in what God does.

More work would need to be done in order to integrate this study of *Life of Moses* 2.160–201 into a more general picture of Gregory's mysticism. However, as regards his tabernacle exegesis, he holds together mysticism, theology, and politics. Under 'mysticism' might be included Moses' ascent to a tabernacle made of spirits which is the radiating centre of holiness and which protects the incomprehensible essence of God; under 'theology' Gregory's exploration of the application of the name 'tabernacle' to both pre-incarnate and incarnate Christ; under 'politics' the heavenly tabernacle as the source of authority to which only the priviledged few have access. This holding together of what might be classed as different categories is typical of heavenly ascent texts. They all combine descriptions of religious experience with claims to authoritative knowledge. For Gregory, the high point of Moses' ascent into the darkness of Mount Sinai is the mystery of Christian doctrine. The heavenly tabernacle is a type of the heavenly Christ. This mystery is beyond intellectual comprehension, it can only be grasped by faith; and only the select few, destined for positions of responsibility, should even attempt to do so. But its benefits are available to all through the community's worship in the earthly tabernacle. Anyone can aspire to wear an airy, angelic robe by living a life of virtue, in which faith and practice go hand in hand.

APPENDIX

Translation of *Life of Moses* 1.46–56, 61; 2.162–201

This is a new translation of the main passages in *Life of Moses* dealing with the darkness on Mount Sinai and the tabernacle not made with hands. There already exists an excellent translation of *Life of Moses* by Abraham Malherbe and Everett Ferguson, published as part of 'The Classics of Western Spirituality' series, which has been used for citations from the rest of Gregory's treatise. This translation too aims 'to stay as close to the Greek text as English style permits'.[1] However, for the purposes of studying Gregory's tabernacle imagery, two specific improvements have been made. Firstly, Gregory's terminology for the constituent parts of the tabernacle and for the priestly vestments has been translated as accurately and consistently as possible. So καταπέτασμα is always rendered 'veil', παραπέτασμα 'hanging', and αὐλαία 'curtain'. Or, to take another example, ποδήρης is translated 'full-length robe', χιτών 'tunic', and ὑποδύτης 'undergarment'. This will then enable a comparison with LXX terminology, which Gregory sometimes follows and from which he sometimes deviates. Secondly, Gregory's biblical quotations are translated as given. Malherbe and Ferguson usually give his scriptural citations according to the Jerusalem Bible, which leads to potential misunderstandings. For the key verse of Exodus 20:21 in 2.164, they have 'Moses approached the dark cloud where God was'. 'Dark cloud' is a translation of the Hebrew ערפל; the LXX and Gregory simply have γνόφος 'darkness'. More confusingly, in 2.191, where Gregory quotes LXX Psalm 38:12, which refers to a spider, despite amending the Jerusalem Bible translation of Psalm 39:11, Malherbe and Ferguson leave its reference to a moth (a translation of the Hebrew עש). Since Gregory is talking about respinning one's bodily nature to make it as light as the thread of a spider's web, a proof text referring to a moth makes little sense. Other than in the case of these two specific strategies, the variations between this translation and Malherbe and Ferguson's simply reflect the range of possibilities open to the translator. There are a number of places where Gregory's syntax is highly complex, not to say obscure, and a measure of conjecture is needed. Daniélou's translation into French has also been consulted, although, as Malherbe and Ferguson remark, it 'is often loose in relation to the Greek text'.[2]

There are two editions of Gregory's Greek text: Jean's Daniélou's in Sources Chrétiennes 1bis, and Herbert Musurillo's in GNO 7,1. This translation is divided up according to Daniélou's paragraph numbers, with the page numbers from Musurillo added in square brackets. Where the editions diverge, Musurillo's text has been followed.

I am extremely grateful to Stuart Hall, experienced translator of Gregory of Nyssa, who went over my draft with a fine toothcomb. He made several corrections, and suggested many improvements. The quality of the translation has been greatly enhanced by his work. Gillian Clark helped me untangle a knotty puzzle about the hem of the

---

[1] Abraham J. Malherbe and Everett Ferguson, *Gregory of Nyssa: The Life of Moses* (New York: Paulist Press, 1978), 23.
[2] Malherbe and Ferguson, *The Life of Moses*, 22.

high priest's robe. Needless to say, I take full responsibility for the errors and infelicities which remain.

Life of Moses 1.46–56, 61

46. [22] Therefore once he was alone, having been stripped of the people's dread as of a burden, [Moses] then boldly approached the darkness itself and found himself inside the invisible realities, where he was no longer discernible to those watching. Stealing into the secret place of the divine mystical initiation, there, unseen, he was with the invisible. He teaches, I think, by the things he did, that whoever intends to be with God must go beyond all appearances and, lifting up his mind to the invisible and incomprehensible as to a mountain peak, must believe that the divine is there where the understanding cannot reach.

47. Once there he receives divine commandments. These were a lesson in virtue, of which the paramount principle therefore was true religion, and to have fitting notions about the divine nature, given that it transcends all knowable concepts and models, and cannot be likened to any known thing. And he was ordered neither to look for the comprehensible when it comes to notions about the divine, nor to liken the nature transcending everything to what can be known by understanding; but rather, while believing that it exists, to leave unexamined questions of kind, quantity, origin, and mode of being, as beyond reach.

48. The Word also adds what are [23] correct ways of behaving, giving the instruction with both general and specific laws. For the law which destroys all injustice is general, namely that one must behave lovingly towards one's compatriot. When this is carried out, it will certainly follow in consequence that no evil will be done by anyone against their neighbour. Among the particular laws, the honour due to parents was stated explicitly, and a list of forbidden transgressions was enumerated.

49. Having been first purified in mind by these laws, as it were, he was led to the more perfect mystical initiation, suddenly being shown a certain tabernacle by divine power. The tabernacle was a shrine, possessing beauty in indescribable variety: entrances, pillars, and hangings; a table, lamps,[3] and an incense altar; an altar and a mercy seat; and the secret and inaccessible core of the holy spaces. So that the wonder might not escape the memory, and might be shown to those below, he was counselled to transmit the beauty and arrangement of all these things not merely in writing, but by reproducing that immaterial creation in a material construction, obtaining the brightest and most radiant materials found on earth. Among these the most abundant was gold, overlaid around the pillars. Taken together with the gold was silver, which in itself beautified the capitals and bases of the pillars, so that, it seems to me, by the variation of colour at each end, the gold when looked upon might glitter more brightly. There were also places where [24] bronze was considered useful, forming the head and base for silver columns.

50. The veils and hangings and the covering round the shrine, and the canopy spread to fit over the pillars—all were completed, each out of the right material, thanks to skilful weaving.[4] The dye of these woven textiles was blue and purple and fiery scarlet

---

[3] Musurillo has lamps (λύχνοι), Daniélou lampstand (λυχνία).

[4] Gregory's terminology does not conform to the LXX, but it seems likely that by 'veils' (καταπετάσματα) he is referring to the material dividing off the holy of holies, talked of in the singular in the LXX (Exod. 26:31); by 'hangings' (παραπετάσματα) he is referring to the fabric at

red,⁵ alongside the brightness of flax, with its natural and unrefined look. For some linen was obtained, and for others hair, according to the function of the textiles. There were also places where the redness of skins contributed to the elegance of the structure.

51. After his descent from the mountain Moses, through his assistants, constructed these things according to the pattern of creation shown to him.⁶ But whilst still in that shrine not made with hands, he received rules on how the priest should be made resplendent by his apparel when setting foot in the secret spaces, the Word having decreed every detail of both inner and visible garments.

52. The pre-eminent garment of the attire was not the hidden but the visible: shoulder pieces woven of various colours,⁷ the same as used in the veil's manufacture, with the addition of gold thread. There were clasps on either side to secure the shoulder pieces, tightly encircling emeralds with gold. The decorative quality of these stones was due to their natural radiance—a certain green glow emanated from them—but the wonder of the engravings was due to art. This was not [25] the art of carving out engravings which represent idols, instead the beauty came from the names of the patriarchs inscribed on the stones, six on each.

53. There were little shields hanging down on the front side of these shoulder pieces; and plaited cords, which were interlaced through each other crosswise in a net-like pattern, suspended on each side from the clasp above the shields, in order, it seems to me, that the elegance of the plaiting might be more conspicuous, set off by the background.

54. There was that ornament wrought of gold positioned in front of the chest, in which were fastened stones of various kinds equal in number to the patriarchs.⁸ They were arranged in four rows, three stones on each, and they exhibited the names of the tribes which were written on them. Beneath the shoulder pieces was the undergarment, stretching from neck to toes, which was suitably embellished with ornamental tassels. The bottom hem was made beautiful not only by variegated woven fabric, but also by gold ornaments.⁹ These were golden bells and small pomegranates, distributed alternately along the hem.

---

the entrance to the tent, which the LXX refers to both as ἐπίσπαστρον and καταπέτασμα (Exod. 26:36–37); by 'covering' (περίβολος) he means the ten coloured inner curtains surrounding the tabernacle (Exod. 26:1–6, cf. *Mos.* 2.84); and by 'canopy' (ὄροφος) he is referring to the skins covering the inner curtains (Exod. 26:7–14).

⁵ Gregory's construction (τὸ πυραυγὲς τοῦ κοκκοβαφοῦς ἐρυθήματος) reflects the 'double scarlet' (κόκκινον διπλοῦν) of LXX Exod. 25:4, itself a misunderstanding of the Hebrew תולעת שני.

⁶ τὸ ... τῆς δημιουργίας ὑπόδειγμα could simply mean 'the design for manufacture'; but it seems likely that Gregory is playing on words, and making reference to the cosmological symbolism of the tabernacle.

⁷ The MT (Exod. 28:6–7) talks of an ephod (אפוד) and two shoulder pieces (כתפת). The LXX translates the first as shoulder piece (ἐπωμίς) in the singular, and the second by the same word in the plural (ἐπωμίδες). Gregory conflates the two, and only refers to the plural 'shoulder pieces'. From *Life of Moses* 2.195 it is clear that he thought of the ephod as being made of two pieces of cloth (δύο πέπλοι). To add to the confusion, however, in 2.189 he refers both to the overgarment (ἐπενδύτης), presumably the ephod, and to the shoulder pieces.

⁸ Gregory is referring to the breastpiece (חשן; περιστήθιον Exod. 28:4, λόγιον / λογεῖον 28:15).

⁹ Gregory seems to be conflating two different undergarments: the tunic, which the MT describes as 'chequered' (כתנת תשבץ) and the LXX as 'tasselled' (χιτὼν κοσυμβωτόν), and the robe (מעיל), which the LXX specifies reaches to the feet (ποδήρης 28:4, ὑποδύτης ποδήρης 28:27). In the MT (Exod. 28:33–34) there are two kinds of ornament on the bottom of the robe: pomegranates made of blue, purple, and scarlet, and golden bells. The LXX (Exod. 28:29–30) has three kinds of ornament: golden pomegranates, bells, and pomegranates made of blue, purple, scarlet,

55. The headband, moreover, was all blue, and over the forehead was a thin plate made of pure gold inscribed with unutterable letters. There was a girdle gathering up the loose folds of the garment, and something decorous for the hidden parts, and everything that educates symbolically, under the guise of clothing, about priestly virtue.

56. Once he had been educated in these and other such things by the ineffable teaching of God, all the while enclosed by that impenetrable darkness, and [26] having become greater than himself with the help of mystical knowledge, he emerged again from the darkness and descended to his people in order to share with them the wonders shown to him in the theophany, to hand over the laws, and to establish for the people the temple and the priesthood according to the pattern shown to him on the mountain.

61. [27] Thus he pitched the tabernacle for them and delivered the laws, establishing the priesthood according to the teaching which came to him from God. And after he had furnished all these things in a material creation, according to the divine guidance—the tabernacle, the entrances, the whole interior, the incense altar, the altar, the lampstand, the hangings, the veils, the mercy seat inside the secret spaces, the attire of the priesthood, the sweet oil, the various sacrificial rites, the purifications, the thank-offerings, rites to avert evil, the propitiations for offences—having arranged everything therein in the right way, he aroused against himself envy, that congenital sickness in human nature, among those close to him.

Life of Moses 2.162–201

162. [86] What does it mean that Moses found himself inside the darkness and thus saw God in it? For what is now recorded seems somehow contrary to the first theophany; for the divine is then perceived in light, but now in darkness. Let us not consider this out of tune with the ascending series of thoughts we have been contemplating. For the Word teaches us by this that religious knowledge at first appears as light to those in whom it springs up. Therefore the opposite of piety is thought to be obscurity; and the escape from obscurity comes with participation in the light. But as the mind advances, and through an ever greater and more perfect attentiveness comes to envisage an understanding of all existence, the nearer it draws to contemplation, the [87] more it sees that the divine nature is not to be contemplated.

163. For leaving behind everything visible, not only what the senses grasp but also what the mind seems to see, he yearns to go ever further in, until, thanks to the mind's curiosity, he slips into the unseen and incomprehensible, and there sees God. For in this is the true knowledge of what is sought, and in this is the seeing which consists in not seeing, that what is sought transcends all knowledge, cut off on all sides by incomprehensibility, as by a kind of darkness. That is why the sublime John, who has been in this radiant darkness, says, 'No one has ever seen God,'[10] affirming by this negation that the knowledge of the divine essence is unattainable not only to human beings but also to any intelligent nature.

---

and linen. These fabric pomegranates are also referred to as 'flower-work' (ἄνθινον), translated 'blossom' by NETS. Since Gregory conflates the two garments, he equates the tassels (κόσυμβοι) of the tunic with the variegated fabric pomegranates of the robe.

[10] John 1:18.

164. When, therefore, Moses grew in knowledge, he declared that he had seen God in darkness, that is, that he had come to know that the divine, by nature, is that which is beyond all knowledge and apprehension. For it says, 'Moses entered into the darkness where God was'.[11] What God? He who 'made obscurity his hideaway',[12] as David says, who was initiated into ineffable mysteries in the same secret place.

165. Once there, he was taught again by the Word what previously the darkness had instilled, in order, I think, that the doctrine on this matter might be made firmer for us through the testimony of the divine voice. The divine [88] word first forbids that human beings liken the divine to anything known, since every concept which derives from a recognizable image by whatever thought process, and by speculation on the divine nature, fashions an idol of God, and does not proclaim God.

166. Religious virtue is divided into two: into the divine and the correct ordering of behaviour—for purity of life is also a part of piety. Having first learnt what it is necessary to know about God—to know that nothing about him can be realized from things known by human apprehension—he was then taught the other kind of virtue, learning the pursuits by which the virtuous life is accomplished.

167. After this he finds himself in the tabernacle not made with hands. Who will follow one who travels through such places, and elevates his mind so high, who as he goes on from peak to peak becomes, through the ascent of the heights, ever higher than before? First he leaves behind the foot of the mountain, separated out from all those unsuited for the ascent. Then as he rises to the summit of the ascent he hears the sounds of the trumpets. At these he steals into the invisible secret place of divine knowledge. And he does not stay there, but carries on to the tabernacle not made with hands. For there the one who is elevated through such ascents truly arrives at the limit.

168. The heavenly trumpet seems to me to become in another sense a teacher for the one who listens, of the access to that which is not made with hands. For the [89] wondrous design of the heavens proclaims the wisdom revealed in all that exists, along with the great glory of God made manifest through visible phenomena, as it is said, 'the heavens proclaim the glory of God'.[13] This [design] by the clarity and sonority of its teaching becomes a loud trumpet, as one of the prophets says, 'the heavens trumpeted from above'.[14]

169. The purified person, whose heart's hearing is keen, welcomes this sound—I am speaking of the growth into knowledge of divine power which comes from the contemplation of all existing things—and, led by it, slips mentally into the place where God is. This is called 'darkness' by Scripture, which means, as already said, the unknown and unseen. Once there, he sees that tabernacle not made with hands, which he shows to those below using a material reproduction.

170. What then is that tabernacle not made with hands, which was shown to Moses on the mountain, and which he was commanded to look upon as an archetype, so that he might present the wonder not made with hands by means of a handmade structure? For it says, 'See, you shall make everything according to the type shown to you on the mountain.'[15] There were golden pillars fixed into silver bases and adorned with similar silver heads; yet other pillars with heads and bases made of bronze, but with silver between the extremities; and the interior of all these was wood not prone to rot, while visibly [90] the radiance of such materials shone out all around.

---

[11] Exod. 20:21.   [12] LXX Ps. 17:12.   [13] LXX Ps. 18:2.
[14] This is not an accurate quotation from a biblical prophet.   [15] Exod. 25:40.

171. Likewise, there was an ark gleaming with pure gold, and the gold layer was again underpinned by wood not prone to decay. In addition there was a lampstand with a single base stem which divided into seven branches at the top, holding up an equal number of lights on the branches. The lampstand was made of gold, neither of hollow construction nor underpinned by wood. In addition to these were an altar and a mercy seat and the beings called cherubim, by whose wings the ark was overshadowed. All these were gold: not just presenting a superficially shiny appearance, but the same all the way through, with the material reaching into the depths.

172. Near these were variegated veils, lovingly crafted of woven fabric, the different colours intertwined with each other to produce the elegance of the weave. By these were separated that part of the tabernacle which was visible and accessible to some of those conducting ceremonies from that which was secret and inaccessible. The name of the front space was 'holy' and the space kept hidden 'holy of holies'. In addition there were washbasins and braziers; the outer covering of curtains, hairy hides, and skins coloured red; and much else that is set out in the Word. Yet what word could apprehend the precise details?

173. Of what things not made with hands are these imitations? And what [91] benefit does the material reproduction of the things seen there by Moses bring to those viewing it? It seems good to me to leave the precise word on these things to those who through the Spirit have the power to search the depths of God,[16] if indeed there be anyone able to speak 'mysteries in the Spirit',[17] as the apostle says. Our speculative suggestions on the matter set before us we refer to the readers' judgement, to be deemed worthless or acceptable, as the mind of the competent judge shall determine.

174. Paul partially disclosed the secret meaning of these things, and therefore, taking a little clue from his words, we say that Moses was educated beforehand by a type in the mystery of the tabernacle which encloses everything. This would be Christ, 'the power of God and the wisdom of God',[18] which in its own nature is not made by hands, yet allows itself to be physically fashioned when this tabernacle needs to be pitched among us, so that, in a certain way, the same is both unfashioned and fashioned: uncreated in pre-existence, but becoming created in accordance with this material composition.

175. Perhaps these words will not seem obscure to those who have received the mystery of our faith accurately. For there is one out of us all who both existed before the ages and came into being at the end of the ages, who did not need a temporal becoming—for how could that which was before all times and ages need a temporal [92] beginning?—yet who, for our sakes, because we had been led astray from true existence by evil counsel, undertook to become like us, in order to draw back into being once again that which had become outside being. This is the Only-begotten God, who encloses everything within himself, yet pitched his own tabernacle among us.

176. If so great a good is named 'tabernacle', let the lover of Christ not be dismayed, as if the expression's literal sense could diminish the splendour of the nature of God. For neither is any other name worthy of the nature of the one designated, but all alike have fallen short of accurate designation, both those considered trivial and those in which it is assumed that lofty concepts are to be seen.

177. But just as all the other names, in keeping with what is being designated, are spoken reverently as an indication of divine power—such as physician, shepherd,

---

[16] Cf. 1 Cor. 2:10.   [17] 1 Cor. 14:2.   [18] 1 Cor. 1:24.

protector, bread, vine, way, door, abode, water, rock, spring, and whatever others are stated of him—so, using a designation fitting to God, he is called by the term 'tabernacle'. For the power which encloses all existence, in whom 'dwells the whole fullness of divinity',[19] the common shelter of all, enclosing everything within himself, is rightly called 'tabernacle'.

178. The vision must have conformed to the name, with each perceived element leading to the contemplation of a concept fitting to God. Since, therefore, the great apostle says that the veil of the lower tabernacle is the flesh [of Christ],[20] because, I suppose, it consists of a blend of colours, that is, of the four elements—he himself probably experienced a vision of [93] this tabernacle in the supercelestial secret places, he to whom through the Spirit the mysteries of paradise were revealed[21]—it would be good, by paying attention to the partial interpretation, to harmonize the whole understanding of the tabernacle with this part.

179. The elucidation of the tabernacle's symbolism may come to us through the very words of the apostle. For he says somewhere about the Only-begotten, who, we have perceived, corresponds to the tabernacle, that 'in him all things were created, visible and invisible, whether thrones or authorities or principalities or dominions' or powers.[22] Surely then the pillars bright with silver and plated with gold, the carrying-poles and rings, and those cherubim, covering the ark with their wings, and all the other elements which the description of the tabernacle's construction contains, if one examines them by looking to things above, are the supercosmic powers, which are contemplated in the tabernacle, and which undergird everything in keeping with the divine will.

180. There are found our true carrying-poles, 'sent forth to serve for the sake of those who are to obtain salvation',[23] which are inserted, as though through rings, through the souls of us who are being saved, and thereby carry those lying on the earth up to the height of virtue. In saying that the cherubim cover with their wings the mysteries lying in the ark of the covenant, the Word confirms the interpretation of the tabernacle we have given. For [94] we have learnt that this is the name of the powers envisaged around the divine nature, as Isaiah and Ezekiel observed. That the ark of the covenant is covered by wings should not be a surprise to our ears. For also in Isaiah the same symbolic understanding of the wings is spoken by the prophet. For the same thing is called 'ark of the covenant' in one place, and 'face' in the other; and in the one it is the ark which is covered by wings, and in the other it is the face; as though what is being apprehended in both cases is the one symbolic representation, so it seems to me, of the impossibility of understanding ineffable things.

181. And should you hear about lamps being held up by many branches stemming from one lampstand, so that ample intense light is projected all around, you would not be wrong to interpret them as the varied sparks of the Spirit shining conspicuously in this tabernacle; as Isaiah says, when he divides into seven the lights of the Spirit.[24]

182. The mercy seat, I think, needs no interpretation, since the apostle exposed what is hidden when he said, 'whom God put forward as a mercy seat' for our souls.[25] Hearing 'altar' and 'incense altar', I understand the adoration by heavenly beings, which is continuously performed in this tabernacle. For he says that not only the tongues of those 'on earth' and 'under the earth', but also of 'heavenly beings', offer praise to the

---

[19] Col. 2:9. [20] Heb. 10:20. [21] Cf. 2 Cor. 12:4.
[22] Col. 1:16, with a slight change of order, and the addition of 'powers'.
[23] Heb. 1:14. [24] Cf. LXX Isa. 11:2–3. [25] Rom. 3:25.

Origin of all things.²⁶ This is the sacrifice pleasing to God, the 'fruit of lips',²⁷ as the [95] apostle says, and the fragrance of prayers.

183. If skin dipped in red dye and woven hairs are seen among these, the continuity of interpretation will not thus be prevented. For he who, with prophetic eyes, finds himself to have the vision of divine things, will behold there foreordained the saving passion, which is indicated by both elements mentioned: the redness representing blood, and the hair death. For hair on the body is without sensation, therefore it rightly becomes a symbol of death.

184. Whenever, therefore, the prophet looks to the tabernacle above, he sees these concepts by means of its components. If one should contemplate the tabernacle below, then, seeing that the church is called Christ by Paul in many places,²⁸ it would be good to consider these terms to refer to the servants of the divine mystery, the apostles, teachers, and prophets,²⁹ whom the Word indeed calls 'pillars' of the church.³⁰ For not only Peter and James and John are pillars of the church, nor was John the Baptist the only 'burning lamp',³¹ but all those who themselves support the church and become 'luminaries',³² by their own works are called 'pillars' and 'lamps'. 'You are the light of the world' says the Lord to the apostles.³³ And again, the divine apostle exhorts others to be pillars, saying, 'Be steadfast and immovable'.³⁴ He built Timothy into a good pillar, making him, [96] as he says in his own words, 'a pillar and foundation of the truth'.³⁵

185. In this tabernacle both a 'sacrifice of praise'³⁶ and an incense of prayer are seen being offered continually at daybreak and at nightfall. Great David also allows us to understand these things, directing the incense of prayer as 'a fragrant offering'³⁷ to God and performing the sacrifice by the stretching out of hands.³⁸ Anyone hearing of the washbasins will no doubt understand them as those who wash away the defilement of sins with sacramental water. John was a washbasin, washing in the Jordan with the baptism of repentance; Peter was a washbasin, leading three thousand down into the water at the same time;³⁹ Philip was the washbasin of Candace's man;⁴⁰ as are all those who administer the grace to all partaking of the gift.

186. As to the curtains, which by being joined to one another encircle the tabernacle, someone suggesting that they are the loving and peaceful unity of the believers would not be far from the mark. For such is David's interpretation, when he says, 'he who made your borders peace'.⁴¹

187. The reddened skin and hairy hides, which contribute to the decoration of the tabernacle, may be interpreted respectively as the death of sinful flesh (of which the reddened skin is a symbol) and the severe life of self-control, by which the [97] tabernacle of the church is especially beautified. For skins which in themselves do not naturally have the power of life become flushed by the dipping in red dye, which teaches that the grace which flourishes through the Spirit is only found in people who make themselves dead to sin. Whether chaste modesty is signified by the Word with the dipping in red dye, I leave for whoever wishes to judge. The intertwining of hairs, which produces a rough and rigid fabric, alludes to this severe self-control which reduces

---

²⁶ Phil. 3:10–11.
²⁷ τὸ κάρπωμα τῶν χειλέων, cf. Heb. 13:15 καρπὸν χειλέων.
²⁸ Rom. 12:4–5; 1 Cor. 12:12–13; Eph. 1:22–23.   ²⁹ Cf. 1 Cor. 12:28.
³⁰ Gal. 2:9.   ³¹ John 5:35.   ³² Phil. 2:15.   ³³ Matt. 5:14.
³⁴ 1 Cor. 15:58.   ³⁵ 1 Tim. 3:15.   ³⁶ Heb. 13:15.   ³⁷ Eph. 5:2; Phil. 4:18.
³⁸ Cf. LXX Ps. 140:2.   ³⁹ Acts 2:41.   ⁴⁰ Acts 8:27–39.
⁴¹ LXX Ps. 147:3.

habitual passions. The life of virginity demonstrates all such things in itself, pummelling the flesh of those who live this way.[42]

188. If the interior, which is called the holy of holies, is not accessible to the multitude, let us not consider this out of tune with the sequence of ideas. For the truth of all existence is truly a holy matter, a holy of holies, incomprehensible and unapproachable for the multitude. Since it is set in the secret and ineffable spaces of the tabernacle of mystery, the understanding of realities beyond apprehension must not be meddled with, for we believe that what is sought exists, and yet is not set before the eyes of all, but remains ineffable in the secret spaces of the mind.

189. Having been educated in these and other such things through the vision of the tabernacle, that eye of Moses' soul, purified and elevated by such sights, is led up again to the peak of other thoughts, [98] as he is educated in the apparel of the priesthood. This consists of the undergarment; the overgarment; that breastpiece, sparkling with the varied glints of precious stones; the headband and on it the thin plate; the breeches; the pomegranates; the bells; then over and above all these the 'oracle', the 'disclosure', and, contemplated in both, the 'truth'; the shoulder pieces holding these together on each side, with the names of the patriarchs secured to them.

190. Most people are prevented from correctly understanding these by the very names of the clothing. For what sort of name for bodily attire is 'disclosure' or 'oracle' or 'truth'? These clearly show that it is not this perceptible clothing that is described for us by the history, but a certain adornment of the soul woven by virtuous pursuits.

191. The dye of the full-length robe is blue. Certain of those who have previously examined the Word say that the dye signifies the air. Whether such vivid colour resembles the colour of the air, I cannot affirm exactly. I do not, however, set the Word aside. For the thought tends towards the interpretation related to virtue, in that it requires one who intends to become a priest of God to bring his own body to the sacrifice and become an unslain victim, in a 'living sacrifice' and 'rational service'.[43] He should not damage the soul with the thick and fleshy clothing of ordinary living, but by purity of life should make [99] all his pursuits as delicate as the thread of a spider's web, and come close to that which ascends and is light and airy. He should respin this bodily nature, in order that when we hear the last trumpet, and are found weightless and light in responding to the voice of the one who urges us on, we may be carried on high through the air together with the Lord,[44] with no weight dragging us back to earth. For the one who, following the advice of the psalmist, 'has melted his soul like a spider's web',[45] has put on that airy tunic which reaches from the head to the extremities of the feet. For the law does not intend virtue to be truncated.

192. The golden bells vibrating around the pomegranates are the sparkle of noble feats. For there are two pursuits through which virtue is acquired: faith as regards the divine, and conscience as regards life. These pomegranates and bells the great Paul bestows upon Timothy's garment, saying that he must have 'faith and a good conscience'.[46] So, on the one hand, let faith ring out loud and clear by the proclamation of the holy Trinity, and, on the other, let life imitate the nature of the pomegranate's fruit.

193. For the outside of this is inedible, covered as it is in a hard and bitter case; but the inside is delightful to look at, with its intricate and orderly arrangement of seeds,

---

[42] Cf. 1 Cor. 9:27.   [43] Rom. 12:1.   [44] Cf. 1 Thess. 4:17.   [45] LXX Ps. 38:12.
[46] 1 Tim. 1:19.

and even more delightful to taste, gratifying the senses. The bitter philosophical life, which is hard to accept and disagreeable to the senses, is yet full of good hopes, and ripens in its own time. When the time comes for [100] our vine-dresser[47] to open up the pomegranate of life and reveal the beauty of hidden things, then the enjoyment of those partaking in their own fruit will be sweet. For the divine Apostle also says somewhere that 'for the moment all discipline seems painful rather than pleasant (that is the impression on first encountering the pomegranate), later it yields the peaceful fruit'.[48] This is the sweetness of the food inside.

194. The law also directs that this tunic be tasselled.[49] The tassels are spherical ornaments attached to it for the sake of decoration, not need. We learn from these that virtue is not to be measured by commandment alone, but that we should find something for ourselves, through original invention, so that extra decoration might be added to the garment. So it was with Paul, who wove his own beautiful tassels into the commandments. Whereas the law directs that 'those attending the altar receive a share from the altar' and 'those proclaiming the gospel make their living' from it,[50] he makes the gospel 'free of charge',[51] undergoing hunger, thirst, and nakedness.[52] These are the tassels, which by their addition adorn the tunic of the commandments.

195. Then two pieces of cloth are set over the full-length robe, coming down from the shoulders as far as the chest and the back; [101] they are joined to each other by two clasps, one on each shoulder. The clasps are stones carrying the names of the patriarchs, six inscribed on each. The weave of the cloths is variegated. Blue is woven with purple, the redness of scarlet mixed with flax. Into all these is interspersed gold thread, so that out of these various dyes a single blended elegance radiates from the fabric.

196. From this elegance through variety we learn that the higher elements of the clothing, those which particularly decorate the heart, are a fusion of many different virtues. The blue is woven with the purple. For royalty is partnered by purity of life. Scarlet mingles with flax, because the radiance and purity of life somehow grow naturally together with the blush of modesty. The gold shining among these colours alludes to the treasure laid up for such a life. The patriarchs written on the shoulder pieces contribute in no small way to such an embellishment for us. Human life is enriched all the more by the models of goodness received from the past.

197. Moreover, there is another decoration set over the decoration provided by these cloths: golden shields hanging from each of the shoulder pieces, themselves holding up a golden object of rectangular shape brightened by twelve stones [102] fixed in rows. There are four rows, each holding three stones. Among these not one was found to be the same as another, but each was embellished by its own particular radiance.

198. Such then is the design of the decoration. As to meaning, that of the shields hanging from the shoulders alludes to the double nature of the armour against the adversary, so that since, as was said earlier, virtue succeeds in two ways—through faith and a good conscience in this life—one is made safe on both sides by the shields' protection, remaining unwounded by such darts, 'by means of the weapons of righteousness for the right hand and for the left'.[53]

199. That rectangular adornment attached to the shields on both sides, on which are the stones engraved with patriarchal name of the tribes, becomes a covering for the

---

[47] Cf. John 15:1.   [48] Heb. 12:11.   [49] See n. 9.   [50] 1 Cor. 9:13–14.
[51] 1 Cor. 9:18.   [52] Cf. 1 Cor. 4:11.
[53] 1 Cor. 6:7. The Greek syntax of this paragraph is unclear.

heart. The Word teaches us through this design that the one who drives away the evil archer with these two shields will adorn his own soul with all the virtues of the patriarchs, each shining on the cloth of virtue in its own way. May the rectangular shape be a sign to you of steadfastness in the good. For such a shape is hard to alter, fixed firm thanks to the right-angled corners based on the straight sides.

200. The straps by which these ornaments are tied to the arms seem to me [103] to supply a principle for the higher life: it is necessary to unite practical philosophy with the work of contemplation. The heart therefore becomes a symbol of contemplation and the arms a symbol of works.

201. The head adorned with the diadem intimates the crown laid up for those who have lived well. It is adorned by the inscription on the thin golden plate with unutterable lettering. Whoever wears an array like this does not put on sandals, so as not to be weighed down for the race and hindered by the covering of dead skins, according to the meaning arrived at in contemplating the mountain. How then could the sandal be intended as a decoration for the foot when it is thrown away at the first mystical initiation as an impediment to the ascent?[54]

---

[54] Exod. 3:5.

Glossary

Not everyone reading this study will be familiar with both Hebrew and Greek. As much as possible is explained in English, with the Greek or Hebrew in brackets for the specialists. But some of the arguments only make sense when reference is made to the original language, whether of the MT, the LXX, or subsequent texts. A few keys terms, therefore, are transliterated. They are always defined the first time they occur, and a list of them is given here. The system of transliteration used for the Hebrew is designed to approximate the correct pronunciation; it is not an accurate guide to the underlying Hebrew letters. The reader is thus warned that in citations from other authors' works the spelling of Hebrew words may differ. For example, a 'b' rather than a 'v' may be used to represent ב.

aduton (pl. *aduta*) Gk., the innermost room of a temple or shrine.

ainigma (pl. *ainigmata*) Gk., riddle, figure, symbol, sign.

akolouthia Gk., orderly sequence.

amora'im Heb., rabbis who feature in either Talmud, but who lived after the final redaction of the Mishnah.

anagōgē Gk., elevation, lifting up. Used in the Alexandrian tradition for the exegetical procedure of elevating one's understanding of the biblical text from the literal to the spiritual.

anthrōpos Gk., man, human being.

apokatastasis Gk., restoration.

apolupragmonētos Gk., not to be meddled with.

devir (pl. *devirim*) Heb., the inner sanctuary of the temple, the holy of holies (e.g. 1 Kings 6:5).

dianoia Gk., thought, understanding, deeper meaning.

diastēma Gk., interval, extension, dimension. (From this root word come the adjectives *diastemic, adiastemic*, and *metadiastemic*.)

eidos Gk., form.

'elim Heb., gods, angels.

'elohim Heb., God, gods, angels.

epinoia (pl. *epinoiai*) Gk., thought, notion, conception.

gnōsis Gk., knowledge.

ḥakham Heb., wise; wise man, sage. In rabbinic terminology it designates an ordained rabbi.

ḥaluq Heb., plain garment. Used in *Hekhalot Rabbati* for the divine garment.

ḥashmal Heb., a mysterious substance mentioned in Ezek. 1:4, 27. The LXX translates it as *ēlektron*, the Vulgate as *electrum*, the RSV as 'bronze', and the NJPS as 'amber'.

ḥayyot Heb., living creatures. In Ezekiel 1 it is *ḥayyot* who carry the chariot throne. Ezekiel 10:20 identifies them as cherubim.

hekhal (pl. *hekhalot*) Heb., palace, temple. Used in the Bible (e.g. 1 Kings 6:5) for the 'nave' of Solomon's temple (i.e. 'the holy place' rather than 'the holy of holies'). In the Hekhalot literature, refers to the palaces through which the adept must pass.

historia Gk., historical narrative.

homoousios Gk., of the same being or essence.

hypostasis (pl. *hypostases*) Gk., substance. Used by the Cappadocians for the persons of the Trinity.

katapetasma Gk., curtain, veil (LXX Exod. 26:31). In the New Testament, *katapetasma* always refers to the inner veil of the tabernacle or temple.

kavod Heb., glory.

kosmos noētos Gk., intelligible world. A Platonic term for the realm of Forms.

logeion Gk., speaking place. Replaces *logion* in some LXX manuscripts and in Philo.

logikos Gk., rational, reasonable.

logion Gk., oracle. Used by the LXX for the high priest's breastpiece (LXX Exod. 28:15–26), which contained the means for determining the divine will.

logos (pl. *logoi*) Gk., word.

ma'aseh bereshit Heb., the work of creation. Exegesis of Genesis 1.

ma'aseh merkavah Heb., the work of the chariot. Exegesis of Ezekiel 1.

merkavah (pl. *markavot*) Heb., chariot. The name given to the vision in Ezekiel 1.

midrash Heb., rabbinic exposition of Scripture.

mishkan Heb., dwelling place, tabernacle.

mitra Gk., band, girdle, headdress (LXX Exod. 28:33).

nous Gk., mind.

oikonomia Gk., management, organization, dispensation, economy. Used of the ordered process of God's self-disclosure (cf. Eph. 3:9).

'ophannim Heb., wheels.

ousia Gk., being or essence. Applied by the Cappadocians to the oneness of God.

paideia Gk., education.

panim Heb., face. Sometimes translated countenance, or presence.

paradeigma Gk., pattern, model, plan.

pardes Heb., garden (Persian loanword).

pargod Heb., curtain. Used in rabbinic Hebrew for the heavenly equivalent of the *parokhet*.

parokhet Heb., curtain, veil. In the tabernacle, the *parokhet* divided off the holy of holies (Exod. 26:31).

peristēthion Gk., around the chest. Used by the LXX for the high priest's breastpiece (LXX Exod. 28:4).

petalon Gk., thin plate (LXX Exod. 28:32).

plērōma Gk., fullness (Col. 1:19; 2:9). Valentinians designate their heavenly world of aeons the 'Pleroma'.

plēthō Gk., To fill (LXX Exod. 40:34).

polupragmosunē Gk., curiosity, meddlesomeness.

prosōpon (pl. *prosōpa*) Gk., face, person.

prostēthion Gk., in front of the chest. Used by Gregory in *Life of Moses* 2.189 for the high priest's breastpiece.

Qedushah Heb., the song of the seraphim in Isa. 6:3.

shakhan Heb., to dwell.

Shekhinah Heb., the manifestation of the divine presence.

skēnē Gk., tent, tabernacle.

skēnōma Gk., tent, tabernacle.

skēnoō Gk., to live or dwell (in a tent). Occurs in John 1:14.

skēnopēgia Gk., the setting up of tents, the feast of Tabernacles.

skēnos Gk., tent, body.

skopos Gk., overarching aim.

talmid ḥakham (pl. *talmidei ḥakhamim*) Heb., the student/disciple of a rabbi.

tanna'im Heb., rabbis from the first and second centuries CE.

tavnit Heb., pattern, plan, design.

theōria Gk., contemplation, meaning, interpretation.

tupos Gk., pattern, model, mould, type.

yored merkavah Heb., descender to the chariot.

Bibliography

Primary Literature

The following texts and translations have been consulted. Translations marked by a * are quoted without specification in the footnotes. The translation of some texts has been taken from secondary sources; these are specified in situ.

Hebrew Bible (MT)
Elliger, K., W. Rudolph, et al., *Biblia Hebraica Stuttgartensia* (1967/1977; repr., Stuttgart: Deutsche Bibelgesellschaft, 1997).
*Revised Standard Version (RSV)
Tanakh: The Holy Scriptures: The New JPS Translation according to the Traditional Hebrew Text (Philadelphia: Jewish Publication Society, 1985). (NJPS)

New Testament
Nestle–Aland, *Novum Testamentum Graece*, 27th edn (Stuttgart: Deutsche Bibelgesellschaft, 1993).
*Revised Standard Version (RSV)

Septuagint (LXX)
Wevers, John William, *Septuaginta: Vetus Testamentum Graecum. Auctoritate Academiae Scientiarum Gottingensis editum*, vol. 2:1: *Exodus* (Göttingen: Vandenhoeck & Ruprecht, 1991).
Rahlfs, Alfred, *Septuaginta: Id est Vetus Testamentum graece iuxta LXX interpretes*, 2 vols (Stuttgart: Württembergische Bibelanstalt, 1935; repr., Deutsche Bibelgesellschaft, 1982).
Pietersma, Albert, and Benjamin G. Wright (eds), *A New English Translation of the Septuagint and the Other Greek Translations Traditionally Included under That Title* (Oxford: Oxford University Press, 2007). (NETS)
Ben Sira (the Hebrew text whose Greek version, which is in the LXX, is known as Sirach or Ecclesiasticus)
Beentjes, Pancratius C., *The Book of Ben Sira in Hebrew: A Text Edition of All Extant Hebrew Manuscripts and a Synopsis of All Parallel Hebrew Ben Sira Texts*, Supplements to Vetus Testamentum, 68 (Leiden: Brill, 1997).
Skehan, Patrick W., and Alexander A. Di Lella, *The Wisdom of Ben Sira*, Anchor Bible, 39 (New York: Doubleday, 1987).

Dead Sea Scrolls
Martínez, Florentino García, and Eibert J. C. Tigchelaar (eds), *The Dead Sea Scrolls Study Edition*, 2 vols (Leiden: Brill, 1997–1998).

Songs of the Sabbath Sacrifice
Charlesworth, James H., and Carol A. Newsom, *Angelic Liturgy: Songs of the Sabbath Sacrifice*, The Dead Sea Scrolls: Hebrew, Aramaic, and Greek Texts with English Translations, 4B (Tübingen: Mohr Siebeck, 1999).

Hellenistic Jewish Authors
Josephus
Thackeray, H. St. J., Ralph Marcus, and Louis H. Feldman, *Josephus in Ten Volumes*, Loeb Classical Library (London: Heinemann, 1926–1965).

Philo
*Colson, F. H., G. H. Whitaker, and R. Marcus, *Philo in Ten Volumes (and Two Supplementary Volumes)*, Loeb Classical Library (London: Heinemann, 1929–1962).

Apostolic Fathers
Barnabas (Barn.)
Ehrman, Bart D., *The Apostolic Fathers: Epistle of Barnabas, Papias and Quadratus, Epistle to Diognetus, The Shepherd of Hermas*, Loeb Classical Library (Cambridge, Mass.: Harvard University Press, 2003), 1–83.

Pseudepigrapha
Ascension of Isaiah (Ascen. Isa.)
Bettiolo, Paolo, Alda Giambelluca Kossova, Claudio Leonardi, Enrico Norelli, and Lorenzo Perrone, *Ascensio Isaiae: Textus*, Corpus Christianorum: Series Apocryphorum, 7 (Turnhout: Brepols, 1995).
Knibb, M. A., 'Martyrdom and Ascension of Isaiah', in James H. Charlesworth (ed.), *The Old Testament Pseudepigrapha*, vol. 2: *Expansions of the 'Old Testament' and Legends, Wisdom and Philosophical Literature, Prayers, Psalms, and Odes, Fragments of Lost Judeo-Hellenistic Works* (New York: Doubleday, 1985), 143–76.

1 Enoch (1 En.)
Milik, J. T., *The Books of Enoch: Aramaic Fragments of Qumrân Cave 4* (Oxford: Clarendon, 1976).
Black, Matthew, *Apocalypsis Henochi Graece*, Pseudepigrapha Veteris Testamenti Graece, 3 (Leiden: Brill, 1970).
Nickelsburg, George W. E., and James VanderKam, *1 Enoch: A New Translation* (Minneapolis: Fortress, 2004).

2 Enoch (2 En.)
Vaillant, A., *Le livre des secrets d'Hénoch: Texte slave et traduction française* (Paris: Institut d'études slaves, 1952).
Andersen, Francis I., '2 (Slavonic Apocalypse of) Enoch', in James H. Charlesworth (ed.), *The Old Testament Pseudepigrapha*, vol. 1: *Apocalyptic Literature and Testaments* (New York: Doubleday, 1983), 91–221.

Testament of Levi (T. Levi)
Greenfield, Jonas C., Michael E. Stone, and Esther Eshel, *The Aramaic Levi Document: Edition, Translation, Commentary*, Studia in Veteris Testamenti pseudepigrapha, 19 (Leiden: Brill, 2004).

Jonge, Marinus de, H. W. Hollander, H. J. de Jonge, and Th. Korteweg, *The Testaments of the Twelve Patriarchs: A Critical Edition of the Greek Text*, Pseudepigrapha Veteris Testamenti Graece, 1.2 (Leiden: Brill, 1978).

Hollander, H. W., and M. de Jonge, *The Testaments of the Twelve Patriarchs: A Commentary*, Studia in Veteris Testamenti pseudepigrapha, 8 (Leiden: Brill, 1985).

Rabbinic Literature
Babylonian Talmud
Epstein, I., et al., *Hebrew–English Edition of the Babylonian Talmud*, 32 vols (London: Soncino, 1962–1990).

Mekhilta
Lauterbach, Jacob Z., *Mekilta de Rabbi Ishmael*, 3 vols (Philadelphia: Jewish Publication Society of America, 1933).

Mishnah
Danby, Herbert, *The Mishnah* (Oxford: Oxford University Press, 1933).

Tosephta
Neusner, Jacob, and Richard S. Sarason, *The Tosefta Translated from the Hebrew*, 6 vols (Hoboken, NJ: Ktav, 1977–1986).

Hekhalot Literature
Schäfer, Peter, *Synopse zur Hekhalot-Literatur*, Texte und Studien zum antiken Judentum, 2 (Tübingen: Mohr Siebeck, 1981).

3 Enoch (3 En.)
Alexander, Philip, '3 (Hebrew Apocalypse of) Enoch', in James H. Charlesworth (ed.), *The Old Testament Pseudepigrapha*, vol. 1: *Apocalyptic Literature and Testaments* (New York: Doubleday, 1983), 223–315.

Philosophical Greek Literature
Chaldean Oracles
Majercik, Ruth, *The Chaldean Oracles: Text, Translation, and Commentary*, Studies in Greek and Roman Religion, 5 (Leiden: Brill, 1989).

Iamblichus: *On the Mysteries*
Des Places, Édouard, *Jamblique: Les mystères d'Egypte* (Paris: Les Belles Lettres, 1966).
Taylor, Thomas, *Iamblichus: On the Mysteries of the Egyptians, Chaldeans, and Assyrians* (London: Bertam Dobell, 1895).

Plato
*Fowler, Harold North, W. R. M. Lamb, R. G. Bury, and Paul Shorey, *Plato in Twelve Volumes*, Loeb Classical Library (London: Heinemann, 1914–1935).

Gregory of Nyssa
Against Eunomius 1 (*Eun.* 1) GNO 1.22–225 (also SC 521, 524)
Hall, Stuart George, '"Contra Eunomium I". Introducción y traducción', in Lucas F. Mateo-Seco and Juan L. Bastero (eds), *El 'Contra Eunomium I' en la producción*

literaria de Gregorio de Nisa. VI Coloquio Internacional sobre Gregorio de Nisa (Pamplona: Ediciones Universidad de Navarra, 1988), 21–135.

Against Eunomius 2 (Eun. 2) GNO 1.226–409
Hall, Stuart George, 'The Second Book against Eunomius (Translation)', in Lenka Karfíková, Scot Douglass, and Johannes Zachhuber (eds), *Gregory of Nyssa: Contra Eunomium II* (Leiden: Brill, 2007), 59–201.

Against Eunomius 3 (Eun. 3) GNO 2.3–311
Hall, Stuart George, 'Contra Eunomium III: Translation', in Johan Leemans and Matthieu Cassin (eds), *Proceedings of the 12th International Colloquium on Gregory of Nyssa (Leuven, 14–17 September 2010)* (Leiden: Brill, 2014).

Against the Macedonians (Maced.) GNO 3,1.87–115
Moore, William, and Henry Austin Wilson, *Gregory of Nyssa: Select Writings and Letters*, NPNF[2], 5 (1892; repr., Grand Rapids, Mich.: Eerdmans, 1976), 315–25.

Against Those Who Defer Baptism (Bapt.) GNO 10,2.355–370
Funeral Oration on Meletius (Melet.) GNO 9.441–457
Moore, William, and Henry Austin Wilson, *Gregory of Nyssa: Select Writings and Letters*, NPNF2, 5, 513–17.

Letters (Epist.) GNO 8,2 (also SC 363)
Silvas, Anna M., *Gregory of Nyssa: The Letters: Introduction, Translation and Commentary*, Supplements to Vigiliae christianae, 83 (Leiden: Brill, 2007).

Life of Gregory the Wonderworker (Thaum.) GNO 10,1.1–57
Slusser, Michael, *St. Gregory Thaumaturgus: Life and Works*, FC, 98 (Washington, DC: Catholic University of America Press, 1998), 39–87.

Life of Macrina (Macr.) GNO 8,1.370–414 (also SC 178)
Silvas, Anna M., *Macrina the Younger, Philosopher of God*, Medieval Women: Texts and Contexts, 22 (Turnhout: Brepols, 2008), 109–48.

Life of Moses (Vit. Moys.) GNO 7,1
Daniélou, Jean, *Grégoire de Nysse: La Vie de Moïse, ou Traité de la perfection en matière de vertu*, SC, 1bis (Paris: Cerf, 2000).
Malherbe, Abraham J., and Everett Ferguson, *Gregory of Nyssa: The Life of Moses*, Classics of Western Spirituality (New York: Paulist Press, 1978).

On Basil (Bas.) GNO 10,1.107–134
Stein, James Aloysius, *Encomium of Saint Gregory, Bishop of Nyssa, on his Brother Saint Basil, Archbishop of Cappadocian Caesarea: A Commentary, with a Revised Text, Introduction, and Translation* (Washington, DC: Catholic University of America Press, 1928).

On Infants' Early Deaths (Infant.) GNO 3,2.65–97
Moore, William, and Henry Austin Wilson, *Gregory of Nyssa: Select Writings and Letters*, NPNF[2], 5, 372–81.

On Perfection (Perf.) GNO 8,1.173–214
Callahan, Virginia Woods, *Saint Gregory of Nyssa: Ascetical Works*, FC, 58 (Washington, DC: Catholic University of America Press, 1967), 91–122.

On the Ascension of Christ (Ascens.) GNO 9.323–327 *On the Beatitudes (Beat.)* GNO 7,2.75–170
Hall, Stuart George, 'Gregory of Nyssa, *On the Beatitudes*, translated by Stuart George Hall', in H. R. Drobner and A. Viciano (eds), *Gregory of Nyssa: Homilies on the Beatitudes* (Leiden: Brill, 2000), 21–90.

On the Christian Mode of Life (Inst.) GNO 8,1.40–89
Callahan, Virginia Woods, *Saint Gregory of Nyssa: Ascetical Works*, 123–58.

On the Lord's Prayer (Or. dom.) GNO 7,2.1–74
Graef, Hilda C., *St Gregory of Nyssa: The Lord's Prayer, The Beatitudes*, Ancient Christian Writers, 18 (London: Longmans, Green & Co, 1954), 21–84.

On the Nativity of Christ (Diem nat.) GNO 10,2.235–269
On the Song of Songs (Cant.) GNO 6
Norris, Richard A., *Gregory of Nyssa: Homilies on the Song of Songs*, Writings from the Greco-Roman World, 13 (Atlanta: Society of Biblical Literature, 2012).

On the Soul and Resurrection (An. et res.) PG 46.11–160[1]
Silvas, Anna M., *Macrina the Younger, Philosopher of God*, 171–246.

On the Titles of the Psalms (Inscr.) GNO 5.24–175 (also SC 466)
Heine, Ronald E., *Gregory of Nyssa's Treatise on the Inscriptions of the Psalms* (Oxford: Clarendon, 1995).

On Those Who Have Died (Mort.) GNO 9.28–68
On Virginity (Virg.) GNO 8,1.247–343 (also SC 119)
Callahan, Virginia Woods, *Saint Gregory of Nyssa: Ascetical Works*, 1–75.

Refutation of the Confession of Faith of Eunomius (Ref. Eun.) GNO 2.312–410
Moore, William, and Henry Austin Wilson, *Gregory of Nyssa: Select Writings and Letters*, NPNF[2], 5, 101–34.

Reply to the Teachings of Apollinarius (Antirrh.) GNO 3,1.129–233
To Ablabius: On Not Three Gods (Abl.) GNO 3,1.35–57
Rusch, William G., 'Gregory of Nyssa's *Concerning We Should Think of Saying That There Are Not Three Gods* to Ablabius', in *The Trinitarian Controversy* (Philadelphia: Fortress, 1980), 149–61.

To Simplicius (Simpl.) GNO 3,1.61–67
To Call Oneself a Christian (Prof.) GNO 8,1.129–142
Callahan, Virginia Woods, *Saint Gregory of Nyssa: Ascetical Works*, 77–89.

---

[1] GNO 3,3 was published too late to be used for this study: Andreas Spira *Gregorii Nysseni: De anima et resurrectione*, GNO 3,3 (Leiden: Brill, 2014).

To Eustathius, on the Holy Trinity and the Godhead of the Holy Spirit (Eust.) GNO 3,1.1–16
Silvas, Anna M., *Gregory of Nyssa: The Letters: Introduction, Translation and Commentary*, 232–45.

To the Greeks from Common Notions (Graec.) GNO 3,1.17–33
Stramara, Daniel F., 'Gregory of Nyssa, Ad Graecos: How It Is That We Say There Are Three Persons in the Divinity But Do Not Say There Are Three Gods (To the Greeks: Concerning the Commonality of Concepts)', *Greek Orthodox Theological Review*, 41: 4 (1996), 375–91.

To Theophilus, Against the Apollinarians (Theoph.) GNO 3,1.117–128

Patristic Writings
Apostolic Constitutions (*Apos. Con.*)
Metzger, Marcel, *Les Constitutions Apostoliques*, tome 3: *Livres VII et VIII*, SC, 336 (Paris: Cerf, 1987).

Basil: *Letters (Epist.)*
Deferrari, Roy J., *St. Basil: The Letters*, 4 vols, Loeb Classical Library (London: William Heinemann, 1926-1939).

Basil: *Letter (Epist.)* 225
Silvas, Anna M., *Gregory of Nyssa: The Letters: Introduction, Translation and Commentary*, 82–4.

Clement of Alexandria: *Canon of the Church* or *Against the Judaisers*
Stählin, Otto, and Ludwig Früchtel, *Clemens Alexandrinus III: Stromata Buch VII und VIII, Excerpta ex Theodoto, Eclogae propheticae, Quis dives salvetur, Fragmente*, GCS, 17 (Berlin: Akademie-Verlag, 1970), 218–9.

Clement of Alexandria: *Excerpts from Theodotus (Exc.)*
Sagnard, F., *Clément d'Alexandrie: Extraits de Théodote*, SC, 23 (Paris: Cerf, 1948).
Casey, Robert Pierce, *The Excerpta ex Theodoto of Clement of Alexandria* (London: Christophers, 1934).

Clement of Alexandria: *Miscellanies (Strom.)*
Le Boulluec, Alain, *Clément d'Alexandrie: Les Stromates, Stromate V*, 2 vols, SC, 278, 279 (Paris: Cerf, 1981).
Wilson, William, *The Writings of Clement of Alexandria*, vol. 2, Ante-Nicene Christian Library, 12 (Edinburgh: T&T Clark, 1869).

Cyril/John of Jerusalem: *Mystagogical Catecheses (Myst. Cat.)*
Cross, F. L., *St. Cyril of Jerusalem's Lectures on the Christian Sacraments: The Procatechesis and the Five Mystagogical Catacheses* (Crestwood, NY: St Vladimir's Seminary Press, 1995).

Eunomius
Vaggione, Richard Paul, *Eunomius: The Extant Works*, Oxford Early Christian Texts (Oxford: Clarendon, 1987).

Eusebius: *Ecclesiastical History* (*Hist. eccl.*)
Deferrari, Roy J., *Eusebius Pamphili: Ecclesiastical History*, 2 vols, FC, 19, 29 (Washington, DC: Catholic University of America Press, 1953–1955).

Eusebius: *Ecclesiastical Theology* (*Eccl. theol.*)
Klostermann, Erich, *Eusebius Werke IV: Gegen Marcell, über die kirchliche Theologie, die Fragmente Marcells*, GCS, 14 (Leipzig: J.C. Hinrichs, 1906), 59–182.

Gregory of Nazianzus: *Letter* (*Epist.*) 11
Silvas, Anna M., *Gregory of Nyssa: The Letters: Introduction, Translation and Commentary*, 90–2.

Irenaeus: *Against Heresies* (*Haer.*)
Rousseau, Adelin, and Louis Doutreleau, *Irénée de Lyon: Contre les hérésies, livre I*, 2 vols, SC, 263, 264 (Paris: Cerf, 1979).
Unger, Dominic J., and John J. Dillon, *St. Irenaeus of Lyons: Against the Heresies*, vol. 1: *Book 1*, Ancient Christian Writers, 55 (New York: Paulist Press, 1992).

Jerome: *Letters* (*Epist.*)
Mierow, Charles Christopher, *The Letters of St. Jerome*, vol. 1: *Letters 1–22*, Ancient Christian Writers, 33 (London: Longmans, Green & Co, 1963).
Fremantle, W. H., *St Jerome: Letters and Select Works*, NPNF[2], 6 (1893; repr., Grand Rapids, Mich.: Eerdmans, 1989).

John Chrysostom: *Homilies on Ephesians* (*Hom. Eph.*)
Schaff, Philip, *Saint Chrysostom: Homilies on Galatians, Ephesians, Philippians, Colossians, Thessalonians, Timothy, Titus, and Philemon*, NPNF[1], 13 (1889; repr., Grand Rapids, Mich.: Eerdmans, 1979).

Justin Martyr: *Dialogue with Trypho* (*Dial.*)
Falls, Thomas B., *Saint Justin Martyr: The First Apology, The Second Apology, Dialogue with Trypho, Exhortation to the Greeks, Discourse to the Greeks, The Monarchy or the Rule of God*, FC, 6 (Washington, D.C.: Catholic University of America Press, 1948), 137–366.

Methodius: *Symposium* (*Symp.*)
Musurillo, Herbert, *St. Methodius: The Symposium: A Treatise on Chastity*, Ancient Christian Writers, 27 (London: Longmans, Green & Co, 1958).

Origen: *Against Celsus* (*Cels.*)
Borret, Marcel, *Origène: Contra Celse*, tome 1: *Livres I et II*, SC, 132 (Paris: Cerf, 1967).
Chadwick, Henry, *Origen: Contra Celsum* (Cambridge: Cambridge University Press, 1980).

Origen: *Commentary on John (Comm. Jo.)*
Blanc, Cécile, *Origène: Commentaire sur Saint Jean,* tome 1: *Livres I–V,* SC, 120 (Paris: Cerf, 1966).
Heine, Ronald E., *Origen: Commentary on the Gospel according to John,* 2 vols, FC, 80, 89 (Washington, DC: Catholic University of America Press, 1989–1993).

Origen: *Commentary on Romans (Comm. Rom.)*
Hammond Bammel, Caroline P., *Der Römerbriefkommentar des Origenes: Kritische Ausgabe der Übersetzung Rufins,* 3 vols, Vetus Latina: Aus der Geschichte der lateinischen Bibel, 16, 33, 34 (Freiburg: Herder, 1990–1998).
Scheck, Thomas P., *Origen: Commentary on the Epistle to the Romans,* 2 vols, FC, 103, 104 (Washington, DC: Catholic University of America Press, 2001–2002).

Origen: *Commentary on Song of Songs (Comm. Cant.)*
Lawson, R. P., *Origen: The Song of Songs Commentary and Homilies,* Ancient Christian Writers, 26 (London: Longmans, Green & Co, 1957).

Origen: *First Principles (Princ.)*
Butterworth, G. W., *Origen on First Principles* (London: SPCK, 1936).

Origen: *Homilies on Exodus (Hom. Exod.)*
Borret, Marcel, *Origène: Homélies sur l'Exode,* SC, 321 (Paris: Cerf, 1985).
Heine, Ronald E., *Origen: Homilies on Genesis and Exodus,* FC, 71 (Washington, DC: Catholic University of America Press, 1982).

Origen: *Homilies on Isaiah* (*Hom. Isa.*)
Baehrens, W. A., *Origenes Werke VIII: Homilien zu Samuel I, zum Hohelied und zu den Propheten, Kommentar zum Hohelied in Rufins und Hieronymus' Übersetzungen,* GCS, 33 (Leipzig: J.C. Hinrichs, 1925), 242–89.

Origen: *Homilies on Joshua (Hom. Josh.)*
Bruce, Barbara J., *Origen: Homilies on Joshua,* ed. Cynthia White, FC, 105 (Washington, DC: Catholic University of America Press, 2002).

Origen: *Homilies on Leviticus (Hom. Lev.)*
Borret, Marcel, *Origène: Homélies sur le Lévitique,* tome 1: *Homélies I–VII,* SC, 286 (Paris: Cerf, 1981).
Barkley, Gary Wayne, *Origen: Homilies on Leviticus 1–16,* FC, 83 (Washington, DC: Catholic University of America Press, 1990).

Origen: *Homilies on Numbers (Hom. Num.)*
Doutreleau, Louis, *Origène: Homélies sur les Nombres,* 3 vols, SC, 415, 442, 461 (Paris: Cerf, 1996–2001).
Scheck, Thomas P., *Origen: Homilies on Numbers,* ed. Christopher A. Hall, Ancient Christian Texts (Downers Grove, Ill.: InterVarsity Press, 2009).

Origen: *Letter to Africanus (Ep. Afr.)*
Harl, Marguerite, and Nicholas de Lange, *Origène: Philocalie 1–20 sur les Écritures et La Lettre à Africanus sur l'histoire de Suzanne*, SC, 302 (Paris: Cerf, 1983).
Crombie, Frederick, *The Writings of Origen*, vol. 1, Ante-Nicene Christian Library, 10 (Edinburgh: T&T Clark, 1869).

Proclus of Constantinople
Leroy, F. J., *L'homilétique de Proclus de Constantinople: Tradition manuscrite, inédits, études connexes*, Studi e testi, 247 (Vatican City: Biblioteca Apostolica Vaticana, 1967).

Pseudo-Justin: *Exhortation to the Greeks (Cohortatio ad Graecos)*
Marcovich, Miroslav, *Pseudo-Iustinus: Cohortatio ad Graecos, De monarchia, Oratio ad Graecos*, Patristische Texte und Studien, 32 (Berlin: Walter de Gruyter, 1990).
Falls, Thomas B., *Saint Justin Martyr: The First Apology, The Second Apology, Dialogue with Trypho, Exhortation to the Greeks, Discourse to the Greeks, The Monarchy or the Rule of God*, FC, 6 (Washington, DC: Catholic University of America Press, 1948), 367–423.

Theodoret of Cyrus: *Questions on Exodus (Quaest. in Ex.)*
Hill, Robert C., *Theodoret of Cyrus: The Questions on the Octateuch, volume 1: On Genesis and Exodus*, The Library of Early Christianity, 1 (Washington, DC: Catholic University of America Press, 2007).

Secondary Literature

Abrams, Daniel, 'The Boundaries of Divine Ontology: The Inclusion and Exclusion of Meṭaṭron in the Godhead', *Harvard Theological Review*, 87: 3 (1994), 291–321.
Adler, William, 'Introduction', in James C. VanderKam and William Adler (eds), *The Jewish Apocalyptic Heritage in Early Christianity*, CRINT, 3:4 (Assen: Van Gorcum, 1996), 1–31.
Alexander, Patrick H., John F. Kutsko, James D. Ernest, Shirley A. Decker-Lucke, and David L. Petersen (eds), *The SBL Handbook of Style: For Ancient Near Eastern, Biblical, and Early Christian Studies* (Peabody, Mass.: Hendrickson, 1999).
Alexander, Philip, 'The Historical Setting of the Hebrew Book of Enoch', *Journal of Jewish Studies*, 28 (1977), 156–80.
Alexander, Philip, '3 (Hebrew Apocalypse of) Enoch', in James H. Charlesworth (ed.), *The Old Testament Pseudepigrapha*, vol. 1: *Apocalyptic Literature and Testaments* (New York: Doubleday, 1983), 223–315.
Alexander, Philip, *Textual Sources for the Study of Judaism* (Manchester: Manchester University Press, 1984).
Alexander, Philip, '3 Enoch and the Talmud', *Journal for the Study of Judaism in the Persian, Hellenistic and Roman Period*, 18 (1987), 40–68. http://search.proquest.com/docview/1308022740?accountid=8630
Alexander, Philip, '"The Parting of the Ways" from the Perspective of Rabbinic Judaism', in James D. G. Dunn (ed.), *Jews and Christians: The Parting of the Ways, A.D. 70 to 135*, Wissenschaftliche Untersuchungen zum Neuen Testament, 66 (Tübingen: Mohr Siebeck, 1992), 1–25.

Alexander, Philip, 'Essay with Commentary on Post-Biblical Jewish Literature', in John Barton and John Muddiman (eds), *The Oxford Bible Commentary* (Oxford: Oxford University Press, 2001), 792–829.

Alexander, Philip, *The Mystical Texts: Songs of the Sabbath Sacrifice and Related Manuscripts*, Companion to the Qumram Scrolls, 7 (London: T&T Clark, 2006).

Alexander, Philip, 'The Qumran *Songs of the Sabbath Sacrifice* and the *Celestial Hierarchy* of Dionysius the Areopagite: A Comparative Approach', *Revue de Qumran*, 22: 87 (2006), 349–72.

Alexander, Philip, '"In the Beginning": Rabbinic and Patristic Exegesis of Genesis 1:1', in Emmanouela Grypeou and Helen Spurling (eds), *The Exegetical Encounter between Jews and Christians in Late Antiquity* (Leiden: Brill, 2009), 1–29.

Alexander, Philip, 'The Dualism of Heaven and Earth in Early Jewish Literature and its Implications', in Armin Lange, Eric M. Meyers, Bennie H. Reynolds, and Randall Styers (eds), *Light against Darkness: Dualism in Ancient Mediterranean Religion and the Contemporary World* (Göttingen: Vandenhoeck & Ruprecht, 2011), 169–85.

Allison, Dale C., 'The Silence of Angels: Reflections on the Songs of the Sabbath Sacrifice', *Revue de Qumran*, 13: 49–52 (1988), 189–97.

Andersen, Francis I., '2 (Slavonic Apocalypse of) Enoch', in James H. Charlesworth (ed.), *The Old Testament Pseudepigrapha*, vol. 1: *Apocalyptic Literature and Testaments* (New York: Doubleday, 1983), 91–221.

Andersen, Francis I., 'Enoch, Second Book of', in David Noel Freedman (ed.), *The Anchor Bible Dictionary* (New York: Doubleday, 1992), 2.516–22.

Anderson, Gary A., 'Towards a Theology of the Tabernacle and Its Furniture', in Ruth A. Clements and Daniel R. Schwartz (eds), *Text, Thought, and Practice in Qumran and Early Christianity: Proceedings of the Ninth International Symposium of the Orion Center for the Study of the Dead Sea Scrolls and Associated Literature, Jointly Sponsored by the Hebrew University Center for the Study of Christianity, 11–13 January, 2004*, Studies on the Texts of the Desert of Judah, 84 (Leiden: Brill, 2009), 161–94.

Arnaldez, Roger, Claude Mondésert, Jean Pouilloux, and Pierre Savinel, *Philon d'Alexandrie: De vita Mosis I–II*, Les oeuvres de Philon d'Alexandrie, 22 (Paris: Cerf, 1967).

Attridge, Harold W., *The Epistle to the Hebrews*, Hermeneia (Philadelphia: Fortress, 1989).

Aubineau, M., *Grégoire de Nysse: Traité de la Virginité*, SC, 119 (Paris: Cerf, 1966).

Balás, David L., *ΜΕΤΟΥΣΙΑ ΘΕΟΥ: Man's Participation in God's Perfections according to Saint Gregory of Nyssa*, Studia anselmiana, 55 (Rome: Herder, 1966).

Balthasar, Hans Urs von, *Présence et pensée: Essai sur la philosophie religieuse de Grégoire de Nysse* (Paris: Beauchesne, 1942); trans. Mark Sebanc as *Presence and Thought: An Essay on the Religious Philosophy of Gregory of Nyssa* (San Francisco: Ignatius Press, 1995).

Bammel, C. P., 'Law and Temple in Origen', in William Horbury (ed.), *Templum Amicitiae: Essays on the Second Temple presented to Ernst Bammel*, JSNTSup, 48 (Sheffield: Sheffield Academic Press, 1991), 464–76.

Barker, Margaret, *The Great High Priest: The Temple Roots of Christian Liturgy* (London: T&T Clark, 2003).

Barr, James, *The Semantics of Biblical Language* (Oxford: Oxford University Press, 1961; repr., London: SCM, 1983).

Barrett, C. K., *The Gospel according to St John*, 2nd edn (London: SPCK, 1978).
Baumgarten, Joseph M., *Studies in Qumran Law*, Studies in Judaism in Late Antiquity, 24 (Leiden: Brill, 1977).
Baumgarten, Joseph M., 'The Qumran Sabbath Shirot and Rabbinic Merkabah Traditions', *Revue de Qumran*, 13: 49–52 (1988), 199–213.
Becker, Adam H., and Annette Yoshiko Reed (eds), *The Ways that Never Parted: Jews and Christians in Late Antiquity and the Early Middle Ages* (Minneapolis: Fortress, 2007).
Boersma, Hans, *Embodiment and Virtue in Gregory of Nyssa: An Anagogical Approach*, Oxford Early Christian Studies (Oxford: Oxford University Press, 2013).
Böttrich, Christfried, 'The "Book of the Secrets of Enoch" (2 En): Between Jewish Origin and Christian Transmission: An Overview', in Andrei A. Orlov and Gabriele Boccaccini (eds), *New Perspectives on 2 Enoch: No Longer Slavonic Only*, Studia Judaeoslavica, 4 (Leiden: Brill, 2012), 37–67.
Boustan, Ra'anan S., 'Angels in the Architecture: Temple Art and the Poetics of Praise in the *Songs of the Sabbath Sacrifice*', in Ra'anan S. Boustan and Annette Yoshiko Reed (eds), *Heavenly Realms and Earthly Realities in Late Antique Religions* (Cambridge: Cambridge University Press, 2004), 195–212.
Boustan, Ra'anan S., 'The Study of Heikhalot Literature: Between Mystical Experience and Textual Artifact', *Currents in Biblical Research*, 6: 1 (2007), 130–60.
Boyarin, Daniel, *Dying for God: Martyrdom and the Making of Christianity and Judaism* (Stanford: Stanford University Press, 1999).
Boyarin, Daniel, *Border Lines: The Partition of Judaeo-Christianity* (Philadelphia: University of Pennsylvania Press, 2004).
Boyarin, Daniel, 'Two Powers in Heaven; or, The Making of a Heresy', in Hindy Najman and Judith H. Newman (eds), *The Idea of Biblical Interpretation: Essays in Honor of James L. Kugel* (Leiden: Brill, 2004), 331–70.
Boyarin, Daniel, 'Rethinking Jewish Christianity: An Argument for Dismantling a Dubious Category (to which is Appended a Correction of my *Border Lines*)', *Jewish Quarterly Review*, 99: 1 (2009), 7–36.
Boyarin, Daniel, 'Beyond Judaisms: Meṭaṭron and the Divine Polymorphy of Ancient Judaism', *Journal for the Study of Judaism*, 41 (2010), 323–65.
Brooke, George J., 'Miqdash Adam, Eden and the Qumran Community', in Beate Ego, Armin Lange, and Peter Pilhofer (eds), *Gemeinde ohne Tempel, Community without Temple: Zur Substituierung und Transformation des Jerusalemer Tempels und seines Kults im Alten Testament, antiken Judentum und frühen Christentum* (Tübingen: Mohr Siebeck, 1999), 285–301.
Brown, Peter, *The Making of Late Antiquity* (Cambridge, Mass.: Harvard University Press, 1978).
Brown, Raymond E., *The Gospel According to John, I–XII*, Anchor Bible, 29 (New York: Doubleday, 1966).
Bucur, Bogdan G., 'The Other Clement of Alexandria: Cosmic Hierarchy and Interiorized Apocalypticism', *Vigiliae christianae*, 60: 3 (2006), 251–68. http://www.jstor.org/stable/20474764.
Canévet, Mariette, 'La perception de la présence de Dieu à propos d'une expression de la XIe homélie sur le Cantique des Cantiques', in Jacques Fontaine and Charles Kannengiesser (eds), *Ἐπέκτασις: Mélanges patristiques offerts au Cardinal Jean Daniélou* (Paris: Beauchesne, 1972), 443–54.

Casey, Robert Pierce, *The Excerpta ex Theodoto of Clement of Alexandria* (London: Christophers, 1934).

Chadwick, Henry, *The Early Church* (Harmondsworth: Penguin, 1967).

Charles, R. H., *The Apocrypha and Pseudepigrapha of the Old Testament in English*, vol. 2: *Pseudepigrapha* (Oxford: Clarendon, 1913).

Charles, R. H., *A Critical and Exegetical Commentary on the Revelation of St. John*, 2 vols, International Critical Commentary (Edinburgh: T&T Clark, 1920).

Charlesworth, James H., and Carol A. Newsom, *Angelic Liturgy: Songs of the Sabbath Sacrifice*, The Dead Sea Scrolls: Hebrew, Aramaic, and Greek Texts with English Translations, 4B (Tübingen: Mohr Siebeck, 1999).

Chavoutier, Lucien, 'Querelle origeniste et controverses trinitaires à propos du *Tractatus contra Origenem de visione Isaiae*', *Vigiliae christianae*, 14 (1960), 9–14. http://www.jstor.org/stable/1582521.

Chazon, Esther G., 'Human and Angelic Prayer in Light of the Dead Sea Scrolls', in Esther G. Chazon (ed.), *Liturgical Perspectives: Prayer and Poetry in Light of the Dead Sea Scrolls* (Leiden: Brill, 2003), 35–47.

Childs, Brevard S., *Exodus: A Commentary* (London: SCM, 1974).

Coakley, Sarah (ed.), *Re-Thinking Gregory of Nyssa* (Oxford: Blackwell, 2003).

Collins, Adela Yarbro, 'The Seven Heavens in Jewish and Christian Apocalypses', in John J. Collins and Michael Fishbane (eds), *Death, Ecstasy and Otherworldly Journeys* (Albany: State University of New York Press, 1995), 59–93.

Conway-Jones, Ann, 'Filled with the Glory of God: The Appropriation of Tabernacle Imagery in the New Testament and Gregory of Nyssa', in Michael Tait and Peter Oakes (eds), *Torah in the New Testament: Papers Delivered at the Manchester–Lausanne Seminar of June 2008*, Library of New Testament Studies, 401 (London: T&T Clark, 2009), 228–38.

Conway-Jones, Ann, 'Uncreated and Created: Proverbs 8 and *Contra Eunomium* III/I as the Background to Gregory's Interpretation of the Tabernacle in *Life of Moses* II 173–7', in Johan Leemans and Matthieu Cassin (eds), *Gregory of Nyssa: Contra Eunomium III: An English Translation with Commentary and Supporting Studies*, Supplements to Vigiliae christianae (Leiden: Brill, forthcoming, 2014).

Cross, Frank M., 'The Tabernacle: A Study from an Archaeological and Historical Approach', *The Biblical Archaeologist*, 10: 3 (1947), 45–68. http://www.jstor.org/stable/3209346.

Crouzel, Henri, *Origen*, trans. A. S. Worrall (San Francisco: Harper & Row, 1989).

Daley, Brian E., '"Heavenly Man" and "Eternal Christ": Apollinarius and Gregory of Nyssa on the Personal Identity of the Savior', *Journal of Early Christian Studies*, 10: 4 (2002), 469–88.

Daley, Brian E., 'Divine Transcendence and Human Transformation: Gregory of Nyssa's Anti-Apollinarian Christology', in Sarah Coakley (ed.), *Re-Thinking Gregory of Nyssa* (Oxford: Blackwell, 2003), 67–76.

Daniélou, Jean, *Platonisme et théologie mystique: Doctrine spirituelle de Saint Grégoire de Nysse*, 2nd edn (Paris: Aubier, 1954).

Daniélou, Jean, 'La chronologie des sermons de Grégoire de Nysse', *Revue des sciences religieuses*, 29 (1955), 346–72.

Daniélou, Jean, *The Bible and the Liturgy* (Notre Dame, Ind.: University of Notre Dame Press, 1956).

Daniélou, Jean, 'Eunome l'Arien et l'exégèse néo-platonicienne du Cratyle', *Revue des études grecques*, 69 (1956), 412–32.

Daniélou, Jean, 'Le Mariage de Grégoire de Nysse et la Chronologie de sa Vie', *Revue des études augustiniennes*, 2 (1956), 71–8. http://hdl.handle.net/2042/617.

Daniélou, Jean, 'Introduction', in Herbert Musurillo, *From Glory to Glory: Texts from Gregory of Nyssa's Mystical Writings* (New York: Scribner, 1961; repr., Crestwood, NY: St Vladimir's Seminary Press, 2001), 3–78.

Daniélou, Jean, *The Development of Christian Doctrine before the Council of Nicaea*, vol. 1: *The Theology of Jewish Christianity*, trans. John Austin Baker (London: Darton, Longman & Todd, 1964).

Daniélou, Jean, 'Grégoire de Nysse à travers les lettres de Saint Basile et de Saint Grégoire de Nazianze', *Vigiliae christianae*, 19 (1965), 31–41. http://www.jstor.org/stable/1582597.

Daniélou, Jean, 'La chronologie des oeuvres de Grégoire de Nysse', in F. L. Cross (ed.), *Papers Presented to the Fourth International Conference on Patristic Studies Held at Christ Church, Oxford, 1963, Part 1*, Studia patristica, 7 (Berlin: Akademie-Verlag, 1966), 159–69.

Daniélou, Jean, *Grégoire de Nysse: La Vie de Moïse, ou Traité de la perfection en matière de vertu*, SC, 1bis (Paris: Cerf, 2000).

Davila, James R., *Descenders to the Chariot: The People behind the Hekhalot Literature*, Supplements to the Journal for the Study of Judaism, 70 (Leiden: Brill, 2001).

Davila, James R., 'The Macrocosmic Temple, Scriptural Exegesis, and the Songs of the Sabbath Sacrifice', *Dead Sea Discoveries*, 9: 1 (2002), 1–19. http://www.jstor.org/stable/4193211.

Davila, James R., *The Provenance of the Pseudepigrapha: Jewish, Christian, or Other?*, Supplements to the Journal for the Study of Judaism, 105 (Leiden: Brill, 2005).

Davila, James R., 'The Ancient Jewish Apocalypses and the *Hekhalot* Literature', in April D. DeConick (ed.), *Paradise Now: Essays on Early Jewish and Christian Mysticism* (Atlanta: Society of Biblical Literature, 2006), 105–25.

Day, John, 'Whatever Happened to the Ark of the Covenant?', in John Day (ed.), *Temple and Worship in Biblical Israel: Proceedings of the Oxford Old Testament Seminar* (London: T&T Clark, 2007), 250–70.

DeConick, April D., 'Heavenly Temple Traditions and Valentinian Worship', in Carey C. Newman, James R. Davila, and Gladys S. Lewis (eds), *The Jewish Roots of Christological Monotheism: Papers from the St. Andrews Conference on the Historical Origins of the Worship of Jesus* (Leiden: Brill, 1999), 308–41.

DeConick, April D., 'The True Mysteries: Sacramentalism in the *Gospel of Philip*', *Vigiliae christianae*, 55: 3 (2001), 225–61. http://www.jstor.org/stable/1584809

DeConick, April D. (ed.), *Paradise Now: Essays on Early Jewish and Christian Mysticism* (Atlanta: Society of Biblical Literature, 2006).

DeConick, April D., 'What Is Early Jewish and Christian Mysticism?', in April D. DeConick (ed.), *Paradise Now: Essays on Early Jewish and Christian Mysticism* (Atlanta: Society of Biblical Literature, 2006), 1–24.

DeConick, April D., et al., '"Early Jewish and Christian Mysticism": A Collage of Working Definitions', in *Society of Biblical Literature: 2001 Seminar Papers* (Atlanta: Society of Biblical Literature, 2001), 278–304.

Dillon, John M., 'The Magical Power of Names in Origen and Later Platonism', in Richard Hanson and Henri Crouzel (eds), *Origeniana Tertia: The Third International Colloquium for Origen Studies, University of Manchester, September 7th–11th 1981* (Rome: dell'Ateneo, 1985), 203–16.

Dimant, Devorah, '4QFlorilegium and the Idea of the Community as Temple', in A. Caquot, M. Hadas-Lebel, and J. Riaud (eds), *Hellenica et Judaica: Hommage à Valentin Nikiprowetzky* (Leuven: Peeters, 1986), 165–89.

Dimant, Devorah, 'Men as Angels: The Self-Image of the Qumran Community', in Adele Berlin (ed.), *Religion and Politics in the Ancient Near East*, Studies and Texts in Jewish History and Culture (Bethesda, MD: University Press of Maryland, 1996), 93–103.

Douglass, Scot, *Theology of the Gap: Cappadocian Language Theory and the Trinitarian Controversy* (New York: Peter Lang, 2005).

Drobner, Hubertus R., 'Allegory', in Lucas Francisco Mateo-Seco and Giulio Maspero (eds), *The Brill Dictionary of Gregory of Nyssa*, Supplements to Vigiliae christianae, 99 (Leiden: Brill, 2010), 21–6.

Dunderberg, Ismo, *Beyond Gnosticism: Myth, Lifestyle, and Society in the School of Valentinus* (New York: Columbia University Press, 2008).

Elior, Rachel, 'The Concept of God in Hekhalot Literature', in Joseph Dan (ed.), *Studies in Jewish Thought*, Binah, 2 (New York: Praeger, 1989), 97–120.

Elior, Rachel, 'From Earthly Temple to Heavenly Shrines: Prayer and Sacred Song in the Hekhalot Literature and Its Relation to Temple Traditions', *Jewish Studies Quarterly*, 4 (1997), 217–67.

Emerton, J. A., 'The Origin of the Son of Man Imagery', *Journal of Theological Studies*, 9 (1958), 225–42.

Ferguson, Everett, 'Progress in Perfection: Gregory of Nyssa's *Vita Moysis*', in Elizabeth A. Livingstone (ed.), *Papers Presented to the Sixth International Conference on Patristic Studies Held in Oxford 1971*, part 3: *Tertullian, Origenism, Gnostica, Cappadocian Fathers, Augustiniana*, Studia patristica, 14 (Berlin: Akademie-Verlag, 1976), 307–14.

Festugière, A. J., *La révélation d'Hermès Trismégiste*, vol. 5: *Le Dieu inconnu et la gnose* (Paris: Gabalda, 1954).

Fletcher-Louis, Crispin H. T., 'Heavenly Ascent or Incarnational Presence? A Revisionist Reading of the *Songs of the Sabbath Sacrifice*', *Society of Biblical Literature Seminar Papers*, 37 (1998), 367–99.

Fletcher-Louis, Crispin H. T., *All the Glory of Adam: Liturgical Anthropology in the Dead Sea Scrolls*, Studies on the Texts of the Desert of Judah, 42 (Leiden: Brill, 2002).

Frankfurter, David, 'Beyond "Jewish Christianity": Continuing Religious Sub-Cultures of the Second and Third Centuries and their Documents', in Adam H. Becker and Annette Yoshiko Reed (eds), *The Ways that Never Parted: Jews and Christians in Late Antiquity and the Early Middle Ages* (Minneapolis: Fortress, 2007), 131–43.

Friedman, Richard E., 'The Tabernacle in the Temple', *The Biblical Archaeologist*, 43: 4 (1980), 241–8. http://www.jstor.org/stable/3209799

Gärtner, Bertil, *The Temple and the Community in Qumran and the New Testament: A Comparative Study in the Temple Symbolism of the Qumran Texts and the New Testament* (Cambridge: Cambridge University Press, 1965).

Geljon, Albert, *Philonic Exegesis in Gregory of Nyssa's De Vita Moysis* (Providence: Brown Judaic Studies, 2002).

Geljon, Albert, 'Divine Infinity in Gregory of Nyssa and Philo of Alexandria', *Vigiliae christianae*, 59 (2005), 152–77. http://www.jstor.org/stable/1584786

Gooder, Paula R., *Only the Third Heaven? 2 Corinthians 12.1-10 and Heavenly Ascent* (London: T&T Clark, 2006).

Gooding, D. W., *The Account of the Tabernacle: Translation and Textual Problems of the Greek Exodus* (Cambridge: Cambridge University Press, 1959).

Goodman, Martin, 'Modeling the "Parting of the Ways"', in Adam H. Becker and Annette Yoshiko Reed (eds), *The Ways that Never Parted: Jews and Christians in Late Antiquity and the Early Middle Ages* (Tübingen: Mohr Siebeck, 2003; repr., Minneapolis: Fortress, 2007), 119–29.

Goodman, Martin, 'The Qumran Sectarians and the Temple in Jerusalem', in Charlotte Hempel (ed.), *The Dead Sea Scrolls: Text and Context*, Studies on the Texts of the Desert of Judah, 90 (Leiden: Brill, 2010), 263–73.

Greenfield, Jonas C., 'Prolegomenon', in Hugo Odeberg, *3 Enoch or the Hebrew Book of Enoch* (New York: Ktav, 1973), xi–xlvii.

Gribomont, J., 'Le *De Instituto Christiano* et le Messalianisme de Grégoire de Nysse', in F. L. Cross (ed.), *Papers Presented to the Third International Conference on Patristic Studies Held at Christ Church, Oxford, 1959, Part 3*, Studia patristica, 7 (Berlin: Akademie-Verlag, 1962).

Grözinger, Karl Erich, 'The Names of God and the Celestial Powers: Their Function and Meaning in the Hekhalot Literature', in Joseph Dan (ed.), *Early Jewish Mysticism: Proceedings of the First International Conference on the History of Jewish Mysticism (Jerusalem, February 1984)*, Jerusalem Studies in Jewish Thought, 6 (1–2) (Jerusalem: Hamakor, 1987), 53–69.

Gruenwald, Ithamar, *Apocalyptic and Merkavah Mysticism* (Leiden: Brill, 1980).

Hagen, Joost L., 'No Longer "Slavonic" Only: 2 Enoch Attested in Coptic from Nubia', in Andrei A. Orlov and Gabriele Boccaccini (eds), *New Perspectives on 2 Enoch: No Longer Slavonic Only*, Studia Judaeoslavica, 4 (Leiden: Brill, 2012), 7–34.

Hall, Robert G., 'The *Ascension of Isaiah*: Community Situation, Date, and Place in Early Christianity', *Journal of Biblical Literature*, 109: 2 (1990), 289–306. http://www.jstor.org/stable/3267019

Halperin, David J., *The Merkabah in Rabbinic Literature*, American Oriental Series, 62 (New Haven: American Oriental Society, 1980).

Halperin, David J., 'Merkabah Midrash in the Septuagint', *Journal of Biblical Literature*, 101: 3 (1982), 351–63. http://www.jstor.org/stable/3260349

Halperin, David J., *The Faces of the Chariot: Early Jewish Responses to Ezekiel's Vision*, Texte und Studien zum antiken Judentum, 16 (Tübingen: Mohr Siebeck, 1988).

Hannah, Darrell D., 'Isaiah's Vision in the Ascension of Isaiah and the Early Church', *Journal of Theological Studies*, 50: 1 (1999), 80–101.

Haran, Menahem, 'The Priestly Image of the Tabernacle', *Hebrew Union College Annual*, 36 (1965), 191–226.

Haran, Menahem, *Temples and Temple-Service in Ancient Israel: An Inquiry into the Character of Cult Phenomena and the Historical Setting of the Priestly School* (Oxford: Clarendon, 1978).

Harl, Marguerite, 'Cosmologie grecque et représentations juives dans l'oeuvre de Philon d'Alexandrie', in Roger Arnaldez, Claude Mondésert, and Jean Pouilloux (eds), *Philon d'Alexandrie: Actes du colloque national sur Philon d'Alexandrie organisé dans le cadre des colloques nationaux du Centre national de la recherche scientifique, à*

Lyon du 11 au 15 septembre 1966 (Paris: Éditions du Centre national de la recherche scientifique, 1967), 189–205.

Harl, Marguerite, 'Moïse figure de l'évêque dans l'Eloge de Basile de Grégoire de Nysse (381): Un plaidoyer pour l'autorité épiscopale', in Andreas Spira (ed.), *The Biographical Works of Gregory of Nyssa: Proceedings of the Fifth International Colloquium on Gregory of Nyssa (Mainz, 6-10 September 1982)*, Patristic Monograph Series, 12 (Cambridge, Mass.: Philadelphia Patristic Foundation, 1984), 71–119.

Harrison, Verna E. F., *Grace and Human Freedom according to St. Gregory of Nyssa*, Studies in the Bible and Early Christianity, 30 (Lewiston, NY: Edwin Mellen, 1992).

Hastings, Adrian, '150–550', in Adrian Hastings (ed.), *A World History of Christianity* (London: Cassell, 1999), 25–65.

Hayward, C. T. R., 'Understandings of the Temple Service in the Septuagint Pentateuch', in John Day (ed.), *Temple and Worship in Biblical Israel: Proceedings of the Oxford Old Testament Seminar* (London: T&T Clark, 2007), 387–400.

Heine, Ronald E., *Perfection in the Virtuous Life: A Study in the Relationship Between Edification and Polemical Theology in Gregory of Nyssa's De Vita Moysis* (Cambridge, Mass.: Philadelphia Patristic Foundation, 1975).

Heine, Ronald E., *Origen: Homilies on Genesis and Exodus*, FC, 71 (Washington, DC: Catholic University of America Press, 1982).

Heine, Ronald E., 'Gregory of Nyssa's Apology for Allegory', *Vigiliae christianae*, 38: 4 (1984), 360–70. http://www.jstor.org/stable/1583672

Himmelfarb, Martha, 'Apocalyptic Ascent and the Heavenly Temple', *Society of Biblical Literature Seminar Papers*, 26 (1987), 210–17.

Himmelfarb, Martha, 'The Temple and the Garden of Eden in Ezekiel, the Book of the Watchers, and the Wisdom of ben Sira', in Jamie Scott and Paul Simpson-Housley (eds), *Sacred Places and Profane Spaces: Essays in the Geographics of Judaism, Christianity, and Islam* (New York: Greenwood, 1991), 63–78.

Himmelfarb, Martha, *Ascent to Heaven in Jewish and Christian Apocalypses* (Oxford: Oxford University Press, 1993).

Himmelfarb, Martha, 'The Practice of Ascent in the Ancient Mediterranean World', in John J. Collins and Michael Fishbane (eds), *Death, Ecstasy and Otherworldly Journeys* (Albany: State University of New York Press, 1995), 123–37.

Hoek, Annewies van den, *Clement of Alexandria and His Use of Philo in the Stromateis: An Early Christian Reshaping of a Jewish Model* (Leiden: Brill, 1988).

Hogeterp, Albert L. A., 'Paul's Judaism Reconsidered: The Issue of Cultic Imagery in the Corinthian Correspondence', *Ephemerides theologicae lovanienses*, 81: 1 (2005), 87–108.

Holder, Arthur G., *Bede: On the Tabernacle*, Translated Texts for Historians, 18 (Liverpool: Liverpool University Press, 1994).

Hollander, H. W., and M. de Jonge, *The Testaments of the Twelve Patriarchs: A Commentary*, Studia in Veteris Testamenti pseudepigrapha, 8 (Leiden: Brill, 1985).

Horbury, William, 'Land, Sanctuary and Worship', in John Barclay and John Sweet (eds), *Early Christian Thought in its Jewish Context* (Cambridge: Cambridge University Press, 1996), 207–24.

Horbury, William, 'The Wisdom of Solomon', in John Barton and John Muddiman (eds), *The Oxford Bible Commentary* (Oxford: Oxford University Press, 2001), 650–67.

Horst, Pieter Willem van der, 'A New Altar of a Godfearer?', *Journal of Jewish Studies*, 43 (1992), 32–7.

Hurowitz, Victor Avigdor, *I Have Built You an Exalted House: Temple Building in the Bible in Light of Mesopotamian and Northwest Semitic Writings*, Journal for the Study of the Old Testament Supplement Series, 115 (Sheffield: Sheffield Academic Press, 1992).

Hurowitz, Victor Avigdor, 'YHWH's Exalted House—Aspects of the Design and Symbolism of Solomon's Temple', in John Day (ed.), *Temple and Worship in Biblical Israel: Proceedings of the Oxford Old Testament Seminar* (London: T&T Clark, 2007), 63–110.

Jonge, Marinus de, 'Levi in Aramaic Levi and in the Testament of Levi', in Esther G. Chazon and Michael Stone (eds), *Pseudepigraphic Perspectives: The Apocrypha and Pseudepigrapha in Light of the Dead Sea Scrolls* (Leiden: Brill, 1999), 71–89.

Joyce, Paul M., 'Ezekiel 40–42: The Earliest "Heavenly Ascent" Narrative?', in H. J. de Jonge and J. Tromp (eds), *The Book of Ezekiel and Its Influence* (Aldershot: Ashgate, 2007), 17–41.

Joyce, Paul M., *Ezekiel: A Commentary*, Library of Hebrew Bible/Old Testament Studies, 482 (London: T&T Clark, 2009).

Katz, Steven T., 'Mysticism and the Interpretation of Sacred Scripture', in Steven T. Katz (ed.), *Mysticism and Sacred Scripture* (Oxford: Oxford University Press, 2000), 7–67.

Kee, H. C., 'Testaments of the Twelve Patriarchs', in James H. Charlesworth (ed.), *The Old Testament Pseudepigrapha*, vol. 1: *Apocalyptic Literature and Testaments* (New York: Doubleday, 1983), 775–828.

Klawans, Jonathan, *Purity, Sacrifice, and the Temple: Symbolism and Supersessionism in the Study of Ancient Judaism* (Oxford: Oxford University Press, 2006).

Knibb, M. A., 'Martyrdom and Ascension of Isaiah', in James H. Charlesworth (ed.), *The Old Testament Pseudepigrapha*, vol. 2: *Expansions of the 'Old Testament' and Legends, Wisdom and Philosophical Literature, Prayers, Psalms, and Odes, Fragments of Lost Judeo-Hellenistic Works* (New York: Doubleday, 1985), 143–76.

Knight, Jonathan, 'The Origin and Significance of the Angelomorphic Christology in the Ascension of Isaiah', *The Journal of Theological Studies*, 63: 1 (2012), 66–105.

Knohl, Israel, 'Between Voice and Silence: The Relationship between Prayer and Temple Cult', *Journal of Biblical Literature*, 115: 1 (1996), 17–30. http://www.jstor.org/stable/3266816.

Koester, Craig R., *The Dwelling of God: The Tabernacle in the Old Testament, Intertestamental Jewish Literature, and the New Testament* (Washington, DC: Catholic Biblical Association of America, 1989).

Kohn, Risa Levitt, and Rebecca Moore, *A Portable God: The Origin of Judaism and Christianity* (Lanham: Rowman & Littlefield, 2007).

Kopecek, Thomas A., 'The Social Class of the Cappadocian Fathers', *Church History*, 42: 4 (1973), 453–66.

Kovacs, Judith L., 'Concealment and Gnostic Exegesis: Clement of Alexandria's Interpretation of the Tabernacle', in Elizabeth A. Livingstone (ed.), *Papers Presented at the Twelfth International Conference on Patristic Studies Held in Oxford 1995*, part 3: *Preaching, Second Century, Tertullian to Arnobious, Egypt before Nicaea*, Studia patristica, 31 (Leuven: Peeters, 1997), 414–37.

Kovacs, Judith L., 'Clement of Alexandria and Gregory of Nyssa on the Beatitudes', in H. R. Drobner and A. Viciano (eds), *Gregory of Nyssa: Homilies on the Beatitudes* (Leiden: Brill, 2000), 311–29.

Kovacs, Judith L., 'Clement of Alexandria', in Robert Benedetto, et al. (eds), *The New SCM Dictionary of Church History*, vol. 1: *From the Early Church to 1700* (London: SCM, 2008), 156–7.

Krabinger, J. G., *S. Gregorii, Episcopi Nysseni: De precatione orationes v, graece et latine* (Landshut: Attenhofer, 1840).

Krivocheine, Basil, 'Simplicity of the Divine Nature and the Distinctions in God, according to St. Gregory of Nyssa', *St. Vladimir's Theological Quarterly*, 21 (1977), 76–104.

Kugler, Robert A., *From Patriarch to Priest: The Levi-Priestly Tradition from Aramaic Levi to Testament of Levi* (Atlanta: Scholars Press, 1996).

Laird, Martin, 'Under Solomon's Tutelage: The Education of Desire in the Homilies on the Song of Songs', in Sarah Coakley (ed.), *Re-Thinking Gregory of Nyssa* (Oxford: Blackwell, 2003), 77–95.

Laird, Martin, *Gregory of Nyssa and the Grasp of Faith: Union, Knowledge, and Divine Presence* (Oxford: Oxford University Press, 2004).

Langer, Ruth, 'Early Rabbinic Liturgy in Its Palestinian Milieu: Did Non-Rabbis Know the *'Amidah*?', in Alan J. Avery-Peck, Daniel Harrington, and Jacob Neusner (eds), *When Judaism and Christianity Began: Essays in Memory of Anthony J. Saldarini*, vol. 2: *Judaism and Christianity in the Beginning* (Leiden: Brill, 2004), 423–39.

Le Boulluec, Alain, *Clément d'Alexandrie: Les Stromates, Stromate V*, 2 vols, SC, 278, 279 (Paris: Cerf, 1981).

Lesses, Rebecca Macy, *Ritual Practices to Gain Power: Angels, Incantations, and Revelation in Early Jewish Mysticism*, Harvard Theological Studies, 44 (Harrisburg, Penn.: Trinity Press International, 1998).

Levenson, Jon D., 'The Temple and the World', *The Journal of Religion*, 64: 3 (1984), 275–98. http://www.jstor.org/stable/1202664.

Liddell, Henry George, Robert Scott, and Henry Stuart Jones, *A Greek–English Lexicon*, 9th edn (Oxford: Clarendon, 1940).

Lieb, Michael, *The Visionary Mode: Biblical Prophecy, Hermeneutics, and Cultural Change* (Ithaca, NY: Cornell University Press, 1991).

Lieu, Judith M., *Neither Jew nor Greek? Constructing Early Christianity* (London: T&T Clark, 2002).

Lilla, Salvatore R. C., *Clement of Alexandria: A Study in Christian Platonism and Gnosticism* (Oxford: Oxford University Press, 1971).

Lim, Richard, *Public Disputation, Power, and Social Order in Late Antiquity* (Berkeley: University of California Press, 1995).

Louth, Andrew, 'The Cappadocians', in Cheslyn Jones, Geoffrey Wainwright, and Edward Yarnold (eds), *The Study of Spirituality* (London: SPCK, 1986), 161–8.

Louth, Andrew, *The Origins of the Christian Mystical Tradition: From Plato to Denys*, 2nd edn (Oxford: Oxford University Press, 2007).

Ludlow, Morwenna, 'Theology and Allegory: Origen and Gregory of Nyssa on the Unity and Diversity of Scripture', *International Journal of Systematic Theology*, 4: 1 (2002), 45–66.

Ludlow, Morwenna, *Gregory of Nyssa, Ancient and (Post)modern* (Oxford: Oxford University Press, 2007).
McGinn, Bernard, *The Foundations of Mysticism: Origins to the Fifth Century* (New York: Crossroad, 1991).
McGinn, Bernard, 'Selective Affinities: Reflections on Jewish and Christian Mystical Exegesis', in Rachel Elior and Peter Schäfer (eds), *Creation and Re-Creation in Jewish Thought: Festschrift in Honor of Joseph Dan on the Occasion of his Seventieth Birthday* (Tübingen: Mohr Siebeck, 2005), 85–101.
McGuckin, John Anthony, *The Westminster Handbook to Origen* (Louisville, Ken.: Westminster John Knox Press, 2004).
Macleod, Colin W., 'Allegory and Mysticism in Origen and Gregory of Nyssa', *Journal of Theological Studies*, 22: 2 (1971), 362–79.
Malherbe, Abraham J., and Everett Ferguson, *Gregory of Nyssa: The Life of Moses*, Classics of Western Spirituality (New York: Paulist Press, 1978).
Maraval, Pierre, *Grégoire de Nysse: Lettres*, SC, 363 (Paris: Cerf, 1990).
Maraval, Pierre, 'Retour sur quelques dates concernant Basile de Césarée et Grégoire de Nysse', *Revue d'histoire ecclésiastique*, 99 (2004), 153–7.
Mateo-Seco, Lucas Francisco, and Giulio Maspero (eds), *The Brill Dictionary of Gregory of Nyssa*, Supplements to Vigiliae christianae, 99 (Leiden: Brill, 2010).
May, G., 'Die Chronologie des Lebens und des Werkes Gregors von Nyssa', in Marguerite Harl (ed.), *Écriture et culture philosophique dans la pensée de Grégoire de Nysse* (Leiden: Brill, 1971), 51–67.
Méhat, André, *Étude sur les 'Stromates' de Clément d'Alexandrie* (Paris: Seuil, 1966).
Meredith, Anthony, *The Cappadocians* (Crestwood, NY: St Vladimir's Seminary Press, 1995).
Meredith, Anthony, *Gregory of Nyssa* (London: Routledge, 1999).
Meredith, Anthony, 'The Language of God and Human Language (*CE* II 195–293)', in Lenka Karfíková, Scot Douglass, and Johannes Zachhuber (eds), *Gregory of Nyssa: Contra Eunomium II*, Supplements to Vigiliae christianae, 82 (Leiden: Brill, 2007), 247–56.
Michaelis, W., 'σκηνή, σκῆνος, σκήνωμα, σκηνόω, ἐπισκηνόω, κατασκηνόω, σκηνοπηγία, σκηνοποιός', in Gerhard Friedrich (ed.), *Theological Dictionary of the New Testament* (Grand Rapids, Mich.: Eerdmans, 1971), 7.368–94.
Mondésert, Claude, *Clément d'Alexandrie: Introduction à l'étude de sa pensée religieuse à partir de l'Écriture* (Paris: Aubier, 1944).
Mondésert, Claude, 'A propos du signe du temple: Un texte de Clément d'Alexandrie', *Recherches de science religieuse*, 36 (1949), 580–4.
Morray-Jones, Christopher R. A., 'Transformational Mysticism in the Apocalyptic–Merkabah Tradition', *Journal of Jewish Studies*, 43 (1992), 1–31.
Morray-Jones, Christopher R. A., 'Paradise Revisited (2 Cor *12*:1–12): The Jewish Mystical Background of Paul's Apostolate', *Harvard Theological Review*, 86: 2, 3 (1993), 177–217, 265–92.
Morray-Jones, Christopher R. A., 'The Temple Within', in April D. DeConick (ed.), *Paradise Now: Essays on Early Jewish and Christian Mysticism* (Atlanta: Society of Biblical Literature, 2006), 145–78.

Mosshammer, Alden A., 'The Created and the Uncreated in Gregory of Nyssa: *Contra Eunomium* 1,105–113', in Lucas F. Mateo-Seco and Juan L. Bastero (eds), *El 'Contra Eunomium I' en la producción literaria de Gregorio de Nisa. VI Coloquio Internacional sobre Gregorio de Nisa* (Pamplona: Ediciones Universidad de Navarra, 1988), 353–79.

Mosshammer, Alden A., 'Disclosing but not Disclosed: Gregory of Nyssa as Deconstructionist', in H. R. Drobner and C. Klock (eds), *Studien zu Gregor von Nyssa und der christlichen Spätantike* (Leiden: Brill, 1990), 99–123.

Mosshammer, Alden A., 'Gregory's Intellectual Development: A Comparison of the *Homilies on the Beatitudes* with the *Homilies on the Song of Songs*', in H. R. Drobner and A. Viciano (eds), *Gregory of Nyssa: Homilies on the Beatitudes* (Leiden: Brill, 2000), 359–87.

Mounce, Robert H., *The Book of Revelation*, New International Commentary on the New Testament (Grand Rapids, Mich.: Eerdmans, 1977).

Mühlenberg, Ekkehard, *Die Unendlichkeit Gottes bei Gregor von Nyssa: Gregors Kritik am Gottesbegriff der klassischen Metaphysik* (Göttingen: Vandenhoeck & Ruprecht, 1966).

Musurillo, Herbert, *From Glory to Glory: Texts from Gregory of Nyssa's Mystical Writings* (New York: Scribner, 1961; repr., Crestwood, NY: St Vladimir's Seminary Press, 2001).

Navtanovich, Liudmila, 'The Provenance of 2 Enoch: A Philological Perspective', in Andrei A. Orlov and Gabriele Boccaccini (eds), *New Perspectives on 2 Enoch: No Longer Slavonic Only*, Studia Judaeoslavica, 4 (Leiden: Brill, 2012), 69–82.

Neusner, Jacob, and Richard S. Sarason, *The Tosefta Translated from the Hebrew*, 6 vols (Hoboken, NJ: Ktav, 1977–1986).

Newsom, Carol A., *Songs of the Sabbath Sacrifice: A Critical Edition* (Atlanta: Scholars Press, 1985).

Newsom, Carol A., 'Merkabah Exegesis in the Qumran Sabbath Shirot', *Journal of Jewish Studies*, 38: 1 (1987), 11–30.

Nickelsburg, George W. E., *1 Enoch 1: A Commentary on the Book of 1 Enoch, Chapters 1–36; 81–108*, Hermeneia (Minneapolis: Fortress, 2001).

Nitzan, Bilhah, 'Harmonic and Mystical Characteristics in Poetic and Liturgical Writings from Qumran', *Jewish Quarterly Review*, 85: 1–2 (1994), 163–83. http://www.jstor.org/stable/1454960.

O'Connell, Patrick F., 'The Double Journey in Saint Gregory of Nyssa: *The Life of Moses*', *Greek Orthodox Theological Review*, 28: 4 (1983), 301–24.

Odeberg, Hugo, *3 Enoch or the Hebrew Book of Enoch* (Cambridge: Cambridge University Press, 1928; repr., New York: Ktav, 1973).

O'Keefe, John J., 'Scriptural Interpretation', in John Anthony McGuckin (ed.), *The Westminster Handbook to Origen* (Louisville, Ken.: Westminster John Knox Press, 2004), 193–7.

O'Leary, Joseph S., 'Logos', in John Anthony McGuckin (ed.), *The Westminster Handbook to Origen* (Louisville, Ken.: Westminster John Knox Press, 2004), 142–5.

Orlov, Andrei A., *The Enoch-Metatron Tradition*, Texts and Studies in Ancient Judaism, 107 (Tübingen: Mohr Siebeck, 2005).

Orlov, Andrei A., 'God's Face in the Enochic Tradition', in April D. DeConick (ed.), *Paradise Now: Essays on Early Jewish and Christian Mysticism* (Atlanta: Society of Biblical Literature, 2006), 179–93.

Orlov, Andrei A., 'The Sacerdotal Traditions of 2 Enoch and the Date of the Text', in Andrei A. Orlov and Gabriele Boccaccini (eds), *New Perspectives on 2 Enoch: No Longer Slavonic Only*, Studia Judaeoslavica, 4 (Leiden: Brill, 2012), 103-16.

Orlov, Andrei A., and Gabriele Boccaccini (eds), *New Perspectives on 2 Enoch: No Longer Slavonic Only*, Studia Judaeoslavica, 4 (Leiden: Brill, 2012).

Pagels, Elaine H., 'Conflicting Versions of Valentinian Eschatology: Irenaeus' Treatise vs. the Excerpts from Theodotus', *Harvard Theological Review*, 67: 1 (1974), 35-53.

Parvis, Sara, 'Christology in the Early Arian Controversy: The Exegetical War', in Andrew T. Lincoln and Angus Paddison (eds), *Christology and Scripture: Interdisciplinary Perspectives*, Library of New Testament Studies, 348 (London: T&T Clark, 2007), 120-37.

Parys, Michel J. van, 'Exégèse et théologie trinitaire: Prov. 8:22 chez les Pères Cappadociens', *Irénikon*, 43 (1970), 362-79.

Parys, Michel J. van, 'Exégèse et théologie dans les livres contre Eunome de Grégoire de Nysse: Textes scripturaires controversés et élaboration théologique', in Marguerite Harl (ed.), *Écriture et culture philosophique dans la pensée de Grégoire de Nysse* (Leiden: Brill, 1971), 169-96.

Pearson, Birger A., *Ancient Gnosticism: Traditions and Literature* (Minneapolis: Fortress, 2007).

Plested, Marcus, *The Macarian Legacy: The Place of Macarius-Symeon in the Eastern Christian Tradition* (Oxford: Oxford University Press, 2004).

Propp, William H. C., *Exodus 1-18*, Anchor Bible, 2 (New York: Doubleday, 1999).

Rapp, Claudia, 'The Elite Status of Bishops in Late Antiquity in Ecclesiastical, Spiritual, and Social Contexts', *Arethusa*, 33: 3 (2000), 379-99.

Reichman, Ronen, 'The Tosefta and Its Value for Historical Research: Questioning the Historical Reliability of Case Stories', in Martin Goodman and Philip Alexander (eds), *Rabbinic Texts and the History of Late-Roman Palestine*, Proceedings of the British Academy, 165 (Oxford: Oxford University Press, 2010), 117-27.

Rooke, Deborah W., 'The Day of Atonement as a Ritual of Validation for the High Priest', in John Day (ed.), *Temple and Worship in Biblical Israel: Proceedings of the Oxford Old Testament Seminar* (London: T&T Clark, 2007), 342-64.

Rowland, Christopher, 'Apocalyptic Literature', in D. A. Carson and H. G. M. Williamson (eds), *It Is Written: Scripture Citing Scripture: Essays in Honour of Barnabas Lindars* (Cambridge: Cambridge University Press, 1988), 170-89.

Rowland, Christopher, 'The Temple in the New Testament', in John Day (ed.), *Temple and Worship in Biblical Israel: Proceedings of the Oxford Old Testament Seminar* (London: T&T Clark, 2007), 469-83.

Rowland, Christopher, and Christopher R. A. Morray-Jones, *The Mystery of God: Early Jewish Mysticism and the New Testament*, CRINT, 12 (Leiden: Brill, 2009).

Runia, David T., *Philo in Early Christian Literature: A Survey*, CRINT, 3:3 (Assen: Van Gorcum, 1993).

Runia, David T., 'Clement of Alexandria and the Philonic Doctrine of the Divine Power(s)', *Vigiliae christianae*, 58: 3 (2004), 256-76. http://www.jstor.org/stable/1584621.

Rusch, William G., 'Church', in John Anthony McGuckin (ed.), *The Westminster Handbook to Origen* (Louisville, Ken.: Westminster John Knox Press, 2004), 78-80.

Sagnard, F., *Clément d'Alexandrie: Extraits de Théodote*, SC, 23 (Paris: Cerf, 1948).

Sandmel, Samuel, 'Parallelomania', *Journal of Biblical Literature*, 81: 1 (1962), 1–13. http://www.jstor.org/stable/3264821.
Sarna, Nahum M., *The JPS Torah Commentary: Exodus* (Philadelphia: Jewish Publication Society, 1991).
Sarna, Nahum M., *Exploring Exodus: The Origins of Biblical Israel* (New York: Schocken, 1996).
Schäfer, Peter, 'The Aim and Purpose of Early Jewish Mysticism', in *Hekhalot-Studien* (Tübingen: Mohr Siebeck, 1988), 277–95.
Schäfer, Peter, 'Tradition and Redaction in Hekhalot Literature', in *Hekhalot-Studien* (Tübingen: Mohr Siebeck, 1988), 8–16.
Schäfer, Peter, *The Hidden and Manifest God: Some Major Themes in Early Jewish Mysticism*, trans. Aubrey Pomerance (Albany: State University of New York Press, 1992).
Schäfer, Peter, 'Merkavah Mysticism and Magic', in Peter Schäfer and Joseph Dan (eds), *Gershom Scholem's Major Trends in Jewish Mysticism 50 Years After: Proceedings of the Sixth International Conference on the History of Jewish Mysticism* (Tübingen: Mohr Siebeck, 1993), 59–78.
Schäfer, Peter, 'From Cosmology to Theology: The Rabbinic Appropriation of Apocalyptic Cosmology', in Rachel Elior and Peter Schäfer (eds), *Creation and Re-Creation in Jewish Thought: Festschrift in Honor of Joseph Dan on the Occasion of his Seventieth Birthday* (Tübingen: Mohr Siebeck, 2005), 39–58.
Schäfer, Peter, *The Origins of Jewish Mysticism* (Tübingen: Mohr Siebeck, 2009).
Schiffman, Lawrence H., 'Community without Temple: The Qumran Community's Withdrawal from the Jerusalem Temple', in Beate Ego, Armin Lange, and Peter Pilhofer (eds), *Gemeinde ohne Tempel, Community without Temple: Zur Substituierung und Transformation des Jerusalemer Tempels und seines Kults im Alten Testament, antiken Judentum und frühen Christentum* (Tübingen: Mohr Siebeck, 1999), 267–84.
Schiffman, Lawrence H., '2 Enoch and Halakhah', in Andrei A. Orlov and Gabriele Boccaccini (eds), *New Perspectives on 2 Enoch: No Longer Slavonic Only*, Studia Judaeoslavica, 4 (Leiden: Brill, 2012), 221–8.
Schoedel, William R., 'Enclosing, not Enclosed: The Early Christian Doctrine of God', in William R. Schoedel and Robert L. Wilken (eds), *Early Christian Literature and the Classical Intellectual Tradition: In Honorem Robert M. Grant* (Paris: Beauchesne, 1979), 75–86.
Scholem, Gershom G., *Jewish Gnosticism, Merkabah Mysticism, and Talmudic Tradition* (New York: Jewish Theological Seminary of America, 1960).
Scholem, Gershom G., *Major Trends in Jewish Mysticism*, 3rd edn (New York: Schoken Books, 1961).
Segal, Alan F., *Two Powers in Heaven: Early Rabbinic Reports about Christianity and Gnosticism*, Studies in Judaism in Late Antiquity, 25 (Leiden: Brill, 1977).
Segal, Alan F., 'Heavenly Ascent in Hellenistic Judaism, Early Christianity and their Environment', in Wolfgang Haase (ed.), *Aufstieg und Niedergang der römischen Welt: Geschichte und Kultur Roms im Spiegel der neueren Forschung. 2. Principat. 23.2* (Berlin: Walter de Gruyter, 1980), 1333–94.
Silvas, Anna M., *Gregory of Nyssa: The Letters: Introduction, Translation and Commentary*, Supplements to Vigiliae christianae, 83 (Leiden: Brill, 2007).

Simonetti, Manlio, 'Exegesis', in Lucas Francisco Mateo-Seco and Giulio Maspero (eds), *The Brill Dictionary of Gregory of Nyssa*, Supplements to Vigiliae christianae, 99 (Leiden: Brill, 2010), 331–8.

Sommer, Benjamin D., *The Bodies of God and the World of Ancient Israel* (Cambridge: Cambridge University Press, 2009).

Spinks, Bryan D., *The Sanctus in the Eucharistic Prayer* (Cambridge: Cambridge University Press, 1991).

Sterk, Andrea, 'On Basil, Moses, and the Model Bishop: The Cappadocian Legacy of Leadership', *Church History*, 67: 2 (1998), 227–53.

Sterling, Gregory E., David T. Runia, Maren R. Niehoff, and Annewies van den Hoek, 'Philo', in John J. Collins and Daniel C. Harlow (eds), *Early Judaism: A Comprehensive Overview* (Grand Rapids, Mich.: Eerdmans, 2012), 253–89.

Stewart, Columba, *'Working the Earth of the Heart': The Messalian Controversy in History, Texts, and Language to AD 431* (Oxford: Clarendon, 1991).

Stone, Michael E., 'Apocalyptic, Vision or Hallucination?', in *Selected Studies in Pseudepigrapha and Apocrypha with Special Reference to the Armenian Tradition*, Studia in Veteris Testamenti pseudepigrapha, 9 (Leiden: Brill, 1991), 419–28.

Stone, Michael E., 'Aramaic Levi Document and Greek Testament of Levi', in Shalom M. Paul, Robert A. Kraft, Lawrence H. Schiffman, and Weston W. Fields (eds), *Emanuel: Studies in Hebrew Bible, Septuagint and Dead Sea Scrolls in Honor of Emanuel Tov*, Supplements to Vetus Testamentum, 94 (Leiden: Brill, 2003), 429–37.

Stone, Michael E., 'A Reconsideration of Apocalyptic Visions', *Harvard Theological Review*, 96: 2 (2003), 167–80.

Strickert, Fred, 'Philo on the Cherubim', *Studia philonica*, 8 (1996), 40–57.

Stroumsa, G. G., 'Form(s) of God: Some Notes on Meṭaṭron and Christ: For Shlomo Pines', *Harvard Theological Review*, 76: 3 (1983), 269–88.

Stroumsa, G. G., 'To See or Not to See: On the Early History of the *Visio Beatifica*', in Peter Schäfer (ed.), *Wege mystischer Gotteserfahrung: Judentum, Christentum und Islam / Mystical approaches to God: Judaism, Christianity, and Islam*, Schriften des Historischen Kollegs Kolloquien, 65 (Munich: Oldenbourg, 2006), 67–80.

Swartz, Michael D., *Mystical Prayer in Ancient Judaism: An Analysis of Ma'aseh Merkavah* (Tübingen: Mohr Siebeck, 1992).

Swartz, Michael D., 'Mystical Texts', in Shmuel Safrai, Zeev Safrai, Joshua Schwartz, and Peter J. Tomson (eds), *The Literature of the Sages*, second part: *Midrash and Targum, Liturgy, Poetry, Mysticism, Contracts, Inscriptions, Ancient Science and the Languages of Rabbinic Literature*, CRINT, 2:3b (Assen: Royal Van Gorcum, 2006), 393–420.

Sweeney, Marvin A., 'Pardes Revisited Once Again: A Reassessment of the Rabbinic Legend concerning the Four Who Entered Pardes', in *Form and Intertextuality in Prophetic and Apocalyptic Literature*, Forschugen zum Alten Testament, 45 (Tübingen: Mohr Siebeck, 2005), 269–82.

Sweet, J. P. M., 'A House Not Made with Hands', in William Horbury (ed.), *Templum Amicitiae: Essays on the Second Temple presented to Ernst Bammel*, JSNTSup, 48 (Sheffield: Sheffield Academic Press, 1991), 368–90.

Taft, Robert, 'The Interpolation of the Sanctus into the Anaphora: When and Where? A Review of the Dossier', *Orientalia christiana periodica*, 57: 2 (1991), 281–308; 58: 1 (1992), 83–121.

Tov, Emanuel, 'The Septuagint', in Martin Jan Mulder and Harry Sysling (eds), *Mikra: Text, Translation, Reading and Interpretation of the Hebrew Bible in Ancient Judaism and Early Christianity*, CRINT, 2:1 (Assen: Van Gorcum, 1988), 161–88.

Trigg, Joseph W., 'Origen', in Robert Benedetto, et al. (eds), *The New SCM Dictionary of Church History, vol. 1: From the Early Church to 1700* (London: SCM, 2008), 479–80.

Tropper, Amram, 'The State of Mishnah Studies', in Martin Goodman and Philip Alexander (eds), *Rabbinic Texts and the History of Late-Roman Palestine*, Proceedings of the British Academy, 165 (Oxford: Oxford University Press, 2010), 91–115.

Tuschling, R. M. M., *Angels and Orthodoxy: A Study in their Development in Syria and Palestine from the Qumran Texts to Ephrem the Syrian*, Studies and Texts in Antiquity and Christianity, 40 (Tübingen: Mohr Siebeck, 2007).

Vaillant, A., *Le livre des secrets d'Hénoch: Texte slave et traduction française* (Paris: Institut d'études slaves, 1952).

Van Dam, Raymond, *Becoming Christian: The Conversion of Roman Cappadocia* (Philadelphia: University of Pennsylvania Press, 2003).

Van Dam, Raymond, *Families and Friends in Late Roman Cappadocia* (Philadelphia: University of Pennsylvania Press, 2003).

VanderKam, James C., '1 Enoch, Enochic Motifs, and Enoch in Early Christian Literature', in James C. VanderKam and William Adler (eds), *The Jewish Apocalyptic Heritage in Early Christianity*, CRINT, 3:4 (Assen: Van Gorcum, 1996), 33–101.

Wade, Martha Lynn, *Consistency of Translation Techniques in the Tabernacle Accounts of Exodus in the Old Greek*, Septuagint and Cognate Studies (Atlanta: Society of Biblical Literature, 2003).

Weinfeld, Moshe, 'כָּבוֹד', in G. Johannes Botterweck, Helmer Ringgren, and Heinz-Josef Fabry (eds), *Theological Dictionary of the Old Testament* (Grand Rapids, Mich.: Eerdmans, 1995), 7.22–38.

Wevers, John William, *Notes on the Greek Text of Exodus*, SBLSCS, 30 (Atlanta: Scholars Press, 1990).

Wevers, John William, *Text History of the Greek Exodus* (Göttingen: Vandenhoeck & Ruprecht, 1992).

Wilcox, Max, '"According to the Pattern (TBNYT)...": Exodus 25, 40 in the New Testament and Early Jewish Thought', *Revue de Qumran*, 13 (1988), 647–56.

Williams, Megan Hale, 'No More Clever Titles: Observations on Some Recent Studies of Jewish–Christian Relations in the Roman World', *Jewish Quarterly Review*, 99: 1 (2009), 37–55.

Williams, Rowan, *The Wound of Knowledge: Christian Spirituality from the New Testament to St. John of the Cross* (London: DLT, 1979).

Williamson, H. G. M., 'The Temple in the Books of Chronicles', in William Horbury (ed.), *Templum Amicitiae: Essays on the Second Temple presented to Ernst Bammel*, JSNTSup, 48 (Sheffield: Sheffield Academic Press, 1991), 15–31.

Wise, Michael O., '4QFlorilegium and the Temple of Adam', *Revue de Qumran*, 15: 57–8 (1991), 103–32.

Wolfson, Elliot R., '*Yeridah la-Merkavah*: Typology of Ecstasy and Enthronement in Ancient Jewish Mysticism', in R. A. Herrera (ed.), *Mystics of the Book: Themes, Topics, and Typologies* (New York: Peter Lang, 1993), 13–44.

Wolfson, Elliot R., 'Mysticism and the Poetic-Liturgical Compositions from Qumran: A Response to Bilhah Nitzan', *Jewish Quarterly Review*, 85: 1–2 (1994), 185–202. http://www.jstor.org/stable/1454961.

Wolfson, Elliot R., *Through a Speculum That Shines: Vision and Imagination in Medieval Jewish Mysticism* (Princeton: Princeton University Press, 1994).

Young, Frances M., 'The God of the Greeks and the Nature of Religious Language', in William R. Schoedel and Robert L. Wilken (eds), *Early Christian Literature and the Classical Intellectual Tradition: In Honorem Robert M. Grant* (Paris: Beauchesne, 1979), 45–74.

Young, Frances M., *Biblical Exegesis and the Formation of Christian Culture* (Cambridge: Cambridge University Press, 1997).

Young, Frances M., and Andrew Teal, *From Nicaea to Chalcedon: A Guide to the Literature and Its Background*, 2nd edn (London: SCM, 2010).

Zachhuber, Johannes, 'Christological Titles—Conceptually Applied? (CE II 294–358)', in Lenka Karfíková, Scot Douglass and Johannes Zachhuber (eds), *Gregory of Nyssa: Contra Eunomium II*, Supplements to Vigiliae christianae, 82 (Leiden: Brill, 2007), 257–78.

Index of sources

Hebrew Bible (MT) and Septuagint (LXX)
Genesis (Gen.)
    1 61, 80
    1:1 100, 102
    3:21 210
    5:24 50
    6:1–4 50
Exodus (Exod.) 15:17
    15:17 83–4, 89
    15:17–18 83
    19 61, 63
    19:9 63
    19:18 63
    19:24 63
    20 63
    20:18–19 63
    20:21 63–70, 80, 232
    24 27, 63
    24:10 63, 68
    24:12 38
    24:15–18 63
    25 228
    25–27 84, 156
    25–28 29, 39, 47, 91
    25:3–7 139
    25:4 45, 157
    25:5 157
    25:8 (LXX 25:7) 39
    25:8–9 2
    25:9 85, 87, 88
    25:10–22 30
    25:12–15 135
    25:18–22 136
    25:22 (LXX 25:21)30, 46, 105, 140, 143, 189
    25:23–30 30
    25:31–39 137
    25:31–40 30
    25:40 85, 88, 90
    26:1 30, 93, 139
    26:1–6 157
    26:4 157
    26:5 157
    26:7 30, 139, 157
    26:14 30, 139, 157
    26:15 155
    26:28 104
    26:29 155
    26:30 88
    26:31 30
    26:32 155
    26:33 188
    26:35 137
    26:36 94
    26:36–37 41
    26:37 155
    27:1–8 30
    27:9 157
    27:10–18 155
    27:16 41, 94
    27:17 155
    28 203, 212, 219, 220, 223
    28:1–4 3
    28:4 31, 203, 204, 207, 209, 212
    28:5 219
    28:8 212, 219
    28:9–10 3
    28:11 219
    28:13 209
    28:13–14 203
    28:14 209
    28:15 31
    28:16 210
    28:22–28 (LXX 28:22–25) 203
    28:25 209
    28:29–30 3
    28:30 (LXX 28:26) 31, 208
    28:31 (LXX 28:27) 31
    28:32 219
    28:33 206
    28:33–34 (LXX 28:29–30) 31, 206
    28:34 (LXX 28:30) 204
    28:35 31
    28:36 (LXX 28:32) 31
    28:37 (LXX 28:33) 31,203, 209
    28:39 (LXX 28:35) 94, 209, 212, 219
    28:40 (LXX 28:36) 209
    28:42 (LXX 28:38) 31
    29–31 27
    29:6 31, 209
    29:9 209
    29:18 172
    29:25 172
    29:41 172
    30:1–10 30
    30:17–21 30
    30:18 156
    31:1–5 89
    31:18 30
    33:13 69
    33:18 106

Index of sources

33:19–20 131
33:20 77
34:1 30
34:29–30 73
35–40 32, 100, 104
35:6 160
39:6 (LXX 36:13) 203
39:15–21 (LXX 36:22–29) 203
39:22 219
39:27 219
39:29 219
40:34 32, 34, 74, 100, 102, 103, 126

Leviticus (Lev.)
7:11–12 173
7:12 (LXX 7:2) 173
8:7 212
8:7–9 212
16 41, 119, 188, 191, 211, 220, 223
16:2–3 188
16:4 32
16:16 188
16:20 188
16:23 188
18 60
20 60
22:21 173
22:29 173
23:34 175
26:21 83

Numbers (Num.)
4 45, 160
4:20 151
7:9 143
17 162

Deuteronomy (Deut.)
5:21–4 77
12:11 131

2 Samuel
7:10–11a 84

1 Kings (1 Kgs)
6:3 94
6:20 94
6:23–28 189
6:29 93
6:29–35 150
8:6–7 189
8:10–11 102
8:12 189
8:13 84, 94
8:27 83, 158
8:39 84
8:43 84
8:49 84
19:12 29, 181

Isaiah (Isa.)
2:18 83

6 47, 111, 137, 143
6:1 77
6:2 41, 137
6:3 59, 180, 183, 184
11:1 141
11:1–3 144, 233
11:2–3 138, 152
14:14–15 114
16:12 83
46:6 83
53:9 143
66:1 83

Ezekiel (Ezek.)
1 32–3, 47, 61, 75, 80, 148, 225, 228
1:22 80
1:26–28 218
1:27–28 218
1:28 74, 199
3:12 59, 180, 184
3:12–13 181
9:2–3 218
9:11 218
10:2 218
10:6 218
10:7 218
10:9–17 148
10:20 33, 148
37:27 29
40–42 4
40–48 94
41:15–26 150
41:20 93
43:3 32

Hosea
14:3 172, 173

Zechariah (Zech.)
4:10 138, 141, 144

Psalms (Ps.)
11:4 84
12:7 (LXX 11:7) 160
18:3 (LXX 17:3) 117
18:11 33
18:12 (LXX 17:12) 65–6, 79, 80, 81, 194, 225
23:2 (LXX 22:2) 117
24 (LXX 23) 57, 226
36:10 (LXX 35:10) 117
39:12 (LXX 38:12) 206
42:9 185
43:3 29
68 61
80:2 33
84:2 29
91:11–12 (LXX 90:11–12) 143
99:1 33
104:2 218
107:22 (LXX 106:22) 173

116:15 200
116:17 (LXX 115:17) 173
118:27 (LXX 117:27) 175
132:9 (LXX 131:9) 212
141:2 (LXX 140:2) 173, 174
147:14 (LXX 147:3) 157
Proverbs (Prov.)
   3:19 100, 101
   8:22 99–102, 104, 171
   8:22–25 99
   8:24–26 102
   9:1 100, 101, 104, 155
Ecclesiastes (Eccl.)
   5:1 71
Song of Songs (Song)
   3:1–4 194
   3:2 6
   4:3 207
   4:13 207
   5:15 155
   6:1 66
   6:7 207
Daniel (Dan.)
   2:22 79
   7 75, 112, 176, 186, 218
   7:9 218
   7:13–14 111
   10:5 218
   10:13 111
   10:21 111
   12:1 111
   12:6–7 218
1 Chronicles (1 Chr.)
   28:11–19 85
   28:18 32, 94, 189
   28:19 85
2 Chronicles (2 Chr.)
   5:1–4 107
   6:30 84
   6:33 84
   6:39 84
Wisdom (Wis.)
   1:7 100, 102
   9:8 84, 56
   9:15 107
   18:24 220
Sirach (Sir.)
   24:8–10 101
   24:10 100

Ben Sira
   3:21-2 80
   49:8 32

<u>New Testament</u>
Matthew (Matt.)
   2:11 172
   4:9 172
   5:14 155
   9:12 117
   18:10 138
   18:26 172
   19:16–22 126
   27:51 126
Mark
   2:17 117
   14:58 82
   14:62 111
   15:38 126
Luke
   2:37 173, 174
   5:31 117
   23:45 126
John
   1 127
   1:1–18 101
   1:1 103
   1:3 100, 101
   1:14 99, 100, 101, 104, 107, 138, 239
   1:14–16 103
   1:16 100, 103, 126
   1:18 64, 103, 138
   2:18–21 159
   2:19–21 90, 107
   2:21 85, 158
   3:14–15 98
   4:13–14 117
   5:35 155
   6:35 117
   10:7 117
   10:9 117
   10:11 117
   12:41 111, 137
   14:6 117
   14:23 117
   15:1 117
   20:21 103
Acts
   2:41 156
   7:44–49 86
   8:27–39 156
   10:25 172
   28:25–27 137
Romans (Rom.)
   3:25 33, 138, 143, 144, 233
   12:1 33, 177, 205
   12:4–5 33, 154
1 Corinthians (1 Cor.)
   1:24 33
   2:9 192
   2:10 33, 97, 197
   3:16 154

4:11 33, 207
7:34 161
9:13–14 33, 207
9:18 33, 207
9:25 209
9:26–27 158
9:27 33, 161
10:4 117
12:12–13 33, 154
12:28 33, 155
14:2 33, 97
14:25 172
15:28 44
15:58 33, 155
2 Corinthians (2 Cor.)
  2:15 172
  3:13 126
  5:1 82, 85
  6:7 33, 209
  6:16 154
  12:2 146
  12:2–5 33, 98
  12:3–4 33
Galatians (Gal.)
  2:9 33, 155, 156, 160, 161
Ephesians (Eph.)
  1:4 145
  1:21 136
  1:22–23 33, 154. 158
  2:19–22 154, 158
  4:12 158
  5:2 33, 172
  6:13–17 220
Philippians (Phil.)
  2:5–8 115
  2:7 115
  2:9 191
  2:10 33
  2:10–11 171
  2:15 33, 155
  3:13 115, 173
  4:18 33, 172
Colossians (Col.)
  1 127
  1:15–18 171
  1:15–20 34, 99, 101, 239
  1:16 33, 34, 100, 102,136, 144, 145, 152, 225, 227, 233
  1:16–19 104
  1:17 33, 100, 101, 102
  1:19 34, 100, 103
  1:24 99
  2:9 33, 34, 100, 103, 239
  2:11 82
  3:12 212
1 Thessalonians (1 Thess.)
  4:17 33, 44, 205
1 Timothy (1 Tim.)
  1:19 33, 206
  2:8 173
  3:15 33, 155, 156
2 Timothy (2 Tim.)
  4:8 209
Hebrews (Heb.)
  1:3 138
  1:14 135,139, 143, 144
  6:19 126
  8:5 86
  9:3 126
  9:5 138
  9:11 3, 82
  9:12 179
  9:24 82, 85
  9:26 85
  10:20 33, 98, 126
  12:11 33, 207
  12:22–23 145
  13:15 33, 172, 173, 187
James (Jas.)
  1:12 209
1 Peter (1 Pet.)
  2:5 158
  2:22 143
  5:4 209
Jude
  1:14–5 50
Revelation (Rev.)
  1:10 236
  1:12–18 111
  2:10 209
  3:5 218
  3:11 209
  4:2–4 218
  4:4 209, 218
  4:5 138, 141, 144
  4:6–11 136
  4:8 173, 180, 183
  4:11 180
  5:6 138, 141, 144
  5:6–14 111
  5:8 173, 178
  5:14 172
  6:9 178
  6:11 218
  7:9 218
  7:11 172
  7:13–14 218
  8:3 178
  8:3b 178
  8:3–4 178
  8:5 178
  9:13 178

11:16 172
14:18 178
16:7 178
19:4 172
19:10 172
19:11–16 111
22:8 172

Dead Sea Scrolls
1 Enoch
 4QEn^c 1 vii 2 218
Pseudo-Ezekiel
 4Q385 4 5–6 32
4QFlorilegium (4Q174)
 4Q174 1 i, 21 2–3 84
 4Q174 1 i 6–7 167
Songs of the Sabbath Sacrifice
 4Q400–407 50
 4Q400 1 i 2 51
 4Q400 1 i 13 95
 4Q400 1 i 15–16 179
 4Q400 1 i 19 51
 4Q400 1 i 19–20 176
 4Q400 1 i 20 51
 4Q403 1 i 41 93, 94, 95, 149
 4Q403 1 i 41–44 150
 4Q403 1 ii 11 95
 4Q403 1 ii 13 94
 4Q403 1 ii 13–15 149
 4Q404 5 5 95
 4Q405 6 2 95
 4Q405 6 2–5 150
 4Q405 7 7 95
 4Q405 14–15 i 4 94, 95
 4Q405 14–15 i 5–7 150
 4Q405 14–15 i 6 94
 4Q405 14–15 i 7 95
 4Q405 15–16 ii 5 95
 4Q405 20–22 ii 3 95
 4Q405 20–22 ii 7–8 181
 4Q405 20–22 ii 7–10 149
 4Q405 20–22 ii 8 94, 95
 4Q405 20–22 ii 10–11 199, 219
 4Q405 20–22 ii 12–13 181
 4Q405 23 i 3 95
 4Q405 23 i 7 95
 4Q405 23 ii 7–10 219
 11Q17 50
 11Q17 6–8 5 150
 11Q17 21–22 4–5 178
Mas1k 50

Hellenistic Jewish Authors
Josephus
Jewish Antiquities (A.J.)
 3.102–203 2

3.165 203
3.170 204
3.179–187 38
3.180 220
3.183 208
3.183–187 211
18.257–260 36
Jewish War (B.J.)
 5.219 189

Philo
Allegorical Interpretation (Leg.)
 1.44 106
 3.96 89, 100, 105
 3.102 88
On Abraham (Abr.)
 48 37
 57 67
 58 37
On Dreams (Somn.)
 1.75 100, 105
 1.125 89
 1.230 117
On Drunkenness (Ebr.)
 134 139
On Flight and Finding (Fug.)
 100–101 91, 100, 104, 140
 101 140
 108 211
 165 67
On Giants (Gig.)
 54 37, 67
On God (Deo.)
 4–9 140
On Moses (Mos.)
 1.158 67
 2.71–135 38
 2.74 38, 90
 2.76 90, 100
 2.81 139
 2.81–108 100
 2.82 191
 2.87 41, 191
 2.88 38, 208
 2.96 38
 2.97 140
 2.97–100 140
 2.98 140
 2.99 38, 140
 2.101–108 139
 2.102 38, 141
 2.102–103 144
 2.109–135 203
 2.112 208
 2.117–135 210
 2.118 204

2.119 204, 206
2.127 104, 210
2.128 213
2.130 214
2.135 211
On Planting (*Plant.*)
  48 89
  50 89
On the Change of Names (*Mut.*)
  7 67
  7–10 67
On the Cherubim (*Cher.*)
  21–29 140
  27–28 140
On the Confusion of Tongues (*Conf.*)
On the Creation of the World (*Opif.*)
  16 89, 90, 100
  20 100, 105, 147
  23 105
  25 100, 105
  36 100, 105, 147
  71 67
On the Embassy to Gaius (*Legatio ad Gaium*) 36
On the Migration of Abraham (*Migr.*)
  4 100, 105
  6 105
  102 211
On the Posterity of Cain (*Post.*)
  14 67, 191
  14–16 67, 68, 69
  15 67
  173 37
On the Preliminary Studies (*Congr.*)
  116 100, 105
On the Special Laws (*Spec.*)
  1.66 88, 174
  1.84 210, 220
  1.84–97 210
  1.207 6, 37
  3.1–3 37
Questions on Exodus (*QE*)
  1.57 140
  2.40 38
  2.51 39
  2.51–124 39
  2.52 90, 100
  2.53–55 39
  2.62–68 140
  2.67 141
  2.68 91, 100, 104, 140, 142
  2.69 139
  2.82 90, 100
  2.83 139
  2.83–85 100

2.89 104
2.91 104
2.94 40, 139
2.108 211, 214
2.112 211
2.114 213
Who is the Heir? (*Her.*)
  166 140
  216 104, 140
  221 144
  225 104, 140, 144

Apostolic Fathers
Barnabas (*Barn*)
  12 98
  16 90
1 Clement
  34:6–7 184

Pseudepigrapha
Ascension of Isaiah (*Ascen. Isa.*)
  1–5 56
  2:4–4:4 56
  3:13 111
  6–11 56
  7–11 56
  7:17 111
  7:25 222
  8:18 111
  9:1–2 222
  9:5 111
  9:7–9 221
  9:36 111
  9:37 74, 75
  9:38 76
  10 115
  10:17–31 113

1 Enoch (*1 En.*)
  1:9 50
  9:1 111
  13:3–6 50
  14 47, 49–50, 75, 93, 176, 186, 199, 218, 232
  14:1 221
  14:2 221, 236
  14:4 221
  14:8 221
  14.11 93
  14.18–20 93
  14:20 74, 218
  14:23 176

2 Enoch (*2 En.*)
  1a:1 55
  1:4–9 221

Index of sources

21:1 180, 181
22:1 74, 76
22:6 55
22:8–10 177, 221
22:10 55
37:2 221
67:2 55
69:15 177
70:26 177
71:19 177

Testament of Levi (T. Levi)
2:5–5:2 53
3:4 48, 74
3:4–6 53
3:5–6 177
3:6 177
4:4 110
5:1 111
5:1–2 53
5:2 177
8 177
8:1–10 53
8:1–19 53
8:2 218
8:2–10 220
18:6–7 110

Rabbinic Literature
Mishnah
m. Avot
 1:13 129
m. Ḥagigah
 2:1 60, 80, 200
m. Yoma
 3:8 130
 6:2 130

Tosephta
t. Berakhot
 1:9 183
t. Ḥagigah
 2:3–4 61

Palestinian Talmud (Yerushalmi)
y. Ḥagigah
 2:1 fol. 77b 61

Babylonian Talmud (Bavli)
b. Ḥagigah
 11b–13a 185
 11b–16a 48, 59–62, 202
 12b 79, 81, 111, 179, 185
 12b–13a 114
 13a 62, 80, 114, 201
 14b 60, 61, 62

 14b–15b 199
 15a 61, 112, 115
 15b 61
b. Menaḥot 110a 111
b. Zevaḥim 62a 111

Mekhilta
Shirata 10.24–28 84

Hekhalot Literature
3 Enoch (3 En.)
 1:1 (§1) 59
 1:11–12 (§2) 184
 5:3 (§7) 75
 6:1 (§9) 59
 12:1–5 (§15) 219
 9:2 (§12) 222
 9:2–4 (§12) 59
 10:1–2 (§13) 59
 15:1 (§19) 222
 15B:1 111
 16 (§20) 59, 112
 16:3 (§20) 59
 18:22 (§27) 221
 22B:5–6 78
 38:1 (§56) 180
 45:1 (§64) 78
Hekhalot Rabbati
 §94 149
 §102 77, 79, 222
 §105 220
 §159 74, 113
 §161 148
 §163 185
 §169 76
 §187 182
 §204–5 128
 §258 113
Hekhalot Zutarti
 §336–7 130
 §349 95
 §350 77
 §352 78
 §360 129
Ma'aseh Merkavah
 §551 180
 §552 129
 §588 131
 §590 130
 §591 77
Material on Metatron
 §390 111, 130

Philosophical Greek Literature
Chaldean Oracles
 Fr. 150 125

Iamblichus: *On the Mysteries*
    7.4 125

Plato
Cratylus
    390DE 120, 124
    391DE 120, 124
Phaedrus (*Phaedr.*)
    246BC 6
    246C 205
Timaeus
    28C 118
    28–29 88, 89

Gregory of Nyssa
Against Eunomius 1 (*Eun.* 1)
    1.55–56 (GNO 1.41) 195
    1.99 (GNO 1.55–56) 215
    1.298–305 (GNO 1.114–17) 99
    1.301–302 (GNO 1.115.25–116.1) 101
    1.306–313 (GNO 1.117–119) 136
    1.307 136
    1.313 136
    1.683 (GNO 1.222) 146
Against Eunomius 2 (*Eun.* 2)
    2.12 (GNO 1.230) 71
    2.93 (GNO 1.254) 71, 81
    2.105 (GNO 1.257) 71
    2.145 (GNO 1.267) 124
    2.294 (GNO 1.313) 117
    2. 300 (GNO 1.314) 117
    2.304 (GNO 1.315) 123
    2.347–349 (GNO 1.327) 117
    2.363 (GNO 1.332)) 124
    2.403–404 (GNO 1.344) 124
    2.605 (GNO 1.403.3) 26
Against Eunomius 3 (*Eun.* 3)
    3,1 99
    3,1.21 (GNO 2.11.4–8) 99
    3,1.21–65 (GNO 2.10–27) 99
    3,1.44 (GNO 2.19.6–8) 101
    3,1.46–48 (GNO 2.19–20) 101
    3,1.49 (GNO 2.20–21) 103
    3,1.56 (GNO 2.23) 102
    3,1.127 (GNO 2.46) 117
    3,3.51 (GNO 2.126.5) 107
    3,5.9 (GNO 2.163) 126
    3,7.8 (GNO 2.217) 106
    3,8.7–9 (GNO 2.240–242) 117
    3,8.10 (GNO 2.242) 117
    3,9.13 (GNO 2.268) 126
    3,9.64 (GNO 2.288) 195
    3,10 (GNO 2.295.1–2) 205
Against the Macedonians (*Maced.*)
    GNO 3,1.110–111 171
    GNO 3,1.111.2–5 172

Against Those Who Defer Baptism (*Bapt.*)
    GNO 10,2.362.15–17 184
Funeral Oration on Meletius (*Melet.*)
    GNO 9.454 190
Letters (*Epist.*)
    3 24
    3.20 (GNO 8,2.25.12) 107
    10 (GNO 8,2.40) 23
    25 (GNO 8,2.79–83) 26
Life of Gregory the Wonderworker (*Thaum.*)
    GNO 10,1.19–20 198
Life of Macrina (*Macr.*)
    GNO 8,1.377.11–12 23
    GNO 8,1.378.2–5 23
    GNO 8,1.382.5–6 205
    GNO 8,1.382.20–383.5 205
    GNO 8,1. 387 147
    GNO 8,1.396 146–7
Life of Moses (*Vit. Moys.*)
    1.2 162
    1.5 115
    1.7 223
    1.11 29
    1.15 22, 27, 35, 161
    1.42 64
    1.43 64
    1.44 64
    1.45 64
    1.45–46 239
    1.46 65, 82, 190, 194
    1.47 87
    1.49 1, 64, 82, 87, 155
    1.49–50 87, 135
    1.50 87
    1.51 82, 87, 93
    1.51–55 203
    1.52 203, 208
    1.53 203, 204, 209
    1.54 204, 207
    1.55 162, 203
    1.56 87, 93, 198, 232
    1.58 87, 236
    1.67–68 98
    2.22 210
    2.45 135
    2.46 135
    2.48–49 163
    2.78 173
    2.84 173
    2.109 196
    2.110 196
    2.130 163
    2.150 173
    2.153 173
    2.160 163, 233
    2.162 63, 64

Index of sources

2.162– 164 2
2.162–169 63–81
2.163 2, 4, 9, 64, 65, 73, 81, 196
2.164 4, 64, 65, 190
2.165 65
2.166 206
2.167 47, 65, 72, 82, 190
2.168 82
2.169 65, 82
2.170 82, 82, 87, 97, 155
2.170–172 82–96, 135
2.170–201 2
2.171 138, 156
2.172 65, 126,156, 157
2.173 1, 33, 82, 87, 97, 98, 154
2.173–179 97–115
2.174 33, 82, 87, 97, 98, 102, 105, 107, 108, 144
2.175 33, 100, 101, 102, 105, 107, 109
2.176 116, 125, 232
2.176–177 116–33
2.177 33, 100, 102, 103, 105, 117, 125, 127, 144, 147
2.178 4, 33, 98, 126, 134, 154, 190, 208
2.178–183 134–53
2.179 33, 98, 100, 102, 134, 136, 176
2.180 4, 65,135, 137, 232
2.181 138, 139, 157, 173
2.182 7, 33, 138, 171–87
2.183 139
2.184 33, 87, 154, 155, 156
2.184–187 154–70
2.184–188 173
2.185 7, 33, 156, 171–87, 205
2.186 157
2.187 33, 157, 158, 215
2.188 65, 87, 188–202, 223
2.189 203, 204, 207, 208, 209, 216, 223
2.189–201 203–24
2.190 203, 214
2.191 33, 35, 204, 205, 206, 210, 216
2.192 33, 162, 204, 206, 234
2.193 33, 207, 215
2.194 33, 204, 207, 215
2.195 207
2.196 208, 214
2.197 203, 208, 209
2.198 33, 162, 209
2.199 208, 209, 213
2.200 203, 209, 214
2.201 119, 203, 209, 210
2.229 65, 82, 173
2.236 106
2.238 106
2.245 82
2.271–277 98

2.288 216
2.312 87
2.315 87, 194
2.316 162
2.319 162
On Basil (*Bas.*)
  GNO 10,1.122.9 205
  GNO 10,1.129 198
  GNO 10,1.131.13–18 6
On Infants' Early Deaths (*Infant.*)
  GNO 3,2.78–79 146
On Perfection (*Perf.*)
  GNO 8,1.212 117
On the Ascension of Christ (*Ascens.*)
  GNO 9.326 57
On the Beatitudes (*Beat.*)
  1 (GNO 7,2.89.2–3) 205
  1 (GNO 7,2.89.4–5) 205
  2 (GNO 7,2.93.2–3) 205
  6 (GNO 7,2.141.25–27) 136
  7 (GNO 7,2.149) 189
On the Christian Mode of Life (*Inst.*)
  GNO 8,1.44 165
  GNO 8,1.78.4–5 206
On the Lord's Prayer (*Or. dom.*)
  3 (GNO 7,2.31.9) 204
  3 (GNO 7,2.31.11) 204, 206
  3 (GNO 7,2.31.24) 204
  3 (GNO 7,2.32) 190
  3 (GNO 7,2.32.1) 204
  3 (GNO 7,2. 32.7–8) 204, 206
  3 (GNO 7,2.32.13–14) 204
  3 (GNO 7,2.32.14) 206
  3 (GNO 7,2.33) 190
  4 (GNO 7,2.49.9–10) 205
On the Nativity of Christ (*Diem nat.*)
  GNO 10,2.236 175
  GNO 10,2.237–238 175–6
On the Song of Songs (*Cant.*)
  1 (GNO 6.15.13–15) 14
  1 (GNO 6.25.6–10) 190
  1 (GNO 6.26.11–12) 189
  6 (GNO 6.181.4–8) 66
  6 (GNO 6.181.7–8) 194
  6 (GNO 6.181.10–16) 195
  6 (GNO 6.182–183) 195
  6 (GNO 6.182.3–11) 6
  7 (GNO 6 .229–231) 207
  9 (GNO 6.282–283) 207
  11 (GNO 6.322.9–12) 71
  11 (GNO 6.323.2–9) 2
  11 (GNO 6.324.10–11) 73
  12 (GNO 6.355.11–14) 73
  14 (GNO 6.415.15–19) 156
  14 (GNO 6.415.21–22) 156
  14 (GNO 6. 416.13–15) 156

14 (GNO 6.416.18) 156
14 (GNO 6.417.3–7) 156
14 (GNO 6.419.9–10) 156
14 (GNO 6.419.12–13) 156
15 (GNO 6.455–456) 207
On the Soul and Resurrection (An. et res.)
  PG 46.108A 206
  PG 46.132B 175
  PG 46.133C 201
On the Titles of the Psalms (Inscr.)
  1.9 (GNO 5.66) 175
  2.6 (GNO 5.86) 175
  2.6 (GNO 5.86–87) 172
  2.6 (GNO 5.87.10) 107
On Those Who Have Died (Mort.)
  GNO 9.62.23–24 205
On Virginity (Virg.)
  4 (GNO 8,1.270.25, 271.2) 107
  16 (GNO 8,1.313) 206
  18 (GNO 8,1.322.10–11) 205
  23 (GNO 8,1.337–338) 164
Refutation of the Confession of Faith of Eunomius (Ref. Eun.)
  110 (GNO 2.538.13–15) 100
  110–113 (GNO 2.358–360) 99
  111 (GNO 2.358.23–26) 100
  124 (GNO 2.365) 117
  191–192 (GNO 2.393) 103
  193 (GNO 2.394) 137
  196 (GNO 2.395) 136
Reply to the Teachings of Apollinarius (Antirrh.)
  GNO 3,1.151.16–20 108
  GNO 3,1.156.14–18 108
To Ablabius: On Not Three Gods (Abl.)
  GNO 3,1.42–43 123
  GNO 3,1.43 116
To Simplicius (Simpl.)
  GNO 3,1.62 117
To Call Oneself a Christian (Prof.)
  GNO 8,1.138.25 216, 223
  GNO 8,1.140.11–14 216
To Eustathius, on the Holy Trinity and the Godhead of the Holy Spirit (Eust.)
  GNO 3,1.12.21–23 172
  GNO 3,1.13 138
To the Greeks from Common Notions (Graec.)
  GNO 3,1.21 137
  GNO 3,1.25.8–10 171
To Theophilus, Against the Apollinarians (Theoph.)
  3,1.123–124 135–6

Patristic Writings
Apostolic Constitutions (Apos. Con.)
  8.12.27 184

Basil: *Letters (Epist.)*
  204.6 44
  225 23

Clement of Alexandria
Canon of the Church or Against the Judaisers
  GCS 3.218–219 158–9
Excerpts from Theodotus (Exc.)
  10 141
  10–12 141
  27 41, 42, 192, 193, 212
  27.1–2 119
  27.2 212
  27.3 142, 192, 212
  27.5 192
  27.6 212
  42–65 42
  63.2 43
Miscellanies (Strom.)
  2.6.1 68
  5.32–40 40, 161, 212
  5.32.3 208
  5.33.2 141, 211
  5.33.3 41
  5.33.4 41
  5.33.5 40
  5.34.5 118, 132
  5.34.7 40, 119, 142, 191
  5.34.8–9 141
  5.35.1 98, 104
  5.35.1–2 141
  5.35.6–7 142
  5.36.3 142, 174
  5.36.4 142, 174
  5.38.2 104
  5.35.6–7 41
  5.36.1 40
  5.36.3 41
  5.36.4 41
  5.37.1 211
  5.37.3 211
  5.37.4 211
  5.37.5 211
  5.38.2 104, 208, 214
  5.38.6–7 119
  5.39.1 104
  5.39.2 211
  5.39.2–3 211
  5.39.3–40.1 192
  5.39.4 191, 236
  5.40.1 41, 192, 212
  5.40.3 192, 212
  5.71.5 69
  5.78.1 118
  5.81.5–6 118
  5.82.1–2 118

Index of sources

Cyril/John of Jerusalem: *Mystagogical Catecheses* (*Myst. Cat.*)
   5.6 184

Eunomius: *Apology*
   8 123

Eusebius
Ecclesiastical History (*Hist. eccl.*)
   5.10–11 40
   6.6 40
   6.30 44
   7.14 44
   7.28.1 44
Ecclesiastical Theology (*Eccl. theol.*)
   3.2 100

Gregory of Nazianzus: *Letters* (*Epist.*)
   11 23

Irenaeus: *Against Heresies* (*Haer.*)
   1.1.1 145
   1.5.2–3 43
   1.7.1 43
   1.7.5 43
   2.1.2 106

Jerome: *Letters* (*Epist.*)
   18A 7.1–2 137
   18B 1.4 136
   64 2
   84 144

John Chrysostom: *Homilies on Ephesians* (*Hom. Eph.*)
   14.4 184

Justin Martyr: *Dialogue with Trypho*
   91 98
   94 98
   112 98

Martyrdom of Perpetua and Felicitas
   12.2 184

Methodius: *Symposium* (*Symp.*)
   5.7–8 2, 98

Origen
Against Celsus
   1.6 119
   1.24 120
   2.64 121
   5.45 120
   5.54 226
   6.17 66
   6.18 137
   6.35 145
Commentary on John (*Comm. Jo.*)
   1.119 121
   2.126 121
   10.226 159
   10.228 159
Commentary on Romans (*Comm. Rom.*)
   3.8 46, 91
   3.8.3 143
   3.8.4 143
   3.8.5 46, 104, 143
   3.8.7 143
   3.8.8 46, 143
   7.11.3 45, 236
Commentary on Song of Songs (*Comm. Cant.*)
   2.8 145
First Principles (*Princ.*)
   1.3.4 46, 143
   4.3.14 46, 143
Fragment on 1 Thessalonians
   PG 14.1302C 45
Homilies on Exodus (*Hom. Exod.*)
   9 45, 160
   9.2 91
   9.3 45, 98, 160, 161, 212, 214, 215
   9.4 91, 160, 193, 212, 213
   10.3 90
   13 45, 160
   13.2 160
   13.3 208
   13.4–5 45, 160
   13.5 45, 160, 161
   13.7 213
Homilies on Isaiah (*Hom. Isa.*)
   1.2 143
   4.1 143
Homilies on Joshua (*Hom. Josh.*)
   17.1 91
Homilies on Leviticus (*Hom. Lev.*)
   6 46
   6.3.5 213
   6.3.6 214
   6.4.2 213
   6.4.3 213, 214
   6.5.2 212
   6.6.1 213
Homilies on Numbers (*Hom. Num.*)
   3.3 145
   5 45, 160
   5.3 98
   5.3.2 45, 160, 174
   5.3.3 143, 160
   10.3.4 91

Letter to Africanus (*Ep. Afr.*) 32
Proclus of Constantinople
Homily 6.17.9 108

Pseudo-Justin: *Exhortation to the Greeks*
29 88

Tertullian: *Prayer*
3.3 184

Theodoret of Cyrus: *Questions on Exodus*
(*Quaest. in Ex.*)
60 2

General Index

Abrams, Daniel 113 n111
Adler, William 50 n17, 226 n3
aduton 65, 126, 147, 189–90, 191, 193–4, 232
  see also holy of holies
Aetius of Antioch 24, 132
Aḥer (Elisha b. Avuyah) 59, 61, 62, 112, 199–200
akolouthia 28
Alexander, Philip 5, 13, 15, 18 n82, 33, 48, 50 n12, 51–2, 55, 58 n65, 75, 83 n12, 94 n86, 95 n101, 96 n103, 102, 112, 113 nn112, 116, 114 n118, 150–1, 152–3, 168–9, 177, 182–3, 199 n72, 218, 221
allegory 28, 35, 38–9, 97, 190
Allison, Dale 181
altar 30, 84, 94, 111, 171, 173, 175–6, 178, 179, 186
altar of incense 30, 45, 119, 160, 171, 173, 174, 178, 186, 212
anagogy 10, 35
Andersen, Francis 54–5, 76, 110 n86
Anderson, Gary 151
angelification 5, 13, 20, 52, 55, 113, 168–9, 205, 216–17, 223, 230–1, 234, 238, 240
angels 46, 48, 50, 53, 55, 56–7, 59, 61, 75, 76, 79, 113, 128, 134–53, 160, 166, 199
  angelic choral dance 172, 175
  angelic clothing 217–24, 231, 234
  angelic liturgy 5, 13, 51, 58, 130, 151, 171–3, 180–7, 227, 228, 229, 230, 234
  angelic priests 51, 88, 142, 168, 174, 176–9, 181–2, 186, 219, 237
  angelic temple 95, 111, 149–51, 152, 170, 225, 226–7, 232
  angelic world 6, 10, 92, 134, 142, 145–7, 192–3, 233
anthropology 89, 159–60, 193, 211
Apocalypse of Abraham 49
Apocalypse of Paul 49
apocalypses 5, 14, 19, 47, 55, 74, 93, 94, 114, 182, 183, 185, 187, 225, 226, 230, 235, 236–7
apokatastasis 44
Apollinarius of Laodicea 24, 25, 108
apophaticism 1, 11, 65, 69, 70, 80, 81, 132, 232, 235, 238
Apostolic Constitutions 184
Aqiva (rabbi) 58, 78, 129, 199–200, 228
Aquila (translator) 100 n21, 207 n38
Aramaic Levi Document 18, 52–3, 177

Arius 24, 99 n19
ark of the covenant 30–1, 33, 86, 166, 189
  in Clement 40–1, 142, 143, 174
  in Gregory of Nyssa 10, 65, 113, 135, 137, 190, 232
  in Origen 45, 46, 143, 160
  in Philo 38, 39, 139, 140
Arnaldez, Roger 38
Ascension of Isaiah 18–19, 47, 55–7, 94
  on Christ's descent 113, 115, 226
  on heavenly robes 221
  on seeing God 75–6
  trinitarian vision 111, 144 n63
ascent 1, 4–5, 8, 19, 37, 44–5, 47–8, 53, 55, 56, 58, 61, 68, 92, 112, 114, 115, 128, 129, 135–6, 146, 176–7, 192, 199, 202, 217, 223, 228, 232, 233, 236, 239
  bodily 113, 221
  as a community 182–3
  into darkness 1–2, 38, 64, 66, 238, 240
  of the gnostic 41, 192–3, 211–12
  to *pardes* 200
asceticism 25, 161, 164, 170, 215–16, 231
Asterius the Sophist 99 n19
Attridge, Harold 83 n9
Aubineau, Michel 22 n4

Balás, David 146
Balthasar, Hans Urs von 44, 146
baptism 156, 165
Barker, Margaret 20
Barmann, Bernard 13
Barr, James 88
Barrett, Charles 101 n25
3 Baruch 49
Basil of Caesarea 6, 22, 23–4, 25, 70, 162, 163, 164–5, 198, 206, 215, 216
Baumgarten, Joseph 178 n46
Bavli, *see* Talmud, Babylonian
Becker, Adam 8, 18 n82
Bede 2
bells (on high priestly robe) 31, 204, 206, 210, 211, 213
Ben Azzai 62, 199–200
Ben Zoma 62, 199–200
Bettiolo, Paolo 56
Boccaccini, Gabriele 53 n35
body of Christ 27, 85, 90, 93, 103 n35, 107–8, 126, 145, 152, 154, 158–9, 169, 227
Boersma, Hans 10–11, 35, 216–17, 223

Book of the Watchers, *see 1 Enoch*
Böttrich, Christfried 54 n43
Boustan, Ra'anan 95 n97, 150
Boyarin, Daniel 8 n33, 15, 18 n82, 111, 112, 115 n122
bread of the Presence (showbread) 30, 157, 165
breastpiece 31, 104, 203, 204, 208, 210, 211, 220, 223
breeches 31
Brooke, George 167-8, 169
Brown, Peter 19 n87
Brown, Raymond 107
burning bush 27, 64, 98

Caesarius 162
Cairo Genizah 18, 52, 57
Canaanite traditions 83, 218 n122
Canévet, Mariette 13 n66, 49
carrying-poles 135
Casey, Robert Pierce 42, 43
chariot, *see merkavah*
Chadwick, Henry 216
Charles, Robert 54, 178
Chavoutier, Lucien 137 n20
Chazon, Esther 182
cherubim 10, 29, 30, 33, 144, 148-9, 151, 189
  in Clement 40-1, 142-3, 174
  in Gregory 65, 81, 113, 135-7, 152, 201, 232, 239
  in heavenly ascent texts 93, 130, 180, 226
  in Origen 45-6, 104, 143, 160, 193
  in Philo 38-9, 140
Childs, Brevard 3
Christ 57, 67, 68, 69, 90, 104, 110-11, 115, 120-2, 137, 141
  as agent/pattern of creation 100, 102
  as fullness of God 100, 103-4, 127
  as high priest 3, 85, 179, 190, 191
  as tabernacle 9, 11, 34, 49, 87, 96, 98-99, 100, 104, 107-8, 109-10, 114, 127, 135, 227, 232, 233, 239
  as wisdom 99-101, 171
  see also body of Christ; incarnation; Jesus; *metadiastemic* intrusion; names; passion
Christology 24, 25, 40, 97-115, 117, 125, 145, 211, 233
church 3, 10, 27, 45, 85, 91, 98, 135, 145, 154-66, 169, 170, 173, 174, 176, 216, 227, 233
clasps 203, 207-8
Clement of Alexandria 39-42
  on the body of Christ 158-9
  on Christ 104
  on darkness 68-9
  on divine names 117-19
  on heavenly powers 141-3, 144
  on heavenly worship 174
  on the holy of holies 191-3, 201
  on priestly vestments 208, 211-12
Coakley, Sarah 11, 49
Collins, Adela Yarbro 94
contemplation 2, 6, 9, 35, 41, 48, 64, 66, 70, 71-2, 142-3, 147, 192, 198, 209, 212, 216, 230, 239
Conway-Jones, Ann 34 n41, 99 n17
colours (of the veil/curtains/ephod) 38, 208, 214, 215, 239
cosmology 38, 40, 55, 59, 89, 90, 93, 104, 107, 139, 140, 142, 145-6, 159-60, 168, 204-5, 208, 210-11, 213, 233, 235, 239
Council of Constantinople 24
Council of Nicaea 24
court(yard) of the tabernacle 30, 139, 155, 157, 161
coverings of the tabernacle 30, 139, 157, 161
Cross, Frank 188 n3
Crouzel, Henri 70
crown, *see* diadem
curtains of the tabernacle 30, 105, 157, 161, 208
Cyril/John of Jerusalem 184

Daley, Brian 25 n19, 108-9
Damascus Document (CD) 168, 227
Daniélou, Jean 2, 6, 9-10, 13, 22 n4, 23-4, 26, 27, 70, 71-3, 81, 92, 98, 107 n64, 124, 132, 134, 145-7, 162, 173 n14, 176, 190 n14, 193-4, 206, 234-5, 238
darkness 63-81, 189, 225, 228
  in Clement 68
  in Gregory 1-2, 9, 11, 27, 64-6, 70-4, 81, 147, 194-5, 232
  in Origen 66-7, 68
  in Philo 37-8, 67, 191
David (king) 4, 33, 85-6, 157, 158, 164, 190, 233
Davila, James 18, 113, 236
Day, John 189 n9
DeConick, April 19-20, 42, 48 nn6,8
Demiurge 43, 88
Denys the Areopagite 67
Deuteronomy 27, 77
devir (inner room) 48, 94, 95, 149, 150, 188-9
  see also holy of holies
diadem (or crown) 31, 59, 119, 129, 203, 209, 219, 220
dianoia 27, 35, 209
diastēma 109-10, 216-17, 224
Didymus the Blind 137 n20
Dillon, John 118 n13, 120
Dimant, Devorah 84 n20, 167 n82, 168, 169, 227 n5, 237 n23

Douglass, Scot 12, 109–10, 114, 126–7, 233
dreams 50, 235, 236, 239
Drobner, Hubertus 35 n2
Dunderberg, Ismo 42 n50, 43 n57

Elijah 135, 239
Elior, Rachel 128, 130 n79, 166–7, 179, 185
Emerton, John 218 n122
'enclosing, not enclosed' 100, 105–6
energies, divine 123, 136, 147
1 Enoch 47–8, 49–50, 111, 221, 226, 235, 236
   discontent with the temple 166
   on the divine garment 75, 199, 218
   heaven as a temple 3, 93, 94, 95, 232
   on heavenly priests 176, 186
2 Enoch 18, 47, 53–5, 110, 180, 181
   on the divine face 74, 76
   on the transformation of Enoch 177, 221
3 Enoch 48, 58–9, 111
   on Aḥer's ascent 61, 112
   on heavenly clothing 219, 221
   on the heavenly *Qedushah* 180, 184
   on Ishmael's ascent 78, 221
   on Metatron's transformation 222
ephod 31, 203, 207–8, 214, 220, 223
epinoiai 121, 122–4
eschatology 10, 20, 40, 43, 84, 164, 166, 167–9, 187, 205, 217
essence, divine 24, 70, 72–3, 81, 109, 113, 116–7, 123–5, 137, 146–7, 196–7, 229, 233, 235
Eucharist 3, 157, 165, 184, 187
Eunomius of Cyzicus 24, 26, 73, 81, 92, 106, 132, 164
   disregard for asceticism 215–16
   on names 122–5
   social status 195–6
   on 'unbegotten' 70–1, 116
Eusebius of Caesarea 40, 100 n21
Eusebius of Nicomedia 99 n19
Eustathius of Sebaste 164
Excerpts from Theodotus 36, 41, 42–3, 141
   on the high priest 119, 142, 192–3, 212
exegesis 11, 14–15, 28, 35, 44–5, 48, 61–2, 80, 200, 228, 230, 235, 238
Ezekiel (prophet) 4, 10, 23–3, 74, 135, 199, 201, 239

face (or countenance) of God 55, 74, 76, 78, 131, 137, 141, 193
faith 9, 14, 65, 72–3, 160, 162, 194–5, 196, 201, 206, 212, 220, 234, 240
Ferguson, Everett 9, 28, 98 n13, 101, 120 n25, 138, 157, 162, 164, 168, 204 n13, 206 n22, 207, 210
Festugière, André-Jean 15 n78

Fletcher-Louis, Crispin 52, 83 n12, 94, 168, 178, 183
flower-work on hem of priestly robe 31, 204, 206
Frankfurter, David 4 n15, 18–19, 55–6
Friedman, Richard 188 n3
fullness of divinity 34, 100, 103–4, 105, 109, 114, 125, 127, 136
furniture of the tabernacle/temple 36, 90, 104, 134–5, 144–5, 148, 151, 155, 159, 160, 193, 227, 233
   see also under individual items

Gabriel (archangel) 55, 111
garment, divine 75, 77, 78–9, 199, 217, 218, 220, 222, 229
Gärtner, Bertil 167 n81
Geljon, Albert 38, 39, 67, 68, 69, 205 n15, 213
girdle 31, 94, 111, 212
glory 32, 48, 51, 58, 59, 62, 63, 74–6, 78–9, 81, 102–3, 107, 110, 131, 182, 198, 199, 217–18, 221, 222, 223, 225, 229, 230–1
   see also Great Glory
gnōsis 9, 40, 191, 201, 212
gnostic Christian 40, 41, 47, 191–2, 193, 201, 211–12
Gnosticism 8, 17, 36, 40, 42, 106, 192
God, *see* energies; essence; face; garment; Great Glory; incomprehensibility; infinity; names; presence; unknowability
Gooding, David 155 n10
Goodman, Martin 15–17, 19, 178 n46
Graef, Hilda 204 n10
Great Glory 48, 50, 53, 56, 74, 75–6, 93, 111, 218
Greenfield, Jonas 55
Gregory of Nazianzus 22, 23, 163–4
Gregory Thaumaturgus 44, 163, 198
Gribomont, Jean 165
Grözinger, Karl 131–2
Gruenwald, Ithamar 76

Hagen, Joost 53
ḥakham (sage) 200–1
Hall, Robert 56
Halperin, David 14, 32, 58, 60, 61, 148, 181, 200, 201 n87, 218, 237
ḥaluq 78–9, 220, 222
hangings of the tabernacle courtyard 155, 157 n23
Hannah, Darrell 111, 143–4
Haran, Menahem 30, 188 nn2, 3, 212 n88
Harrison, Verna 9, 12, 13, 14, 73, 136 n14, 232 n2
ḥashmal 62, 75, 199, 200, 226
Ḥasidei Ashkenaz 57 n59

Hastings, Adrian 25
Hayward, Robert 88
hayyot (living/holy creatures) 32–3, 59, 79, 80, 114, 130, 136, 148, 177, 180, 181, 184
heavenly ascent, *see* ascent
heavenly clothing, *see* robes, heavenly
heavenly temple 5, 51–2, 83–5, 90–1, 94–5, 149–51, 152, 166, 168–9, 176, 178, 182, 218, 226–7, 236
Hebrews 3, 33, 82, 85, 86, 87, 90, 98, 111, 135, 143, 145, 172, 173, 179, 187, 207
Heine, Ronald 9–10, 13, 14, 26, 27, 72, 73, 97 n7, 97 n8, 156, 161, 162, 164, 197, 215, 235, 238
Hekhalot literature 3, 5, 13, 48, 57–9, 61, 62, 95, 111, 113, 114, 151–2, 166–7, 179, 181–2, 183, 199, 200, 229, 236, 237
  on the divine face 74
  on the divine garment 78–9, 220, 222
  on divine names 128–32, 133, 180
  on the living divine throne 149
  on the *Qedushah* 184–5
  on seeing God 76–9
Hekhalot Rabbati 58, 74, 76, 77–8, 113, 128, 148, 149, 182, 185, 220, 222
Hekhalot Zutarti 57, 58, 61, 62, 77, 78, 95, 129, 130, 151
heresiology 18, 36, 115
heuristic comparison 5–6, 7–9, 49, 167 n81, 225–6, 231, 238
high priest 31, 41, 42, 90, 111, 118–19, 189, 191–2, 193, 211–12, 223
Himmelfarb, Martha 4 nn14, 16, 14, 47–8, 50, 83 n12, 93, 94, 166, 176, 177, 218, 235
Hippolytus 36
historia 27, 35, 203, 208
Hoek, Annewies van den 39, 40, 89, 142 n49, 191
Hogeterp, Albert 167 n81
hoi polloi 190, 195, 202, 228, 234, 239
Holder, Arthur 2 n7
Hollander, Harm 52, 53 n30
holy of holies 12, 30, 40, 43, 48, 50, 65, 91, 105, 110, 119, 127, 139–40, 166, 176, 182, 188–202, 218, 223, 228, 232, 234
Holy Spirit 46, 56, 103 n37, 111, 136, 137–8, 143, 157, 165, 196–7
Horbury, William 83–4
Horst, Pieter van der 82 n5
Hurowitz, Victor 86 n28, 188–9
hypostases 24, 137

Iamblichus 124–5, 132
incarnation 40, 44, 98, 101, 104, 107, 109–10, 114, 115, 126–7, 158–9, 175, 193, 233, 239

incomprehensibility, divine 2, 14, 64–5, 67–8, 71, 72, 81, 132, 194–7, 229, 232, 233, 234
infinity, divine 14, 106–7, 201, 233
Irenaeus 36, 42–3, 106, 145 n68
Isaiah (prophet) 3, 4, 10, 56–7, 75, 77, 111, 148, 201, 221–2, 239
Ishmael (rabbi) 57–9, 78, 221, 222

James (apostle) 155
Jerome 2, 26, 50, 53, 136, 137 n17, 144, 226
Jerusalem 24, 91
  heavenly 90–1, 111, 145, 159, 179
  temple of 20, 50, 51, 86, 90–1, 159, 166, 170, 177, 178 n46, 227, 235, 237
Jesus 25, 33, 82, 85, 107, 109, 111, 119, 121, 143, 158–9
Jewish–Christian boundaries 15–19
John (apostle) 4, 101, 155, 164, 201, 233
John the Baptist 155, 156
John Chrysostom 184, 197
Jonge, Marinus de 18, 52, 53 nn29, 30
Josephus 2, 36 n7, 38, 94, 132, 189 n9, 203 n4, 204, 205 n15, 208 n40, 211, 220
Joyce, Paul 4 n16, 75 n86
Justin Martyr 36

katapetasma 30, 126, 190
  see also veil
Katz, Steven 238
Kee, Howard Clark 52
Klawans, Jonathan 3 n12
Knibb, Michael 56
Knight, Jonathan 56, 76
Knohl, Israel 181, 189
Koester, Craig 85, 107, 139–40
Kohn, Risa Levitt 167 n80
Kopecek, Thomas 196 n54
kosmos noētos 6, 10, 40–1, 92, 100, 145, 147, 201, 232
Kossova, Alda Giambelluca 56 n57
Kovacs, Judith 40 nn33, 34, 41, 42, 69 n51, 192–3, 212
Krabinger, J. G. 204 n11
Kugler, Robert 53 n29

Laird, Martin 11, 13–14, 70 n53, 72–3, 194–5, 196 n57, 232 n2, 238
lampstand 30, 38, 45, 104, 137–8, 140, 141, 144, 152, 156, 160
Langer, Ruth 184
Langerbeck, Hans 13
Le Boulluec, Alain 142, 191
leadership:
  of the church 10, 156, 162–4, 198, 228
  of the Jerusalem temple 86, 227

General Index

Leonardi, Claudio 56 n57
Lesses, Rebecca 151–2, 237
Levenson, Jon 148
Liddell and Scott (lexicon) 6
Lieb, Michael 10
Lieske, Aloysius 13
Lieu, Judith 18 n80
light 9, 11, 64, 66, 67, 70, 71, 73, 74, 75, 79, 138, 218, 225
Lilla, Salvatore 42, 68–9, 192
Lim, Richard 195–7, 201–2, 235
living creatures, *see ḥayyot*
Logos 25, 108, 112–13, 115, 122, 147
   in Clement 69, 142, 192–3, 214
   in Origen 66, 120–1, 145
   in Philo 39, 68, 89, 91, 100, 104–5, 140–1, 210–11
Louth, Andrew 1, 66 n32, 67
Ludlow, Morwenna 11–12, 27–8, 126 n62

maʿaseh bereshit (the work of creation) 60, 79–80, 114, 185–6, 202, 239 n32
maʿaseh merkavah (the work of the chariot) 14, 48, 60, 61–2, 202, 237
Maʿaseh Merkavah 58, 77, 129, 130, 131, 180
McGinn, Bernard 5, 19, 29, 44, 70, 162 n47, 238
McGuckin, John Anthony 44 n59, 46
Macleod, Colin 9, 12, 15 n78, 27, 28, 44, 49, 65, 74
Macrina the elder 44
Macrina the younger 23, 25, 146, 205, 223
Malherbe, Abraham 28, 98 n13, 101, 120 n25, 138, 157, 162, 164, 204 n13, 206 n22, 207, 210
Maraval, Pierre 22 n3, 23
Marcellus of Ancyra 99 n19
Marcovich, Miroslav 88 n45
Marcus, Ralph 38 n17
May, Gerhard 26 n26
Méhat, André 69
Mekhilta 84
mercy seat 30, 38, 45–6, 104, 138–9, 140, 143, 144, 152, 160, 174, 189, 193
Meredith, Anthony 9, 68, 122 n35, 123 n38
merkavah (chariot) 3, 10, 32–3, 48, 51, 58, 59, 60, 61–2, 75, 76, 94, 95, 113, 128, 129, 140, 148–9, 152, 169, 189, 198–9, 200, 201, 202, 219, 228, 232
Messalianism 8, 165 n73
metadiastemic intrusion 12, 109–10, 115, 127, 233
Metatron 59, 61, 78, 111–12, 115, 130, 219, 222

Methodius 2, 98 n10
Michael (archangel) 55, 111, 179, 221
Michaelis, Wilhelm 30, 107–8
Milik, Józef 54
mitra 31 n19, 203, 204, 209
Mishnah 59–62, 80, 129, 200
model *see* pattern
monasticism 25, 162, 164–5, 216
Mondésert, Claude 40, 159
Moore, Rebecca 167 n80
Morray-Jones, Christopher 4 n16, 14–15, 51–2, 57, 62, 149–50, 151, 182, 183, 200, 222, 227 n4, 230
Moses 29, 30, 63, 85–6, 131
   in Gregory 4, 10, 11, 27–8, 64, 72, 73, 82, 87, 116, 135, 152, 161–4, 170, 187, 197–8, 201, 228, 232, 233, 234, 239
   in Hekhalot literature 129
   in Philo 37–8, 67–8, 90
Mosshammer, Alden 26–7, 92, 115 n124, 122 n34, 123 n37, 126, 127
Mounce, Robert 178 nn39, 41
Mühlenberg, Ekkehard 13, 14
Musurillo, Herbert 157, 162
mysticism 5, 12–15, 19–21, 230, 236, 238–9
   Gregory's mysticism 9, 11, 26–7, 70, 71, 73, 81, 115, 194, 230, 234–5, 238–40
   merkavah mysticism 19, 78, 130–1, 184–5, 199–200
   Origen's mysticism 44, 70
   see also 'transformational mysticism'; *unio mystica*

names, divine 24, 58, 78, 110, 116–33, 146, 152, 179, 180, 225, 229, 232–3
Navtanovich, Liudmila 54 n37
Neḥuniah ben ha-Qannah 58, 128
neoplatonism 8, 70, 120, 124–5, 132, 230
Neusner, Jacob 183 n72
Newsom, Carol 51, 83 n12, 94, 95, 149 n96, 177, 182, 183
Nickelsburg, George 4 n16, 50 n14, 176, 218 n125
Nitzan, Bilhah 51
Norelli, Enrico 56
'not made with hands' 82–3, 85, 87

O'Connell, Patrick 197–8
Odeberg, Hugo 55
Ogdoad 43, 145
O'Keefe, John 44 n61
O'Leary, Joseph 121 n31
ʾophannim 79, 148, 181, 226

Origen 43-6
  on the church 159-61
  on darkness 66-7, 70
  on divine names 119-22, 124
  on the heavenly church 145
  on heavenly powers 143-4
  on the holy of holies 193
  on prayer 174
  on the priestly vestments 212-13, 214
  on the temple 90-1
Orlov, Andrei 18 n84, 53 n35, 54, 55, 74, 76
ousia 24, 71, 137, 147
  see also essence

Pagels, Elaine 42 n50, 43
paideia 207
paradeigma 85, 87-91, 94, 100, 105
  see also pattern
paradox 64, 65, 76, 81, 94, 96, 106, 107, 114, 127, 133, 190, 217, 232, 233, 238, 239
parallelomania 8
pardes 61, 62, 199-200, 228
pargod (heavenly veil) 78
parokhet 30, 78, 93, 95, 188 n3
  see also veil
participation in the divine 10, 11, 13-15, 35, 66, 92, 117, 146-7, 218, 223-4, 240
Parvis, Sara 99 n19
Parys, Michel van 99 n19
passion, Christ's 139, 157
pattern (or model) of the tabernacle 3, 29, 63, 85-6, 89-90, 93, 96, 100
Paul (apostle) 44, 69, 97, 121, 136, 145, 158, 206, 207, 215
  ascent to third heaven 4, 33, 98, 135, 164, 190, 197, 201, 233
  body imagery 85, 107, 154, 158, 170, 227
  on sacrifice 172, 186
  tabernacle/temple imagery 34, 82, 99, 154, 158, 167, 170, 239
Pearson, Birger 36 n6, 42
perpetual progress 11, 92, 115
Perrone, Lorenzo 56 n57
petalon (plate) 31, 118-19, 133, 209, 210, 212, 213, 220, 233
Peter (apostle) 155, 156, 159
Philip (apostle) 156
Philo 36-9
  on darkness 67-9
  on 'enclosing not enclosed' 105-6
  on God's transcendence 117, 132
  on heavenly powers 139-41, 144, 174
  on the holy of holies 190-1
  influence on Clement of Alexandria 40, 68-9, 142-3
  influence on Gregory 67-8, 105-6, 204-5, 213-14, 232, 233
  on the Logos 100, 104-5
  on *paradeigma* 88-90
  on the priestly vestments 203-5, 208, 210-11, 213-14
pillars 41, 45, 93, 95, 135, 149, 155-6, 160, 180, 226, 233
plate, *see petalon*
Platonism 5, 6, 17, 20, 38, 40, 44, 67, 88, 89, 92, 118, 120, 132, 134, 140, 145-6, 147, 205, 232
Pleroma 43, 201
plērōma, *see* fullness
Plested, Marcus 164-5
Plotinus 23, 67, 92
politics 195, 197, 228, 235, 237, 239, 240
polupragmosunē (curiosity) 196-7
pomegranates (on high priestly robe) 31, 204, 206-7, 210
presence, divine 9, 12, 13-15, 30, 38, 72-3, 75, 81, 85, 107-8, 110, 140, 151, 158, 233, 238
Priestly source 29, 75, 131
priesthood 20, 50, 95, 159, 162, 163, 166, 169, 177, 198, 220, 223
Prince of the Divine Presence 55, 58, 59, 128
Proclus of Constantinople 108 n71
Propp, William 83
prosōpon 137
Pseudo-Justin 88
Pseudo-Macarius 8, 165

Qedushah 59, 180, 183-5
4QFlorilegium (4Q174) 84, 167, 227
Qumran 5, 18, 50-2, 84, 152, 167-9, 170, 178, 183, 227, 237

Rapp, Claudia 196 n54
Reed, Annette Yoshiko 8, 18 n82
Reichman, Ronen 60 n72
resurrection 20, 25, 109, 205-6, 216-17
Revelation (book) 3, 18, 33, 56, 111, 115, 136, 138, 141, 172, 173, 177-8, 179, 180, 186, 187, 218, 236
Revised Common Lectionary 3
righteous dead 55, 217, 218, 221
robe, high priestly 31, 204-6, 207, 210, 211, 212, 213, 215, 223, 234, 240
robes, heavenly 59, 85, 111, 216, 217-24, 231, 234, 239, 240
Rooke, Deborah 220 n136
Rowland, Christopher 103 n35, 154, 158 n31, 236-7, 239
Rufinus 46, 161
Rule of the Community (1QS) 168, 227

Runia, David 36 n9, 37 n10, 39 n30, 69, 142–3
Rusch, William 145 n70

sacrifice:
   animal 3, 25, 27, 172
   heavenly 51, 52, 177–9, 186–7
   spiritual 156, 159, 164, 167, 172–3, 174, 205
Sagnard, François 42, 141 n44
Sanctus, *see* Qedushah
sandals 209–10
Sandmel, Samuel 8
Sarason, Richard 183 n72
Sarna, Nahum 31 nn16, 22, 24, 188n3
'scarlet doubled' 45, 160
Schäfer, Peter 4 n16, 12, 13, 14, 48 n4, 50, 52, 57, 58, 61, 74, 75 n87, 76–7, 78, 79, 80, 81 n118, 95 n99, 112, 114, 128, 129 n76, 130–1, 166, 167, 177, 178–9, 183, 184–6, 199, 200, 201 n88, 229, 230, 231, 238, 239 n32
Schiffman, Lawrence 54, 178 n46, 237 n24
Schoedel, William 106
Scholem, Gershom 12–13, 48, 130, 199, 222
Segal, Alan 5, 8, 37, 113 n111
seraphim 29, 46, 136–7, 143, 152, 180, 184, 239
Shekhinah 75, 77
shields on priestly vestments 208–9, 216
shoulder pieces of the ephod 31, 203, 207–8, 211, 214
silence 71, 119, 127, 180–1, 185, 189
Silvas, Anna 22, 23 nn8, 13, 16, 235
Similitudes of Enoch 49
Simonetti, Manlio 35
skēnē 30, 66, 82, 107–8, 110, 175
skēnōma 107
skēnos 82, 107
skopos 28
Solomon 85–6, 101, 158, 189
   temple of 30, 33, 84, 86, 93–4, 110, 114, 150, 159, 188–9
Sommer, Benjamin 30 n4, 75
Songs of the Sabbath Sacrifice 29, 48, 50–2, 198, 226–7
   on the community as a temple 168–9
   on heavenly clothing 218–19
   on heavenly priests 176, 178–9
   on a living heavenly temple 95, 148–52, 225
   rhetorical devices 94–5
   on sharing in angelic worship 182–3, 187, 230
   on silent angelic worship 180–1
   temple terminology 93–4
Spinks, Bryan 183 n71
Sterk, Andrea 163–4, 216
Sterling, Gregory 36 n8

Stewart, Columba 165 n73
Stone, Michael 14, 53 n29, 236
stones on priestly vestments 31, 203 n4, 204 n10, 208–9, 210, 211, 213, 220
straps 203, 209, 214
Stroumsa, Guy 20–21, 103 n35
Strugnell, John 51
Swartz, Michael 58 n66, 128, 130 n81
Sweeney, Marvin 200 n86
Sweet, John 82 n5, 85
Symmachus (translator) 100 n21
synagogue 130, 167, 169, 183–5, 229

Tabernacles (feast) 175–6
table for the bread of the Presence 30, 45, 157, 160
Taft, Robert 183 n71
Talmud, Babylonian 48, 59–62, 111, 114, 179, 227–8, 239 n32
   on Aḥer's ascent 112–13, 115
   on darkness 79–80, 225
   on *pardes* 199–201
   on worship 185–6, 187, 228, 230
Talmud, Palestinian 59, 61, 200
tassels of the tunic 31, 204, 207
Testament of Levi 18, 47, 48, 52–3, 75, 94, 110, 226
   critical of the temple 166
   on heavenly clothing 218, 219–20
   on heavenly sacrifices 177, 179
Thanksgiving Hymns (1QH) 168, 227
Theodoret 2
Theodotion (translator) 100 n21
theophany 27, 64, 87, 93, 137, 164, 198, 232, 238
theōria 27, 35, 147, 203
   see also contemplation
theurgy 48, 58, 125, 128
throne, divine 3–4, 31, 32–3, 48, 50, 53, 58, 77–8, 79, 93, 95, 111, 148–9, 198–9, 218, 226, 229, 236–7
throne, Metatron's 59, 112
Timothy (apostle) 155, 206
Tosephta 60, 61, 183, 200
Tov, Emanuel 87 n43
transformation 20, 59, 108, 112, 113, 115, 148, 177, 183, 216–17, 221–2, 223, 229, 230, 231, 234
   see also angelification
'transformational mysticism' 222, 223, 230, 234
Trigg, Joseph 43 n58
Trinity 137, 138, 143–4, 206
Tropper, Amram 60 n72
tunic, high priestly 31, 204, 207, 211, 212–13
turban 31, 203, 209, 220
Tuschling, Ruth 183 n71
'twisted linen' 45, 160, 161

typology 2–3, 35, 87, 96, 98, 104, 134, 154, 158–9, 173, 198, 227

unio liturgica 13, 183, 228, 230, 234, 238
unio mystica 12–13, 14, 228, 230, 238
unbegotten 24, 70–1, 81, 116, 122–3
union with the divine 12–15, 49, 73, 92, 147, 194, 230–1, 235, 238–9
unknowability, divine 1, 24, 67, 69, 116, 117
Urim and Thummin 31, 208, 213

Vaillant, André 54
Valentinianism 8, 36, 42–3, 47, 48, 145, 201
Van Dam, Raymond 22, 195 n53
VanderKam, James 226 n1
veil 30, 41, 93, 95, 98–9, 104, 119, 126, 188, 190, 193, 201, 208, 239
vestments, priestly 2, 3 n11, 31, 38, 102, 203–24
  see also under individual items
virginity 158, 160, 161, 214, 215
virtue 10, 27, 35, 135, 160, 162–3, 197, 204, 205–9, 211, 212, 214, 215–17, 220, 223, 234
Völker, Walther 13

Wade, Martha Lynn 32 n30, 155 n10
washbasin(s) of the tabernacle 30, 156, 165
Weinfeld, Moshe 131
Wevers, John William 32 n30
Williams, Megan Hale 18
Williams, Rowan 67–8, 92 nn64, 65, 193 nn34, 35, 223
Williamson, Hugh 85–6
Wilson, William 191
wisdom 98, 99–102, 104, 105, 112, 121, 156, 213
Wise, Michael 168 n84
Wolfson, Elliot 13, 14–15, 62, 79, 230–1

Yerushalmi *see* Talmud, Palestinian
Yoḥanan b. Zakkai 60, 61–2
yored merkavah (descender to the chariot) 57, 58, 76, 77–8, 185, 229, 236
Young, Frances 71 n56, 116 n3, 121 n26, 122, 123 n39, 125–6, 132

Zachhuber, Johannes 116 n2, 121–2